# TRADE UNIONS AND THE LABOUR PARTY
## SINCE 1945

# TRADE UNIONS
## AND
# THE LABOUR PARTY
## SINCE 1945

by

MARTIN HARRISON
Research Fellow of Nuffield College
Oxford

Detroit – Wayne State University Press – 1960

# PREFACE

El hacer bien á villanos es echar agua en la mer.
SPANISH PROVERB

'IT is surprising', said Mr David Butler, pacing his room in Nuffield College on that autumnal day in 1954. 'It is surprising how little has been written about the political work of the unions.' Such was the beginning not only of the present volume, but of my numerous debts to those who have contributed to it in one way or another. My principal debt of gratitude is to the Warden and Fellows of Nuffield College, Oxford, for making it possible for this book to be written and for encouragement in the writing of it.

I wish also to thank the Chief Registrar of Friendly Societies, without whose cooperation the chapters on trade union political finance and the political levy could not have been attempted. In his Search Room, that engaging backwater in North Audley Street, his friendly and helpful staff provided me with desk space, supplied me with files, and sustained me with countless cups of Civil Service tea.

It would be invidious to single out all those who have helped within the trade union and Labour movement. They include members of more than sixty unions, and national, regional and local representatives of the Labour Party. One general secretary, it is true, would not even say whether any members of the union had been candidates at the 1955 election, declaring 'This is a confidential matter, reserved to members of the Executive Council'. But this was exceptional. Though some unions were nursing painful memories of certain previous research workers, most of my informants were surprisingly communicative, and gave generously of their time and specialized knowledge.

I am further indebted to all those who have discussed particular sections with me at union summer schools or WEA lectures. Among my colleagues I wish to express my particular thanks to Mr Hugh Clegg and Mr David Butler, who suffered with my successive drafts, and to Mr Philip Williams, Mr Rex Adams and Mr Frank Bealey who read the later versions. Some union officials have kindly read the sections on their own

7

organizations. To all of them I owe a great debt for their criticisms and encouragement. This book appears in its final form as a result of—and sometimes in spite of—their ready advice. But mine is the final responsibility, and this volume should not be taken to express the views of any of those I have mentioned.

My warmest thanks are also due to the members of the college secretarial staff who struggled with the manuscript, but notably to Miss Jean Brotherhood who toiled the longest. Finally, I wish to add my special thanks to my wife, not only for the sustained encouragement she gave to a husband who seemed at times to have contracted a bigamous marriage with a typewriter, but for mountains of arithmetical calculations.

# CONTENTS

# INTRODUCTION

AFTER the expectant hush came happy pandemonium. Scrambling on their seats, waving their hats, delegates cheered the outcome of the crucial vote. The scene was the Trades Union Congress of 1899; the vote was on whether the unions should take independent political action. So far the TUC had always stood aside from the series of bodies which had been set up to win representation in Parliament for the working class. Now, after the long years of struggle by Keir Hardie and the Socialists, it was rejecting the traditional insistence that trade unionism and politics did not mix. By 546,000 votes to 434,000, it adopted a motion whose terms still merit recalling for all their lugubrious phrasing:

'This Congress, having regard to its decisions in former years, and with a view to securing a better representation of the interests of labour in the House of Commons, hereby instructs the Parliamentary Committee to invite the cooperation of all cooperative, socialistic, trade union, and other working organizations to jointly cooperate on lines mutually agreed upon, in convening a special congress of representatives from such of the above-named organizations as may be willing to devise ways and means for securing the return of an increased number of labour members to the next Parliament.'

And so the Labour Party was born. For this was the decision which brought trade union and Socialist society delegates to that gloomy 'Cathedral of Non-conformity', the Memorial Hall in Farringdon Street, on February 27, 1900. Out of that meeting came the Labour Representation Committee.

To introduce an account of the Labour Party's relations with the unions today by recalling that enthusiastic scene at the TUC sixty years ago may seem a little less than kind. But these beginnings are still important. They are a reminder that the traditional claim of trade union orators that 'the Labour Party is the child of the trade union movement' is no idle boast. And yet even at birth the Labour Party was never exclusively a trade union preserve. Throughout its history it has been profoundly marked by being a party within which union and non-union elements have had to live together. It is also worth recalling the ambivalence in which the Party was born. The founders' deliberate ambivalence, without which the Party could scarcely have existed, still lingers to explain many of its internal tensions. The TUC motion indicates significantly what first persuaded many unions to support political action: it was 'the return of an increased number of labour members to the next Parliament'.

Some of the unions attending that inaugural meeting in 1900 were already under Socialist leadership. They saw the new party as the nucleus of a broad-based Socialist movement which was to transform society. But they were a minority. To many union leaders the views of Hardie and his friends were anathema. They were not consciously assisting at the birth of a Socialist party; political action was more a matter of bread and butter than of ideology. Their aims were more limited, reformist, sometimes expressed directly in terms of class. For years the unions had been wanting to send working men to the House of Commons to propose reforms and put their point of view in debates which affected their members. After appealing to the Liberals and Conservatives with signally little success they were now prepared to work for working class representation through a new political party.

It was to be years before Labour could hope to hold the bulk of the unions within its ranks and embrace a fully Socialist creed. Only in 1918 was the Party formally to adopt a Socialist constitution. From the very beginning Labour developed as a party within which 'socialist' and 'labour' preserved distinct meanings, in which there were both reformers and transformers, supporters of a class movement and believers in a national party—and in which the diverse threads were never neatly identifiable with either the unions or the political movement. But, most important, Labour developed into a party which the unions had not only helped to found and rear, but in which they found themselves organically embedded, forming part of the Party but also in constitutional and practical terms quite distinct from it. Here was an alliance which was to become the most controversial relationship in British politics. For after the struggle over the 'wage freeze', the Bevanite revolt, and the nuclear weapons controversy—to take only three post-war examples—could anyone term the adjective excessive?

It is just sixty years since the first unions decided to support the 'political action' which took them in time into the Labour Party. Throughout those six decades, for the great majority of these unions 'political action' has meant effectively the trade union-Labour alliance. Against the 373,000 trade unionists who affiliated to the Labour Representation Committee in 1900, unions now associated with the Party have over eight million members. Today only five unions of more than one hundred which operate special political funds are not also affiliated to the Labour Party. There have been aberrations: the unions have flirted with syndicalism, held a general strike during which the Trades Union Congress kept the Party at arm's length, and they have mused from time to time about the joys of independence. Yet the link with the Labour Party has become so embedded in tradition that today in most of the larger unions it is an unspoken assumption.

While the trade union-Labour partnership may be taken almost for granted within the unions, the old belief that the unions should leave politics to the politicians and stick to their industrial affairs has never completely disappeared. 'Our object is to keep politics out of the unions', Mr 'Ted' Leather tells Conservatives.[1] 'Surely the business of politics should be left to the powers that be while we get on with winning improved conditions', writes a railwayman.[2] 'Our job is to win higher wages and better conditions—not to get mixed up with politics', objects a member of the AEU.[3] Such judgments spring either from woolly thinking or from a complete misapprehension of trade unionism. The unions have never been wholly isolated from politics, even in the days of purest *laisser faire*. In 1867 the Trades Union Congress found itself involved at birth with the Royal Commission on the Trade Unions. By the end of the century the unions were pressing for the State to introduce regulation of sweated labour, improved safety regulations, even

---

[1] *Advance*, August 1950.
[2] *Railway Review*, July 23, 1954.
[3] *AEU Journal*, October 1953.

nationalization. Such essentially industrial aims could not be achieved without the intervention of the State.

Today there is less possibility than ever of a union avoiding involvement in politics. Even if we accept that the mission of trade unionism is just to 'win higher wages and better conditions' the idea that these can be won without intrusion into 'politics' bears no relation to reality. As the activities of government have multiplied to the point where Ministers influence wage settlements in nationalized industries, and mediate in major disputes in private industry, politics and 'better conditions' have become inextricably linked. Even such a union as the National & Local Government Officers' Association—so steadfastly non-political that it declines to affiliate even to the TUC—found itself caught up in a political storm in 1957 when the responsible Minister refused to implement recommended salary increases for its members employed in the National Health Service. Far from keeping the unions at a distance governments continually seek their opinion on a wide range of questions. Union representatives must figure on innumerable committees in Whitehall and on every Royal Commission. Today it is unthinkable that this movement, which has been hailed by Sir Winston Churchill as an estate of the realm, should become 'non-political' in the sense in which some of its critics use the term.

But the unions are more than simple by-standers, caught up in the political battle. They are combatants. Most of them are in direct partnership with the Labour Party; the decision taken in 1899 has led them a long way. 'Political action' has meant not only electing working class Members of Parliament and 'winning better conditions', but making pronouncements on education and Africa, and helping to shape Labour's policy on nuclear weapons and a host of other issues which have a tenuous connection at best with the unions' industrial interests.

Within the Labour Party the suggestion that the unions could fruitfully be 'in politics' without being linked so intimately with the Party is greeted with either incomprehension or derision. Yet it is clear that although the unions can never avoid being caught up in political debates, their traditional association with the Labour Party is a question of choice and political judgment. It may be self-evident to Labour supporters that the unions have most success in attaining their ends by affiliating to the Labour Party, but which party best serves the working class is clearly a matter of opinion. It is worth recalling that between one fourth and one fifth of trade unionists vote either Liberal or Conservative (while the proportion of non-Labour voters in the whole working class is rather higher). Many unions have persistently held aloof from association with the Labour Party.

Yet the Labour-union alliance exists. Our purpose is not to debate its wisdom but to explore it. It is a strange relationship. Here is a movement more than eight million strong, connected intimately with the political party which forms now the government now the opposition. The questions their alliance provokes are as important as they are numerous. Around it have turned some of the most bitter debates of recent years. It is next to impossible to understand the strains and cross-currents in the Labour Party without exploring its relationship with the unions. For example, the extraordinary character taken by the struggle over policy and the succession to Mr Attlee which rent the Party from 1951 to 1956 was inseparably connected with the terms on which Labour lives with the unions. For years the air has been loud with cries about trade union 'bosses', block votes, and the clash between the unions and the Party's intellectuals. Yet, for all the angry polemic there has been surprisingly little attempt to weigh the unions' contribution to the life of the Labour Party. As a result the myths have flourished luxuriantly. How rife and contradictory these had become was most clearly revealed in the Bevanite controversy, but the commentaries provoked by Mr Frank Cousins' leadership of the TGWU show that as many misconceptions remain within the Party as outside. It is time they were cleared away.

Not everyone would agree: 'Look', said a respected union leader, stubbing his fingers emphatically on the desk and glaring at his interrogator. 'Look. What this union does in the way of politics is purely a matter for the members of this union. If they are satisfied that's an end of it. No one coming from outside has any right to know what we are doing, or to say otherwise.' And he leaned back with an air of ponderous, immovable finality. This attitude may have made sense sixty year ago. But today, such is the importance of both the trade unions and the Labour Party that the terms on which they live together are no simple cosy domestic affair. They have lost the right to privacy.

Moreover, the questions which the Labour-union alliance provokes are as important for those within the Party as for outsiders. The Movement has had a spate of furious recrimination and wild generalization, and a certain amount of what can only be termed devotional literature. But in many Labour circles serious discussion of union-Party relationships is tacitly avoided in the interests of unity. The assumption is revealing. While members of the Labour Party may have lost some of the illusions which are held by outsiders, there is still little conception of the real and possible relations between the industrial and political wings.

It is fashionable within the Labour Party to wish that the skeletons of old feuds be left in the cupboard. But episodes like the Bevanite revolt are more than an unhappy accident or a calamitous departure from the Party's normal life. Although many of its ingredients rose from the specific political situation, it brought to the surface long-standing tensions and suspicions. These did not die as Mr Bevan and Mr Gaitskell stood shoulder to shoulder again on Party platforms. They remain, either latent or active but concealed from the eyes of the general public. In taking many examples from that period and more recent quarrels we shall not be idly raking over past history but looking at forces and problems with which, whether in power or in opposition, Labour must live. If ever Labour is bitterly divided again they could flare into the open.

Controversy may well return. 'It is inevitable', wrote Mr Attlee. 'It is inevitable that there should from time to time be misunderstandings between the industrial and the political sides of the Movement.'[1] The Party's history has not failed to confirm that laconic observation. If conflicts are to be expected they may at least be less serious if both sides understand the limita-

[1] *The Labour Party in Perspective*, Gollancz, 1937, p. 71.
'Movement' refers to the alliance of unions, Party and Cooperatives, while 'movement' refers either to the political or industrial wings according to context. Similarly 'Conference' and 'Party' refer throughout to the Labour Party Conference and the Labour Party.

tions of their partners. After surveying the record of the running battle in the Labour Party up to 1956, it is hard to doubt that both Deakinites and Bevanites misunderstood the Movement of which they were members. It is time not only that outsiders should begin to see the Labour Movement 'warts and all', but that the Labour Party should begin to know itself.

Within a single volume it is scarcely possible to answer every question which the unions' association with Labour raises. This would demand a review of a large slice of the work of the TUC and of the Party itself, as well as a study of many of the unions' industrial activities. But we shall go to the heart of many of the most controversial issues by concentrating on what is materially the most substantial side of the partnership. Inevitably such a scrutiny reveals some of the bases of union power in the Party and the way in which this power is exercised. However, this will not be primarily an examination of the ways in which union pressure is brought to bear—for the most important single source of pressure is exercised directly on the Party leadership by the General Council of the TUC, quite outside the Party's normal constitutional circuits. Accordingly we shall not attempt a systematic exposure of union power or trace the historical development of the alliance more than incidentally. We shall be trying to find how, as individual organizations, the unions contribute to the life of the Labour Party—enquiring into the health of the Labour Movement today, into its material expression.

We shall start, logically enough, with the political levy. Collected in every union which affiliates to the Labour Party, it forms the essential basis of union political activity. While trade unionists' enthusiasm for the Movement cannot be directly measured, examining the way they pay the political levy—the minimum commitment—will give a fairly clear indication of the support that political action commands today. This discussion of the payment of the levy leads naturally to its spending. That the unions pay large sums to the Labour Party is commonplace. How large, how important, and how generous these sums are has never previously been revealed. Finance, we shall see, is one of the alliance's most delicate problems.

We shall then turn to the unions' part in the making of

B

Labour policy. For years Labour dissidents have grumbled about the unions' power within the annual Labour Party Conference—the celebrated dispute over the 'block vote'—or criticized the way that the unions made their own policy decisions or join in the Party's local activities. We shall see what truth there is in such myths and criticisms, considering not just how the unions join in the policy-making process, but how far they are really capable of doing so.

Recalling the terms of the original motion of the 1899 TUC, we shall see how working class representation has fared. How close to fulfilment are the aspirations of the Party's founders? How far are the unions themselves still interested in sending their men to Westminster? Finally, after looking at the part that unions play in electing some of the Party leadership we shall glance briefly at the unions which have stood aside from the Movement. These often-forgotten non-political unions raise a question which the Movement normally prefers to forget.

To examine the relationship between the unions and the Labour Party largely in material terms admittedly does less than justice to the moral backing that the Party has drawn from the unions. No one who has worked among active trade unionists could fail to be aware of how often affiliation with Labour is taken as a natural and undiscussed part of union life. The association between union membership and Labour voting is assumed to be automatic. Even an enquiring research worker is likely to be taken for a Labour supporter simply because he shows a sympathetic interest in the unions. In electoral terms the 'rub-off' effect of such an atmosphere within the unions must be appreciable.

Yet, in affiliating to the Party the unions have assumed certain obligations, just as any individual who becomes a member. Indeed, the whole theory of 'The Movement' requires it. Labour is always critical of the Conservatives' connections with business and manufacturing interests. By contrast, Labour apologists say, the unions' association with the Labour Party is not that of a simple pressure group which is seeking to promote narrow sectional interests. The Movement rises above such sordid aims simply because it integrates the unions intimately into its whole life. They are part of the Party itself, sharing its burdens and tribulations as well as the rewards. The course of the following pages will reveal the measure in which this ideal is realized, and the extent to which the unions are structurally capable of playing their part in the Movement. And in looking in turn at the political levy, Labour Party finance, Parliamentary representation and the making of policy we may fairly ask: do the unions pull their weight? Do the unions take their share of the burdens, or are they sleeping partners? Does the link with Labour still seem important enough for the unions to be willing to make sacrifices to maintain it? The answers will give some indication of the vitality of the Movement at the end of its first sixty years.

# CHAPTER I

# THE POLITICAL LEVY

'We require unity, and we go so far as to say that unity must
sometimes be imposed upon men in their own interests.'

J. R. CLYNES

'If I believed that the development of Socialism meant the
crushing of liberty, I should plump for liberty.'

ERNEST BEVIN *

ONE of the most puzzling problems of the trade union-Labour
Party alliance is what the ordinary trade unionist thinks of it all.
After all, he is the very basis of the Movement. It is in his name
that decisions are made and trade union leaders will claim to
speak. The extent to which the vision of a Labour Movement
corresponds to reality depends essentially on the degree to
which he not only knows that the relationship exists, but accepts
it and is ready to breathe life into it.

For all the brave words of official propagandists and fraternal
delegates it would be unfair to set expectations too high. It
would be unreasonable to look for the Movement to rouse the
fervour in its seventh decade that it could apparently stir in its
first. Obviously, as in all voluntary movements, the proportion
of members actively engaged in meetings and conferences will
be small. Yet this only makes it the more important to know
what the average passive trade unionist thinks. Until a more
systematic direct study of working class attitudes is made one of
the few indications of the ordinary member's feelings which is
available is the way in which he accepts the very minimum
association with the Movement: payment of his union's political
levy.[1] The way in which the unions recruit support for their
political funds is some measure of the basis on which the Move-

* (a) Clynes' speech on the political levy in 1913 (41 H.C. Deb. 5s. col. 3020).
For a less succinct but more recent expression of these views see Mr. Tom O'Brien's
speech in 1946, at 419 H.C. Deb. 5s. cols. 231–2.

(b) Ernest Bevin, December 22, 1947.

[1] These unions have political funds but no affiliation with the Labour Party:
Aeronautical Engineers' Association, Liverpool Victoria Workers' Union,
National Union of Commercial Travellers, National Federation of Insurance
Workers, Association of Scientific Workers. They are generally excluded from
the following discussion.

ment is built. Accordingly we turn first to examining the way the political levy is collected—which also gives the chance to outline the legal framework within which the unions have been allowed to engage in politics over the years.

In the earliest days of political action the law set few limits. One by one the unions began supporting Parliamentary candidates, then affiliating to the Labour Party. Once the decision to intervene in politics had been taken the individual trade unionist could not escape. He had to pay the political levy whatever his opinions. At first the complaints were few, but Conservative and Liberal members grew increasingly restive as it became clearer that almost all political expenditure was favouring the Labour Representation Committee. Then, in 1908, the pertinaceous Mr A. V. Osborne of the Amalgamated Society of Railway Servants (forerunner of the present National Union of Railwaymen) successfully challenged in the courts his union's power to operate a Parliamentary Representation scheme. The House of Lords not only found the Railway Servants' political rules *ultra vires* the Trade Union Acts, they plainly considered that their subsidizing of 'tied' Members of Parliament was contrary to public policy. In the Court of Appeal Lord Justice Cozens-Hardy had already commented on another aspect of the unions' political activities, the compulsory levy:

'I cannot think that it is the intention of the Legislature that it should be competent to a majority of the members to compel a minority by their votes, and still less by their subscriptions, to political views which they may abhor.'[1]

Over the next year or so a series of like-minded injunctions paralysed the political funds of almost every large union. A few, such as the Miners and the Railway Servants, continued to collect contributions unofficially but, for the moment, trade union political action was all but crippled. Poverty-stricken at the best of times, the Labour Party now saw the chief sources of its income gradually drying up. Fortunately the Liberals, partly in Labour's debt for support, promised relief. Payment of Members of Parliament, many of whom were dependent on maintenance grants from their unions, was a partial help after 1911.

---

[1] [1910] A.C. 87 at p. 108.

But the unions' full return to political activity took longer. The Liberal Government found it hard to strike a balance between the dark suspicions of its own right wing and Labour's demand that the unions be given the widest possible freedom. Ill-drafted and imprecise, the Bill which emerged from the months of delicate negotiation bore all the marks of compromise. Nevertheless it has survived. The Trade Union Act, 1913 still effectively determines the conditions on which unions can engage in political activities.

It is an odd mixture of restriction and license. It lays down that before a union may spend any money to further those political objects which come within the Act,[1] it must secure the approval of its members, through a general ballot, for the setting up of a political fund. (Whether a union affiliates to the Labour Party is, in law, a separate issue decided through the union's normal policy-making processes.) The ballot must be held under rules approved by the Chief Registrar of Friendly Societies, who insists on rigorous provisions to ensure that the vote is secret, that voting and counting are honest, and that every attempt is made to publicize the ballot throughout the union. Before they vote members must receive a copy of the proposed political fund rules—which must also be approved by the Registrar. On several occasions the Registrar has shown his determination to ensure a fair vote by his investigation of members' complaints, and even by quashing ballots where there had been purely technical infringements of the rules.[2]

Most unions which have political funds today set them up immediately after the 1913 Act was passed. Ballots were almost always successful. By 1939 over 200 unions had voted on political action, and only thirteen failed to obtain a majority—although some had to try several times. The Association of Engineering & Shipbuilding Draughtsmen went to the polls in 1920, 1921, 1923 and 1940, before it succeeded at last in 1944. There has only been a slow trickle of ballots since the war. Of the twenty-four unions which have voted since 1945 only seventeen have

---

[1] For an outline of the scope of the Act see Chapter II. A full examination of the Act is contained in N. Citrine, *Trade Union Law*, Stevens, 1950.

[2] For example, the Registrar rescinded his approval of the CSCA ballot rules because they did not require the stamping of the branch stamp on each ballot. *Red Tape*, October 1949.

shown a majority for political action—often by small majorities on low polls. In some unions the opposition to political funds has been so strong that motions to hold a ballot have been rejected at their conference or not even submitted. This relative lack of enthusiasm is scarcely surprising, for most strongly political unions set up their political funds long ago.

Few trade unionists have had a direct say about whether their union should join in political activity. This is far from saying that they are bound unwillingly to continue a fund to which they have never given their assent. Constitutionally it is much easier for a union to suppress or to emasculate its political fund than to introduce it. No ballot is necessary. Following their normal procedure for amending rules unions can delete their political fund rules (or simply omit them from the next printing of the rule book). They may retain the political rules, but make them a dead letter by declining to collect contributions. All these courses have been adopted.[1] Contributors to the political fund can cripple it by refusing to agree to higher contributions, or they can insist that the union either disaffiliate from the Labour Party or even stop spending its money on any party political purpose at all.[2] So long as a union is democratically run there is scope for any opposition to political action to show itself. However, although renunciation of political action is simple on paper, in practice once a political fund has been established it rapidly becomes a union tradition, with all

---

[1] In *Edwards and the National Federation of Insurance Workers* Mr Edwards, a member, complained that the union was not collecting the political levy. This was admitted by the NFIW. At the Annual General Meeting in April 1947 a proposal to begin the collection of the political levy, according to rule, had been defeated by a simple majority. The Registrar ruled that this was not an amendment to rule (requiring a two-thirds majority) but a refusal to exercise power, and that the collection of the levy was not mandatory. Registrar's decision, January 21, 1948, *Report of Selected Disputes etc.*, p. 241.

The Executive of the Musicians' Union reported in 1957 that 'of the union's branches many did not operate a political fund'. *The Musician*, July 1957. This is a long-standing failing.—Cf., *Report of the Chief Registrar*, 1924, Part IV.

The Amalgamated Society of Woodcutting Machinists let its political fund lapse during the 1930's by publishing a new rulebook without political rules.

In 1955 the Medical Practitioners' Union voted that 'No part of the subscription of the Union shall be used for the furtherance of the political objects . . .', effectively negativing the political rules.

[2] Notably the Association of Scientific Workers.

the advantages that sheer inertia and the argument that 'We've always had a political fund' can give.[1]

The Trade Union Act provides two other major safeguards. Once the political fund has been set up it must be kept rigorously separate from the industrial funds. The Act and the Registrar insist categorically that only political contributions may be paid into the political fund. Finally there is relief for the dissenters. Liberals, Conservatives, and those trade unionists who simply want to save a shilling or so per year may be excused payment of the levy by handing a 'contracting-out' form to their branch secretary. New members may contract out at any time; others can claim exemption from the following January 1. Simple though it is, this system led to forty years of heated controversy.

In 1913 it was unthinkable that the Conservatives should welcome the incursion of the unions into politics, or that they should be quickly reconciled. This hostility crystalized in the contracting-out issue. The long, unhappy debate constitutes the history both of political action before the law in recent years, and of the attitude of the political parties to trade union political action.

## Contracting-Out

From the beginning the Conservatives fought contracting-out, insisting that it gave protesters a wholly inadequate protection against victimization by their fellows. Labour, meanwhile, termed the provisions for dissent a 'blacklegs' charter', a reflection on the unions' honour, and a subversion of the principle of majority rule. MacDonald demanded that whatever their views all members should be forced to pay the levy.[2]

As the unions set up their political funds the marked discrepancy between the number of votes cast against their being

---

[1] There have been repeated attempts in the Association of Engineering & Shipbuilding Draughtsmen to end political affiliations, or to hold a further ballot. Cf., *Report of the Representative Council Conference*, 1947, p. 96; 1948, p. 259; 1949, p. 324; 1950, p. 244; 1952, p. 382; 1953, p. 363; 1955, p. 342; 1958, p. 395. The majorities against a further ballot have fallen steadily. There have been other attempts, less substantially backed, in the Amalgamated Union of Building Trade Workers and the Association of Supervisory Staffs, Executives & Technicians.

[2] 26 *H.C. Deb. 5s.* col. 949.

established and the number of members subsequently contracting-out hardened the Conservative belief that many were
paying only under duress. But for the moment the war imposed
a lull in the debate.

Peace, and the return of industrial unrest brought with them
a militant Conservative Right, suspicious of the unions and
determined to curb abuses of power. The first attacks, led by Sir
Frederick Banbury, were broad and repeated. Every session
brought at least one private member's Bill to prohibit trade
union political action, or to sweep away the privileged position
at law granted to the unions by the Trade Disputes Act of 1906.
However, the Lloyd George Coalition and subsequent governments refused to grant further time for their discussion.
Gradually the hostility to political action narrowed, concentrating on the contracting-out rule.

In measures like the flamboyantly styled Trade Unionists'
(Restoration of Liberty) Bill the Right called for annual contracting-in, by which the levy would have been paid only by
members who signified their willingness afresh each year. Conservative opinion hardened. By 1925 it was no longer clear
where the majority in the Parliamentary Party lay, and the
Conservative Party Conference was pressing for action to 'curb
the unions'. But an active moderate wing still urged Baldwin to
oppose the latest attack—the Macquisten Bill—which proposed
a straight switch to annual contracting-in. Baldwin rallied behind him a cabinet containing a sizeable revisionist element, and
then carried the House. He was later to say that this speech, one
of the few which may genuinely have swayed votes, gave him
the greatest satisfaction of all his Parliamentary performances.[1]
He argued:

'I want my party to make a gesture to the country . . . and to
say to them: "We have our majority; we believe in the justice
of this Bill which has been brought in today, but we are going
to withdraw our hand, and we are not going to push our
political advantage home at a moment like this. . . . We, at any
rate, are not going to fire the first shot." '[2]

[1] See A. Duff Cooper, *Old Men Forget*, Hart-Davis, 1953, p. 142 f. G. M.
Young, *Stanley Baldwin*, Hart-Davis, 1952, p. 91.
[2] 181 *H.C. Deb. 5s.* col. 840.

Baldwin carried the day on expediency, leaving the principle conceded. The controversy might well have petered out but, as Baldwin remarked, 'There was a shot fired the next year, and a very heavy shot'.[1] The General Strike gave the Right the ascendancy. Baldwin's temporizing could do little more than limit the drastic reprisals that were urged upon him. The Trade Disputes and Trade Unions Act, 1927, was primarily concerned with the events of the previous year. It sought to outlaw political and sympathetic strikes, to prohibit the enforcement of the closed shop by public authorities, and to tighten the laws on intimidation. The financial support given to the strikers by some of the Civil Service unions (none of whom came out on strike), led to a provision that they might not affiliate to bodies outside the Service. The Post Office Workers, the Tax Officers, and the Civil Service Clerical Association were forced to abandon their affiliation to the Labour Party, cease political action, and wind up their political funds. All Civil Service unions were obliged to withdraw from the TUC. Finally, and wholly unconnected with the General Strike, contracting-in was imposed in place of contracting-out.

Despite the reservations of some courageously thoughtful Conservatives such as Mr Oliver Stanley,[2] the Bill was carried against implacable Labour opposition, with the Liberals divided.[3] The second Labour Government twice tried to honour its pledge to return to contracting-out. Both attempts foundered ignominiously in committee. During the 'thirties motions to repeal the 1927 Act became part of the pious ritual of trade union conferences and Labour election addresses, much as demands for the repayment of post-war credits have been faithfully reiterated in more recent years. But there was no hope of a change.

During the war the unions' hopes rose, and the TUC approached both Mr Chamberlain and Mr Churchill, hinting that labour's contribution to the war effort might be recognized by relaxation at least of the closed shop provisions, and the ban on Civil Service unions affiliating to the TUC (though not to the Labour Party). After prolonged meetings between Conservative Party officials and union leaders, Mr Churchill wrote to Sir

[1] 247 H.C. Deb. 5s. col. 416.       [2] 206 H.C. Deb. 5s. col. 2068.
[3] For Clynes' speech pledging repeal see 205 H.C. Deb. 5s. col. 1340. For the Liberal attitudes see 247 H.C. Deb. 5s. col. 875.

Walter Citrine, then General Secretary of the TUC, 'I fear that there is no possibility of amending the Trade Disputes Act . . . I have ascertained that the overwhelming mass of Conservatives would not support such an amendment'. The forthcoming election would indicate the mood of the electorate.[1]

Although repeal of the 1927 Act was undoubtedly part of Labour's programme, it was little debated during the 1945 campaign.[2] However, in due course the Labour Government claimed its mandate to introduce 'a modest little Bill',[3] repealing the 1927 Act outright. The Conservatives professed themselves scandalized at Labour's haste to attack this problem, when the economic situation was so grave. But already the unions and the Labour rank and file, who understood little of the difficulties of the Parliamentary timetable, had been growing restive. While the Conservatives fought every section of the Bill, the return to contracting-out drew particularly violent attack: 'A devastating comment on the fitness of the Labour Party to govern' thought Mr Quintin Hogg.[4] 'A stab in the back for democracy', cried Lord Willoughby de Eresby.[5] Liberal opposition was tinged with embarrassment, since the original 1913 Act was the work of the last Liberal Government. A few trade union Labour MPs still hankered after the suppression of all right to refuse to pay the levy, but the party leadership was firm.[6] The repeal

[1] There are several versions of these wartime exchanges, differing slightly. See: Mr Tom O'Brien's account, see 419 *H.C. Deb. 5s.* cols. 228–231. Mr Arthur Deakin's account, see *Report of the Labour Party Conference* 1951, p. 92. Minutes of the National Council of Labour, *Report of the Labour Party Conference*, 1945, p. 3. *Repeal of the Trade Disputes Act*, Labour Party, 1946. *Notes for Speakers & Workers*, Conservative Central Office, 1945, pp. 131–6.

[2] It is not mentioned in R. B. McCallum and A. Readman, *The British General Election of 1945.* OUP, 1947.

[3] Sir Hartley Shawcross, 419 *H.C. Deb. 5s.* col. 193.

[4] 419 *H.C. Deb. 5s.* col. 296.          [5] 419 *H.C. Deb. 5s.* col. 241.

[6] Mr Tom O'Brien and Mr J. Haworth, trade unionists with no reputation for extremism, regretted that the government had failed to abolish all exemption. (419 *H.C. Deb. 5s.* cols. 231–2 and 258).

Mr E. J. Hill criticised the return to the 1913 compromise in the *Annual Report* of the Boilermakers for 1946.

The Scottish Horse & Motormen's Association voted unanimously in 1953 that trade union law should be amended to give trade unionists 'the right to participate in unfettered political action.' *The Highway,* May 1953.

Among the more interesting examples of double-think that this issue stimulates is an account in *The Woodworkers' Journal,* June 1952. This remarks that 'In 1913 the Liberal Government . . . had the object of hampering trade union interest in politics and making it more difficult for unions to finance Labour candidates than it was before the Osborne case. . . . That Liberal Government was so anxious to

passed, the 1913 Act was restored, and with it contracting-out. But the battle was not yet over.

The Conservatives pledged amending legislation when they returned to power; singling out specifically the contracting-out clause and the affiliation of Civil Service unions to the Labour Party. Even then not all Conservatives shared Mr Hogg's dogmatism. Mr Selwyn Lloyd observed simply, 'Personally, I do not attach quite the importance to this particular measure that I suspect my honourable and learned friend would like me to, but I think that it would be most seemly and decent if this alteration had not been proposed'.[1] Conservative publications promised insistently that the Party would, after consultation with the unions, re-establish contracting-in—'on which', as the Conservative Campaign Guide, 1950 pointed out, 'we have strong convictions of principle'.[2]

The 1950 election over, the Conservative Party's Weekly Newsletter reaffirmed, 'We want a round-table conference with the unions on a number of questions—how to ensure that no man pays to the funds of a political party unless he wants to. . . .'[3] Later that year, however, it remarked that 'contracting-out is a very personal matter, and the Conservative Party have always made it of secondary importance compared with the necessity to attend branch meetings'.[4] Sir David Maxwell Fyfe, the chief spokesman on trade union affairs, wrote that 'we deny to none the right to contribute to a union's political fund if he or she desires'.[5] Early in 1951 Mr David Eccles, speaking of union political activities said, 'I reject the idea of legislation to make

handicap the trade unions that they introduced one of the most unfair methods in democratic practice. . . .' The denunciation merges into an attack on the 1927 Act, but the article concludes with a thankful note about Labour's repeal of the 1927 Act, without mentioning that in so doing it re-established 'one of the most unfair methods in democratic practice'. The case for compulsion rests on the contention made in a letter to The Post (Union of Post Office Workers), October 24, 1953, that 'Anyone withholding the political levy is gaining the benefit of political action without doing anything about it'. This puts him in the same category as non-unionists. The arguments come from industrial need and experience, and carry the common union tendency to consider the methods used in industrial action as appropriate in politics.

[1] 419 H.C. Deb. 5s. col. 272.

[2] The Campaign Guide, 1950, p. 180. See also 50 Things the Tories will Do (1949), This is the Road (Popular Version) (1950). For the importance of the issue during the election, see H. G. Nicholas, The British General Election of 1950, Macmillan, 1951, p. 180.

[3] March 4, 1950.    [4] November 11, 1950.    [5] Ibid, November 18, 1950.

any radical change in the unions' structure and rules'.[1] Yet official literature still insisted that 'Conservatives are pledged to restore this lost political freedom'.[2] However, when the *Conservative Campaign Guide*, 1951 was published, the Party's industrial policy had been almost totally excised; the political levy was not so much as mentioned. On the eve of the election Sir David Maxwell Fyfe reiterated the pledge to seek round-table talks with the unions.[3] Mr Arthur Deakin, Mr Aneurin Bevan, and then the *TGWU Record* challenged him to reveal what the Conservatives proposed to do if they gained power.[4] A major campaign issue was brewing. Sir David announced almost at once, on October 8, that there were no issues pressing for immediate discussion between the Conservatives and the unions.[5] His speech caught the *Weekly Newsletter* dated October 13 in the press saying 'Sir David Maxwell Fyfe and others have made it quite clear that one of the first actions of a Conservative government would be to call a round-table conference with the unions on a wide variety of questions'. Now, in Mr Churchill's words, the Party's attitude was:

'We do not think this is fair. But the Conservative and Liberal membership of the Trade Unions is growing so steadily, that a wider spirit of tolerance has grown up and the question may well be left to common sense and the British way of settling things.'[5]

This was the opening of the Monckton era when Conservatives hoped to get on even better with the unions than Labour. A small group of younger MPs, such as Mr 'Ted' Leather, a member of the Association of Supervisory Staffs, Executives & Technicians (and a Canadian) were urging that Conservatives should be encouraged to be good trade unionists. If the unions were to be weaned away from the Labour Party, it would be through Conservatives working within the movement for political neutrality—much as some Cooperative societies had

---

[1] *The Times*, March 21, 1951.
[2] *All the Answers for the Election*, Conservative Research Department, 1951.
[3] *The Listener*, September 27, 1951.
[4] Respectively: *Report of the Labour Party Conference*, 1951, p. 92. *The Times*, October 9, 1951. *TGWU Record*, October 1951.
[5] *Daily Notes*, Conservative Central Office, October 12, 1951.

been taken out of politics. But Conservatives could not hope for peaceful cooperation with the unions if they insisted either on contracting-in or on the so-called 'Industrial Charter'. Finally the Conservative Party realized that contracting-out just did not interest the electorate. It was expendable ballast. Even without Mr Deakin's challenge it was unlikely, by October 1951, that the Party would have restored contracting-in. It would probably have been quietly shelved, like the promise to re-introduce the university seats.

Conservative hostility had always reflected general suspicion of the unions' fitness to exercise power rather than any appreciation of the specific problem. After forty years of dispute contracting-out, and with it the terms on which unions engage in politics, seems accepted. Conservative policy still holds, naturally enough, that the unions should keep out of party politics. But when the Party's hopes of harmony with the unions faded amid the major strikes of the mid-fifties, the demands that abuses of trade union power must be curbed centred on such industrial problems as shop stewards' activities and the closed shop. Contracting-out was a forgotten battle. While the system of political action is subject to amendment from within the trade union movement itself the possibility that it might be crippled or abolished from without seems to have passed.

## Who Pays the Levy—and Why?

Mr Clement Davies might well remark, as the House of Commons debated contracting-out in 1946, 'I do not think that any deep principle is involved'.[1] It was not principle that impassioned the debates. Behind the highly-coloured controversy both parties were campaigning lustily in their own interest. Every Labour or Conservative partisan knew that the adoption of one or other system of paying the political levy led to large variations in the numbers of members contributing—to much more, or much less money being given by the unions to the Labour Party.[2]

---

[1] 419 H.C. Deb. 5s. col. 266.
[2] Duff Cooper recorded in his diary for January 25, 1926: 'Later some of us went to see Jackson and Blair at (Conservative) Central Office, who crudely confessed that their object was to deplete the funds of the Labour Party.' Old Men Forget, p. 143.

Nevertheless, Conservative criticisms seemed devastatingly justified when the effect of the 1946 Act was reported by the Chief Registrar. The proportion of contributors, in unions with political funds, rose from 48·5 per cent in 1945 to 90·6 per cent in 1947.[1] Conservatives could claim that three million workers were paying the political levy against their will. But it was typical of the whole confused controversy over the political levy that the debate was fed by inaccurate statistics.

To know how many members were led to contribute to their union's political fund simply because of the change from contracting-in to contracting-out is not just a matter of historical interest. It affects the whole relationship between the unions and the Labour Party. The number of members a union affiliates to the Labour Party depends on its number of political contributors. The overwhelming voting power of the unions at the Party Conference, and the financial well-being of the Labour Party also depend on how many members pay the levy. Trade union leaders will claim to speak for these members. How far they contribute willingly and how far they pay the levy only as a result of this minor administrative change, is obviously an indication of the importance that trade unionists attach to political activities and to the link with the Labour Party.

## TABLE 1

### TRADE UNIONISTS PAYING THE POLITICAL LEVY[a]

| Year[b] | Registered Trade Unions with Political Funds | | Members Paying the Political Levy in Unregistered Trade Unions[c] | Total Paying the Political Levy[d] | Per cent Paying Political Levy[e] |
| | Membership | Contributing to the Political Fund | | | |
| --- | --- | --- | --- | --- | --- |
| 1925 | | | | | |
| 1926 | | | | | |
| 1927 | | | | | |
| 1928 | 2,801,434 | 1,634,019 | 581,444 | 2,088,000 | 58·3 |
| 1929 | 2,822,537 | 1,668,796 | 583,530 | 2,119,000 | 59·1 |
| 1930 | 2,840,000 | 1,683,457 | 590,044 | 2,144,000 | 59·2 |
| 1931 | 2,701,000 | 1,587,452 | 582,310 | 2,045,000 | 59·7 |
| 1932 | 2,553,283 | 1,493,495 | 542,404 | 1,916,000 | 58·5 |
| 1933 | 2,597,455 | 1,481,402 | 548,585 | 1,915,000 | 57·0 |

[1] *Report of the Chief Registrar of Friendly Societies*, 1947. Part IV, *Trade Unions*.

| 1934 | 2,731,846 | 1,575,865 | 525,443 | 1,983,000 | 57·7 |
|------|-----------|-----------|---------|-----------|------|
| 1935 | 2,965,442 | 1,671,060 | 525,343 | 2,078,000 | 56·5 |
| 1936 | 3,297,797 | 1,779,537 | 544,980 | 2,325,000 | 54·0 |
| 1937 | 3,729,011 | 1,921,623 | 569,538 | 2,491,000 | 51·5 |
| 1938 | 3,935,080 | 1,974,903 | 574,724 | 2,550,000 | 50·2 |
| 1939 | 4,074,939 | 2,016,674 | 562,221 | 2,579,000 | 49·8 |
| | | | | | |
| 1943 | 5,705,835 | 2,385,417 | 515,502 | 2,901,000 | 41·8 |
| 1944 | 5,619,728 | 2,426,499 | 523,514 | 2,950,000 | 43·2 |
| 1945 | 5,928,674 | 2,846,150 | 95,813 | 2,917,000 | 48·0 |
| 1946 | 6,904,000 | .. | .. | .. | .. |
| 1947 | 7,413,000 | | | 5,613,000 | 75·6 |
| 1948 | 7,529,000 | | | 5,773,000 | 76·8 |
| 1949 | 7,477,000 | | | 5,821,000 | 77·9 |
| 1950 | 7,433,000 | | | 5,833,000 | 78·4 |
| 1951 | 7,688,000 | | | 5,936,000 | 77·1 |
| 1952 | 7,712,000 | | | 5,962,000 | 77·5 |
| 1953 | 7,678,000 | | | 5,924,000 | 77·2 |
| 1954 | 7,707,000 | | | 5,949,000 | 77·2 |
| 1955 | 7,854,000 | | | 6,173,000 | 79·6 |
| 1956 | 7,859,000 | | | 6,245,000 | 79·5 |
| 1957 | 7,923,000 | | | 6,329,000 | 80·0 |
| 1958 | 7,735,000 | | | 6,280,000 | 81·3 |

[a] From 1925–45 the source is the Chief Registrar of Friendly Societies. From 1947 the figures are revised calculations by the author. The Chief Registrar gives the following figures for these years:

| 1947 | 6,738,000 | 1950 | 6,683,000 | 1953 | 6,787,000 | 1956 | 6,903,000 |
|------|-----------|------|-----------|------|-----------|------|-----------|
| 1948 | 6,890,000 | 1951 | 6,839,000 | 1954 | 6,808,000 | 1957 | 6,947,000 |
| 1949 | 6,814,000 | 1952 | 6,857,000 | 1955 | 6,907,000 | 1958 | 6,813,000 |

[b] Figures are not available for 1940–2. The figures for 1925–7 contain substantial double counting and should be taken as only a rough indication.

[c] The National Union of Mineworkers became a registered trade union in 1945 and separate figures for unregistered unions were no longer published.

[d] From 1928–34 the total of contributors is less than the sum of the two columns of contributors because the Chief Registrar has eliminated some double counting.

[e] Until 1945 this percentage refers to registered trade unions only, thereafter to all unions.

It is unfortunate, since the point is so politically important, that the official statistics are gravely inaccurate.[1] Up to 1945 they were acceptable enough. Unions reported to the Chief Registrar the numbers of their political contributors, and the totals were

[1] The production of any trade union statistic is open to error. There is no standard definition of what constitutes a member, and union practices vary widely. Some unions give year-end membership figures—which are possibly affected by seasonal factors. Others calculate figures of average membership, allowing elaborately for turnover. Though few unions nowadays claim inflated membership figures for prestige reasons, many unions cannot state their membership precisely. Their figures are honest approximations at best. My statistics reflect this imprecision, as do those of the Chief Registrar of Friendly Societies.

C

printed in the Registrar's Annual Reports. Since 1946, however, unions have reported the number of members who have 'obtained exemption from contributing to the Political Fund', that is, those who have contracted-out. Deducting this total from the membership of unions with political funds, the Registrar has published annually a statistic of 'Members contributing'.

This is far from telling the whole story. Some unions automatically exempt whole classes of member by rule, such as juniors or apprentices, the sick and the unemployed, members serving in the armed forces, and those living in the Republic of Ireland or overseas. Contracting-in remains in force in Northern Ireland, and only about 37,000 of the 150,000 members of English-registered unions contribute to the political funds.[1] For these and other reasons the number of effective contributors often falls far below the numbers reported to the Chief Registrar. The United Society of Boilermakers reported to the Chief Registrar in 1957 that 4,518 of its 93,706 members had contracted-out. But it also excused 587 temporary and honorary members, 10,651 apprentices, and 4,031 superannuated members. None of the 325 members in the Republic of Ireland paid, and only 250 of the 3,200 Ulster members contracted-in. Altogether 18,544 more members were excused than was reported. Contributions finally collected represented payment by 57,030 members.[2] The Typographical Association, with 57,324 members, of whom only 9,425 contracted-out had, in fact, 31,442 contributors to its political fund.[3] In the Amalgamated Engineering Union (AEU), about 100,000 overseas members are apparently counted as paying the political levy, although they never contribute a penny, and the National Union of Mineworkers (NUM) returns include some 90,000 retired and 'Power Group' members who do not pay the levy.[4] Some unions report all their exemptions, whatever the cause, as 'contracting-out'. Others return only the numbers who have signed the

---

[1] *Reports of the Registrar of Friendly Societies* (Northern Ireland).
[2] *Annual Financial Report*, 1957.
[3] 219th *Half-Yearly Financial Report*, March–September 1958.
[4] The NUM Power Group includes colliery members of the TGWU and NUGMW, on behalf of whom the NUM exercises negotiating rights, who normally contribute to their own union's political fund. They are apparently double-counted in the membership figures.

official contracting-out form. The result is statistical chaos.[1] Since 1946, in the last type of union, members who are excused payment of the political levy by rule are counted in the official statistics as paying it. In the extreme case, the unions which have a political fund but collect no contributions, the number of contributors was officially nil in 1945 but, since there were no contractors-out, it became 100 per cent, for official purposes, from 1947.[2]

It is quite impossible to tell from the published statistics either how many people pay the political levy, or how many have refused to do so by signing a contracting-out form. It is quite evident, however, that the number of trade unionists who have contracted-out in the officially prescribed manner falls far short of the Registrar's figure of just under one million. Some other yardstick is essential. The best available means of gauging the effect of the switch from contracting-in to contracting-out is to measure its consequences, not on contributors—who may exist only on paper—but on contributions. By measuring the importance of the 1946 change through the increase in the political levy collected we can also take account of the 'silent contractor-out'—the member who simply will not pay the political levy, but never fills in a contracting-out form. The Shipwrights' Association shows what a problem these members can be. Slightly over 1,500 of its 25,000 members have contracted-out—yet only about 5,100 pay the political levy. No amount of cajoling by the union has persuaded them to 'regularize their position'.[3]

Making contributions collected the standard presents certain difficulties, because of the problem of 'fractional members', and the averaging of contributions—as a result 20,000 contributions do not necessarily indicate exactly 20,000 contributors. It has proved a reliable index during the postwar years, when unem-

[1] The attention of the Chief Registrar of Friendly Societies was drawn to this point in 1925, by Captain Waterhouse. Cf., 181 *H.C. Deb. 5s.* cols. 33 and 624, and *Report of the Chief Registrar of Friendly Societies*, 1924, Part IV.
[2] This appears to have been the case for the National Federation of Insurance Workers and the Medical Practitioners' Union.
[3] *Report of the SSA*, 1947, 1948 and 1951. See also *The Highway*, May 1948. The Scottish Horse & Motormen's Association complains that although 20,000 members out of 21,000 should have been paying the political levy because 'only a few hundred' had contracted-out, they had nowhere near so many contributors.

ployment has been low for most unions, arrears have probably been relatively constant, and the expansion or contraction of total membership has been slow. According to the Registrar's calculation (which was then accurate), there were 2,917,000 political contributors in 1945; the revised method produces a figure of 2,903,000.[1]

The true consequences of the 1946 Act are now more evident. The proportion of contributions collected rose from forty-eight per cent to seventy-six per cent—not to ninety-one per cent as the official statistics have it.[2] The number contributing to political funds rose by 3,800,000 between 1945 and 1947, on the Chief Registrar's reckoning. About 700,000 of these were new members who would have paid the levy in any case. But the *true* rise was equivalent to 2,700,000 members—of whom, again, some 700,000 would have paid in any event. In short, the simple change from contracting-in to contracting-out was worth 2,000,000 contributors to the unions. Among those eligible, one trade unionist in four who would not have paid the political levy under contracting-in, paid it under contracting-out.

## TABLE 2

HOW THE RETURN TO CONTRACTING-OUT AFFECTED THE AMALGAMATED ASSOCIATION OF OPERATIVE COTTON SPINNERS AND TWINERS

| District Association | Percentage of Members Paying the Political Levy | |
| --- | --- | --- |
| | April 1947 % | July 1947 % |
| Bamber Bridge | 32 | 82 |
| Bolton | 73 | 96 |
| Bury | 46 | 99 |
| Heywood | 50 | 94 |
| Hyde | 52 | 97 |
| North-East Lancs—Accrington | 42 | 98 |
| North-East Lancs—Blackburn | 27 | 100 |
| Oldham Cop Packers | 0 | 92 |
| Oldham Provincial | 58 | 96 |
| Oldham Roller Coverers United | 0 | 0 |
| Preston | 27 | 100 |
| Rochdale | 52 | 54 |

[1] Under contracting-in many unions, unable to say how many members contributed to their political funds, calculated their political membership on the basis of contributions collected. The revised calculation continues this practice.

[2] Henceforward we shall refer to 'contributors' and 'proportion contributing' for convenience's sake, although this is not completely precise.

| | | |
|---|---|---|
| South-East Lancs | 79 | 99 |
| Stockport | 43 | 100 |
| Wigan | 78 | 77 |
| Whole AAOCST | 58 | 89 |

It seems legitimate to attribute the whole of this rise to the return to contracting-out. It might be argued that the unions would have collected a higher proportion of contributions in any case once they had settled down to peace-time standards of administration, or that the achievements of Labour in office would have stimulated members to pay the political levy. This seems unlikely: in unions which delayed the switch to contracting-out until 1947 there was an increase of only 0·4 per cent. On the other hand, the proportion of members paying the political levy had fallen steadily from 1930 to 1946, with little apparent regard to the political or economic situation. This decline might well have continued unchecked had the 1946 Act not intervened. The effects of the Act, though less than generally believed, are still large enough to call for an explanation.

TABLE 3

EFFECTS OF THE CHANGE TO CONTRACTING-OUT IN THE
BRITISH IRON, STEEL AND KINDRED TRADES' ASSOCIATION

| Division | Percentage of Members Paying Political Levy | |
|---|---|---|
| | 31/3/1947 %| 30/6/1947 % |
| 1. (Scotland) | 21·97 | 86·88 |
| 2. (Teeside) | 25·56 | 82·13 |
| 3. (South Yorks, Lincolnshire) | 62·68 | 92·83 |
| 4. (Midlands) | 38·72 | 87·90 |
| 5. (South Wales) | 38·26 | 89·30 |
| 6. (South Wales) | 47·95 | 92·78 |
| 7. (North Wales, Cumberland) | 30·98 | 86·33 |
| 8. (Home Counties) | 78·79 | 90·98 |
| Whole of BISAKTA | 41·10 | 88·71 |

It is typical of the discussions of the part that the unions play in politics that the facts have been given widely varying and contradictory interpretations. A Conservative source could claim:

'The immense jump (in political contributors) and the restoration of the invidious system of contracting-out is clear proof of the difficulty which non-Socialists find in practice in declaring their unwillingness to subscribe to Socialist Party funds.'[1]

Looking at the Transport & General Workers' Union, Mr J. Goldstein thought that 'this fantastic increase is startling but undeniable evidence of apathy . . .'[2] To a Labour spokesman, naturally enough, 'The figures . . . demonstrate that there is not a rag of evidence that anyone was being compelled to contribute to political funds against his will.'[3]

Intimidation was once the most favoured explanation of why contracting-out produces so high a proportion of contributors. Conservative speakers brought forward harrowing tales to prove their case. There was the Miners' lodge which forced its contractors-out to parade once a year under a rain of insults to collect their shilling, the South Wales miners who were set upon and beaten, the men who went in terror of their jobs. As late as 1946 some Conservatives could accept Lt-Col Bromley-Davenport's picture of 3,500,000 unwilling trade unionists subscribing to the political levy only for fear of reprisals on their wives and children.[4]

It has never been possible to gauge how far trade unionists were intimidated. Labour apologists, loath to admit the unions capable of victimization, considered the tiny trickle of complaints reaching the Registrar of Friendly Societies convincing proof that the problem was negligible. But the number of complaints to the Registrar means almost nothing. Few members know that they have the right to complain, and fewer still, among those who have suffered intimidation, will incur the expense, and the even greater unpopularity of appealing to the Registrar for the sake of two shillings per year. The safeguards in the 1913 Act were little comfort to the occasional Liberal miner in a Durham pit village in the thirties. To many miners, the man who did not pay his political levy was a blackleg—to be treated as such. It made little difference in this kind of atmosphere

---

[1] *The Campaign Guide*, 1950, p. 181.
[2] J. Goldstein, *The Government of British Trade Unions*, Allen & Unwin, 1950, p. 124.
[3] Sir Hartley Shawcross, 419 *H.C. Deb. 5s.* col. 209. His remark refers, strictly, to the period before the 1927 Act.
[4] 419 *H.C. Deb. 5s.* col. 278.

whether contracting-in or contracting-out was in force. As Mr
Oliver Stanley, a Conservative, noted in 1927:

'You still have the knowledge, which is the essential preliminary to intimidation—you may charge people and you may
mark them in instead of out; you may tick them off with a red
pencil instead of a blue pencil—that, in fact, there are two lists
still there. . . . There are many ways in which trade union
leaders, if they want to intimidate, can still do it.'[1]

Changing to contracting-in only safeguards members where
there are enough dissenters to put the task of coercing them
beyond the capacity of local officials and militants. Contracting-
in can eliminate intimidation only if the trade union machine is
less efficient, or the militants less determined, than many of the
unions' critics have allowed.

It is true that the 'weight' of contracting-in and contracting-
out is different. Stanley Baldwin shrewdly noted that:

'. . . a man has a loyalty—and it is a very good loyalty—to his
fellows who work with him, and it is a very hard thing for him
in any way to feel that he is throwing them over. That is a kind
of pressure which, under the old system of contracting-out, hit
him very hard and made it difficult for him either to claim or to
get the exemption to which, I think, he was fully entitled.'[2]

The conclusion was not so sound. Contracting-out does
dissociate the member from his fellows more directly than
simply neglecting to contract-in. But it is fair enough that
members should feel some pressure of loyalty, which should be
broken for the sake of principle rather than to save a shilling or
so a year. Contracting-in lets the member evade this choice.

At times the frustration by a union's administration of members who want to contract out falls little short of intimidation.
Branches may be 'out of stock' of contracting-out forms. As
ominously late as 1954, the Bakers' Union report stated that
'It was agreed to inform all districts that the rules of the Political
Fund are to operate, and all branches must be supplied with
contracting-out cards'.[3] Now and then branch secretaries jib at

[1] 206 H.C. Deb. 5s. col. 2072.
[2] 247 H.C. Deb. 5s. col. 421.                    [3] at p. 60.

accepting contracting-out forms prepared by the Conservative Party, or by the member himself. At one time there were frequent reports of contracting-out forms being 'accidentally' burned or lost.[1] Today these are rare.

There seems to be general agreement that intimidation of all kinds has declined since the war, though pockets may still exist. Members may tremble at the shop steward's frown—against which no legislation can be wholly effective—or they may simply hesitate to show themselves 'different' from their workmates. But official Conservative circles make few complaints about the treatment of contracting-out members. The Party's announcement of its change of policy in 1951 was couched in optimistic terms, and the *Weekly Newsletter* has confided to Party workers that 'contracting-out is not difficult'.[2]

The energy of a branch committee or a group of active members often makes all the difference between a high and low proportion of contributors. 'If it wasn't for the Commies I don't know how we would collect our political levy', confessed the Assistant General Secretary of a large craft union. 'They're the only ones who whip it in.' Elsewhere the enthusiasm of branch officials sometimes depends on whether they are allowed commission on the political contributions they collect. The branch's efficiency can be all-important. Just as enthusiastic militants can see that the levy is paid, so in some unions groups of Conservatives successfully encourage their fellow-members to contract-out. Under contracting-in the whole weight of

[1] *Nutter and the National Union of Railwaymen*, Registrar's decision December 4, 1947. The Registrar dismissed the complaint that a contracting-out form was not supplied. (*Report of Select Disputes etc.*, p. 240). See complaint in AESD *Report of the RCC*, 1947, p. 101. For an appeal to the Registrar on refusal of a union to accept a contracting-out form supplied by the local Conservative Association, see *Hewett and another and the Electrical Trades Union* (*Report of Select Disputes etc.*, p. 222) and *Valentine and the Electrical Trades Union*, in *Report of the Chief Registrar of Friendly Societies*, 1957, Part IV, p. 3.

[2] December 6, 1952. It is pleasing to note that Mr Churchill, who as Liberal Home Secretary introduced the 1913 Act, was among the strongest enthusiasts for contracting-in in the twenties, and finally announced the reversal of his Party's policy in 1951. His words in 1951, previously quoted, had a strange similarity to what he said in 1913: 'There never was a time when public opinion was more vigilant, when publicity was more searching, and when intolerance in all its forms was so absolutely lacking in defenders of any kind, and any attempt to trample upon the political convictions of individuals is more severely censured and condemned and more effectively pilloried at the present time than it ever has been in any country.' 26 *H.C. Deb. 5s.* col. 1017.

inefficiency or inertia in a union's administration, or of lethargy among its members, tends constantly to depress the numbers contributing. Under contracting-out they just as surely inflate the proportion who pay the levy.

The members' ignorance counts in the same way. The Trade Union Act, 1913, lays down that a member must be given a current rule book which clearly states the amount of political levy, how he can contract out, and how he can complain to the Registrar. Normally members do receive rule books on joining their union—but how many read and understand the long pages of legal phraseology? Goldstein claimed that only one in three of the members of the Transport & General Workers' Union (TGWU) he interviewed had read either the rules or the *Member's Handbook*.[1] As a Typographical Association official openly admitted to his union's conference: 'There are a great many people who pay the $\frac{1}{2}$d to the Labour Representation Fund unknowingly.'[2] While the proportion of ignorant members might be disputed no one in the movement seriously denies that many trade unionists have not the least idea that they pay a political levy, have never heard of contracting-out, and would want to be excused payment if they did know. Immediately after the passing of the 1946 Act the Conservatives tried to publicize the possibility of contracting-out. Although the 'interference' by Conservative Associations or by the 'British Workers' Information Bureau' irritated trade union militants from time to time there is little evidence that the drive has had much success. The most effective campaigning is confined to a few unions— notably the Association of Engineering & Shipbuilding Draughtsmen, where Conservative branch officials telling new members that they can contract out have aroused the ire of Labour supporters, who consider it disloyal to let a member know his rights.[3]

Most unions give only the scantiest information about the number of their political contributors. The records of the few which publish branch or district contribution figures show a wide

---

[1] *The Government of British Trade Unions*, p. 231. Goldstein says that one in three inactive members of the TGWU he interviewed claimed not to have received a rule book (p. 230).
[2] *Report of the Delegate Meeting*, 1953, p. 137.
[3] *Report of the RC Conference*, 1947, p. 101 and 1953, p. 270.

range of experience. It is sometimes suggested that certain types of union, or organizations recruiting among a given kind of worker, are more likely to have a high or low proportion of members paying the levy. In fact there is little consistent experience among the general, craft or industrial unions, between growing and shrinking unions, or between white collar unions and the rest. The white collar group, for example, contains several unions with no party affiliation, the Association of Supervisory Staffs, Executives & Technicians (ASSET), which has a high contracting-out rate because of its high levy and the dual membership of many of its members in other unions, and the Transport Salaried Staffs' Association, whose record for contracting-in used to outshine even the Miners.

Within most unions there were wide variations in the numbers paying the levy between branches and districts. The National Union of Furniture Trade Operatives' record shows how wide

TABLE 4

COLLECTION OF THE POLITICAL LEVY IN THE NATIONAL
UNION OF FURNITURE TRADE OPERATIVES, 1954

| Division | Per cent of Possible Contributions Collected % |
|---|---|
| Eire and Northern Ireland | 1 |
| Scotland | 14 |
| North Western | 25 |
| North Eastern | 4 |
| Midlands and East Anglia | 18 |
| Mid-South and South East | 10 |
| Wales | 10 |
| South West | 18 |
| London | 47 |
| Whole NUFTO | 28 |

these differences may be. The problem is similar in the National Union of Printing, Bookbinding & Paper Workers where, in 1957, there were:

19 branches with 75 per cent or more contributors
15      ,,        ,, 50–74 per cent contributors
36      ,,        ,, 25–49 per cent contributors
159     ,,        ,, 24 per cent or fewer contributors

At one time the Boilermakers' Society's branches in Sunderland had records varying between 0·4 per cent and 88 per cent of contributions collected. On the other hand, the NUM shows a monolithic solidarity worthy of Eastern Europe—with the exception of the Tradesmen's Groups, and the Colliery Officials' and Staffs' Association which have come into the union since

TABLE 5

PAYMENT OF THE POLITICAL LEVY IN THE NATIONAL UNION
OF MINEWORKERS—1958

| Area | Members Paying Political Levy | Members Contracting-Out |
|---|---|---|
| Cokemen | 7,029 | 69 |
| Cumberland | 5,016 | 10 |
| Derbyshire | 35,731 | 5 |
| Durham | 84,574 | 190 |
| Kent | 6,727 | 0 |
| Lancashire | 40,019 | 1 |
| Leicester | 6,588 | 0 |
| Midlands | 47,053 | 2 |
| Northumberland | 33,141 | 1 |
| North Wales | 7,506 | 0 |
| Nottinghamshire | 47,841 | 4 |
| Scotland | 73,027 | 0 |
| Somerset | 2,630 | 0 |
| South Derbyshire | 5,483 | 0 |
| South Wales | 93,655 | 59 |
| Yorkshire | 125,581 | 0 |
| Durham Mechanics | 11,360 | 16 |
| Durham Enginemen | 3,796 | 9 |
| Northumberland Mechanics | 4,702 | 41 |
| Yorkshire Enginemen | 1,069 | 18 |
| Yorkshire Winders | 95 | 465 |
| Lancashire Colliery Tradesmen | 3,997 | 3 |
| Lancashire Enginemen | 1,786 | 4 |
| Derbyshire Enginemen | 1,578 | 0 |
| Derbyshire Winders | 67 | 211 |
| Scottish Enginemen | 9,591 | 9 |
| Colliery Officials' & Staffs' Association | 8,210 | 24,693 |
| WHOLE NUM | 667,852 | 25,810 |

the war. The general result of imposing contracting-out was to narrow the range of variation between branches where it had been marked. In 1946, for example, South Yorkshire branches of the British Iron, Steel & Kindred Trades' Association collected sixty-three per cent of its contributions, while Scotland collected only twenty-two per cent. Once contracting-out came into force the gap narrowed, to ninety-three per cent and eighty-seven per cent. The Typographical Association and the Cotton Spinners' Amalgamation had very similar experiences. Some branches, which had no more than one or

TABLE 6

EFFECTS OF CHANGE TO CONTRACTING-OUT
IN THE TYPOGRAPHICAL ASSOCIATION

| Proportion of Eligible Members Contributing % | Number of Branches | |
|---|---|---|
| | July 1946 | December 1946 |
| 0–19% | 15 | 16 |
| 20–39% | 21 | 5 |
| 40–59% | 21 | 14 |
| 60–79% | 45 | 57 |
| 80% and over | 85 | 106 |
| | 197 | 198 |

two political contributors for years suddenly reached 100 per cent political membership in 1947.

The statistics cannot reveal how such complete reversals of branch habits came about—but no one would attribute them to a change of heart. It seems inescapable that the choice of contracting-in, or contracting-out profoundly affects the number of members who pay the political levy. It is legitimate enough that, once a union has democratically decided to take part in political activities, those who dissent should have to dissociate themselves from the decision. There seems no case for requiring a second consent from those who support political action—as contracting-in does. For all that, about 2,000,000 trade unionists pay the political levy purely as a result of the return of contracting-in. The change may be attributed to inertia, inefficiency, intimidation, or ignorance—or all at once. No other explanations have been advanced. They are an inglorious acquisition. Nothing permits us to conclude that a sizeable number of trade unionists pay the levy unwillingly, but neither can it be claimed that members who support political action only through an administrative 'gimmick' have any enthusiasm for the political activities which are conducted in their name.

## The Trend

Despite the significant fraction of trade unionists whose 'support' for political action rests on laziness, ignorance or fear, many members pay—or refuse to pay—quite consciously and deliberately. Accordingly, once the change from contracting-in to contracting-out had been made, fluctuations in the support for the political fund can cast some further light on the members' attitude to political activity. It is remarkable, for instance, how often branches with a poor contribution record in 1945 have remained below their union's average since 1946, while branches which always collected a high proportion of contributions under contracting-in usually retain a slight lead even now.

TABLE 7

PROPORTION OF MEMBERS PAYING THE POLITICAL LEVY

| Per cent Paying Political Levy | Number of Unions | | | | | | |
|---|---|---|---|---|---|---|---|
| | 1945 | 1947 | 1949 | 1951 | 1953 | 1955 | 1957 |
| 91–100% | 1 | 13 | 16 | 17 | 16 | 18 | 20 |
| 81– 90% | 3 | 11 | 10 | 13 | 13 | 14 | 16 |
| 71– 80% | 5 | 10 | 13 | 9 | 13 | 12 | 11 |
| 61– 70% | 9 | 12 | 25 | 21 | 18 | 19 | 19 |
| 51– 60% | 7 | 11 | 10 | 13 | 13 | 10 | 10 |
| 41– 50% | 8 | 6 | 4 | 4 | 6 | 6 | 7 |
| 31– 40% | 13 | 4 | 4 | 5 | 4 | 6 | 7 |
| 21– 30% | 10 | 3 | 4 | 4 | 5 | 6 | 7 |
| 11– 20% | 10 | 4 | 2 | 3 | 4 | 4 | 4 |
| 1– 10% | 18 | 4 | 4 | 5 | 4 | 3 | 0 |
| TOTAL UNIONS | 84 | 78 | 92 | 94 | 96 | 98 | 101 |

Superficially the statistics of contributing membership should, therefore, comfort those who believe in political action. But although the Chief Registrar's figures show a fall from 90·6 per cent contributors in 1947 to 87·5 per cent in 1957, the revised calculation reveals that it has risen irregularly over this period from seventy-seven per cent to eighty per cent. But this slight rise is largely attributable to administrative changes in several large unions.[1] Closer examination reveals a rather different picture. Of eighty-nine unions for which the 1947 and 1957

[1] See p. 49.

figures were comparable, seventeen had the same proportion contributing in 1957 as in 1947, twenty-five had a higher proportion, and in forty-seven the proportion fell. These movements were all small—but they may be significant.

In 1957 only twenty unions collected political contributions from ninety per cent or more of their members, while twenty-five had fifty per cent or fewer contributors. For one cause or another some 3,500,000 members of trade unions with political funds pay no political levy. Exemptions by rule apart, voluntary non-contribution is increasing.

How significant these changes are is not yet fully clear. Possibly more trade unionists know that they can contract out, while others may be less hesitant to apply for exemption. It seems unlikely that the unions have become less efficient, but their enthusiasm for chasing defaulters has doubtless reflected the general decline in political militancy. Although, therefore, the fairly widespread fall may not indicate that trade unionists are drifting away either from Labour or political action, there is little to comfort the enthusiasts.

Since the war the small rise in union membership has kept political revenues buoyant. In few unions has the proportion paying the levy dropped more than five per cent. Few have realized that they have a problem. The Transport Salaried Staffs' Association, where contributions fell from ninety-three per cent to ninety per cent of membership, was one of the first to become concerned at the slow erosion. It began a campaign to interest its members in the political levy. The union's Members of Parliament addressed meetings, leaflets were distributed outlining the benefits that Parliamentary representation had brought the union, and the TSSA's *Journal* has always tried to show what political action has won. The Association seeks to counter the cry that the unions should keep out of politics by showing that political action brings solid *industrial* benefits.

The Amalgamated Engineering Union has also been troubled by a large number of non-contributors. Its National Committee has called for a campaign to stress the levy's importance at every level in the union. The Executive Council has circulated pamphlets, published articles in the *AEU Journal*, and distributed large quantities of Labour Party literature in the branches. But in the AEU, as in the TSSA, the results have been slender.[1] The Association of Engineering & Shipbuilding Draughtsmen has sent appeals to its junior members, as they became eligible to pay the political levy, and has published several series of articles in *The Draughtsman*. Yet all the while the numbers paying the political levy have steadily fallen, until they are well under half the membership. Other unions have made scattered appeals, published occasional articles, and distributed a few leaflets, but nothing approaching a sustained campaign.

Some attempts to persuade members to pay the levy fail because so many trade union militants, living in a world in which 'The Movement' is either taken for granted or is an article of faith, are quite incapable of comprehending another point of view. Often they prefer to abuse the opposition rather than convert it. Here is a member of the AEU addressing Conservative trade unionists in his union's *Journal*:

'I wonder if you know what the vast majority of your fellow members think of you. Maybe your best friends won't tell you. . . . Some of your fellow trade unionists look upon you with open contempt. They believe that you are a member only for what you can get from the Movement. . . . Others do not condemn you—they pity you, because they think you are ignorant. . . . If, being cognisant with these things, you still give the Tories your vote, brother, you can be regarded as the Judas in our midst.'[2]

Discussion is carried on as if the working class were politically united apart from a derisory handful of backsliders. There is almost no understanding that one trade unionist in four or five votes Conservative. Perhaps discretion is the best course. So long as many members are unaware that they can contract-out, campaigns for contractors-out to repent may be unwise. Ignorance does help keep the proportion of contributors high. The safest course for a union which wants to keep its political fund healthy is to insist continually on the value of its link with the Labour Party and the importance of the political levy,

[1] *Minutes of the Proceedings of the National Committee*, 1954, p. 188.
[2] *AEU Journal*, February 1950.

keeping contracting-out in the background—unless it is so well known that no harm can be done by admitting it is possible.

Many unions are still worried by the problem of members who neither contract out nor pay the political levy.[1] Some members flatly refuse to pay political contributions, although they keep a 'clean card' industrially. Collectors usually prefer to clear up industrial arrears before insisting on payment of the levy. It is widely—and erroneously—believed that the law prohibits action against such defaulters. In any case unions are reluctant to discipline their members purely over political arrears. In the past few years a growing number of unions have solved the problem by merging or 'compounding' their political and industrial contributions.

At one time most unions collected the levy in separate quarterly or annual instalments. When the levy is compounded it is merged into the normal weekly contribution, or one or two weekly contributions are allocated to the political fund each year. Compounding is popular with collecting stewards because it usually simplifies the structure of contribution rates. But, like the contracting-out system itself, it also makes the member less conscious than ever that he is paying a political levy. As a delegate to the Bakers' conference suggested:

'If the levy could just be embodied, say put a penny per week on the total subscriptions, then I think everybody will agree to pay, but it is because it stands out on its own as Political Levy that people seem to be afraid to pay it. . . .'

In 1954 the National Union of General & Municipal Workers (NUGMW), which had a compounded contribution, collected the political levy from ninety-nine per cent of its members, while the TGWU, which collected it each quarter, effectively had

---

[1] The position had deteriorated so far in the Musicians' Union by 1958 that the union's conference found it necessary to vote that 'unless he had given notice to contract out', every member should pay the political levy. *The Musician*, May 1958.

In 1957 the National Union of Furniture Trade Operatives' conference noted 'with regret the failure of branches and members to observe the rule on payment of political levy'. *NUFTO Record*, August 1957. The Bakers also reminded their District Secretaries that members must be made to pay up or contract out, *Annual Report*, 1955, p. 74. The General Secretary of the Association of Blacksmiths, Forge & Smithy Workers complained that of 126 branches making returns sixty-seven had made no contribution to the political fund. *The Anvil*, December 1955–March 1956.

eighty-four per cent contributors. When the TGWU switched to a compounded contribution in 1957 and *doubled its levy*, the proportion paying rose to ninety-six per cent. The National Union of Tailors & Garment Workers and the National Union of Public Employees, both with compounded contributions, claim that ninety-nine per cent of their members pay the political levy. Efficient though it is, the compounding system is not universally popular. 'What do I think of compounding?' echoed the General Secretary of a printing craft union. 'Frankly, these people are up to a bloody swindle. They know their members wouldn't pay the money if they knew what they were paying for. I'd sooner we didn't have a political fund than get money that way.' Swindle or not, there seems little doubt that compounding will spread, that it will be on the basis of such 'support' that the Movement makes its way.

## The Politically Active

Theoretically the unions' political activities are run by the six million or so members who pay the political levy. The rest have no share at all in the unions' political life. If only Labour-minded members contributed to a fund which is so largely spent in aid of the Labour Party, it would be the Labour section of trade union membership, which nominated Labour candidates, decided how the unions shall vote at the Party's conferences, and contributed to its election funds. But this is far from true in practice.

The 1913 Act has provided the safeguard for a member who contracts-out, that he 'may not be put at any disadvantage compared with other members, purely by reason of his not contributing to the political fund, except in relation to the control and management of the political fund'. Some such rule was obviously necessary to prevent members being victimized because of their political views. At the same time it is legitimate that trade unionists who refuse to pay the levy should have no share in debates on the rate of political levy, how much allowance is to be paid to Members of Parliament, or who the Treasurer of the Labour Party should be. But the exact scope of the restriction has been disputed for many years.

At one time the Chief Registrar held that contractors-out

D

could not be fairly excluded from a ballot to choose a union's Parliamentary candidate—though he subsequently changed his mind.[1] Later he felt unable to uphold the complaint made by a Mr Johns, a member of the National Union of Railwaymen, that he had been held ineligible for a branch office because he had contracted-out.[2] A similar issue was raised by Mr Birch, another member of the NUR, a Conservative branch chairman. He had refused to countersign his branch's nomination of a candidate to a Parliamentary selection conference. He was unseated, under the union's rules, on the ground that his office involved control of the political fund and, since he had contracted-out, his original nomination had been invalid. The Chief Registrar found that the chairman did control the political fund in some respects since, with the secretary and a majority of members of the branch, he sanctioned any withdrawal of funds, including political expenditure, and could exercise the chairman's power over meetings. Mr Birch was accordingly not being put to a greater disadvantage than the Act authorized. He rejected the complaint.[3]

Normally the Registrar's decisions are subject to no appeal. Had the decision stood, in the *Birch* and *Johns* cases, contracting-out members could have been excluded from *any* union office which carried any discretion in relation to *any* political activity. Contractors-out would have been excluded from almost every office: they would have been second-class members. Mr Birch was able to bring action against the union through the courts, on the grounds that the NUR Rules, which had been approved by the Chief Registrar, were *ultra vires*. He was successful. The Court found that the deprivation went beyond the 1913 Act by excluding Mr Birch from an office which did not *solely or mainly* involve the control or management of the political fund.[4]

Other restrictions, some informal, are still imposed on mem-

---

[1] *H. F. S. Jackson and the National Union of Vehicle Builders.* Registrar's decision, April 24, 1945. See also *Quarterly Report of the NUVB*, July 1945. According to counsel for the union there had been only one political contributor in the protesting branch out of 600 members. The single contributor stood for the Parliamentary Panel and the branch asked for 600 ballot papers.

[2] *Johns and the National Union of Railwaymen, Report of Selected Disputes, etc.*, p. 221.

[3] *Birch and the National Union of Railwaymen*, ibid, p. 221.

[4] *Birch* v. *National Union of Railwaymen and Others* [1950] 2 All E.R. 253.

bers who contract-out. Some unions forbid them to vote on certain questions at their conferences. The Union of Shop, Distributive & Allied Workers (USDAW), and the Fire Brigades' Union, give their conference delegates 'industrial' and 'political' voting cards, carrying the number of 'industrial' or 'political' members of the branch, which are used according to the issue. At one conference where abstention is forbidden, contracting-out delegates must leave the hall during 'political' votes.[1] Some of these 'political' issues are in fact raised subsequently at the Trades Union Congress—the preparation for which has nothing at all to do with the political levy. How far the 1913 Act applies to such questions is not always understood. One General Secretary, stoutly declaring that no member of his union should be prevented from joining in the formation of any of its policies, since it created unhealthy distinctions, shook his head sadly and said, 'But it's in the Act, isn't it?' It is doubtful whether it is.

After the *Birch* decision the *Weekly Newsletter* remarked:

'In future Socialist chairman will not be able to tell contracted-out members that they cannot speak or vote on political issues. . . . Conservative trade unionists should bear this point in mind when they attend their branch meetings.'[2]

But the full implications of the *Birch* decision have not been felt. Many branches still refuse to let contracting-out members speak on any motion dealing with political issues, whether it is addressed to the Constituency Labour Party, the local Trades Council, or simply the union's own Executive. It is doubtful whether there is any legal justification for excluding contracting-out members from any discussion of political policy— even if it is directly aimed at the Labour Party. Discussion is neither 'control' nor 'management' of the political fund. The exclusion of contractors-out from voting on certain 'political' motions which will later be debated at the TUC has no legal justification whatsoever. The contracting-out member clearly often enjoys less than his rights. Yet to grant them is difficult,

[1] *Report of the 36th Conference of the Amalgamated Union of Operative Bakers, Confectioners and Allied Workers*, p. 44.
[2] July 1, 1950.

since it implies that people who refuse to contribute to the Labour Party's funds should have the right to shape its policies.[1]

But the position is complicated by the fact that many of those who do pay the political levy—and fully qualify to join in political activities—are as bitterly anti-Labour as those who refuse. Many Communists, and some Conservatives and Liberals, contribute (knowingly) to their union's political fund. Unless the union's rules provide otherwise they have full rights to help choose Labour's candidates and to form its policies. The one, general, restriction is that they cannot represent the union at Party meetings.[2]

Some unions have partly avoided the dangers. One or two apply 'blanket' discriminations to both political and industrial activities. Among these are the bans on Communists and Fascists holding office adopted by such unions as the TGWU. Others effectively eliminate groups of members from holding certain important posts. Thus, the National Association of Operative Plasterers refused to accept the candidature of a Conservative member for the post of Assistant General Secretary. Its Executive argued that this official had to be able to deputize for the General Secretary, whose duties included attendance at the Labour Party Conference and the admin-

---

[1] This problem has troubled the AESD particularly, in choosing a selection committee for the Parliamentary Panel. After consulting a solicitor and an official of the Registry of Friendly Societies the union took advice from counsel: it was not within its rules to refuse a nomination of a candidate on the ground that he was not a member of the Labour Party. Since the union was affiliated to the Labour Party members of the conference might feel that the selection committee should be composed of members of the Labour Party. If they held this view they could give effect to it by their votes, and it would be permissible to ask each candidate whether or not he was a member of the Labour Party, though a negative answer would not disqualify.

There was a long and confused debate at the union's conference about whether members of the selection committee should 'accept the principles and policies of the Labour Party', be 'individual members' of the Party or simply pay the political levy. All were rejected and eventually the President simply put the question to candidates whether or not they belonged to the Party. *Report of the RCC*, 1954, p. 347 ff.

When a member of the Clerical & Administrative Workers' Union complained that contractors-out had been allowed to vote on the nomination of Mr. Aneurin Bevan for the Treasurership of the Labour Party, at his union's conference, the Chief Registrar ruled that he had no *locus standi*, since the Trade Union Act, 1913, covers only cases where members are put at a disadvantage. *Report of the Chief Registrar of Friendly Societies*, 1956, Part IV.

[2] This restriction is imposed by the Party's own standing orders.

istration of the political fund.[1] In 1953 a Communist organizer in the National Union of Railwaymen (NUR), explained that he could not stand for the post of Assistant General Secretary because the rules laid down that he must be able to deputize for the General Secretary at the Labour Party Conference.[2] Similarly the General Secretary of the Amalgamated Union of Building Trade Workers told his National Delegate Conference, 'Our rules declare this Union to be affiliated to the Labour Party. We work strictly in conjunction with the Labour Party, and with no other Party, and any other political party which attempts to involve this union in its meshes is doing a disservice to the union. The General Secretary must undertake the industrial and political work, and unless he subscribes to the policy of the Labour Party he could not do this'.[3]

Such rules are far from universal. Indeed, the unions cannot systematically eliminate every Conservative, Communist or Liberal member from office or discussions, simply because they are affiliated to the Labour Party. In many unions the activities of these minorities have never been important in any case. But sometimes they have. It is common knowledge that the Communist Party effectively controls the Electrical Trades Union, and that Communists or fellow-travellers control, or have controlled the policies of other unions for periods since the war. It is immaterial that they find suitably-qualified Labour spokesmen to register within Party meetings decisions that they have taken. Other unions, such as the Amalgamated Engineering Union, or the Union of Shop, Distributive & Allied Workers, have had influential Communist minorities within their executives or their conferences, which have sometimes swung their decisions, and more frequently have accentuated them further to the left. Although the unions, as organizations, are bound by their affiliation to the Party to be loyal, their militants, and their leading personalities may not be.

Though the substantial support among the unions for a Communist-Labour alliance did, for a moment in 1945–6,

---

[1] T. Vaughan and the National Association of Operative Plasterers, Report of the Chief Registrar, 1932.
[2] The Railway Review, May 22, 1953. NUR Rulebook, Rule 4(6).
[3] Report of the National Delegate Conference, 1950, p. 229.

bring the Party close to disaster, the spectre of the Labour Party being controlled through the unions by its own worst enemies has never come close to realization. This is chiefly because the majority of unions are controlled by Labour-sympathizing militants and officials. It is only on these terms that the link between the Labour Party and the unions remains tolerable to the Party.

# CHAPTER II

# PAYING THE PIPER

'It would be very bad for the Labour Party if its relationship with the unions came to be regarded as predominantly that of the "sugar daddy" . . . I do not think that there is much danger of that.'   MR. HUGH GAITSKELL

'We shall find the money and see that the Labour Party is not short.'   SIR THOMAS WILLIAMSON

'The plain truth is that the unions own the Labour Party practically lock, stock and barrel.'   A MEMBER OF THE AEU

'We have all subscribed to, and propagated, the idea that the overwhelming bulk of the Party's money comes from the affiliation fees and grants paid by the trade unions.

THIS ISN'T JUST WRONG—IT'S A MYTH.'

MR. IAN MIKARDO *

POLITICAL or revolutionary strikes apart, trade union political action could be little more than an oratorical gesture without the backing of substantial finance. Even in the Labour Party's halcyon days of street-corner fervour election expenses had to be paid, Members of Parliament maintained, and the poverty-stricken organization supported. In those days the Party had nowhere else to turn for funds but the unions. But is the unions' contribution still so important today? As the quotations which head this chapter show even within the Party the financial relationship between Labour and the unions stirs quite contradictory judgments. In the following pages we shall try to show the real measure of the Party's debt to the unions today—to see whether, in fact, the unions still 'pay the piper'.

Not since the earliest days of political action have the unions been wholly free of restrictions on their political spending. Not, in fact, since the Osborne Judgment cut off a large slice of the Party's income in a matter of months—its first, painful reminder of its dependence on the unions. Later the Trade Union Act, 1913, that laboured compromise, laid down the hurdles that unions must jump before they could spend money on politics.

* (a) Report of the ADC (ASW), 1955, p. 231.
  (b) Report of Congress (NUGMW), 1957, p. 275.
  (d) Tribune, October 7, 1955.

Industrial and political funds must be kept rigorously separated and only the political fund may be drawn on for expenditure on 'political objects'. According to the Act this includes:

> paying expenses incurred directly or indirectly by a candidate or prospective candidate for any public office, before, during or after his election in connexion either with his candidature or his election,
>
> holding meetings or distributing literature or documents in support of a candidate or prospective candidate to public office,
>
> maintaining any Member of Parliament or other holder of public office,
>
> the selection of a candidate for Parliament or any public office, 'the holding of public meetings of any kind, or the distribution of political literature or political documents of any kind, unless the main purpose of the meetings or of the literature or documents is the furtherance of statutory objects within the meaning of this Act. . . .'[1]

These are the only activities on which expenditure *must* be taken from the political fund. Unions may spend what they like on other political matters—no matter how controversial—providing they fall within their statutory objects, without touching a penny of their political funds.[2] Within limits they can use their industrial funds to campaign for the nationalization of their industry, to fight de-nationalization, demand equal pay for women, attack the government's wages policy, provide Labour (or Communist) oriented educational facilities, or publish strongly 'committed' journals. The exact extent to which unions could venture into political propaganda in the guise of furthering industrial objects has never been quite clear, but one of the Registrar's rulings suggests that the limits are wide. He observed:

[1] The full text of S.3(3) of the Trade Union Act, 1913, is printed and commented on in Citrine, *Trade Union Law*, pp. 331-2.

[2] 'Statutory objects' means 'the objects mentioned in section 16 of the Trade Union Amendment Act, 1876, namely, the regulation of the relations between workmen and masters, or between workmen and workmen, or between masters and masters, or the imposing of restrictive conditions on the conduct of any trade or business, and also the provision of benefits to members'. Cf., Trade Union Act, 1913, S.1(2).

'. . . trade unions have become more and more identified with the politics of a particular party. But [this] fact . . . does not justify us in sweeping this proviso aside and saying that everything they do and everything they advocate must be "political" within the meaning of the Section. This would not be construing the Act, but amending it, and the logical result would be that the unions would have all their funds in the political fund and no general funds at all. . . . If a matter lies within the statutory objects of the trade union it is not "political" although it may be part of the programme of a political party. The "political" objects, therefore, which are contrasted by the proviso with statutory objects must be those party political objects which are not also statutory objects.'[1]

This ruling offers an engaging number of loopholes. Since the information we have about the unions' expenditure on politics comes from studying their political funds, to the extent that they spend money out of industrial funds on these often controversial 'other political objects', we shall be underestimating their efforts. In fact most unions lean over backwards to keep the spirit of the law rather than its more accommodating letter, and over ten per cent of the sums spent from union political funds could legally be taken from the industrial funds. These include not only administrative costs, but such items as gifts to the Hungarian Relief Appeal or the Sir Stafford Cripps Memorial Fund, and subscriptions to the Royal Institute of International Affairs.[2] Despite the laxity of the Act, many keenly political trade unionists would resent the large-scale use of industrial funds for essentially political campaigns—though the

[1] *J. F. Forster and the National Amalgamated Union of Shop Assistants, Warehousemen and Clerks. Report of the Chief Registrar of Friendly Societies*, 1925, p. 3. The Registrar found that an affiliation fee to the TUC was not 'political expenditure' even though the TUC had spent money on running a joint Research Department and a Library with the Labour Party, had affiliated to the Socialist International, had publicized the Industrial Workers' Charter, and had spent £3 on an election tract (which was disregarded: *de minimis*). The TUC's investment in the *Daily Herald* was also queried. After examining a typical issue he concluded that the paper was a commercial venture and not political literature.

[2] In *Corrigan and the Union of Shop, Distributive & Allied Workers* the Registrar ruled that payment of £1,000 to Hungarian Relief funds, from the political fund, was permissible under the 1913 Act, whether or not the object was 'political' within the terms of the Act. *Report*, 1957, Part 4, p. 5.

strongly pro-Labour line taken by most union journals is usually considered legitimate.

Once they set up a political fund unions are not normally bound to use it solely for political purposes. After the First World War the Engineers and Miners were reduced by prolonged strikes to paying benefits from the political fund, and several AEU Parliamentary candidates had to withdraw from the 1923 election because the political fund was exhausted.[1] To this extent, therefore, the contribution of some unions to politics may be less than the crude figures suggest.

There are a few exceptions to these normally law-abiding ways. Some union branches collect local levies of a few pence per year 'for benevolent and industrial purposes'. Since the war the Tobacco Workers' Union, the Amalgamated Society of Lithographic Printers, the National Union of Heating, Ventilation & Domestic Engineers, the Amalgamated Society of Woodcutting Machinists, and several smaller organizations, have all had branches affiliated to Constituency Labour Parties at times when they had no political funds.[2] Elsewhere branches of unions with political funds have collected extra local levies when the normal political contribution was too small to allow them to affiliate to their local Parties. Some Executives have sagely turned a blind eye to these practices. In 1949, when the Chief Registrar intervened to suppress local levies in a number of branches of the Amalgamated Society of Woodworkers, the General Secretary admitted:

'Your Executive Committee were aware over the years, due to the fact that they were unable to make payments in respect of local affiliations, in various districts throughout the Society, certain subterfuges have been taken in connection with the method of payment for affiliation to the local Labour Parties.'[3]

---

[1] *Report of the Annual Conference of Delegates* (*NUM*), 1949, p. 54. Jeffereys, J. B. *The Story of the Engineers*, Werner Laurie 1946, p. 240. Pugh, Sir Arthur, *Men of Steel*, BISAKTA 1953, p. 360. Webb, Beatrice, *Diaries, 1912–1924*, Longmans 1952, p. 210.

[2] If these affiliations were made through personal donations by members they would probably be legal.

[3] *Report of the ADC*, 1949, p. 48. A union may not charge a higher levy than the rules allow, without acting *ultra vires*. For suppression of such a practice see *Special Report of the Auditors of Kent Area of the NUM*, attached to the union's annual return to the Chief Registrar for 1952.

Now and then other branches spend money from their industrial funds on politics, in ignorance of the law and their own rules. Several shop stewards' organizations have set up funds from which political expenditure is made, including affiliation to Constituency Labour Parties, which escapes the control of the Trade Union Acts. Although it is hard to gather full information there is no reason to believe that these irregular forms of expenditure between them involve appreciable sums of money.

Often the unions' own accounts are the most serious obstacle to finding how much is spent on politics. Statute binds them to make an annual financial statement to their members and to the Registrar of Friendly Societies—but nothing binds them to make it either comprehensive or comprehensible. While accounting standards have risen since the war, a few unions are still so afraid of giving anything away to 'the other side' that they withhold the most elementary facts from their own members.[1] 'In any case', they say, 'there is no demand for such information.' As the leader of one of the most discrete unions remarked, 'After all, the more details we put in the accounts, the more questions people ask. . . .' Even the more conscientious unions may not provide a full picture. For example, the National Union of Mineworkers, one of the highest spenders, bravely tries to tell the full story, but probably no one within the union knows exactly how much it really spends on politics.

The limitations of these sources prevent either the Registrar or the layman from saying with complete accuracy how much the unions spend from their political funds. Nevertheless, the general outlines are clear enough for us to be able to show how more than ninety per cent of their political expenditure has been distributed since 1945.[2]

[1] e.g. The *Financial Report*, 1955 of the Association of Correctors of the Press made no mention of the political fund.

[2] The information on which this chapter is based derives from the Annual Returns made to the Registrar of Friendly Societies by about 150 unions with registered political funds for the years 1944–58. These have been supplemented and corrected by inspection of the printed accounts of about 100 of these unions, and of the unregistered unions (whose returns to the Registrar are not public). Further information is derived from trade union journals, reports of Regional Councils of the Labour Party, constituency party accounts, and in some instances interviews with union treasurers.

The chief obstacles to giving full information are, beside the inadequacy of some unions' accounts, the complexity of the accounting in a small number of unions, notably the NUM. The NUM Central Accounts list the share of political contri-

POLITICAL INCOME

By any British standard the unions' political income is formidable. Now running at about three-quarters of a million pounds per year—and backed by reserves equal to two years expenditure—it has almost quadrupled since the war. In 1945 the total income of union political funds was £219,000. Increased membership and the return to contracting-out brought it up sharply to £465,000 by 1948. Then, after a more gradual rise, a general increase in contributions after 1956 raised it rapidly to £770,000 in 1958.

TABLE 8

INCOME OF TRADE UNION POLITICAL FUNDS: 1945–1958

| Year | Contributions £ | Other Sources £ |
|------|------|------|
| 1945 | 211,009 | 8,346 |
| 1946 | 247,254 | 5,681 |
| 1947 | 404,742 | 8,191 |
| 1948 | 458,745 | 6,141 |
| 1949 | 464,992 | 6,408 |
| 1950 | 466,784 | 5,827 |
| 1951 | 475,743 | 5,224 |
| 1952 | 498,875 | 5,652 |
| 1953 | 535,249 | 6,245 |
| 1954 | 541,373 | 8,215 |
| 1955 | 536,247 | 15,937 |
| 1956 | 563,571 | 15,633 |
| 1957 | 732,174 | 18,228 |
| 1958 | 746,000* | 24,300* |

* estimate.

butions which are due to be retained by Areas as if they had in fact been collected and *expended*. Much of this money has not, in fact, been spent and remains in the reserves of Area unions, which are not included in the reserves which the National Union reports to the Registrar. In normal years NUM expenditure is substantially less than reported, and in election years it is more.

Some Areas do not collect the full levy. Accordingly at times money which figures as income in Head Office accounts has never been collected at all. If an Area contributes to the Head Office election fund from the share it receives of the contributions, and the Head Office then gives this sum to the Labour Party it passes through the National Union accounts twice as income and twice as expenditure. Though the practices of the NUM accountants are fully justified, the consequence is that the Registrar's figures include some double counting.

The same problem arises in the NUR in 1948–50, and to a lesser degree in some other unions. I have included the United Textile Factory Workers' Association, and organisation of textile unions, as one unit, but the Registrar receives reports on only the component unions.

The statistics compiled in this chapter accordingly differ slightly from those previously published by the Registrar of Friendly Societies.

All but £20,000, mostly arising from investments, comes from contributions. The insignificance of this investment income is remarkable. Although political fund reserves stood at over £1,400,000 throughout 1958, they earned only £23,000 —a net return of about 1½ per cent. It may be relevant to note that the unions are liable to income tax on their political funds, but not on their industrial funds, under the Trade Union Act, 1871.

Such are the sums of which the unions dispose. In the following pages we will see how they spend them.

### POLITICAL EXPENDITURE

The money the unions spend falls conveniently into four main categories: national, regional, local and internal. In all but a handful of unions this expenditure is directed in one way or another to supporting the Labour Party. There are therefore two yardsticks by which it must be measured: is it sufficient to further the unions' own interests, and does it meet the Labour Party's needs?

### THE NATIONAL PARTY

#### 1 *Affiliations*

One of the few charges that have kept pace with the cost of living is the Party's affiliation fee. Rejecting a proposed shilling-a-year levy, the Labour Representation Committee fixed its first affiliation fee at a penny per member per year. By 1918 it had jumped to threepence. The fall in affiliations after the 1927 Trade Disputes Act led to a rise to fourpence in 1931. Later came increases to 4½d (1937), fivepence (1940) and sixpence (1948). Since 1957 the fee has been ninepence. This ninefold rise has been needed not only to meet rising costs but to match the expansion of the Party's activities and organization since the days when Ramsay MacDonald and James Middleton set up party headquarters with a tiny staff in dismal offices at the top of Victoria Street.

In 1958 186 unions affiliated 8,177,000 of their members to the Trades Union Congress. In the same year eighty-seven unions affiliated 5,628,000 members nationally to the Labour

Party (and eight more unions affiliated at regional or constituency level only). The rise in numbers affiliated—from 2,510,000 in 1945—and increased fees have quadrupled the Party's affiliation income from the unions since the war. While the unions are often reluctant to accept new obligations they are traditionally prompt to honour those that they have assumed. Of the £210,000 they paid in affiliation fees in 1958 only £3,969 represented arrears. By contrast the constituencies' arrears were £11,609 in a total payment of only £35,300—one of the many signs of their chronic financial instability.

TABLE 9

PROPORTION OF TRADE UNIONISTS PAYING POLITICAL LEVY
AFFILIATED NATIONALLY TO THE LABOUR PARTY, 1945–1958

| Year | Trade Unionists Paying Political Levy | Trade Unionists Affiliated Nationally to the Labour Party | Percentage of Paying Members Affiliated % |
|---|---|---|---|
| 1945 | 2,903,000 | 2,510,000 | 87 |
| 1946 | .. | 2,636,000 | .. |
| 1947 | 5,613,000 | 4,387,000 | 78 |
| 1948 | 5,773,000 | 4,752,000 | 82 |
| 1949 | 5,821,000 | 4,947,000 | 85 |
| 1950 | 5,833,000 | 4,972,000 | 85 |
| 1951 | 5,936,000 | 4,938,000 | 83 |
| 1952 | 5,962,000 | 5,072,000 | 85 |
| 1953 | 5,924,000 | 5,057,000 | 85 |
| 1954 | 5,949,000 | 5,530,000 | 93 |
| 1955 | 6,173,000 | 5,605,000 | 91 |
| 1956 | 6,245,000 | 5,659,000 | 91 |
| 1957 | 6,329,000 | 5,645,000 | 90 |
| 1958 | 6,280,000 | 5,628,000 | 90 |

The unions are often criticized for their failure to affiliate fully to the Party. The Party's Constitution clearly commits organizations to affiliate their entire levy-paying membership.[1] Not all do. Some of the largest unions have been backsliders. In 1945 six large unions affiliated less than seventy-five per cent of their eligible membership: the NUGMW, the National Unions of Public Employees, Seamen, and Agricultural Workers, the Amalgamated Union of Operative Bakers, Con-

[1] The Constitution (Clause X(1)), says rather ambiguously 'Each affiliated organization . . . shall pay an affiliation fee of 9d. per member per annum to the Party'.

fectioners and Allied Workers, and the Mental Hospital & Institutional Workers' Union (now Confederation of Health Service Employees). Ten years later three of the six were still lagging: NUPE (sixty-four per cent), NUS (twenty-nine per cent) and CHSE (twenty-six per cent), while they were joined by the Musicians' Union (seventy-one per cent) and the

TABLE 10

NUMBERS OF POLITICAL CONTRIBUTIONS AFFILIATED NATIONALLY
TO THE LABOUR PARTY

| Proportion of Political Contributors Affiliated Nationally | Number of Affiliated Unions* | | | | | |
|---|---|---|---|---|---|---|
| | 1945 | 1947 | 1949 | 1951 | 1953 | 1955† |
| 91% and over | 43 | 48 | 47 | 54 | 56 | 58 |
| 71–90% | 13 | 9 | 13 | 11 | 12 | 14 |
| 51–70% | 5 | 4 | 8 | 5 | 12 | 7 |
| 50% or less | 2 | 5 | 7 | 11 | 3 | 3 |
| TOTAL | 63 | 66 | 73 | 81 | 83 | 82 |

* excluding a small number of unions for which a precise calculation cannot be made.
† 1955 is the last year for which the Labour Party published details of trade union affiliations.

National Union of Dyers' Bleachers & Textile Workers (seventy-five per cent). Most of these unions had fixed their contributions so low that affiliating fully would have rapidly bankrupted their political funds.

Under-affiliation was fairly widespread for several years after the war. Several unions failed to raise their affiliations to match the rise in contributing membership after 1946. But the record has improved. By 1958 only about ten per cent of levy-paying trade unionists were not affiliated to the Party, taking the revised calculation of the numbers paying. Part of this small gap is due to the normal time-lag of a year or so in adjusting union affiliations to increased membership. In 1945, forty-three of the sixty-three unions for which there was adequate data affiliated ninety-one per cent or more of their political members. In 1955, fifty-eight out of eighty-two unions had ninety-one per cent or more affiliated. Apart from those already mentioned most of the defaulters were small.

In 1957 a handful of smaller unions preferred to reduce their affiliation rather than increase the political levy when the Party raised its affiliation fee. But the only brazen backslider is the National Union of Public Employees. Its 1951 Biennial Delegate Conference rejected a proposal to affiliate fully. Mr Bryn Roberts, General Secretary, argued that if the union affiliated fully it 'would not be able to help Labour's cause in the backward areas as it had been doing in the past'. This was close to claiming that the union could put the money to better use than the Party.[1]

A handful of unions affiliate on more than the true figure. Oddest of all is the National Union of Mineworkers, whose Labour Party affiliation is actually higher than its TUC membership despite the numerous contractors-out in the Colliery Officials' & Staffs' Area. This discrepancy is said to be due to contributions by retired members who are not counted as full industrial members. At least one observer had suggested that the NUM's over-affiliation is not unconnected with the extra votes which are attached.[2] But most unions which over-affiliate have simply maintained their affiliation despite falling membership or have so few members paying their political levy that their 'true' affiliation would be derisory.

That affiliation is a question of political power as much as finance was made clear by the controversy that broke out when some unions raised their affiliations in 1955. At the 1954 Party Conference there had been strong support for a National Agency Service, for which the Party had not sufficient funds. Arthur Deakin suggested that though the unions could not increase their regular commitments for some time for constitutional reasons, there was scope for emergency aid if the National Executive and the unions were to meet for discussions. Despite a chilly rejection from Mr Ian Mikardo, Mr Deakin received the warmest reception the Conference ever gave him. The following spring Mr Deakin and Mr Williamson announced increases in TGWU and NUGMW affiliations totalling 350,000. NUPE and the ETU followed, and a few smaller unions brought the total increase to 470,000.

---

[1] *Report of the BDC.* The affiliation was raised in 1954, but is still low.
[2] Cf., B. Hennessey. 'Trade Unions and the British Labor Party'. *American Political Science Review*, Vol. XLIX, January 1956.

These increases followed hard on the Executive's narrow escape from defeat on German rearmament, and Mr Bevan's high poll in the contest for the Party Treasurership at the 1954 Conference. The AEU, whose support of Mr Gaitskell had aroused an acrimonious dispute within its ranks, appeared likely to defect to Mr Bevan in the next election.[1] At that moment it seemed that a switch in AEU support might bring Mr Bevan victory. Alternatively, should Mr Bevan be expelled from the Party—which seemed possible at the time—the leadership would need all the votes it could muster to survive the ensuing battle at the 1955 Conference. Even the least suspicious might look askance, and critics talk of 'questionable morality'.[2] Official spokesmen could find only 'financial reasons' for the decision— a claim which imputed to Mr Deakin and Mr Williamson an improbable degree of ingenuousness. For years the Party had been asking the unions to raise their affiliations. Now they increased them retroactively, paying in 1955 for 1954 affiliations—which gave them the right to vote on the higher membership at the next Conference. To take a wholly cynical view does less than justice to Arthur Deakin's loyalty to the Party, which urgently needed the money. Such an increase was a once-for-all coup, not one that the unions can bring out of the hat every time they face defeat.

Constituency enthusiasts sometimes grumble that the unions do not pull their weight. Unfortunately they would scarcely be content if the unions did affiliate completely. For because voting power at the Party Conference is linked to the number of members affiliated the result would simply be to aggravate the problem of the block vote—particularly since most of the backsliders are right-of-centre. Moreover, in raising their affiliations some unions lay themselves open to the charge that they are buying votes at Conference. In 1953 the political income of the TGWU was 1s 1½d for every member affiliated to the Labour Party. After raising the affiliation in 1954 it fell to 11d— while *expenditure* per head was even less. Morally organizations should supplement the sums they pay the party in affiliations by election grants and donations to the constituencies. Some unions

[1] See pp. 147–8 and 316–9.
[2] *The Economist*, March 12, 1955. *The New Statesman*, March 19, 1955.

E

with low contributions were concentrating almost all their political expenditure on affiliations, leaving little to help the Party in other ways. This was close to 'buying votes at sixpence a time', as one critic put it, in practice if not in intent. Subsequent increases in contributions have let most unions—including the TGWU—affiliate fully and give generously in other ways, but some laggards remain.

## 2  By-Election Fund

Since pre-war days the Labour Party has spread the burden of fighting by-elections through this 'insurance' fund. Every organization contributes on a sliding scale ranging from 5s for the smallest to £150 for unions with over 400,000 members. The unions contribute the lion's share. In 1945 they paid about forty per cent of the fund's income; in 1958 about sixty per cent. But the sum involved remains relatively unimportant—some £5,000 per year.

## 3  Election Appeals

As each general election approaches the Labour Party launches its 'Victory' or 'Fighting' Fund to provide the money which will subsidize the campaign in poverty-stricken constituencies, bolster the marginal seats, send cheap propaganda almost everywhere, and pay the higher cost of running Transport House during the campaign. This is the unions' proudest moment. Here is a world where the constituencies cannot

TABLE 11

DONATIONS TO LABOUR'S NATIONAL GENERAL ELECTION FUND

| Sources | Amount Contributed | | | | |
|---|---|---|---|---|---|
| | 1945 | 1950 | 1951 | 1955 | 1959 |
| | £ | £ | £ | £ | £ |
| Trade Unions | 111,154 | 156,178 | 101,199 | 99,815 | 325,678 |
| All Other Sources | 14,284 | 15,603 | 17,981 | 5,065 | 20,000* |
| TOTAL | 125,438 | 171,781 | 119,180 | 104,880 | 345,678 |

* estimate.

compete. They must watch and mark the moral as the leaders of the great unions pledge their thousands. How important the unions' contributions are is amply shown in Table 11. Seventeen

shillings and sixpence in every pound subscribed for the first
four post-war elections came from the unions. (Eighty per cent,
ninety-one per cent, eighty-five per cent and ninety-six per
cent respectively). The remainder comes mostly from individuals, with a small amount from the Cooperative Movement
and next to nothing from the constituency parties.

TABLE 12

CONTRIBUTIONS BY MAJOR UNIONS TO THE LABOUR PARTY
GENERAL ELECTION FUND

| Union | Amount Contributed | | | | |
|---|---|---|---|---|---|
| | 1945 | 1950 | 1951 | 1955 | 1959 (provisional) |
| | £ | £ | £ | £ | £ |
| TGWU | 10,000 | 20,000 | 10,000 | 2,000 | 35,000 |
| NUM(C)* | 23,506 | 30,100 | 20,100 | 10,000 | 42,000 |
| NUGMW | 10,000 | 20,000 | 10,000 | 4,000 | 25,000 |
| AEU | 3,000 | 10,000 | 5,000 | 10,000 | 50,000 |
| USDAW | 5,300 | 15,832 | 5,000 | 15,000 | 26,152 |
| NUR | 10,000 | 15,400 | 7,000 | 7,000 | 14,630 |
| ETU | 500 | 2,500 | 10,000 | 5,000 | 25,000 |
| UPW | 110 | 5,000 | 2,000 | 5,000 | 10,000 |
| UTFWA(C)* | 2,600 | 4,000 | 4,000 | 5,100 | 3,000 |
| NUAW | 1,500 | 1,000 | 500 | 500 | 1,000 |
| Other | 44,638 | 32,346 | 27,599 | 36,215 | 93,896 |
| TOTAL | 111,154 | 156,178 | 101,199 | 99,815 | 325,678 |

* Throughout (C) indicates a composite figure for the central union and all
its component unions.

Almost every union contributes. Naturally the bulk of the
money comes from the 'Big Six' unions. The Miners alone gave
twenty per cent of the Fund's income in 1945, 1950 and 1951—
but not in 1955. Some of the smaller unions are notably open-
handed. The Electrical Trades Union, which gave £25,000 in
1959, is always generous, while some of the tiniest organizations
raise a gallant £100. However, the General Election grant is
not a sure indication of how a union honours its obligations. The
Clerical & Administrative Workers' Union, for example,
prefers to distribute small grants to members who are candidates. The United Textile Factory Workers' Association,
although a generous contributor to central funds, also sends a
substantial sum direct to the Lancashire & Cheshire Region for

use on its home ground. While some of the poorest givers are generous in other ways, a few unions give almost nothing between elections so that they can make an impressive 'splash' every five years.

The Election Fund has had a rather uncertain passage in recent years. In 1945, though they had fewer contributing members, the unions could dig into reserves accumulated during the war and be generous. In 1950 (despite the heavy demands of the Party's Development Fund) they were enjoying the benefits of the 1946 Act and could afford to be generous again. In 1951, understandably enough, they spent cautiously, for they wanted to keep something in hand lest there be another election. Even so, they gave £100,000. But in 1955 with their reserves at the record level of nearly one million pounds they gave less than £100,000—the lowest total since 1936. There were several reasons for the unions' poor showing. Some, aware that affiliation fees were going to rise, clung to their money. Others decided to spend it in such a way that they won more kudos. One General Secretary said frankly, 'It may be wrong of us, but when the elections come we know who has helped us, and we like to spend our money accordingly'. From his union's viewpoint he was doubtless right, but the Labour Party would soon find it intolerable if many unions were to split up their gifts in so inefficient and self-seeking a way.

Not every union has appreciated Transport House's financial policies since the war. The Labour Party set itself out frankly to build reserves. There were sound enough reasons for such a course. In 1943 the Election Fund had a balance of only £110. This gave the Party little room for manoeuvre. When an election can be predicted there is time to canvass the unions for donations. When it comes suddenly the Party must be able to launch its campaign without waiting for the money to come in. In 1955 several large unions had still to agree on their grants on polling day. In turn, Transport House has often left the constituencies unsure about how much they could hope to receive until well on in the campaign, perhaps because it wanted them to rely on their own resources as far as possible. Such uncertainty is no encouragement to efficient campaigning. Accordingly the Party set out to build up its election fund. From 1945 Transport

House leaders took pride in 'running the election at a profit'. At each election grants to the constituencies fell below the unions' donations. By 1955 the £110 of 1943 had swelled to about £200,000. Some union leaders were now feeling that the Party's need was less than theirs, and when the 1955 appeal was made they were far less ready to loosen their purse strings. At least one union felt that the Party might be encouraged to act too independently if its reserves became too comfortable. Its cut in a normally generous contribution was meant as a gentle reminder to the Labour leaders that they would be in a sorry state without union finance.

Although this union's leaders were more frank than most there was little doubt that the unions' failure to give freely in 1955 reflected their irritation at the Party's failure to come to grips with the dissidents, as well as their own reactions to the Monckton era of industrial relations. Conservative rule had proved less painful than they had feared and their election contributions expressed their weakened militancy. The unions' election donations again reflected their own moods more than the Labour Party's needs in 1959. Within three months of the election fund being opened a record sum of over £200,000 had been received from the unions. This was much more a flamboyant declaration of the unions' renewed hostility towards the Conservatives than a response to Mr Aneurin Bevan's persuasive appeals.

The Party has used this election fund in a curious way. As the balances mounted the Wilson Committee, enquiring into the Party's organization after the 1955 election, recommended that in the short run the renovation of the Party machine should be financed from the election fund.[1] There is no logical distinction between building organization between elections and fighting the election campaign itself. The Wilson Report marked a step away from Labour's traditional tendency to treat elections as set-piece battles which are fought for one month every four or five years. Even though the Party's funds have often been limited it was always doubtful economy to shepherd them for

---

[1] Its correct title was the Sub-Committee on Party Organization. It investigated Party organization under the chairmanship of Mr Harold Wilson after the 1955 General Election. Its report is published in the *Report of the Labour Party Conference 1955*, pp. 63–105.

one great electoral effort. Yet even since the Wilson Report, Transport House has remained painfully conservative. Although it improved the organization it would not dip boldly into the Election Fund. By the end of 1957 this held more than enough to finance two campaigns at the normal rate. A quarter of a million pounds is an astonishingly large sum to keep sterilized in a party which is always pleading poverty. Then in October 1958 Labour appealed for a further £500,000 to fight the next election. Despite the unions' generous response the Party showed yet again that it has little idea of how to employ such relative riches successfully. Far too little was employed for long-term campaigning, and while £25,000 was spent on an inadequate poster campaign early in 1959, the bulk of the money was hoarded until it could not be put to the best use.

Elections apart the unions rarely make gifts to the Party. In recent years there have been occasional grants of £500 from the ETU, and £250 from the Fire Brigades' Union. The only remarkable grant was £1,000 from the Association of Engineering & Shipbuilding Draughtsmen in 1953. 'Our political fund is there to be spent. We collected the money for the Labour Party. They know how to use it, and there is no point in letting it lie idle in the bank', said an AESD official. The Labour Party must often wish other unions were as clear-thinking.

## 4 *The Development Fund*

The Party has made one other appeal for help. Just after the war it found the organization inefficient and antiquated, and it was clear that the Party would face a rejuvenated Conservative machine in the next election. Labour might be swept out as it had been swept in. Rising costs and increased commitments had to be met with inadequate income and negligible reserves.[2] Accordingly the Party went through the indispensable preliminary to asking the whole Party for more money—it called a meeting of union executives. The unions agreed, and the 1947 Conference concurred, in establishing the Development Fund. Supported by a shilling per head levy it was to finance the expansion of the organization, which would subsequently be

---

[1] The *Daily Telegraph*, and the *Manchester Guardian*, January 8, 1959.
[2] The General Fund balance fell to only £8,771 at the end of 1947.

maintained through higher membership and increased affiliation fees.

The unions met their commitments punctiliously. They were due to contribute £131,767; they gave £150,386, eighteen shillings in every pound of the fund's income. One or two unions defaulted, but others gave more than their due. But while the fund was so faithfully supported Sir William Lawther voiced a common union outlook:

'Where a trade union makes a subscription of X thousand pounds to the Labour Party's Development Fund, there will be a lessening of the grant to someone else. . . . We hope that there are not going to be too many demands such as we have already heard at this Conference. . . .'[1]

Supporting the Party's central organization absorbs over one-third of the unions' political expenditure. Even Mr Ian Mikardo was bound to make this grudging concession:

'The unions pay the bulk of the cost of running our central machine (which, according to the special committee, is the least effective part of our organization).'[2]

Since the war the national organization has always drawn at least two-thirds of its income from the unions. Although their share has fallen away slightly in recent years this does not mean that the Party has found alternative sources of finance. Rather, its investment income—derived largely from money given by the unions—has risen from £1,300 in 1945 to £5,000 (net) in 1957. Setting this aside the unions' share of Transport House income has been steady since the war.[3]

It may seem ungracious to ask whether the unions give enough, for the Party's central reserves have risen elevenfold since 1944. But the financial position is not as healthy as it seems at first glance. The reserves have been built up chiefly through special appeals. Between 1950 and 1958 there was a deficit on general fund in every year but two. The Party

---

[1] *Report of the Labour Party Conference*, 1947, p. 132.
[2] *Tribune*, December 2, 1955.
[3] With the exception of 1946 (the effect of the Trades Disputes Act) and 1950 (since the unions' election donations were chiefly made in 1949, and the 'other' donations fell chiefly in 1950).

## TABLE 13

### TRADE UNION CONTRIBUTIONS TO CENTRAL LABOUR PARTY FUNDS

| Year | Trade Union Affiliation Fees | By-Election Fund Subscriptions | Grants | Total | Per cent of Central Income Given by Trade Unions* | Labour Party Central Expenditure* | Labour Party Central Balances |
|---|---|---|---|---|---|---|---|
| | £ | £ | £ | £ | % | £ | £ |
| 1943 | — | — | — | — | — | — | 33,275 |
| 1944 | 49,343 | 2,450 | 34,187 | 85,980 | 89 | 56,833 | 74,420 |
| 1945 | 51,307 | 2,483 | 66,967 | 120,757 | 73 | 100,424 | 151,846 |
| 1946 | 50,633 | 3,255 | 250 | 54,138 | 68 | 92,219 | 138,830 |
| 1947 | 81,274 | 3,497 | 54,002 | 138,773 | 86 | 107,323 | 193,436 |
| 1948 | 129,476 | 4,427 | 68,483 | 202,386 | 86 | 133,101 | 315,498 |
| 1949 | 125,829 | 4,603 | 175,317 | 305,749 | 86 | 200,658 | 461,571 |
| 1950 | 126,681 | 4,830 | 8,262 | 139,773 | 72 | 292,546 | 347,525 |
| 1951 | 124,306 | 4,217 | 101,199 | 229,722 | 82 | 244,093 | 377,869 |
| 1952 | 126,299 | 4,945 | 250 | 131,494 | 76 | 202,232 | 347,525 |
| 1953 | 125,840 | 4,822 | 1,750 | 132,412 | 77 | 172,574 | 347,473 |
| 1954 | 138,669 | 4,932 | 250 | 143,851 | 80 | 182,659 | 345,115 |
| 1955 | 140,931 | 5,182 | 99,815 | 245,928 | 90 | 219,204 | 374,540 |
| 1956 | 141,271 | 4,943 | — | 146,214 | 81 | 182,603 | 328,131 |
| 1957 | 209,409 | 4,899 | 300 | 214,708 | 84 | 274,961 | 306,823 |
| 1958 | 209,549 | 4,967 | 149,051† | 363,567 | 84 | 328,829 | 355,993 |

\* Interest and trading items counted net.

† Includes £44,000 received by the Labour Party in 1959.

obviously needs an adequate steady income much more than periodic fund-raising drives. Its over-cautious financial stewardship may be attributable to its continued uncertainty whether its income will cover future commitments. In 1957 the Party succeeded, for the second time since the war, in raising its affiliation fee. The increase brought in £80,000 per year. Yet even when Mr Gaitskell first proposed the rise to Conference in 1955, £15,000 to £20,000 was mortgaged to meet existing commitments.[1] The Wilson Committee's proposed modernization of the Party machine—including a marginal constituencies' scheme, more staff, better equipment—would obviously cost money. Political television would become more expensive. In the measure that it accepted the Wilson Committee proposals the Party was committing itself permanently to a higher standard of living, even if higher membership or more efficient collection of contributions should spread the burden. Already the Party's central expenditure had risen about £90,000 per

[1] *Report of the Labour Party Conference*, 1958, p. 204.

year between 1946 and 1954. It seemed clear that the rise in affiliation fees would be sufficient for only a few years.

So it proved. In 1958, with £80,000 additional income to hand, the Party found itself yet again running a General Fund deficit of about £25,000. Political parties can live up to any income they may be given. By Liberal standards Labour's income represents undreamt of riches; by Conservative standards the Party is still poor.[1] It is hard to avoid the conclusion that even in 1955 a shilling affiliation fee was necessary. Yet when a trial balloon suggesting the doubling of the existing fee of sixpence was sent up the reception was so hostile that the proposal was never formally advanced. By no objective standard could a contribution of one shilling per member per year to the running of the central party machine be called exorbitant. But it was not practical politics. Within months of the introduction of the ninepenny fee, however, the Executive had to admit that its income was again inadequate: 'It will be necessary, at an early date, to consider an increased annual income'.[2]

At the same time as it introduced the ninepenny fee the Party raised the minimum affiliation for Constituency Labour Parties from £6 to £30. Even so, the local parties' contribution to the central machine is pitifully small—particularly in comparison with the Conservatives. In 1958 the £35,000 paid by the constituencies was £5,000 less than they received back from Transport House through the marginal constituencies scheme alone. Hopes that with higher membership the local parties would take a greater share of the burden have always been disappointed. Although the constituencies will have to pay their share if affiliations rise again, it is the unions that the Party will have to convince of its needs. By the time the delicate canvassing of the unions is completed even a shilling fee may well look inadequate. But whether the Party has to cut its coat to suit its cloth, or whether it convinces the unions its needs are genuine, for many years to come the Labour Party will have to rely predominantly on trade union funds to run Transport House.

[1] The Conservatives, whose accounts are not published, are oddly reluctant to admit publicly that they are richer. (Cf., *Onward*, December 1955). It is so apparent that Conservative salaries are higher, their employees more numerous, and their premises more spacious that there seems little point in attempting formal proof.
[2] *Report of the Labour Party Conference*, 1958, p. 137.

## FINANCING THE REGIONS

Labour has completed its regional organization only since the war; now ten regions cover the country. The regional councils are primarily intended to bring national Party officials within easy reach of every constituency, but they also provide a link between the Party and trade union regions or districts, and a forum for the discussion of regional problems. By their constitutions they are forbidden to debate national political issues, though the Scottish and Welsh Councils at least find adequate material to discuss. Some regional councils—notably London—take an active part in financing or coordinating county council elections.[1]

Scotland and London excepted the Regions are not economically viable. They have never been conceived as paying their way—even though the officials' salaries are paid by Transport House. Although subscriptions are generally kept low (3d per member per year in the London Labour Party, £1 to £1 5s 0d per thousand members elsewhere) to attract affiliations—these are substantially short of the maximum. As usual the unions' performance is patchy. While the Miners and the United Textile Factory Workers' Association are almost completely affiliated, many unions do not know what their membership is within each region, because (except in Wales, Scotland and London) party and union boundaries rarely coincide. Some unions like the National Union of Seamen and the Prudential Staff Union, maintain a nominal affiliation in almost every region, so that they can have their say on any issue that interests them, but several smaller unions have few or no regional affiliations. The TGWU, NUGMW, the Woodworkers, and even such normally punctilious unions as the AEU, USDAW and the Transport Salaried Staffs' Association, have never troubled to affiliate fully.

Although a few regions—notably Lancashire & Cheshire—have zealously rounded up the unions' affiliations, others have been less conscientious. The negligible income that affiliations bring gives regional officials little incentive to pursue the de-

---

[1] Though it is not constitutionally a region London Labour Party is included here for convenience.

## TABLE 14

### TRADE UNION AFFILIATIONS TO REGIONS OF THE
### LABOUR PARTY: 1945–1958

| Year | Trade Union Regional Affiliations | Per cent of National Affiliations % | Year | Trade Union Regional Affiliations | Per cent of National Affiliations % |
|---|---|---|---|---|---|
| 1945 | 2,069,000 | 83 | 1952 | 4,166,000 | 82 |
| 1946 | 2,409,000 | 92 | 1953 | 4,198,000 | 83 |
| 1947 | 3,239,000 | 73 | 1954 | 4,264,000 | 77 |
| 1948 | 3,713,000 | 78 | 1955 | 4,309,000 | 77 |
| 1949 | 3,793,000 | 77 | 1956 | 4,412,000 | 78 |
| 1950 | 4,019,000 | 81 | 1957 | 4,415,000 | 78 |
| 1951 | 4,025,000 | 82 | 1958 | 4,445,000 | 79 |

faulters. The unions often have a similar attitude. Commenting on the failure of twenty-three AEU District Committees out of about thirty in the Southern Region to affiliate a member said it was 'probably because they have never heard of the Regional Council, and have no knowledge of what it does'.[1] Other unions, well aware that regional councils exist, have never considered affiliation worth while.

Yet affiliations have risen steadily since the war, as new regions were established, and the 1946 Act had its effect. Affiliation income has risen equally, through rising membership more than by increased fees.[2] The unions contributed about £3,000 in 1945; in 1958 their affiliations were over £7,000.

## TABLE 15

### ESTIMATED TRADE UNION PAYMENTS TO REGIONS OF
### THE LABOUR PARTY, 1945–1958

| Year | Affiliation Fees £ | Grants £ | Year | Affiliation Fees £ | Grants £ |
|---|---|---|---|---|---|
| 1945 | 2,950 | 7,042 | 1952 | 6,885 | 4,236 |
| 1946 | 3,340 | 5,000 | 1953 | 6,782 | 532 |
| 1947 | 4,429 | 150 | 1954 | 7,093 | 1,114 |
| 1948 | 5,473 | 1,235 | 1955 | 6,755 | 21,215 |
| 1949 | 6,169 | 9,154 | 1956 | 7,267 | 1,006 |
| 1950 | 5,977 | 11,286 | 1957 | 7,329 | 1,064 |
| 1951 | 5,949 | 1,035 | 1958 | 7,356 | 4,389 |

[1] *AEU Journal*, May 1950.
[2] The London Labour Party affiliation fee was increased from 2d. to 3d.

Affiliated membership has kept close to eighty per cent of the national figure. While the unions normally set aside only two per cent of their political expenditure for the regions, it is nonetheless sixty-five per cent to seventy-five per cent of the regions' autonomous income.[1]

A few unions—notably the NUM, AESD, and the United Textile Factory Workers' Association—support regional election appeals generously. The UTFWA has always found it useful to give money and propaganda material—dealing with the problems of the cotton industry—for distribution in Lancashire constituencies. Although the unions support both the London Labour Party's LCC Election Fund and the Scottish Council's election fund generously, they usually prefer to give directly to the local parties and the other regions have had little success with their fund raising. Outside election years few unions make grants to the Regional Councils—although the donations the regions receive come almost exclusively from the unions.

The Party's main interest in the regions is organizational. Perhaps that is why affiliation fees have been kept so low. Even if the whole trade union movement were to affiliate regionally, the Party would only receive about £12,000 per year. Nevertheless, affiliation *is* cheap, most unions could afford a rise, and the regional offices run at a loss. If it really wanted to the Party could reduce the deficit.

## UNION FUNDS IN THE CONSTITUENCIES

Just how much the Constituency Labour Parties draw from the trade union movement is not wholly clear, since some expenditure is lost in the vagueness of trade union accounts.[2] Yet a reasonably full picture can be obtained—with reserves that will become evident.

---

[1] That is, omitting the proportion of regional office expenses borne by Transport House.

[2] Several large unions, notably the AEU and the TGWU, list the money *allocated* to their Districts or Regions, and not the money actually *spent*. (This fault is reproduced in the official statistics of union expenditure.) It is not possible to allow completely for this, but by information obtained in the constituencies, and a degree of extrapolation, it has been minimised. The expenditure of these unions was found to be higher than reported in election years, lower in normal years. This is reflected in the full statistics.

Within many unions how much the branches shall have to spend in the constituencies is often a matter for lively debate. The NUGMW has discussed the issues at seven congresses and has changed the shares five times, varying between half to the head office and half to the districts, and a division of 70:30. Anxious to keep a tight hand on the purse strings and spend the political funds strategically instead of letting it be frittered away in dribs and drabs Executives often prefer to control the fund. Rank and file members naturally want to have funds immediately to hand in the branch (or district) to allow them to cut a respectable figure in local politics. Prestige counts as much as the local Party's needs. As a member of the Amalgamated Society of Woodworkers said:

'I have stood with an NUR man and with a TGWU man. Their contribution to the local party had been £10. When I scratched the bottom of my pot and mortgaged the next quarter's affiliation fees, I could only hand over £2 10s 0d, and I am almost ashamed to do it.'[1]

Normally the head office, which has to pay the national affiliation fees and grants takes the larger share, though the range lies between a division of 85:15 in the Amalgamated Union of Building Trade Workers and 50:50 in the NUM.[2] These settlements are the results of pressures and tradition within the union, and correspond to no clear idea of the 'best' division of the money available. Often the real source of the controversy is not how the levy should be split, but that the levy is too small to meet all the calls on it. Both sides are trying to take a quart from a pint pot.

The branches' freedom to spend as they like varies. Some unions give them full discretion, providing only that expenditure must be compatible with the union's affiliation to the Labour Party. (Though occasionally anti-Labour candidates *are* given local election grants, the sums involved are insignificant.) Other unions allow branches to spend up to a certain sum, and retain the balance, otherwise branches may spend their money

[1] *Report of the ADC*, 1954, p. 50.
[2] The division in other major unions is TGWU and NUFTO, 75:25; USDAW, 70:30; AEU, ASW, Boilermakers' 2:1.

aimlessly, or active members may corner the political fund to further their own ambitions on the local council, or an apathetic branch lets the fund lie idle. Within these limits most branches have between threepence and sixpence a year per member to spend on all their local political activities—though some have as much as two shillings. Even where no formal allocation is made it is a rare union that will not find funds for its branches to affiliate to a Constituency Labour Party, or to support a member's campaign for election to the local council.

## 1 *Affiliation in the Constituencies*

There is no way of telling how many trade unionists are affiliated to Constituency Labour Parties, since some unions pay a fixed sum—which naturally represents a different number of affiliations depending on whether the fee is 3d or 6d. Sometimes members are affiliated to more than one constituency at a time. It is clear enough that many individual branch affiliation fees are painfully small. In 1957 the fees paid by the fifty-five affiliated branches of the National Union of Furniture Trade Operatives amounted to only £194—the lowest payment was 1s 10d.[1] The sixty affiliated branches of the National Union of Tailors & Garment Workers paid sums ranging from £117 to 2s—£466 in all. The Power Group of the TGWU had forty-eight branches affiliated at a cost of £135, and thirty-eight branches of the Scottish Painters' Society paid £130 in fees. These are not isolated examples. The forty-five branches of Blastfurnacemen paid a total of £110 in fees. While USDAW does not release detailed figures, the £3,300 it spent on affiliations in 1958 was spread over 1,800 branches; similarly the 1,400 branches of the NUR spent £4,100 in affiliating. While the average fee is around £3, unions with heavily concentrated membership often pay sizeable sums. In 1958 Blyth CLP received £100 from the Northumberland Miners in affiliation fees, and Ince CLP took £120 from affiliated lodges of the NUM Lancashire Area (in addition to a £491 grant which brought the Miners' contribution up to about half the Party's income). In areas where the AEU, TGWU, the cotton

[1] This and subsequent references are taken from the accounts of the organization referred to in the stated year.

unions, or the Boot & Shoe Operatives are strong similar payments are common.

One of the largest Borough Labour Parties in the country, Birmingham, had 154 trade union affiliations in 1954, which brought in almost £1,000, while in 1958 the Liverpool Trades Council and Labour Party took slightly over £800 from 165 union branches.[1] The exceptionally rich and successful Woolwich Borough Labour Party received £200 in fees from sixty-eight trade union branches in 1957. But although a large Borough Party like Leeds can take £900 in affiliation fees, many urban constituencies receive no more than £50, and in 1958 one remote rural constituency received as little as £9, a working class residential Labour constituency in North London collected £24, a prosperous South Midlands farming seat took only £35, while even in the relatively prosperous constituencies of Oxford and West Lewisham union affiliations came to only £60 and £41. Yet these modest sums are much more than many received when the 1927 Act was in force. Branches could often pay only a few shillings.[2] In 1944 a CLP in industrial Lancashire got a mere £26, while a Trades Council & Labour Party covering two north London constituencies received only £23 in affiliations. Many rural parties had even less.

Since the war the average income of the constituencies from union affiliations has risen from about £48 in 1945 to about £106, a total of £30,000 and £66,000 respectively. Full affiliation would have brought in £38,000 and £85,000 respectively. Though the average affiliation income has risen, it is still only equivalent to the average contribution that would be *collected* from 700 individual members of the Party. In only a handful of constituencies—mostly safe Labour seats where individual membership is minute—do union affiliations exceed members' subscriptions. However, though persuading the unions to affiliate is not always easy, their fees are usually more easily gathered than a comparable sum in individual members' subscriptions.

[1] There were twenty-two payments of under £1; seventy-eight of £1 to £5; and fifty-four of over £5.

[2] In 1944 Doncaster CLP had an affiliation income of £89; Darlington had £44 in 1945 and Halifax £64. Edinburgh City Labour Party had thirty-two affiliations of under £1; eighteen of £1 to £5; and only four of more than £5.

Affiliation fees have risen little since the war. Rather more are sixpence per year than formerly, but many remain at three-pence or fourpence. This seems far too little. The constituencies have always been financially frail because their regular income is too small—even more inadequate than the national Party. The unions might fairly say that the constituencies' poverty is the result of their own inertia. This may be so, but threepence, or even sixpence a year is not generosity. Many of the smaller affiliations cost more in postage than they bring in. On financial grounds the case for local affiliation fees being at least double their present levels is hard to contest. The unions' responsibility is the greater because they are unable—as organizations—to contribute in other ways to the work of the local Party. Regular income is preferable to sporadic gifts, however generous. Although affiliations would doubtless fall if fees are raised, not every constituency member would blanch at the prospect. In the past many unions could not afford to pay more to con-stituency parties. Today that is no longer true.[1]

## 2  The sponsored candidates

While the financial support that unions give to constituencies which adopt their candidates is not the largest item in their local expenditure, it is surely the most controversial. Later we shall discuss the issues the system raises;[2] for the moment we shall outline how much sponsorship is worth to the constitu-encies.

How much the unions may contribute to local parties to support their candidates is limited by the 'Hastings Agreement' which, after successive rises, now permits a maximum grant of £350 per year in borough, and £420 per year in county, constituencies.[3] These are maxima. Sponsoring bodies are free to agree on any terms they wish within those limits. Several unions, in consequence, make no annual grants at all, mostly

---

[1] See p. 103.

[2] For a full discussion see Chapter 6.

[3] The Hastings Agreement, adopted at the 1933 Conference lays down the terms under which affiliated organizations may sponsor candidates. A separate agreement governs the adoption of Labour & Cooperative candidates.

The original maximum annual payment for maintenance of a constituency was £150 (borough) £200 (county). This was raised progressively to £250 and £350 respectively in 1948, and to the present level in 1957.

small unions putting forward few candidates.[1] But the National Union of Mineworkers, which sponsors most candidates of all, rarely pays the full grant. Some of its Areas pay nothing, and others, such as Derbyshire and Yorkshire, give far less than the Hastings Agreement rate. Durham Area, though contributing £100 per year to the funds of Bishop Auckland, South Shields, and Easington constituencies, which have no miners' candidate, makes very small grants to its own 'miners' ' seats. A constituency which adopts a candidate from one of the more open-handed unions cannot invariably count on a fat sponsorship cheque. Sponsorship normally ends with defeat at the polls. Candidates who are adopted at the beginning of an election campaign, and are defeated at the polls, bring no maintenance grant, only a share of election expenses.

If allowance is made—arbitrary though it must be—for the altering of constituencies that resulted from the 1948 and 1955 redistributions of seats, it seems that some 220 constituencies have received trade union maintenance grants since 1945. (A further forty-five seats have had Cooperative sponsorship, and about ten have been personally financed by the candidate.)[2] As few as sixty seats were continuously sponsored for ten years or more within the period 1945–59, and just half of these were miners' seats. Outside the coalfields sponsorship is clearly a short-term relationship, since many of the remaining seats owe their continuous sponsorship to the longevity of the sitting Member. In a handful of seats the adoption of a succession of sponsored candidates over the years may be a sign of venality.[3]

Rumour often has it that some unions are willing to outbid rivals by paying over the Hastings Agreement rates. A few constituencies undoubtedly receive more than the normal rate. USDAW paid Westhoughton CLP £878 in support of Mr J. T. Price in 1958, and USDAW constituencies can count on a bonus of £50 to £100 after a general election, while at one time some of its seats also received a £100 'propaganda allowance'.[4] The NUGMW, too, used to pay more than the

---

[1] Notably the National Union of Public Employees, Clerical & Administrative Workers' Union, ASSET, and the United Patternmakers' Association.

[2] See p. 276.   [3] See pp. 270–8.

[4] Cf., *Accounts of the Doncaster Divisional Labour Party*, 1944. In 1958 other USDAW seats received between £150 and £220 over normal Hastings Agreement rates.

F

## TABLE 16

SCALE OF TRADE UNION MAINTENANCE GRANTS TO CONSTITUENCY LABOUR PARTIES, 1945–1958

| Amount of Grant* | Number of Payments in Each Year | | | | | | | | | | | | | |
|---|---|---|---|---|---|---|---|---|---|---|---|---|---|---|
| | 1945 | 1946 | 1947 | 1948 | 1949 | 1950 | 1951 | 1952 | 1953 | 1954 | 1955 | 1956 | 1957 | 1958 |
| Over £600 | — | — | — | — | 2 | — | — | — | — | 1 | 1 | 1 | 1 | 3 |
| £551–£600 | — | — | — | — | — | — | — | 1 | 1 | — | — | — | — | — |
| £501–550 | — | — | — | 2 | — | 2 | 2 | 1 | 1 | — | — | — | — | 4 |
| £461–£500 | 3 | 2 | 2 | 1 | 6 | 3 | — | 2 | 1 | — | 2 | — | — | 3 |
| £401–£450 | 3 | 2 | 2 | 2 | 6 | 6 | 3 | 4 | 3 | 1 | 2 | — | — | 19 |
| £351–£400 | 3 | 3 | 2 | 7 | 4 | 4 | 6 | 2 | 1 | 4 | 4 | 2 | 17 | 2 |
| £301–£350 | 4 | 10 | 10 | 3 | 25 | 21 | 27 | 22 | 26 | 27 | 17 | 21 | 48 | 56 |
| £251–£300 | 16 | 8 | 7 | 22 | 49 | 48 | 46 | 45 | 47 | 49 | 43 | 46 | 18 | 4 |
| £201–£250 | 30 | 22 | 28 | 37 | 4 | 4 | 6 | 5 | 5 | 3 | 3 | 3 | 2 | 1 |
| £151–£200 | 22 | 34 | 35 | 10 | 16 | 16 | 9 | 9 | 10 | 11 | 21 | 12 | 9 | 1 |
| £101–£150 | 24 | 6 | 3 | 13 | 10 | 17 | 10 | 9 | 6 | 7 | 6 | 6 | 7 | 16 |
| £51 –£100 | 6 | 17 | 20 | 11 | 2 | 2 | 2 | — | — | — | 6 | — | — | 1 |
| £50 and under | — | 7 | — | — | — | — | 2 | 4 | 6 | 5 | — | 6 | 5 | 4 |
| **TOTAL** | 111 | 111 | 109 | 108 | 124 | 123 | 113 | 104 | 107 | 108 | 105 | 97 | 107 | 114 |
| **TOTAL PAYMENTS** £ | 20,000 | 23,000 | 22,000 | 26,000 | 32,000 | 27,000 | 30,000 | 26,000 | 26,180 | 26,930 | 23,307 | 22,606 | 28,082 | 37,447 |
| **AVERAGE PAYMENT** £ | 180 | 207 | 202 | 241 | 259 | 220 | 265 | 250 | 246 | 249 | 222 | 233 | 262 | 328 |

* Including Payments for part-years but excluding cases where no maintenance grant was paid for a sponsored candidate.

## TABLE 17

TRADE UNION MAINTENANCE GRANTS TO CONSTITUENCIES, 1945–1958

| Sponsoring Union | Sums Paid to Constituency Labour Parties | | | | | | | | | | | | | |
| --- | --- | --- | --- | --- | --- | --- | --- | --- | --- | --- | --- | --- | --- | --- |
| | 1945 £ | 1946 £ | 1947 £ | 1948 £ | 1949 £ | 1950 £ | 1951 £ | 1952 £ | 1953 £ | 1954 £ | 1955 £ | 1956 £ | 1957 £ | 1958 £ |
| Transport & General Workers' Union | 4,164 | 4,289 | 4,351 | 5,164 | 5,775 | 5,175 | 4,835 | 4,538 | 3,871 | 4,750 | 4,475 | 4,163 | 5,205 | 6,720 |
| National Union of Mineworkers (C) | 2,851 | 3,773 | 3,689 | 4,042 | 4,633 | 4,047 | 4,419 | 4,260 | 4,043 | 3,722 | 2,404 | 2,598 | 2,379 | 2,690 |
| National Union of General & Municipal Workers | 2,812 | 3,384 | 3,122 | 3,505 | 4,559 | 2,267 | 3,153 | 2,463 | 1,974 | 1,688 | 1,704 | 1,418 | 2,123 | 3,105 |
| Amalgamated Engineering Union | 504 | 871 | 754 | 686 | 1,614 | 2,197 | 3,725 | 1,864 | 2,717 | 2,690 | 1,929 | 1,928 | 3,094 | 4,150 |
| Union of Shop, Distributive & Allied Workers | 2,383 | 3,045 | 3,068 | 2,852 | 3,626 | 3,001 | 3,376 | 3,153 | 3,150 | 3,081 | 4,026 | 3,000 | 3,314 | 6,102 |
| National Union of Railwaymen | 2,425 | 2,400 | 2,150 | 2,900 | 3,150 | 2,725 | 2,900 | 2,992 | 3,200 | 3,200 | 2,800 | 2,319 | 2,530 | 3,453 |
| Electrical Trades Union | — | 150 | 200 | 250 | 400 | 750 | 500 | 250 | 925 | 800 | — | 300 | 334 | 548 |
| United Textile Factory Workers' Asso. (C) | 829 | 528 | 497 | 500 | 550 | 883 | 1,055 | 850 | 788 | 600 | 480 | 600 | 700 | 870 |
| Transport Salaried Staffs' Association | *1,500* | *2,500* | *2,500* | *3,500* | *4,000* | *2,600* | *2,700* | *2,600* | *2,600* | *2,500* | *2,700* | *2,400* | *2,650* | *3,300* |
| Other | *2,532* | *2,060* | *1,669* | *2,601* | *3,698* | *3,355* | *3,337* | *3,080* | *2,912* | *3,949* | *2,789* | *3,880* | *5,753* | *6,402* |
| TOTAL | *20,000* | *23,000* | *22,000* | *26,000* | *32,000* | *27,000* | *30,000* | *26,000* | 26,180 | 26,930 | 23,307 | 22,606 | 28,082 | 37,447 |

Italic indicates estimated expenditure.

permitted rate to constituencies employing agents. But most unions' accounts lend little credence to allegations that *sub rosa* payments are made.

In recent years sponsorship has been severely attacked as much because of its effects on party organization as because it may lead to 'buying' of seats. The Wilson Committee commented on the practice of candidates making contributions to constituency funds:

'Quite apart from the undesirability of this practice on general grounds, the dependence of CLP finance on such a source of income has had a detrimental effect on organization. We recommend that early steps be taken to end this practice.'[1]

R. T. McKenzie has also suggested that maintenance grants have an 'enervating effect on the parties'.[2]

Such allegations are plausible but hard to either verify or to disprove. By the one yardstick available they seem dubious. In 1955, when average membership of all constituency parties was 1,365, the average membership of sponsored constituencies was almost identical, 1,372. This figure was unduly depressed by the NUM seats, whose average was 942—though many of them receive well below the full grant. Figures printed by the Lancashire & Cheshire Regional Council suggest that party membership is, on the average, a higher proportion of the Labour Party's vote, in the sponsored constituencies than in the remainder.[3]

Mining constituencies are particularly criticized. Though they are often comfortably supplied with Miners' money, a large part of their income is affiliation fees, which would still be paid and still 'sap the initiative', whether the candidate was a sponsored miner or not. Many sponsored CLPs *are* 'enervated' and inefficient, but since many of them are also safe seats, where membership is often low, or are in cities where the Borough Party's predominance has caused the withering away

[1] *Report*, para. 68.
[2] The *Observer*, September 25, 1955.
[3] A *Report of the Lancashire & Cheshire Regional Council* for 1952 divides the constituencies in the area into four divisions according to their success in building membership. Six of the twenty sponsored seats came in the top division of twenty-one, six in the second, and five in the bottom division.

of the constituencies, it is premature to lay all the blame against the sponsorship system. At least until the launching of the Marginal Constituencies Scheme in 1956, sponsored constituencies were more likely to have a full-time agent—one sign of a healthier Party—than the unsponsored.[1] Many agencies are established or survive only through payment of sponsorship grants.

The clash of opinion within the Party about the continuing of sponsorship is understandable enough. At any moment about one constituency in five has a maintained candidate, and many more have hopes. On the other hand, a majority of local parties are unlikely to have the chance of adopting a sponsored candidate, and some of the richer parties prefer to retain their independence. Though the criticism of sponsorship comes almost wholly from the constituency side of the Party the initiative for higher grants in 1955–6 came primarily from the constituency parties. The controversy over the rate of grants was mainly fought between the have and the have-not constituency parties. The unions kept discreetly silent, though in 1955 the Wilson Committee had found trade union Members of Parliament almost unanimously opposed to a rise.[2] Despite the most recent increases, the maximum payment looks less attractive to most constituency parties than it did a quarter of a century ago.

### 3 Sponsored Elections

Not only do the unions contribute to the maintenance of many constituencies, they pay a sizeable proportion of the election expenses where their candidates are adopted. Under the Hastings Agreement they pay a constituency eighty per cent of the election expenses incurred, up to a maximum of eighty per cent of the limit laid down by the Representation of the People Acts. The limit was imposed to discourage constituencies spending wastefully in the comfortable knowledge that it would come out of someone else's pocket.

Allowing as far as possible for redistribution of seats, about 230 constituencies were sponsored in one or more of the

---

[1] In Lancashire & Cheshire Region there were thirty-four agents, and eighty-one constituencies in 1955. Of twenty union constituencies fifteen had agents. There were eleven agents in the forty-seven non-union sponsored constituencies (eight agents were employed by Borough Labour Parties).
[2] Report, para. 127.

elections 1945–1955. The sums involved have held fairly steady: £65,000 for 124 candidates in 1945; £75,000 for 128 candidates in 1950; £70,000 for 136 candidates in 1951, and £65,000 for 127 candidates in 1955. On average, then, a constituency which adopts a sponsored candidate received £550 when the election comes.[1]

But the actual payments vary widely, as does the observance of the Hastings Agreement. At the 1951 election USDAW paid:

> 100% of all election costs to Jarrow CLP ( £696)
> 86% of all election costs to Leigh CLP ( £724)
> 83% of all election costs to Edinburgh (Pentlands) CLP ( £723)
> 102% of all election costs to Bradford (South) CLP ( £686)

At the same election the Woodworkers contributed eighty-two per cent of the cost of Mr Sam Viant's campaign at Willesden West, but 110 per cent of the costs incurred by Mr A. S. Moody in fighting Gateshead. But most large unions kept strictly to the eighty per cent limit, while the AEU is said to have a maximum payment of £600. Smaller unions frequently give less than the maximum. Thus, Mr R. H. Edwards, fighting Chertsey for the National Union of Vehicle Builders in 1955, paid the local party only £400, and the President of the United Patternmakers' Association has always received less than the maximum for his campaigns at Stoke.[2]

The Miners have the most complicated system of all. It dates from days when nominations were easily won. Their central political fund grants £500 to Areas for county constituencies and £450 for boroughs, with a limit of one candidate for every ten thousand members. Areas who run more than their 'quota' of candidates either pay the costs themselves or, more often, spread the grant more thinly over the greater number of seats. Constituencies which adopt Miners' candidates often receive

---

[1] In 1954 East Ham North and Workington CLPs proposed rises of £50 and £100 respectively. In 1956 the UPW proposed a £100 rise, and three CLPs demanded an unspecified increase. *Agenda for the Labour Party Conference*, 1954, pp. 22–3 and 1956, p. 3.

[2] £500 in 1945, 1950 and 1951; £600 in 1955.

well under the NUM allowance.[1] In 1955, rather than pump
money into safe seats, Nottingham and Derbyshire Areas gave
money to their Regional Council to distribute to needy marginal
seats.

Here is the real problem of the sponsorship system. Logically
Labour should shepherd its resources, to concentrate them where
they are most needed. This has never been practical politics.
Rich constituencies cannot be made to share their wealth with
poor areas, and scarcely any do so voluntarily. The Marginal
Constituencies Scheme has brought a degree of equalization,
but the system of election and maintenance grants still leads
inherently to the payment of large sums to constituencies which
should be fully self-supporting or are rock-solid Labour seats.
In 1955 the Miners' candidate at Ince, Mr Tom Brown, who
was returned with a formidable majority of 18,000 votes, spent
£829 on his campaign. The USDAW candidate at Westhoughton, Mr J. T. Price, who had a majority of 12,000 votes,
spent £938. Mr James Griffiths, another NUM candidate, at
Llanelly, elected by the comfortable margin of 24,000 votes,
spent £905. Mr Ernest Thornton, United Textile Factory
Workers' Association MP for Farnworth, spent £920. Every
one of these candidates spent well over the Party's national
average of £620; all were among the small number of Labour
candidates who spent more than their Conservative opponents.

Theoretically the constituencies' obligation to find the
twenty per cent of expenses which are not paid by the sponsoring
union should be a check on extravagance. In practice almost
every Party can count on receiving this remainder in grants
from other unions. In consequence few sponsored constituencies
show the restraint of Mr John Parker, who won Dagenham at
the same election by 25,000 votes, but spent only £309.
Maintenance grants and election expenses are poured into seats
which are completely safe and should stand on their own feet,
while until the past few years many marginal seats have been
desperately short of funds. Many local parties are even now in
almost constant debt. It is natural that the unions want their
candidates to stand in safe seats. Their clear interest lies in
continuing the system. But as the Wilson Committee and many

[1] But NUM lodges are usually generous.

trade unionists have recognized, sponsorship is inherently a grossly wasteful way of financing a political party.[1]

The Hastings Agreement apart, most trade unionist parliamentary candidates can count on a grant from their union at a general election. The Clerical & Administrative Workers' Union in fact prefers to distribute its money to its members' campaigns rather than make a grant to national funds. Almost every union gives at least £25, while some give as much as £50 or £100 to all who claim it. It is indicative of the tenuous character of some Labour candidates' trade union membership that although thirty-nine candidates said they were members of USDAW at the 1955 election, only twenty-three claimed the union's £25 grant or were officially sponsored. Occasionally a lucky candidate receives support from two unions at once. Mr Stubbs, who fought Cambridgeshire in 1945 and 1950 was partly maintained by the TGWU, while he received election expenses from the Typographical Association. Mr George Isaacs had the support of both the London Typographical Society and the National Society of Operative Printers & Assistants (Natsopa) at Southwark, and the English and Scottish Bakers' Unions jointly supported a candidate in 1951. Quite often unions make grants to candidates run by unions organizing in an allied craft, as an expression of solidarity, particularly when they have no candidates of their own.

These sums have little effect on the results. Many of the seats that receive them are immovably Conservative; the unions can certainly not be suspected of 'buying' nominations here. But the £5,000 to £7,000 involved at each election does spread union money to constituencies which normally have little share in it. Though £25 may be chicken-feed to the union or the large city party, it is rare enough to be viewed with gratitude by a struggling rural constituency.

---

[1] *Report*, para. 127. 'The trade union movement ignores [the rural areas] altogether, as regards candidates with financial assistance behind them, and to this extent the movement, by its selfishness on such issues, deserves what it has got. . . . Although [the unions] may pick and choose their constituencies, all their money is wasted unless the rural areas can be won as well.

Give them some of the money wasted by the trade unions on safe seats. Let the trade unionists stand by their principles and make their contribution to ensuring trade union conditions for those rural agents who at present work for half the agreed rate for the job.' *The Railway Review*, March 10, 1950.

## 4 *Grants by the Branch*

To the gifts from the unions' national offices can be added donations from branches and districts, in those unions which allow a share of the levy to be spent locally. Naturally the amounts they can give vary widely. Most District Committees try to see that every Party in their area receives something, even if it be only a nominal £5, and they can usually be counted on for an extra grant if one of their own members is the candidate. The sums involved are sometimes sizeable. One or two AEU District Committees have been able to make grants of up to £150 to a single constituency party. The grants made by USDAW have averaged £8, £11, £13 and £15 per constituency at the first four elections since the war—but USDAW is among the most openhanded of unions.

Though separating municipal and general election grants from union accounts is not always possible, the average sum received by the constituency parties in grants from branches and districts has clearly risen since the war. It averaged about £40 in 1945, £140 in 1950, £95 in 1951 and £150 in 1955.

### TABLE 18

ESTIMATED TRADE UNION CONTRIBUTIONS TO CONSTITUENCY
LABOUR PARTIES, 1945–1958

| Year | Affiliation Fees | Maintenance of Sponsored Candidates | General Election Grants to Sponsored Candidates | Local and Other General Election Grants* | Total |
|---|---|---|---|---|---|
| | £ | £ | £ | £ | £ |
| 1945 | 30,000 | 20,000 | 65,000 | 58,000 | 173,000 |
| 1946 | 35,000 | 23,000 | — | 22,000 | 81,000 |
| 1947 | 38,000 | 22,000 | — | 29,000 | 89,000 |
| 1948 | 38,000 | 26,000 | — | 16,000 | 80,000 |
| 1949 | 44,000 | 32,000 | — | 57,000 | 133,000 |
| 1950 | 44,000 | 27,000 | 75,000 | 93,000 | 239,000 |
| 1951 | 48,000 | 30,000 | 70,000 | 92,000 | 240,000 |
| 1952 | 52,000 | 26,000 | — | 35,000 | 112,000 |
| 1953 | 55,000 | 26,000 | — | 39,000 | 120,000 |
| 1954 | 58,000 | 27,000 | — | 31,000 | 116,000 |
| 1955 | 60,000 | 23,000 | 65,000 | 127,000 | 285,000 |
| 1956 | 62,000 | 23,000 | — | 39,000 | 124,000 |
| 1957 | 66,000 | 28,000 | — | 54,000 | 148,000 |
| 1958 | 66,000 | 37,000 | — | 57,000 | 161,000 |

\* Excluding sums reaching the constituencies through the Regional Councils, and the constituencies' share of the national General Election Fund.

By contrast to this relatively generous support, the unions' grants towards local government elections are modest. There is no Hastings Agreement for local elections, and candidates are not normally officially sponsored. The unions' grants are an expression of solidarity rather than an effective contribution to campaign costs. Most unions manage to find something, although until recently a union as important as the Amalgamated Society of Woodworkers had so small a political levy that it could not afford to make local government grants. The standard scale, little changed since the war, ranges between £1 for a Parish Council election to £5 for a contested county council seat, though a few unions, such as BISAKTA and the Plasterers pay £10. The only notable exception is London, where the unions are often prepared to recognize the higher cost of LCC elections by making grants of £25 or more and supporting the LCC Election Fund generously.[1]

The most active and generous unions are directly interested in local government. The Fire Brigades' Union (particularly when it was fighting off the rival Junior Fire Officers' Association), the National Union of Public Employees and the National Union of General and Municipal Workers all spend relatively large sums on local elections. In 1953 the FBU actually spent more than its political income for the year on municipal elections.

The amounts that individual constituencies receive in local election grants, and other special donations from the unions vary considerably. Individual constituencies may also find their local election income fluctuating widely from year to year. How much the local branches give depends not only on the local Party's needs and energy, but on such unpredictable factors as relations between the unions and the Labour group on the council, whether there are trade union candidates, and on the enthusiasm of the leading figures in the branches. Yet over the country as a whole the constituencies have been receiving increasing support for local elections since the war. From about £20,000 in 1946 such grants rose to over £50,000 in 1958, an average of about £85 per constituency. In addition the unions

---

[1] The London Labour Party election fund received grants of £5,242 in 1946; £7,198 in 1949; and £4,399 in 1952.

give from £3,000 to £5,000 per year towards the cost of by-elections.

## EXPENDITURE WITHIN THE UNIONS

Since most of the unions' internal political expenditure is rather humdrum outlay on administration, income tax, and political education it deserves only brief mention. Yet, arising directly from the unions' affiliation to the Labour Party, it must in fairness be included as part of their political effort, just as much as comparable outlay by a constituency party.

One of the largest 'internal' items is the cost of the Labour Party Conference, some £20,000 (compared with only £7,000 in 1945), nearly four per cent of total political expenditure. The Miners' delegation alone costs over £3,000, while in 1958 the AEU delegation cost more than £45 per head.[1] Even so the union delegations are far below strength. Had they sent their complete delegations to every conference from the end of the war to 1958 the total extra cost would have exceeded £150,000. Delegations to the Labour Party Women's Conference and to Regional conferences must also be paid for, and some unions pay fees to their delegates to Constituency Labour Parties. Normally these amount to only a few shillings to cover expenses, and are no real incentive to attend. Most unions pay nothing. With these further outlays included the movement is spending almost £30,000 on delegates and conferences.

Political education claims a small share. Most educational activity, whether biased or not, can be reconciled with the unions' industrial objects. A few unions think the instruction provided by the National Council of Labour Colleges is so politically oriented that it is best paid for from the political fund. Scholarships to Labour Party Summer Schools, and the organization of political weekend schools within unions must also come out of the political funds. But the sums involved are always small, some £12,000 per year, a total which, it must be emphasized, underestimates the political impact of trade union education. Most unions believe that directly political education

---

[1] The cost of sending a delegate is, on average, £35 compared with £25 in 1945.

TABLE 19

POLITICAL EXPENDITURE WITHIN THE UNIONS, 1945–1958

| Year | Conferences and Delegations | Retainers and Candidates' Expenses | Political Education | Income Tax | Administration |
|---|---|---|---|---|---|
| | £ | £ | £ | £ | £ |
| 1945 | 11,978 | 6,247 | 3,141 | 2,684 | 22,334 |
| 1946 | 11,470 | 5,572 | 819 | 2,713 | 24,904 |
| 1947 | 13,954 | 4,741 | 6,229 | 2,391 | 28,043 |
| 1948 | 13,703 | 5,236 | 5,151 | 1,279 | 28,619 |
| 1949 | 17,178 | 5,428 | 7,312 | 2,417 | 29,345 |
| 1950 | 18,375 | 6,010 | 8,318 | 2,019 | 35,899 |
| 1951 | 18,535 | 7,207 | 8,276 | 2,082 | 33,807 |
| 1952 | 20,758 | 7,523 | 7,712 | 1,869 | 41,564 |
| 1953 | 23,738 | 8,654 | 7,732 | 1,855 | 41,093 |
| 1954 | 25,430 | 10,333 | 8,224 | 2,398 | 38,064 |
| 1955 | 28,419 | 9,380 | 8,138 | 3,202 | 42,738 |
| 1956 | 28,725 | 9,310 | 8,380 | 3,566 | 39,890 |
| 1957 | 32,082 | 10,240 | 13,179 | 4,058 | 49,566 |
| 1958 | 34,500 | 9,934 | 14,300 | 5,350 | 58,800 |

is not their concern. When the NUGMW Congress was asked to vote that a political propagandist be employed to improve the union's political work, Mr Tom Williamson crisply replied: 'This is a job for the Labour Party'. The motion was lost.[1]

Another modest share of the political funds is absorbed by the traditional payment of retainers to Parliamentary representatives. Before the payment of Members of Parliament some grant was essential if there was to be working class representation. Since the introduction of Parliamentary salaries in 1911 trade union retainers—like those paid by other organizations with representatives in the House—have been a recognition of services rendered, a supplement to Parliamentary salaries. Union aid to Members of Parliament cannot be precisely evaluated. Some unions provide their Parliamentary spokesmen with offices, secretarial and research facilities, postage and stationery. In the AEU these services replace a retainer; elsewhere they may supplement it. Other unions, such as the Union of Post Office Workers provide secretarial help at a fraction of

[1] *Report of Congress*, 1950, p. 259.

cost. Most unions charge such costs against their industrial funds.

Retainers are much more common since the war, perhaps because Executives have started to look for ways of encouraging members to go into Parliament, perhaps because their Members of Parliament felt the Parliamentary salary at times to be inadequate. Now the smaller unions, such as the Typographical Association or the National Union of Public Employees make an annual payment of £50, while the NUR and the British Iron, Steel & Kindred Trades' Association both pay £100 per year.[1] The TGWU, NUGMW and USDAW all give their officer-MPs £200 per year from general funds.[2] The Miners' annual grant of £225 is now the highest in the movement.

In the past few years the payment of retainers has spread quickly. Unions have been more ready to assume the responsibility of nursing constituencies by paying their candidates' expenses before they are elected. The Transport Salaried Staffs' Association gives every member of its parliamentary panel selected under Constituency Labour Party sponsorship £50 personal expenses allowance, and any other member who is adopted receives £15. The NUGMW not only pays its sponsored candidates £75 per year to cover constituency expenses, it gives £52 per year to its Unofficial Panel of selected Members of Parliament—most of them 'intellectual' members of the union. More recently the Blastfurnacemen have been paying £100 per year to Mr Hilary Marquand. This former professor of industrial relations, has been closely connected with the union for years, and is now Member for Middlesbrough, where the union has its headquarters.

[1] BISAKTA was first approached by its MPs in 1946, but decided the Parliamentary salary was sufficient. In 1950 they agreed to pay £100, and this was raised in 1952. As soon as Parliamentary expense allowances were introduced the retainer was again cut. See *Quarterly Report* for the quarters ending June 1946, September 1950, December 1950, March 1951, December 1953 and September 1954.

[2] In *McCarthy and the National Association of Theatrical & Kine Employees* the aggrieved member contended that NATKE had infringed its rules, and S.3 of the Trade Union Act, 1913 by paying the salary of Sir Tom O'Brien, its General Secretary, out of the General Fund, while he was a Member of Parliament. The Registrar held that since the General Secretary's salary had not been increased to take account of his Parliamentary duties there was no question of his being 'maintained' within the Act. This ruling would apparently apply to officials on part-pay. *Report*, 1957, Part 4, pp. 3–4.

In 1958 the unions paid more than twice as much in retainers and candidates' expenses than in 1945, although the number of trade union MPs had fallen slightly. However, many grants still look modest by the standards of other interest groups which are represented in the House of Commons. Although by crude comparison with union salaries MPs often seem well paid, trade unionists often fail to grasp how many calls a Member of Parliament has to meet, which do not trouble a trade union official with an expense allowance and the use of a car. Although many Members of Parliament can work part-time at their professions or supplement their salary by journalism or broadcasting, few manual trade unionists have any sizeable earnings outside their Parliamentary salaries, and those who have are often strongly criticized.[1] Union MPs felt more keenly than many of their colleagues the failure at certain periods, of Parliamentary salaries to respond to rises in prices. The unions consider responsibility for paying MPs adequately lies with the public rather than with them. So it does, but some unions might profitably ask themselves whether the present level of grants, £10,000 per year, brings them as many Parliamentary candidates as they would like.[2]

Although unions are not bound to make a return of their administrative costs against the political fund, about ten per cent of their political expenditure is classed as 'administration'.[3] While the National Union of Public Employees spent almost £9,000 of its total outlay of £17,250 in 1958 on collecting subscriptions and running its political fund, some unions, such as the TGWU, make no charge at all. Union accounts rarely reflect fully the real cost of administration. With all overheads considered it seems probable that the expenditure of £60,000 reported in 1958 was little more than half the true cost—and that the unions' political efforts were to that extent underestimated.

---

[1] The strongest criticism arose from the acceptance by Mr Jack Jones (BISAKTA) of a post as welfare supervisor to the Lancashire Steel Corporation: 'What do they think we pay our contributions to the Labour Party for? To sponsor MPs to become labour advisers to recalcitrant employers?' (Boilermakers' conference). *The Times*, May 29, 1957.

[2] Some unions (notably the NUM) still make allowances to their local government representatives. About £3,500 is spent in this way.

[3] In Great Britain only direct political expenditure need be returned. In Northern Ireland indirect expenditure falls within the Act and must be returned.

A few items fall conveniently into no category; gifts to memorial appeals, affiliations to bodies like the Fabian Society and the British-Asian Socialist Fellowship. About £1,500 per year is spent in Northern Ireland and a few hundred pounds per year in Eire. These are included in Table 20 as 'Other expenditure'. Finally because of the inadequacy of some union accounts, a further sum, never exceeding about £20,000 had had to be classed as unassignable although the bulk of it represents 'useful' political expenditure that should have been allocated under other headings. Such is the unions' outlay on politics.

TABLE 20

CONSOLIDATED TRADE UNION POLITICAL INCOME, EXPENDITURE
AND RESERVES, 1945–1958

EXPENDITURE

| Year | The Labour Party | | | | Total | INCOME | RESERVES at December 31 |
|------|------------------|----------|-------------|----------------------|-------|--------|-------------------------|
|      | National | Regional | Constituency | Internal and Other |       |        |                         |
|      | £ | £ | £ | £ | £ | £ | £ |
| 1945 | 121,000 | 10,000 | 173,000 | 67,000 | 371,000 | 220,000 | 634,000 |
| 1946 | 54,000 | 8,000 | 81,000 | 60,000 | 203,000 | 253,000 | 483,000 |
| 1947 | 139,000 | 4,000 | 89,000 | 79,000 | 311,000 | 413,000 | 533,000 |
| 1948 | 202,000 | 6,000 | 80,000 | 70,000 | 358,000 | 465,000 | 635,000 |
| 1949 | 305,000 | 15,000 | 133,000 | 77,000 | 530,000 | 470,000 | 742,000 |
| 1950 | 139,000 | 17,000 | 239,000 | 85,000 | 480,000 | 473,000 | 682,000 |
| 1951 | 230,000 | 7,000 | 240,000 | 89,000 | 566,000 | 481,000 | 675,000 |
| 1952 | 131,000 | 11,000 | 112,000 | 111,000 | 365,000 | 505,000 | 590,000 |
| 1953 | 133,000 | 8,000 | 120,000 | 108,000 | 369,000 | 542,000 | 730,000 |
| 1954 | 144,000 | 8,000 | 116,000 | 104,000 | 372,000 | 550,000 | 904,000 |
| 1955 | 246,000 | 28,000 | 285,000 | 97,000 | 656,000 | 552,000 | 1,082,000 |
| 1956 | 146,000 | 8,000 | 124,000 | 106,000 | 384,000 | 579,000 | 978,000 |
| 1957 | 214,000 | 8,000 | 148,000 | 124,000 | 494,000 | 750,000 | 1,173,000 |
| 1958 | 364,000 | 12,000 | 161,000 | 154,000 | 692,000 | 770,000 | 1,430,000 |
|      |         |        |         |         |         |         | 1,508,000 |

* The equivalent figures given by the Chief Registrar of Friendly Societies—who has been misinformed by several large unions about the sums they were spending—systematically exaggerate expenditure, except in election year, when they underestimate it. The degree of error in election years is not apparent from the table above because some double-counting has been eliminated. The Chief Registrar's figures are:

| Year | Expenditure £ | Income £ | Balance £ | Year | Expenditure £ | Income £ | Balance £ |
|------|---------------|----------|-----------|------|---------------|----------|-----------|
| 1944 | — | — | 583,000 | 1952 | 374,000 | 508,000 | 689,000 |
| 1945 | 353,000 | 230,000 | 460,000 | 1953 | 405,000 | 548,000 | 834,000 |
| 1946 | 207,000 | 254,000 | 506,000 | 1954 | 410,000 | 555,000 | 981,000 |
| 1947 | 325,000 | 409,000 | 590,000 | 1955 | 638,000 | 561,000 | 906,000 |
| 1948 | 390,000 | 465,000 | 666,000 | 1956 | 416,000 | 588,000 | 1,078,000 |
| 1949 | 534,000 | 494,000 | 626,000 | 1957 | 535,000 | 753,000 | 1,298,000 |
| 1950 | 472,000 | 492,000 | 647,000 | 1958 | 707,000 | 773,000 | 1,366,000 |
| 1951 | 583,000 | 490,000 | 554,000 |      |         |         |         |

*Who Pays the Piper?*

Seven pounds in every ten that the Labour Party receives centrally and at least two in every three that it receives regionally come from the trade unions. But what of the Party as a whole? No wholly accurate figure can be given. Although the Labour Party publishes far more information about its finances than the Conservatives, it does not—as it is wont to claim—publish its accounts for the world to see. It is doubtful whether even Transport House knows the Party's total income and expenditure. Certainly members of the National Executive Committee are incompletely informed.[1]

The main obstacle is the constituencies' accounting methods. Drawn up in no standard form, they are frequently either incomplete or strikingly misleading. So-called 'constituency' accounts sometimes completely omit to mention the finances of the ward parties. One North-Eastern CLP produced accounts showing an apparent income of only £76 for the year; its true income was nearer £500. Another local party which claimed an income of more than £3,000 per year had lumped in the gross receipts from its football pool and the annual draw. There is little wonder that estimates of the Party's income have so often been ill-informed.

The constituencies' income is drawn from several main sources: members' subscriptions; trade union and Cooperative Party affiliation fees; donations from members and affiliated organizations; proceeds of lotteries, polls, bazaars and dances. Some information is available on the first two, a little on the third, and very little on the fourth. Like the Labour Party the Cooperative Party publishes only national accounts, and does not collate the income and expenditure of its local branches. Although its contribution to the Party is therefore hard to assess it is clear that only a small part of Cooperative expenditure directly benefits the Labour Party. Most is used within the Cooperative Movement for propaganda and political education. Cooperative contributions to the Labour Party can be roughly

---

[1] The Wilson Committee clearly did not have complete information, while Mr Ian Mikardo (a member of the NEC with a special interest in organization) had to rely on accounts collected by friends when estimating the Party's income at £1,200,000 per year. Cf., *Tribune*, October 7, 1955.

estimated from the accounts of a selection of the larger Cooperative Societies' accounts, bearing in mind that by no means all
Cooperatives are 'political', and from the accounts of constituency parties. In an ordinary year the Cooperatives spend
at least £130,000, and possibly as much as £175,000 on
political activities, but only about £30,000 reaches the Labour
Party.[1]

Commenting on members' subscriptions the Wilson Committee reported that:

'It is widely known that the recorded membership of many
CLPs is considerably in excess of the actual contributing membership paying a full subscription all the year round. Compared
with a theoretical annual subscription of 6s per annual member,
the average receipts are probably nearer half that sum.'[2]

Constituency accounts tend to confirm that 3s to 3s 6d per
head of stated membership is about the average for the whole
country. No one in the Party hides the fact that the collection of
subscriptions is one of its least efficient activities. This thankless
task is usually dependent on volunteers or pensioners working
on commission. Some energetic parties like Eastleigh, Erith &
Crayford, and Petersfield regularly collect over 5s per head.
Many more—largely in the Southern counties—can collect over
4s.[3] But against these must be set constituencies like Bolton
East, which was said, before a recovery drive, to be 'in debt,
its membership and collection system collapsed, and with four
of its nine wards for all practical purposes defunct'.[4] One county-
constituency in the North-East with 1,750 nominal members in
1954 collected only £108 in subscriptions—1s 3d per head.
Solihull and Kidderminster CLPs were well pleased with

[1] This expenditure is heavily concentrated in the London area, where the
London Cooperative Society and the Royal Arsenal Cooperative Society are ex-
tremely active politically. Elsewhere Cooperative affiliations are often very small.
Cooperative contributions to national and regional funds are negligible. The failure
of the Cooperatives to put a significant fraction of their money into the Labour
Party has been one of the causes of irritation at the Cooperatives' sponsorship of
Parliamentary candidates. See p. 305.

[2] Para. 122.

[3] The Southern Region set its 'target' for 1958 at 4s. 2d. per head.

[4] In another constituency, Ludlow, there were only eight paying Party members
in a population of 6,500. Several small Parties scarcely have any real existence.
They affiliate on the minimum membership, which was 240 until 1957 and 800
thereafter, but some do not have even this number.

G

average subscriptions of 3s 1d (1952) and of 2s 8d (1954) respectively. Some of the 'success' stories are revealing. Exeter CLP reported a rise from 2s 1d per head in 1951 to 3s 7d in 1952 and 3s 8d in 1953. Hemel Hempstead was proud of raising its average collected subscription from 1s 4d in 1951 to 1s 10d in 1957. Although the Party's efficiency in collecting contributions is probably increasing, there are always many backsliders to set against the successes. Many of the tiny constituency parties which eke out a hand to mouth existence in safe seats or remote areas are often reluctant to admit how low their income is. The average contribution of 11½d reported to have been collected in Woking in 1958 shows how weak their position can be. The figure of 3s 3d per head per year can be taken with some confidence as a working average that does not do the constituencies an injustice. This suggests that with Party membership between 850,000 and 900,000,[1] members subscribe between £140,000 and £150,000—or from £225 to £240 per constituency.

The constituencies' income from special events also varies widely. Again the suburban constituencies are the most successful. Fulham can make £200 on its Christmas Draw, St. Marylebone looks to its Derby and Christmas draws as its main source of income. Other parties have an annual income from dances, bazaars and socials running into several hundred pounds (garden parties are mainly a Conservative activity). Colne Valley once took £400 on its gift day while, although many Scottish constituencies are among the poorest, Selkirk & Peebles once reported a profit of over £700 on its bazaar. But these are the widely reported successes. One of the largest borough parties was recently making only £100 profit from such 'events'. Many constituency accounts show them as a negligible proportion of their income.

Many local parties have been increasing their income from lotteries and football pools in the past few years. Gillingham CLP claims to take £80 per week from its schemes, while a South Wales constituency reckons to make £1,000 from its

---

[1] In 1957 membership was officially 913,000, but at least 57,000 of these were 'phantom' members, affiliated solely because the minimum affiliation had been raised to 800 from 240.

football pools. A considerable number of constituencies regularly net £20 per week during the football season. But again the results are patchy. On one hand West Lewisham can report that its profits from football ( £1,206) and draws ( £289) were almost two-thirds of its total income in 1958; on the other are many constituencies with scattered membership or religious or socialist scruples against the profit motive which have no such income. Only a handful of local parties, mostly in the Home Counties, can count regularly on taking more from gambling and 'events' than from affiliation fees and subscriptions.

From the evidence of constituency, union, and Cooperative Party accounts it seems that the income of the constituency parties at present runs at about £450,000[1] made up of about £145,000 from the trade unions, £150,000 from subscriptions, £125,000 from gifts, 'events' and 'gambling', and £30,000 from the Cooperatives. This is an average of about £750—but the average covers a spread of between £200 and £3,500, and perhaps higher. The unions' contribution to the constituencies is relatively much less important (just over thirty per cent) than their national or regional payments. Its inadequacy is a matter of frequent complaint in the local parties.

Taking this estimate we can calculate the unions' share of the Party's total income. Double counting has to be eliminated at every level, leaving only autonomous income at national and regional level (net income from trading items, interest) and allowing for Transport House grants to the constituency parties. For 1957 the Party's income was divided approximately as follows:

| | £ |
|---|---|
| Autonomous Central and Regional Income | 10,000 |
| Autonomous constituency income | 275,000 |
| Cooperative donations to Labour Party | 30,000 |
| Trade union donations to Labour Party | 370,000 |
| | £685,000 |

Thus, the unions contributed between fifty per cent and fifty-five per cent of the Party's total income. However, calculating

[1] This is based on 1957. Both union contributions to the constituencies and the constituencies' autonomous income have been rising steadily since the war. The picture would be little different if other years had been chosen.

the unions' contribution solely on the basis of what they pay to the Party does them less than justice. Their political expenditure also includes outlay on administration and joining in Party activities. If this is reckoned too, giving a total outlay of £490,000 their share of combined Party income and union expenditure comes to almost exactly seventy per cent.[1]

It is more difficult to estimate the unions' share in an election year. In 1955 their special grants amounted to £272,000—seventy per cent of the Party's direct election expenses. But both Transport House and many constituencies run the election at a profit; many local parties receive far more than they could legally spend. Consequently the unions' share of the Party's total election *income* is probably about the same in an election year as in a normal year.

While estimates cannot pretend to complete accuracy, their general significance is solidly enough established. For even were it assumed that the constituencies themselves raised twice the amount estimated—£550,000—and their total income was accordingly £725,000 exclusive of Transport House grants; even then the unions would still be contributing forty per cent of the Party's income. Finding exactly how large is the unions' share is obviously relevant to any discussion of whether they are honouring their obligations. Some members would think it relevant to the controversy over voting rights. Yet the essential political fact is that, whether the correct figure be forty per cent, fifty-five per cent or seventy per cent, this is overwhelmingly the largest single element in the Labour Party's finances.

### Do the Unions Pull Their Weight?

Fifty or more years ago the first political levies were fixed at one shilling per year. At the beginning of 1959 there were still twenty-five affiliated unions whose adult male members paid one shilling per year political levy. Many female and juvenile members pay less. Even after the TGWU raised its political contribution in 1957 its female and junior members paid only 8d per year to the political fund, less than it cost to affiliate them

[1] It is reasonable to make this calculation for the unions, while omitting the Cooperative Party's expenditure because the unions' expenditure is wholly the consequence of their affiliation to the Party, while the Cooperatives spend most of their money on their own activities.

to the national Labour Party alone. At the top of the scale the position has improved. In twenty-three unions adult male members contributed as much or more than the annual average of 3s collected from individual Party members, compared with six in 1945.[3]

### TABLE 21

RATES OF POLITICAL CONTRIBUTION IN TRADE UNIONS AFFILIATED TO THE LABOUR PARTY

| Annual Adult Male Contribution | Number of Unions* 1945‡ | 1955‡ | 1959‡ | Number of Members Eligible to Contribute at 1959 rates§ |
|---|---|---|---|---|
| over 4s 6d | 0 | 3 | 4 | 434,718 |
| 4s 1d–4s 6d | 5 | 3 | 11 | 703,515 |
| 3s 7d–4s 0d | 0 | 2 | 4 | 654,529 |
| 3s 1d–3s 6d | 1 | 1 | 1 | 352,333 |
| 2s 7d–3s 0d | 0 | 7 | 6 | 231,650 |
| 2s 1d–2s 6d | 5 | 12 | 9 | 269,049 |
| 1s 7d–2s 0d | 12 | 20 | 25 | 3,551,209 |
| 1s 1d–1s 6d | 8 | 7 | 2 | 561,000 |
| 1s 0d and under | 43 | 30 | 25 | 1,097,718 |

* Component unions of the United Textile Factory Workers' Association reckoned separately.
‡ At January 1.
§ Based on membership in 1957. Where unions have lower contribution rates for women the male and female memberships have been allocated separately according to contribution due.

The political levy is part of the unions' continual problem of keeping contributions in line with rises in costs. Contrary to the general impression political contributions have, on average, kept pace rather better than the industrial.[2] For some years after the war the problem was avoided. The 1946 Act, coupled with higher membership, boosted political income. Although it rose from £221,000 in 1945 to £538,000 in 1954, only £97,000 (thirty per cent) came from higher contributions.

Nevertheless, after 1950 several union political funds ran into difficulties; the Typographical Association could spare nothing for the Party's election fund in 1955. The Bakers failed twice to

[1] The highest contributions in 1959 were Northumberland Area of the National Association of Colliery Overmen, Deputies & Shotfirers (8s 8d), and Durham Area of the NUM (8s 4d).
[2] Taking 1938 as 100, political contributions paid in 1958 were 160, industrial contributions collected in 1958 were 150, and the London & Cambridge Economic Service's index of weekly wage rates stood at 305 in December 1958.

carry an increase in political contributions by a ballot of their members. The Painters, Building Trade Workers, and the National Union of Furniture Trade Operatives all thought of raising contributions but gave up the idea. The Typographical Association conference agreed to a higher levy, but the members rejected it. Although several unions, such as the Miners, had little difficulty in carrying increased contributions, the Woodworkers needed three conferences and two ballots before their levy could be raised.

Many militants objected to paying more while other members paid nothing: 'We must tackle the blacklegs first', they argued. Others complained of the burden of paying both the levy and the Party subscription. Many trade union leaders also claim that the burden of the two contributions justifies a low rate of political levy. This is a red herring. Not more than one political fund contributor in ten is also an individual member of the Labour Party.[1] Others feared that higher contributions would lead to a rise in contracting-out. As a Woodworkers' branch official so ingloriously put it, 'We branch secretaries draw money from people who would not pay it if they knew what they were paying it for'.[2] He was afraid a higher contribution would be noticed.

By 1955 the issue had to be met squarely. With a national affiliation fee of ninepence it would be impossible to affiliate members nationally, regionally and locally and sponsor candidates on the traditional shilling contribution. A union which kept its levy at a shilling would be forced to cut its Party affiliation and other activities. Matters could drift no longer. Most large unions took the increase in their stride during 1956–8. The two general unions, the Miners and USDAW all raised their levies. But one or two Executives left the attempt until the Party had actually increased its affiliation fees, so that they could tell their members, 'Unless we put the levy up at once the political fund will collapse in a few months, and we shall be

---

[1] Officially Party membership was 888,955 in 1958, although true membership was substantially less. This includes housewives, non-unionists, and members of unions which have no political fund. Since 6,280,000 trade unionists contributed to the political levy in 1958 it seems evident that not more than one in ten were double contributors.

[2] *Report of the ADC*, 1950, p. 67.

## TABLE 22

POLITICAL INCOME, EXPENDITURE AND RESERVES OF TWELVE LARGE UNIONS IN 1958

| Union | The Labour Party — National Affiliations* (£) | Grants (£) | Regional (£) | Constituencies (£) | Conferences, Delegations (£) | Candidates & MPs (£) | Political Education (£) | Administration Income Tax (£) | Other & Unassignable (£) | Total (£) | Income (£) | Reserves at 31/12/58 (£) |
|---|---|---|---|---|---|---|---|---|---|---|---|---|
| TGWU* | 37,650 | 35,000 | 2,050 | 24,775 | 1,500 | 6,400 | — | .. | .. | 100,975 | 107,197 | 72,000 |
| NUM (C) | 25,891 | 35,050 | 1,716 | 21,077 | 6,986 | — | 3,100 | 8,300 | 7,605 | 116,125 | 152,909 | 362,034 |
| AEU‡ | 26,641 | — | 1,100 | 18,044 | 2,839 | — | 1,892 | 3,422 | 25 | 59,963 | 65,713 | 185,054 |
| NUGMW‡ | 24,525 | — | 1,740 | 16,523 | 2,812 | — | 113 | 11,871 | 32 | 57,616 | 71,777 | 137,000 |
| USDAW | 12,478 | 26,152 | 231 | 14,916 | 4,738 | — | 209 | 4,644 | 526 | 63,894 | 55,030 | 80,849 |
| NUR | 10,430 | — | 271 | 17,089 | 1,187 | 1,516 | — | 3,289 | 50 | 33,831 | 62,644 | 126,411 |
| UPW | 6,200 | 10,000 | — | 2,862 | 422 | — | 54 | 1,211 | 25 | 20,786 | 15,436 | 13,179 |
| ETU | 5,375 | 500 | 613 | 7,767 | 867 | 117 | 5,000 | 7,140 | 833 | 28,212 | 33,191 | 98,009 |
| UTFWA (C) | 4,878 | 1,000 | 210 | 2,000 | 1,560 | — | — | 1,190 | 100 | 10,938 | 12,263 | 51,608 |
| ASW | 4,619 | 5,000 | 211 | 2,582 | 871 | 317 | 82 | 221 | 232 | 14,136 | 12,753 | 28,024 |
| NUPE | 3,875 | — | 187 | 3,684 | 544 | — | — | 8,965 | — | 17,250 | 23,806 | 60,323 |

Estimates are printed in italic.

* Including by-election contribution.

‡ These unions' accounts simply show sums allocated to regions or districts, not the amount spent. These figures attempt to correct that presentation. Expenditure is lower, and reserves higher than reported to the Chief Registrar.

## Table 23

### Political Expenditure per Contributing Member, 1945–1958

| Union | 1945 s | d | 1947 s | d | 1948 s | d | 1949 s | d | 1950 s | d | 1951 s | d | 1952 s | d | 1953 s | d | 1954 s | d | 1955 s | d | 1956 s | d | 1957 s | d | 1958 s | d |
|---|---|---|---|---|---|---|---|---|---|---|---|---|---|---|---|---|---|---|---|---|---|---|---|---|---|---|
| National Union of Agricultural Workers | 1 | 5 | | 10 | | 11 | | 9 | 1 | 0 | 1 | 1 | | 10 | | 9 | | 10 | 1 | 7 | | 11 | 1 | 2 | 1 | 6‡ |
| Electrical Trades Union | 2 | 5 | 1 | 5 | 1 | 3 | 2 | 5 | 3 | 1 | 4 | 5 | 2 | 0 | 2 | 6 | 2 | 6 | 2 | 9 | 1 | 7 | 2 | 2 | 3 | 3 |
| Amalgamated Engineering Union | 1 | 4 | 1 | 0 | 1 | 5 | 2 | 1 | 1 | 7 | 1 | 11 | 1 | 5 | 1 | 5 | 1 | 5 | 2 | 0 | 1 | 4 | 1 | 10 | 1 | 11 |
| National Union of General & Municipal Workers | 2 | 2 | | 10 | | 11 | 1 | 6 | 1 | 0 | 1 | 3 | | 11 | 1 | 0 | 1 | 0 | 1 | 3 | 1 | 0 | 1 | 5 | 1 | 8 |
| British Iron, Steel & Kindred Trades' Association | 2 | 7 | 1 | 1 | 1 | 2 | 2 | 2 | 1 | 6 | 2 | 2 | 1 | 3 | 1 | 4 | 1 | 6 | 2 | 7 | 1 | 5 | 1 | 8 | 1 | 10 |
| National Union of Mineworkers (C) | 3 | 4 | 1 | 9 | 2 | 11 | 2 | 11 | 2 | 6 | 3 | 1 | 2 | 2 | 1 | 11 | 1 | 11 | 3 | 2 | 2 | 0 | 2 | 5 | 3 | 6‡ |
| Union of Post Office Workers* | — | | | 10 | 1 | 0 | 1 | 2 | 1 | 6 | 1 | 7 | | 9 | | 10 | | 9 | 1 | 9 | | 10 | 1 | 3 | 2 | 6‡ |
| National Union of Public Employees | 1 | 7 | 1 | 0 | 1 | 0 | 1 | 3 | 1 | 6 | 1 | 6 | 1 | 3 | 1 | 3 | 1 | 5 | 2 | 1 | 1 | 6 | 1 | 9 | 2 | 0 |
| National Union of Railwaymen | 5 | 10 | 2 | 2 | 2 | 3 | 3 | 3 | 3 | 4 | 3 | 10 | 2 | 0 | 2 | 5 | 2 | 0 | 3 | 8 | 2 | 3 | 2 | 3 | 2 | 6 |
| Union of Shop Distributive & Allied Workers | .. | | 1 | 8 | 1 | 7 | 2 | 11 | 2 | 2 | 2 | 8 | 1 | 8 | 1 | 8 | 1 | 8 | 3 | 8 | 1 | 11 | 1 | 11 | 4 | 0‡ |
| National Union of Tailors & Garment Workers | | 11 | | 11 | 1 | 3 | 2 | 0 | 1 | 0 | 1 | 1 | | 10 | | 9 | | 9 | 1 | 3 | | 11 | 1 | 3 | 1 | 3 |
| United Textile Factory Workers' Association (C) | 1 | 3 | 1 | 0 | 1 | 0 | 1 | 10 | 1 | 7 | 2 | 2 | 1 | 4 | 1 | 4 | 1 | 5 | 2 | 2 | 1 | 1 | 1 | 3 | 1 | 6 |
| Transport Salaried Staffs' Association | 4 | 5 | 2 | 7 | 2 | 9 | 4 | 4 | 5 | 2 | 6 | 11 | 2 | 7 | 2 | 8 | 3 | 1 | 6 | 6 | 2 | 6 | 3 | 3 | 4 | 7‡ |
| Transport & General Workers' Union | 1 | 5 | 1 | 1 | | 11 | 1 | 2 | | 11 | 1 | 1 | | 9 | | 9 | | 10 | 1 | 0 | | 9 | 1 | 2 | 1 | 10‡ |
| Amalgamated Society of Woodworkers | 2 | 2 | | 5 | | 11 | 1 | 2 | 1 | 0 | 1 | 5 | | 11 | 1 | 3 | 1 | 4 | 1 | 7 | 1 | 2 | 1 | 8 | 2 | 5‡ |
| All Unions with Political Funds | 2 | 6 | 1 | 1 | 1 | 1 | 1 | 10 | 1 | 8 | 1 | 11 | 1 | 2 | 1 | 3 | 1 | 3 | 2 | 1 | 1 | 4 | 1 | 7 | 2 | 1 |

* Affiliated 1947    ‡ Election grant paid in 1958.

forced to go back on our obligations'. Most of the laggard
unions were now able to put up their levy—helped by the
militants' greater hostility to the Conservatives which had
followed the deterioration in industrial relations after 1955.
Yet several—notably the National Union of Printing, Bookbinding & Paper Workers and the Patternmakers—still did not
come into line.

Since most of the unions clinging to the traditional shilling
contribution are small the political levy is now pegged to the two
shilling standard. But this is only twice the normal contribution
at the turn of the century and in real terms it is worth far less.
No objective yardstick can measure the correct financial obligations of the constituencies and the unions. The former do the
hard work of campaigning and organizing, while the unions
contribute propaganda and maintain an atmosphere favourable
to Labour within their ranks, which is of unquestionable electoral importance. Yet, there is no genuine reason why trade
union affiliated members should contribute so much less than
individual members. Of the six largest unions only two levy
more than the average collected from individual members.
When the movement's rolling hundreds of thousands of political
income are broken down into a *per capita* rate they look far less
impressive, while the unions' *expenditure* per head is less impressive still. Table 23 is so revealing that it needs no comment. There is little question that even after the increased
payments they have been making to the Labour Party for the
past few years, the unions have been enjoying the benefits of
political action on the cheap. They cannot fairly claim to be
pulling their weight.

## The Role of Trade Union Finance

Between 1954 and 1957 the unions' political income rose by
£200,000—thirty-five per cent. While this solved some
problems it raised others.

Trade union leaders are often uneasy about the way that the
Party treats their help. At times they have felt that the Con-

[1] The annual political contributions of these unions are: TGWU 2s (adult male),
8d (juniors and females); NUGMW 2s (adult male), 1s (juniors and females);
AEU 2s; NUM 4s (full members), 2s (half members); USDAW 3s 4d; NUR
4s 4d.

stituency Labour Parties are only interested in them in so far as they can wring money out of them. A heckler once stung Arthur Deakin into the revealing remark, 'You would listen if you wanted to get money from the trade unions'.[1] A Labour Party regional officer admitted that 'for too long some of our constituency parties have looked upon trade union branches as fee-paying agents'. The Assistant National Agent once wondered:

'How much effort do the CLPs really make towards encouraging the maximum help and interest from trade union branches? Three approaches are taken for granted—the annual request for affiliation fees, the appeal for local government elections, and financial assistance for a General Election.'[2]

Union executive minutes are full of incidents which explain the unions' feelings: East Grinstead CLP wants help in maintaining a member's wife and children; Wembley South CLP wants money for central premises; Penistone CLP wants an election grant but does not reply to an enquiry; Scarborough CLP wants money for a Party headquarters; Rotherham CLP wants a maintenance grant above the Hastings Agreement rate; Rotherham CLP—again—is dissatisfied with an offer to take up £100 in its nursery; South West Regional office needs furniture; Ince CLP asks for money to celebrate the Parliamentary Party's Fiftieth anniversary; Rotherham CLP, yet again, wants money towards premises; the London Labour Party is entertaining two Austrians; Middlesbrough Borough Labour Party wants new premises; Ebbw Vale Trades Council & Labour Party asks for a grant in addition to affiliation fees; Middlesbrough BLP writes 'referring to the cost of local elections and new premises', and later bemoans 'the depletion of funds for various reasons'; Rotherham CLP, once more, 'having regard to the unusually heavy expenses incurred in respect of the municipal elections' appeals for 'more generous assistance'.[3] So they turn to the unions. Not all requests are unreasonable, but

[1] *Report of the Labour Party Conference*, 1952, p. 78. Also *Report of the Conference of the Political Section of the London Society of Compositors*, 1951.

[2] *The Labour Organiser*, September 1953.

[3] Taken from: *Quarterly Reports* of the AUBTW, quarters ending June and Dec. 1952, March 1954. *Quarterly Executive Minutes* of BISAKTA, quarters ending: Sept. 1948, Dec. 1951, June and Dec. 1952, Sept. 1954, March 1956, June 1957, June and Dec. 1958, Sept. 1959. *The New Dawn*, March 24, 1956.

added to the routine appeals for election grants, they make some
trade unionists feel that the local parties are far too ready to prey
on them. 'They're the greatest failure in the Labour Movement',
exclaimed a union President as he threw a constituency's beg-
ging letter into the fire. It was no isolated judgment.

Though the constant demands of a minority of Constituency
Labour Parties irritate the unions, the real problem lies
deeper. The Party has persuaded the unions to pay higher
affiliation fees and constituency maintenance grants, and to
contribute handsomely to its election funds. But they hesitate
to take on even heavier contributions—the last rise in affiliation
fees was three years in coming to fruition—and they prefer to
use their money at their own discretion. The Party has far more
need of a high assured income than of massive grants every five
years. The majority of the unions can afford to be generous
regularly *and* special occasions. At the end of 1958 the unions'
political reserves stood at £1,500,000. Far exceeding any
forseeable calls, this sum was being held frustratingly sterilized.

Due to the unusual system of affiliation the unions can control
eight out of every ten votes at the Party Conference although
they contribute only about half the Party's income. There is no
simple moral law equating the money contributed with the
votes that organizations should hold—again the local parties'
and the unions' intangible contributions to the work of the
Movement must be counted in. Tradition and the realities of
power within the Party explain why the unions have not been
under pressure to give more—but they cannot make such a
situation just. The unions are fortunate, however, that the
absolute size of their gifts, and the fillip given them by the 1946
Act, have obscured the degree to which some of them have been
dragging their feet.

Yet what if the unions did match the constituency members'
subscriptions? With an average contribution of 3s 3d per year,
their political income would be over £1,000,000. This would
amply satisfy the Party's every want—although doubtless it
would find more. Yet although the organization might flourish,
there would be little stimulus left for workers in the constituencies to continue the voluntary work and fund raising.
The boast that 'the unions own the Labour Party, lock, stock and

barrel' would be almost literally true. The Party's financial tutelage would inevitably be reflected in its policies. It would be harder than ever for a party so deeply in the unions' debt to remember that it had a duty to other groups in the community, which might require it to cut across the unions' interests. It is scarcely conceivable that any party which becomes heavliy dependent on the goodwill and finance of a single interest group —however numerous its members—can develop into the truly national party it aspires to be.

For the health of Labour, and in the wider, national, interest it may be preferable that the unions do not fully honour their obligations. Even now the Party's heavy financial dependence is obvious. Although the unions might cut off the Party without a penny and meet no immediate disaster, the short-term effects on the Labour Party (particularly on Transport House) would be little short of calamitous. From time to time the question is asked: 'Will the Party and the unions split?' Perhaps the unions could go their own way, but so long as the Party is so heavily dependent on trade union money there can be little doubt what its choice must be.

_What is a constituency labour party?_

# CHAPTER III

# POLITICS IN THE BRANCH

'What do we talk about? Long and interminable discussions
on the football competition, the Party social, the outing, and
the best way of getting the crockery back from the public
hall.'

A MEMBER OF A CONSTITUENCY LABOUR PARTY *

IN the branch, as at national level, the unions have the chance to
take part in the Labour Party's work. To all practical purposes
the Party's Constitution gives them the same rights as individual members. Branches may affiliate, send their delegates to
join in the local Party's discussions, and even help to choose
Labour candidates.[1] Indeed the union branches have a privileged
place in the Labour Movement. On one hand affiliation to a
Constituency Labour Party gives a branch the chance to influence
the constituency's decisions on policy at the annual Party Conference. On the other, the branch can work through its union's
own constitutional procedures to determine the union delegation's vote at the Party Conference.

The vitality of the branches is therefore doubly important.
On their interest or apathy depends the extent to which those at
the 'grass roots' of the movement effectively share in the formation of policy. On them depends also whether 'the Movement' is
a living relationship between trade unions and constituency
parties, or merely a sentimental rallying cry. These are the
problems which we shall be examining: what is the relationship
between the branches and the local Parties; how politically alive
are the branches; what are the unions doing to make the
relationship closer?

Inevitably the myth flatters reality. Apathy afflicts the unions
as heavily as other voluntary organizations. Sometimes it seems

---

* The _Manchester Guardian_, November 9, 1954.
[1] Below Constituency Party level the Labour Party has Local Labour Parties in
county constituencies and Ward Labour Parties in boroughs. The unions normally
affiliate to Local Labour Parties, but not to Ward Parties.
Only individual members of the Party may be nominated for public office.

that the major impression that post-war research into trade unionism has made on public opinion has been to reveal the extent of apathy. Perhaps the insistence that so many Labour apologists make, that the movement is massively democratic, and its decisions should compel respect by the sheer size of the numbers involved, has provoked such over-zealous debunking. Yet, for all the head-wagging talk of the 'good old days' there is little evidence that apathy has been increasing. Political activity in the branch is now, as in the past, the concern of a small minority of active members. Mr J. Goldstein, whose *Government of British Trade Unions* is largely a study of one branch of one union, the TGWU, suggests that between 1942 and 1949 an average of four per cent of the membership attended union meetings. Mr B. C. Roberts has concluded that about one trade unionist in twenty (some 500,000) takes anything approaching an active part in the life of his branch.[1]

It may be fortunate for the unions' critics in the constituencies that no comparable figures are available for the local parties, although they may attract a slightly higher proportion of members to meetings because membership is entirely voluntary. Veteran agents often suggest that only about ten per cent of Party members attend meetings with any frequency; the rest just pay their subscriptions and may be prevailed upon to help at elections.[2] Ten per cent may simply be a convenient round figure. While some local Parties number their active militants in hundreds, others are run by a majority of the thirty or so 'keen' members who turn out to meetings. Many local Parties, led

---

[1] B. C. Roberts. *Trade Union Government and Administration, Great Britain*, LSE, 1956, pp. 95–9.

[2] Attendance at the 1954 Annual General Meeting of the 'Ashton' Local Labour Party was 26; there were 153 at the annual dinner. Dennis, Henriques and Slaughter, *Coal is Our Life*, Eyre & Spottiswoode, 1956, p. 67.

Mr A. H. Birch remarks in *Small Town Politics* (Glossop) that: 'Problems of national policy are clearly discussed in local parties, for resolutions resulting from them are submitted in large numbers to the regional and national conferences, but our inquiries into the work of Manchester branches have shown that this is by no means the general practice. . . . In practice there are hardly any organized discussions of general policy within the party [in Glossop]'. (pp. 71–2.)

Similar reflections on the relatively small role of discussions of national policy in Constituency Labour Parties are made by J. Gould in 'Riverside: A Labour Constituency', *Fabian Journal*, November 1954, Wilfrid Fienburgh, and the Manchester Fabian Society, 'Put Policy on the Agenda', *Fabian Journal*, Feb. 1952, and in D. V. Donnison & D. E. G. Plowman, 'The Functions of Local Labour Parties', *Political Studies*, June 1954.

by semi-oligarchic cliques, have no better claim that their
decisions are 'representative' than some of the unions which
they reproach for being out of touch with the rank and file.
It is with a full acceptance of the limitations that apathy
imposes on both wings that the unions' local activities must
be assessed.

## Branches and Constituencies

The formal link between the unions and the Labour Party is
the branch's affiliation to the local constituency. Constitutionally
the unions should affiliate their whole political membership to
their local Party. In practice it is almost impossible to say how
many trade unionists are affiliated. One or two unions give their
local Party a flat sum to cover affiliations: the maximum
NUGMW grant of £8 represents 320 members (at 6d in some
constituencies but 480 (at 4d) in others. Other unions spread
their affiliations evenly over all the constituencies within a
District, so that the number affiliated to each of the Parties may
bear no relationship to the number paying the political levy
within any constituency. Some members are affiliated more
than once.

But it is abundantly clear that the number of trade unionists
affiliated to the Party is far less than it could be. Constituency
representatives are forever complaining that union branches are
not affiliated, or are affiliated on far less than their true membership. Sometimes the complaints are misguided. Constituency
members are inclined to forget that contracting-out and inefficient collection of contributions cut the members that can
be affiliated. But the Boilermakers, a politically militant union,
had to concede that 'not *all* our branches affiliate to the local
Labour Party, and most of those who do don't affiliate on the
full number allowed them by the Labour Party constitution'.[1]
A 1949 survey in the AEU revealed that of 2,034 branches
making returns only 1,667 were affiliated, often on far less than
their full membership. The following brief table gives a
reasonably fair impression of the range:

[1] All the following instances are taken from the relevant annual report of the
union referred to.

| Union | Number of Branches | Branches Affiliated to CLPs | Year |
|---|---|---|---|
| Amalgamated Society of Woodworkers | 1,414 | 547 | (1954) |
| Electrical Trades Union | 664 | 135 | (1955) |
| London District of NUGMW | 292 | 161 | (1952) |
| United Society of Boilermakers, etc. | 281 | 254 | (1957) |
| National Union of Furniture Trade Operatives | 280 | 55 | (1957) |
| National Union of Tailors & Garment Workers | 244 | 60 | (1957) |
| Power Group of the TGWU | 196 | 48 | (1957) |
| National Union of Sheet Metal Workers & Braziers | 104 | 58 | (1958) |
| Scots Painters' Society | 98 | 38 | (1957) |

Until their political levy was increased in 1951 the Wood-workers could not afford to affiliate at all. Even now the Theatrical & Kine Employees (NATKE) and the Patternmakers have not affiliated a single member to a constituency Party. Some small and scattered unions like the National Union of Scalemakers do not find it practical to affiliate. On the other hand the NUR and USDAW affiliate nearly fully, and the Miners have a traditionally good record. Few unions can claim, as the National Union of Seamen has, to have affiliated every one of its branches. Even fewer constituency Parties can say—as Woolwich did in 1948—that they have brought almost every trade union branch in the borough into affiliation. Much more common are the towns like Glossop where, 'of the thirty-five union branches in the town, only six are affiliated to the local Labour Party'.[1]

The picture is not quite as gloomy as the figures may suggest. It is chiefly the smaller branches and the smaller unions which are not affiliated. More branches are affiliated now than before the war—and the numbers have increased slightly in recent years.[2]

Sometimes Communist or Conservative branch officers are responsible for non-affiliation. In some branches bitter political divisions among the membership make it unwise. But more often

---

[1] *Small Town Politics*, p. 168.
[2] In the National Union of Sheet Metal Workers & Braziers only twenty out of seventy-nine branches were affiliated in 1945. The Boilermakers improved rapidly from 144 out of 234 branches affiliated in 1954.

the real cause is the indifference of both the unions and the local Parties. Some branch officials do not even know that their branch can affiliate to a constituency. Many parties have taken the attitude that 'If the unions want to affiliate, let them. If not, we won't lose any sleep over it'. This indifference leads some trade unionists to complain in turn of the constituencies' cliquishness. The political wing is well-armed with complaints in return. 'We have made repeated attempts to bring in the unions, without the least success' protested a Scottish agent. 'I can't even get them to reply to my letters, let alone affiliate', said another Party official. The reluctance of union officials to cooperate is a well-known complaint.[1]

Nationally the unions do urge their branches to affiliate. However, their encouragements cannot amount to much: a few circulars, appeals in the union journal, a reminder at the annual conference. It is well-meaning but ineffectual. The real responsibility rests with the branches. How can their frequent failure even to affiliate to their local Constituency Labour Party be reconciled with that image, cherished by the Labour left, of a militant rank-and-file campaigning for the adoption of progressive policies?

Even when the unions are affiliated it is far from sure that the relationship with the Party functions according to theory. The weakness of the trade union movement in the countryside is widely understood. A 'typical' rural county constituency contains a number of branches of the National Union of Agricultural Workers, an USDAW branch if the Cooperative movement is strong, and building craft union branches. There will be few trade unionists in shops and offices; most of the factories and workshops will be small. The general unions usually have a rather diverse membership, and there will probably be a branch of the NUR. But there are few sizeable groups of workers where the trade union movement can firmly establish itself. Even if the unions all affiliate to the local Party, they often find it hard to play an active part in its affairs, because their membership is so small and scattered. Often even their financial help is limited.

In a few areas—chiefly its strongholds in East Anglia—the

[1] Cf., *The Labour Organiser*, August 1954.

H

National Union of Agricultural Workers constitutes an exception. There the NUAW is built on strong radical traditions. Its branches are to be found in almost every village and hamlet. Encouraged by the union many branch secretaries and officers represent the Labour Party in areas where the rarity of Party members makes the formation of Local Labour Parties difficult. In these few areas the Labour vote has been nurtured, and its organization sustained by the presence of a powerful union.

The same is true of some mining areas, although not all sections of the National Union of Mineworkers are equally active politically. South Wales and Scotland have a long tradition of political militancy, while the Midlands have never shown as much interest as some of the older and more concentrated coalfields. For some years after 1926 George Spencer's 'non-political' union organized the Nottinghamshire coalfield. However, transfers from regions like Durham since the war have spread political interest. Many of these mining constituencies are run almost completely by miners. They have almost all the affiliated membership, and they contribute the bulk of the Party's income. In some areas some of the functions of the constituency General Management Committee are effectively exercised by the miners' lodges. Sometimes the NUM has the 'right' to nominate half the candidates in local government elections, subject to the automatic approval of the GMC. In other seats they simply nominate as many candidates as they please—not necessarily miners—knowing that the Party will accept them. In such areas nomination is tantamount to election. Although these privileges are fast disappearing in Yorkshire they seem as entrenched as ever in parts of Durham. One day two men met in a Durham pit village, one the NUM lodge secretary, the other a corporation plumber. 'Jack', said the secretary, 'the lads at the lodge had a meeting last night. We're going to put you on the council.' And they did. Yet, in most coalfields it is the assiduity of the miners in affiliating and sending delegates, coupled with the loyalty of miners and their families attending as individual Party members, which explains the NUM's ascendancy rather than any crude domination.

The unions may be no better placed in the towns than in the countryside to join in political work. Large areas of the major cities are occupied by shops, offices, and small workshops, which are traditionally under-unionized. Elsewhere, the organization may be better, but workers may have to travel long distances. Though union branches are usually willing to affiliate to the City Labour Party, they have much less interest in the individual Constituency Parties. Several safe Labour seats in London have dismally small trade union affiliations. One Labour working-class residential seat in London has only nine small branch affiliations. Another, near a main line terminus, has only four. Apathy is partly to blame, but often the constituency means little or nothing to branch members living miles away, scattered all over London. Some branches, such as the Central London branches of the CAWU and the TSSA, affiliate to several suburban seats where their members live. These affiliations may give individual members the chance to join in the Party's work, and constituencies welcome the income they bring, but members living in Surbiton are unlikely to take a lively interest in the work of delegates to the East Harrow Constituency Labour Party. Certainly the members of such branches are quite unable to give the constituency active help in elections. Even in smaller cities it is hard to stimulate interest in such artificial constituencies as Leeds Central or Bradford South. Thus, while many branches are affiliated to their constituencies, there are many structural reasons, in addition to sheer apathy, which prevent the movement from joining fully in the work of the Party.

Yet after all allowances are made the unions' participation in the constituencies falls short of what could be achieved. Trade unionists themselves are usually ready to admit that their record has been 'shameful', 'lamentable', or 'pitiful', or to say that 'where we really fall down is in the branches'. Some blame the constituencies. Mr Victor Feather, Assistant Secretary of the TUC, has alleged that:

'. . . in some of the rural areas and the more recently established parties in dormitory and residential areas, there seems to be a desire on the part of some Party members to keep themselves pure, undefiled by association with trade unionists. . . . The trouble seems to be that if a trade union branch is affiliated to the local Labour Party, it sends delegates to meetings; delegates have votes, and if the trade union delegates were to get together they would out-block vote the dentist, the headmaster, and the business executive, or maybe jolt the obscure thinking about abstract politics in which some of the so-called intellectuals so earnestly delight.'[1]

Mr Feather was not alone. The 1947 conference of the National Union of Public Employees was asked to 'view with grave concern the attitude adopted towards the trade unions by the Labour Party', including 'the growing indifference to trade union delegates at Party meetings'.[2] Yet such complaints about discrimination in suburbia sound oddly like the protests made by individual members in some of the industrial seats; ruling cliques rarely look kindly on potential challengers.

The attendance of trade union delegates at constituency party meetings is notoriously erratic. Sometimes they even fail to attend when their union is putting up a candidate for Parliamentary nomination.[3] Apart from paying their affiliation fees some branches are not heard from for years. In one West Country constituency whose General Management Committee met four times in the year two trade union delegates attended all four meetings, three came to three meetings, and the other twenty-three delegates registered twenty-four attendances between them. Ten other branches did not even appoint a delegate, and twenty-six branches (though repeatedly asked) either refused or would not answer letters. Merton and Morden once reported it had twenty-one affiliated branches; sixteen appointed a total of nineteen delegates. Five attended meetings. In one northern constituency three out of fifteen branches sent delegates, in another twelve out of nineteen. These are bad cases. Often the trade union delegates on General Management Committees have a record as good, or better, than the Ward Party

[1] *The Labour Organiser*, July 1954.
[2] *Report of the Biennial Conference*, 1947, p. 101.
[3] The difficulty of getting members to act as delegates to the CLP is sometimes used as an argument to justify the lifting of proscriptions preventing Communists from acting as delegates. One Communist claimed to have been approached repeatedly by members of his branch to be its delegate because no one else was willing. The writer knows of one case where a Conservative councillor was invited to become delegate to his local CLP. For the former case see *Report of the ADC (ASW)*, 1953, p. 177.

delegates. In some towns a union has earned itself a reputation for consistent and loyal attendance, while another is scornfully dismissed as moribund. In a neighbouring seat the positions may be reversed. No union has a uniform reputation. Even the most 'militant' have backward areas where their representatives are either apathetic or 'right wing'. The 'progressive' AEU is frequently condemned as politically dead in the constituencies, while the ETU is stigmatized as 'reactionary'. Such local reputations usually reflect the enthusiasm of a handful of leading personalities.

The unions' readiness to affiliate and send their delegates is directly reflected in the composition of the constituencies' General Management Committees. As a result, even in areas where the unions are industrially strong, they may be poorly placed on the local Party's GMC. In one northern Labour seat with a 20,000 majority in 1955 and a 90-strong GMC only thirty delegates represent the trade unions, while in another, marginal, Labour constituency they have 140 out of 200 members. In another seat, where the Conservative majority is 10,000, the unions hold half the places on the GMC. The failure of their delegates to attend means that often the *effective* working strength of the unions on the GMC is far less impressive than it looks on paper. In practice the unions dominate far fewer constituencies than their numbers suggest.

Some constituencies try to encourage branches to participate by circulating reports of their activities. They arrange for MPs or candidates to visit branches periodically to discuss current affairs, and to thank them for their help. But most prefer to preach to the outside world rather than hold revivalist campaigns within their own ranks. Even the constituencies which do set out to cultivate the unions are not always successful; some branches will not answer letters, some never meet, and some refuse to receive visitors. Few trade union branches feel that they can really help the local Party, apart from making occasional grants of money. Neither side makes the enlisting of union support a matter of sustained concern. This is no new problem: it is one of the accepted facts of the Party's existence.

The formal share of the unions in the life of the local parties is limited, but trade unionists often form a majority of the

Party's individual members. All post-war studies of Constituency Labour Parties in action have agreed on this—although some found the trade unionists less numerous among the Party's office holders.[1] This modifies the observations we have made, without vitiating them. Many experienced agents confirm the impressions of the various surveys, but make an emphatic distinction between the trade union delegate and the trade unionist member of the Labour Party. The latter may be 'Party-minded' or 'Coop-minded', and leave his trade unionism behind him when he goes to a Party meeting. Julius Gould made a similar remark about trade unionist members of 'Riverside' CLP: 'Still less are they Trade Union stereotypes. They may belong to Trade Unions, but such membership does not play a large part in their lives. . . .'[2] Even the trade union delegates are often more 'political' than their branch members, since many industrially active members have little time for political activities too. Many a local Party carries out its work in isolation from the organized trade union movement and the main stream of trade union thought.[3] Trade union delegates who come from branches which do not require a report, conscientious though they may be, may represent no one but themselves. In many constituencies the contribution of union delegates who are out of sympathy with their own union has intensified the misunderstandings between the two wings.

The existence of City Labour Parties in the larger towns has aggravated this situation (with the notable exception of Birmingham). The unions normally affiliate not to the constituencies but to the City Party, which is a more meaningful unit to them than the local Parties. Their affiliations and attendances are usually above average. An old agent explained: 'They can get together there and talk for hours, and they never have to do a damn thing about it'. The City Labour Parties' most useful work is the organizing of municipal elections; at other times they tend to become talking shops which attract delegates who would have little taste for more practical forms of political action. But the unions are scarcely to blame for this over-centralization,

---

[1] See the works already cited and Benney, Gray and Pear, *How People Vote*, p. 28.
[2] *Fabian Journal*, November 1954.
[3] Gould remarks, for instance, that some trade union members of 'Riverside' CLP 'view the unions with distrust or distaste'.

which—the Wilson Committee alleged—had led to the withering away of the local Parties in some cities. The Committee's proposal that the City Parties should be replaced by 'Coordinating Committees' found little favour. Although it 'hoped that trade unions would be willing to divide their present affiliations equally among the CLPs covered by the City or Borough Party', and suggested expedients to encourage the unions to pay their full fees, it was clear that the adoption of the Wilson proposals would have brought a reduction in the union's affiliations, simply because the unions have less interest in the individual constituencies, and would scarcely have welcomed a central body (of the sort that the Committee proposed) which would have seemed a device for extracting money from them.[1] So far the Party has made little progress in finding a solution.

In formal terms the link between the unions and the constituencies is tenuous. On a personal level there is far greater contact than the analysis has suggested, by frequent meetings between Party agents and union officials, and branch committeemen, both within the Party and on local government bodies. This can ensure a frequent coordination on issues, but it is no substitute for effective, organized union participation in the full life of the Party, and it has little relevance to the formation of national policies. Though many constituencies do express themselves satisfied with their relations with their local unions, the establishment of an amicable *modus vivendi* falls far short of what the term 'Labour Movement' really implies.

## Politics Within the Branch

Most of the branches' political activities are tuned to the affiliation with the local Labour Party: the briefing of delegates, the report back, and the voting of resolutions for consideration by the Constituency Labour Party, Trades Council, or the union's Executive Committee. Discussion of the union's annual conference agenda provides a further, though hurried, chance for political debate, while occasionally a political figure may come from outside to lead a discussion. Naturally there is a great

[1] *Report*, paras. 110–2. The degree to which the Committee's proposals were adopted is outlined in *Report of the Labour Party Conference*, 1957, p. 15.

variation between branches and unions. Some branches never discuss politics, either because they never hold meetings, or from lack of interest, or because political issues arouse such violent controversy that for the sake of unity they are best avoided. Others seem far more interested in protesting at the latest American diplomatic initiative, or demanding the withdrawal of foreign troops from Britain, or with conditions in Kenya, than in their bread and butter. Morris' and Plowman's conclusions about trade union branches in Glossop would hold true in most areas; 'Political activities are the exception rather than the rule. Only one union, the Electrical Trades Union, discusses political matters regularly at its meetings and forwards resolutions to the Glossop Trades Council and the local Labour Party. A few other unions discuss politics on occasions when industrial matters are involved. . . . Those few unions that do engage in politics do so largely because of the influence of one or two enthusiasts among their members'.[1] The *Woodworkers' Journal* gives the most revealing indication of the form that branch discussions often take. It is the last union journal to retain the old-fashioned practice of printing branch resolutions and the voting on them. Although publication is a stimulus to enthusiasts to put down motions, the Woodworkers' experience seems typical. During 1956 and 1957 the *Journal* recorded 257 original or supporting resolutions on questions which required political rather than industrial action for their fulfilment. There are some hardy annuals: pensions, abolition or reduction of national service, east-west trade, post-war credits; and there are the affairs of the moment: atomic weapons, the Rent Act, Hungary and Suez.

The wording is often quaint. A Dublin 11 branch resolution once declared with fine impartiality, 'We strongly condemn the British terror in Kenya, and also call for the disbandment of the Mau-Mau'. This common conviction that the pen is mightier than the sword was revealed in a motion that 'we wholeheartedly support the TUC resolution in throwing out the Rents Bill and request the EC to take immediate action'. Taken at their face value such sweeping motions can be quite frightening. There are the calls to 'support *any* action that can be taken to prevent

[1] *Small Town Politics*, p. 168.

[the Rent Bill] becoming law', for the TUC to 'cease any further contact with the Government until it shows sign of giving equal consideration to the opinions of the workers as well as the employing classes', for 'a General Strike to turn out the government'; demands that old age pensions be paid 'without restrictions of any nature'; suggestions that 'all automated plant shall be either nationalized or brought under some method of Government supervision', and a growing tendency to back the claims of other interest groups, voiced in resolutions of the sort that support the British Legion in its campaign to restore war pensions to 1938 value and 'all organizations calling and working for an increase in the pensions rate'.[1]

During 1956–57 housing, rents and rates, on which there were forty-one resolutions, were the most common subjects—because of the passing of the Rent Act and rises in interest rates to mortgage-holders and local authorities. An increase in National Health Service prescription charges brought in twenty-seven resolutions, more than Suez (twenty), nuclear weapons (twenty), or Hungary (eleven). Eighteen resolutions amounted to nothing but general abuse of the government, demands for its resignation, or threats to turn it out by 'industrial action'.

The evidence of these resolutions casts serious doubts on the belief that policy is formed from the branch upwards. Motions which could conceivably have been stimulated by the Labour Party's policy statements issued between 1956 and 1958 could be numbered on one hand. Most spring from a desire to support or attack an attitude already struck by the Parliamentary Party, rather than from any wish to fashion future policy. Almost all deal with the economic, foreign or colonial crises of the moment. A tiny number tackle matters like education in the colonies, or handicapped children, about which Executives and unions would not normally think. Others are quite trivial. These resolutions are the result of individual members' enthusiasms; they attract little discussion.

---

[1] In the past few years union branches have shown an interesting readiness to endorse the claims of such professional organisations as the National Union of Teachers and the British Medical Association.

Where the resolutions diverge from official policy it is almost always to the left. A small group of branches normally follow a Communist Party line.[1] They are the most prolific. Several are influenced by minority Socialist groups like the Independent Labour Party and the Socialist Party of Great Britain. By contrast to the energy of the left, there were only eleven attacks on Soviet intervention in Hungary, and the only right-wing deviations were one attack on the amount of political material in the *Journal*, a criticism of Dr Edith Summerskill's visit to Port Said in 1957, and a protest at contributions to the defence of arrested Cypriots made by several other unions. To these may be added demands for restriction of West Indian immigration which were voted by some branches (but rejected by others, and by the union's Annual Delegate Conference). Although every Labour leader was uncomfortably aware that a large proportion of the Party's working class supporters approved the Suez intervention there seems no trace, in any union, of a motion directly supporting the government. For the most part the wording of resolutions lies in the no-man's-land between left-Socialist and Communist thought.

During 1956–57 144 of the 1,400 ASW branches in the United Kingdom sent in 257 resolutions. The total participation in the 121 votes for which figures are given is 3,080. (The 144 branches had 28,000 members; the 121 recorded votes came from branches with 24,000 members, out of 100,000 to 110,000 in the whole union.) The average participation in the 121 votes was 12·5 per cent (with a range of twenty-eight per cent to five per cent).[2] At the lower levels probably members of the branch committee made up a majority of those present. Of the 3,080 participating 2,934 voted for proposals, forty-four voted against, and the remaining 102 either abstained or were absent when the vote was taken. Votes were cast against only eighteen motions; the rest were carried unanimously or *nemine contradicente*. There was only one close vote, on a motion carried at Deptford 2 branch (210 members) by ten votes to nine, with

[1] Thirty-three branches nominated the Communist candidate for General Secretary in 1958. *Woodworkers' Journal*, April 1958.

[2] Roberts analysed 198 political and industrial resolutions voted in January to June, 1949. He found an average participation of rather under 13 per cent. *Trade Union Government & Administration in Great Britain*, (pp. 95–6).

three abstentions, proposing that the TUC attack the government more 'positively' over Suez. It seems unlikely, therefore, that many resolutions were rejected by branch meetings.

The voting shows such unanimity that it seems unlikely that the motions were carefully discussed. Many must have been carried in circumstances such as Goldstein has described:

'By this time many of the members have left, and those remaining, chilled from sitting in the cold, are anxious to leave. The Chairman asks is there any other business. As most members shake their heads Brother Ward jumps to his feet, brandishing a daily paper containing pictures of Greek trade unionists being tortured. With an energy which belies the hour he reads a resolution calling upon the Government to end the foreign policy now being pursued in Greece and to stop the murder of leading Greek trade unionists. Brother Vinson seconds the motion without comment. One dissident voice proclaims that the murder of Communists is the real issue, and that it is not a Branch concern. The Branch votes in favour of the resolution with the proviso that it be sent to the Southboro Trades Council with a request that the London Trades Council approach members of the Government on this matter.'[1]

This picture will be readily recognized by anyone with experience of committees. Within the branch it often leads—since there is little enough sympathy at the best of times with members who quibble with textual amendments—to the voting of ambiguous or crudely violent motions. But even where the discussion takes place in more favourable conditions members expect short speeches—two or three minutes—and few trade unionists would claim that the debate reaches a high standard.

In the Woodworkers, as in other unions, branch resolutions are often in glaring contradiction with the decisions of the union's annual conference. The ASW's Annual Delegate Con-

[1] *The Government of British Trade Unions*, pp. 193–4.

This incident compares with an account of an 'Ashton' Local Labour Party meeting in 1953, which includes the following passage:

'I've a letter here about British Guiana', the Secretary said, 'it's a bit of a long letter. Does anyone want me to read it?'

'Don't bother,' one of the ladies cried out, 'we've enough trouble in Ashton'. The letter was accordingly left unread. *Coal is Our Life*, pp. 166–7.

ference, which normally follows a slightly left-of-centre line within the Labour Party, almost never accepts immoderate resolutions. It is highly improbable that a union in which only sixty per cent of the members contribute to the political fund could be as homogeneously left-wing as the branch resolutions suggest. This contrast was most marked in the controversy over German rearmament. Branch resolutions attacking re-armament flowed in from February to May 1954, when the Annual Delegate Conference voted decisively to oppose re-arming Germany. But in October the ASW delegation supported German rearmament at the Labour Party Conference. Reso-lutions poured in; 152 branches condemned the Executive, seventeen demanded a statement, thirteen wanted the Con-ference recalled. Two sent congratulations. In all, 184 of the 1,414 United Kingdom branches joined in. This was by far the biggest storm on a political question in the union for years, and it was aggravated by raising the long-vexed question of whether the Annual Delegate Conference was a full policy-forming conference. But only thirteen per cent of the branches voted motions, involving some 4,500 members, or about $2\frac{1}{2}$ per cent of the membership. When the issue came before the 1955 con-ference the ASW Executive won its support by a substantial majority.[1]

If Executives were to follow the demands of their branches on such matters the tail would be wagging the dog indeed. Most Executives pay little heed to what their branches say on strictly political issues unless it suits their purpose. They may endorse branch resolutions for forwarding to the government or other outside organizations, or inform the branch of their opposition; usually political motions are simply 'noted'. Executives are well aware which branches support an extreme-left line, which are Communist or Conservative-minded. They recognize the Communist line no matter how cleverly sub-merged—sometimes they discern it too readily. The enthusiasts may still think the effort worthwhile. Voting motions helps them build up a picture of a vigilant rank and file, which can be con-trasted with the lethargy of the leaders. It makes a useful paragraph for the *Daily Worker*, or it provides support for a

[1] See pp. 171-3

friend on the Executive, who then claims to have rank and file backing. In time it may even influence union (or public) opinion. Branches which persist in voting motions long enough sometimes win their way simply by exhausting the patience of everyone else.

However ill-informed it may be at times branch political discussion does at least provide a frequent reminder that political and industrial matters are inter-related, and that both are the unions' business. This, at least, is in accordance with the theory of the Labour Movement. Its greatest failure is in stimulating new thinking or widening members' horizons. But if this reproach is to be made, the unions are clearly not the only section of the Labour Movement to be criticized.[1]

## Towards a Recovery?

A few unions, realizing the weakness of their branch political life have tried to stimulate political interest and discussion. Some circulate Party statements to their branches, although some of the Communist-led unions also distribute documents in direct opposition to official policy.[2] Most Head Offices foster the least sign of interest, but few have the staff to make sustained or extensive efforts. Not all unions think it wise to turn their branches into political debating clubs. A few have tried to use their journals to stimulate thought and discussion on political issues—*The Post* (UPW) and *The New Dawn* (USDAW) have made notably gallant efforts. At the end of the war it was common for journals to devote long articles to discussing policy. But then came the years when the unions, like the Party, were occupied with factionalism rather than future policy. Though a few journals, such as the two mentioned, and *The Draughtsman* (AESD) were ready to discuss colonial

---

[1] Gould remarks (Riverside: A Labour Constituency) 'That [the members] work on a narrow front in a rather narrow way does not trouble them too much. . . . For the bigger things they, like everyone else, are living on their emotional capital, on their inherited ideals. The Labour Party cannot draw new life or ideas from its grass roots in the constituencies'.

[2] In 1953 the Fire Brigades' Union distributed, in addition to Labour Party material, six publications of the Communist World Federation of Trade Unions, two publications of the Labour Research Department (which is proscribed by the Labour Party but not by the TUC) and two from the British-China Friendship Society.

matters and the work of the United Nations, most simply
abused the Conservatives, recalled the 'bad old days' and
printed yet again their pictures of the Jarrow marchers and the
dole queue. Only after the Party itself returned to reconsidering
its policies in 1956 did the unions also turn to policy discussion
again. As successive policy statements were produced, most
unions loyally printed summaries (usually prepared by Transport House's Labour Press Service), but only a bare handful
made the slightest attempt to discuss the issues involved, and
they were almost all on the disgruntled left. Few trade unionists
could have grasped that *Personal Freedom* had implications for
their own movement. A few unions have produced material on
the problems of their own industries. There has been the
Draughtsmen's *Plan for Engineering*, a discussion of the Confederation of Shipbuilding & Engineering Unions' ('Confed')
plan for public ownership, and the same union's *Advance of
Living Standards*. ASSET has produced *Automation—A Challenge to Trade Unions & Society*. The Fire Brigades' Union has
on several occasions proposed to its members long policy statements as alternatives to official Labour Policy.[1] But most unions
have not even provided their branches with material to discuss
the possible forms of nationalization in their own industry.
Usually they simply reiterate familiar slogans. It is small
wonder that the meaning of nationalization was not fully recognized in the industries that have already been taken over by the
State.

Some unions have tried to meet the problem of local political
activities by forming district organizations. The Transport
Salaried Staffs' Association has Political Advisory Councils in
London, Glasgow, Manchester and Merseyside. Their purpose
is to encourage branch affiliation to local Parties, to discuss
policies, and to stimulate branch leaders. The London council,
the most successful, has the incentive of affiliation to the London
Labour Party. It has organized meetings with Members of
Parliament throughout each winter, held weekend schools and
speakers' classes. It is responsible for making representations
to the LCC and for distributing political literature to the
branches. By all trade union standards it is a flourishing body—

---

[1] See *Annual Report*, 1953, p. 32ff; 1954, p. 28ff; 1958, p. 69ff.

but it touches directly only a small fraction of the Association's London membership.

The Union of Shop, Distributive & Allied Workers tries a different approach. Each of its Divisions holds an annual political conference, while the Quarterly Divisional Conferences on industrial issues usually find time for discussing some political questions. Local federations of branches hold weekend schools mixing political and industrial sessions—such an immixture is characteristic of USDAW. Though most other unions have District Councils they usually have no political functions, they are limited to organizing the election of the union's candidates to the Regional Councils of the Labour Party. There are a few other activities, such as the annual county conferences in several unions, where political matters are introduced.[1] There are also small islands like Mr Sam Watson's 'Bible class', a National Council of Labour Colleges class run by the NUM Area Secretary on winter Sundays in a Durham cinema, which attracts miners from the whole Durham coalfield. Other such exceptions may be found here and there. Unions can try, as the TSSA does, to increase branch political activities and find new leaders, in separate political organizations. Alternatively they can integrate industrial and political activities as USDAW has done. The USDAW approach has the merit of being more in keeping with the idea of a 'Labour Movement'. Many trade unionists would feel, though, that it is too political an approach for a union's industrial health.

Such local bodies fail if they recruit only a handful of the faithful. Their purpose is to revive political interest—at present so weak that there are usually insufficient resources for recovery to begin within the branch itself. Outside critics of the unions suggest that the unions must make a concentrated drive to awaken interest, and to make their votes at the TUC and Labour Party representative. They rarely grasp the magnitude of the task. Political activity is now so weak that it is probably beyond the unions' capacity to stimulate a direct revival. Unions with hundreds or thousands of branches have not the resources to re-create activity within each one. The most they can do is to

[1] Notably the National Union of Agricultural Workers, National Union of Public Employees, and BISAKTA.

encourage the growth of a cadre of militants by cooperative efforts between the branches. Even this is immensely difficult.

Only if the unions could find some solution to the intractable problem of general apathy could they hope for a marked decline in political apathy. The unions' critics have been slow to grasp that almost every decision a trade union makes, whatever its political hue, must be a minority decision. It will never be possible to interest the entire industrially active membership in the Labour Movement. Some members think that politics and trade unionism do not mix, others belong to anti-Labour parties, and others have no time to spare for the political side. If the number who join from time to time in industrial activities is rather under a million, as Roberts has suggested, it seems extremely unlikely that more than two-thirds are even potentially likely to take part in political activities. Even so, it must be admitted that no union is at present attracting anywhere near the maximum political participation.

By the standards of many voluntary associations the unions' record is not unhealthy. For all that, it is the active trade unionists (far fewer than the occasional participants) who begin the process of deciding how ten to fifteen times their number of votes shall be cast at the Labour Party Conference. At every Party Conference the unions cast a *minimum* of five million votes on behalf of men who have never made the slightest attempt to participate in the decision, many of whom have no idea what is being said and voted in their names, and who never will know. This cannot glibly be dubbed 'undemocratic'. It is not necessarily unrepresentative. There is no clear evidence that the unions are, relatively, worse offenders than the local parties. But this basis of participation should be some check to the common feeling in Labour circles that decisions taken in the names of so many members have some peculiar validity, some special claim to be taken seriously by the government or public opinion. The reality of branch political life is far from confirming the more roseate conceptions of the Labour Movement. There is little evidence that it is likely to change.

# CHAPTER IV

# THE MAKING OF POLITICAL POLICY

'Do not let the union leaders think that they alone speak for
their members. We speak for them as much as they do.'

MR ANEURIN BEVAN*

'The British trade union movement is a shining example of
democracy at its best.'

SIR THOMAS WILLIAMSON*

WHEN Aneurin Bevan talked angrily of 'a travesty of the
democratic vote', and union leaders were stung to bitter insistence that 'We have a mandate', they had one belief in common at least. These warring factions made the common
assumption that trade unions can, and should, form their policies
'democratically'. In doing so they voiced one of the Labour
movement's most deeply rooted principles. However, in recent
years readier acceptance has been given to views such as V. L.
Allen has put forward, that 'The end of trade union activity is
to protect and improve the general living standards of its
members, and not to provide the workers with an exercise in
self-government'.[1] Thinking of trade unions as purely industrial organizations Allen may be right in treating
representative democracy as a luxury, subsidiary to a union's
achieving its objects either directly or through political action.
But when a union accepts political affiliation it also assumes the
obligation implied in the traditional insistence that:

'The Labour Party is founded on democratic notions . . . [It]
is a collective expression of democratic sentiment based on the
working-class movement, and on the constituency organizations
of the workers by hand and brain.'[2]

Membership of the wider Labour Movement does require an
'exercise in self-government'. It clearly implies that the
decisions taken in a union's name should correspond to the
wishes of its members. From 1951 to 1955 the gravest charge

* (a) Speech, September 29, 1954.    (b) NUGMW Journal, May 1954.
[1] Power in Trade Unions, p. 15.
[2] Facts and Figures for Socialists, The Labour Party, 1951, pp. 303–4.

that Bevanites made against such leaders as Deakin and Lawther was that the machinery of union democracy had ceased to function, and that they were no longer truly representing their members.

These, and later critics, seem convinced that the problem of union democracy is at bottom one of good faith. It is one of the Labour Party's misfortunes that so few members of its political wing have any wide knowledge of how trade unions make their decisions. In the absence of solid knowledge myth and legend have flourished. Probably the making of specifically political decisions is least known of all, for it often differs widely from the forming of industrial policy. A union often decides whether it will accept a wages settlement by procedures very different from those appropriate to deciding whether the public schools should be abolished. For this reason studies of industrial policy-making have rarely revealed all the problems which surround the process of deciding how a union's vote shall be cast at the Labour Party Conference. Clearly we need to look at the course that policy-making on political questions takes within the unions before we can pass any judgment on whether their decisions are 'representative'—or even on what we mean by a 'representative' decision. How far can the ideal of the democratic Labour Movement be translated into reality?

During the long discussions about 'democracy in the unions' six unions, the so-called 'Big Six', were the most controversial. Between them they hold a majority of the votes at the Labour Party Conference. Although none is 'typical', collectively their experience amply reveals the unions' problems in making the decisions that they register at the Party Conference. Let us first look at how they make their policies as a background to the discussion of the whole movement.

## 1 *The Transport & General Workers' Union*[1]

Casting one million votes at the Labour Party Conference, the TGWU is by far the largest union in the country, with a

[1] Information about the TGWU is drawn from the Union's Rule Book, Member's Handbook, Annual Reports, Minutes of the Biennial Delegate Conferences and press reports of the BDCs (the transcript is not published), from J. Goldstein's *The Government of British Trade Unions*, V. L. Allen's *Trade Union Leadership*, and numerous interviews with officers and members.

strong claim to be considered one of the most politically controversial. Yet its policy-forming machinery differs little in
essence from that of many lesser unions. Subject to a quinquennial Rules Revision Conference, the TGWU's supreme
policy-making body is the Biennial Delegate Conference.
Representation at the BDC, resting on a structure conceived by
Ernest Bevin at the union's formation, and modified only in
detail since, is based on thirteen geographical regions and
fourteen trade groups, representing industries or groups of
allied industries.

Direct representation of all the 5,000-odd branches is out of
the question. Although any branch may make a nomination,
conference delegates are elected by a ballot of members of the
trade group in each region, with a quota of one delegate per
thousand members up to five, and one for each full two thousand
members thereafter. The system has its critics—particularly
from groups like the taxi drivers who are swamped by the
busmen in their trade group. But such discontents are probably
inevitable in any attempt to represent geographically and
occupationally every element in a highly diverse membership.

The seven hundred or so delegates meet at a seaside resort,
nominally for five days, effectively for less. Time must be found
for the Chairman's address, courtesy calls from the Mayor and
the local Trades Council, protracted elections of tellers, scru-
tineers and standing orders committee, votes of thanks and
presentations. Traditionally the conference ends early on the
final day. Its real work must be crammed into four days.

The most important single item of business is the report of
the General Executive Council for the two previous years,
running to over 200 pages.[1] The rest of the agenda is crowded.
In 1955, for example, it included 460 motions, of which thirty-
six were withdrawn, seventy-eight referred to the GEC, 104
sent to Trade Group conferences, and 218 were discussed—
although compositing reduced the actual number of motions to
fifty-eight. Domestic issues usually have priority although
some—such as wages policy—are also politically controversial.

---

[1] The TGWU GEC is a lay body of regional representatives elected in the
proportion of about 1:50,000 members, plus one representative from each trade
group. The General Secretary is the only full-time official to attend all its meetings.

Strictly political motions come far behind. In 1955 eighty-seven minutes were recorded, of which sixty-seven were internal union business or 'industrial', twelve were political-industrial, and only eight were essentially political. Yet although the time given to political discussion is so limited, there has been a coherent thread in the decisions under both Arthur Deakin and Frank Cousins.

The public image of the TGWU is essentially the impression made by its general secretary on opinion. In Deakin's time the 'T and G' stood for militant anti-communism and an only slightly diminished hostility to left-wing policies. For this Deakin consistently won the support of his conference. In both 1945 and 1947 the Biennial Delegate Conference rejected the fashionable pleas for 'progressive unity' (the euphemism for Communist Party affiliation to the Labour Party) by over-whelming majorities. Deakin's anti-Communism was steadily sharpened by his experience in the TUC, at the World Federa-tion of Trade Unions, and on his own General Executive Council. But the initiative to ban Communists from office in the union in 1949 came from the branches, and not directly from Deakin.[1] Its adoption by 426 votes to 208 was not wholly expected. Deakin also won handsome majorities for his refusal to recommend the TUC's return to the WFTU, from which it had withdrawn because the WFTU was a Communist tool, in 1949. Later conferences have decisively crushed the few attempts to raise the 'bans and proscriptions' within the Party or the union itself.

When in 1949 and 1951 Communists or fellow-travellers attempted to swing conferences against NATO, the Marshall Plan, the presence of American troops in Britain, the rearming of Germany, or strategic controls on East-West trade, they were routed. With the Communists excluded the Biennial Delegate

---

[1] Deakin had been attacking the Communists with increasing bitterness for several years. He was one of the chief promoters of the TUC's statement, *Defend Democracy*, which he persuaded the 1949 TGWU conference to accept by 508 votes to 123. Deakin refused to get the union's General Executive Council to propose banning Communists, and even opposed the attempt by Communist members of the GEC to make him agree to an Executive recommendation being made to the 1949 conference when the resolutions proposing banning the Com-munists were discussed. He realised that this would be tactically unwise, and preferred to wait for a rank-and-file initiative. However, delegates could have had no doubt of his views. Cf., *The Record*, July 1949.

Conference became at times so docile that Deakin himself felt the need to 'stir it up'. He had relatively little difficulty in persuading his delegates to follow him in support of wage restraint during the late forties and early fifties. Although Deakin led the TGWU's fierce opposition to the denationalization of road haulage, and the union remained committed in principle to an extension of public ownership, every attempt by militant delegates to win support for a 'shopping list' of industries to nationalize failed.

During Deakin's long feud with the Bevanites he was only once challenged directly at the BDC. In 1953 an attempt was made to repudiate two of his more fulminating anti-Bevanite utterances (at the 1952 Party Conference, and at Bristol in February 1953). Whatever delegates' attitude to the Bevanites may have been, it was scarcely surprising that a motion cast in such terms failed miserably,[1] Deakin's successor, Arthur Tiffin, persuaded the 1955 conference, over the protests of a militant minority, that it was not competent to nominate for the Treasurership of the Labour Party, which was vested in the General Executive Council by 'custom and practice'. Under Deakin the TGWU Biennial Delegate Conference never once strayed from the orthodox Labour line. On only one issue could there have been any doubt that the votes cast by the TGWU's delegates to the Labour Party Conference were in line with what the union's conference would have decided. This was German rearmament. In 1951 conference rejected two extreme attacks on rearming Germany. In 1954 these decisions were used to justify support for German rearmament at the Party Conference. In 1955, when the issue again came before the BDC, the official line prevailed, but there was a large minority. Had the BDC met to take a decision and not to repudiate one when the issue was at white heat in 1954, the opposition might possibly have won. Yet the platform did not exert itself in 1955 as it would have done in 1954, and Deakin's death had removed its most forceful advocate.

Arthur Tiffin, who succeeded Deakin in 1955, died soon after taking office and left little permanent mark on the union's

[1] Such a resolution, involving the prestige of the union itself, obviously would not indicate the true opposition to Deakin's policies.

political line. But soon after Mr Frank Cousins became General Secretary in 1956 the union seemed to be heading steadily left-wards. This impression was a compound of fact and over-simplification. Few would have guessed from the Press that Mr. Cousins had repeatedly urged moderation on his London busmen before they decided to strike in 1957. It matters rela-tively little if Mr Cousins is cast as chief bogey man in succession to Mr Bevan; it is disastrously misleading to interpret industrial disputes as grave as the London bus strike in the highly per-sonalized form that has become fashionable.

The record of Cousins' first two conferences, in 1957 and 1959, shows an undoubted move to the left (in an industrial climate which had changed profoundly since Deakin's day) but relatively few clear-cut differences. Both conferences voted the perennial motions for repayment of post-war credits, abolition of petrol tax, and defeat of the Conservatives. Both disposed of demands for a reconciliation with the WFTU, criticism of purchase tax, calls for higher pensions, 'reaffirmation of the principle of public ownership of the essential parts of the road haulage and road passenger transport services' and motions on colonial policy in the same fashion as they would have been treated in Deakin's time.

While the atmosphere of these two conferences was more militant than their predecessors, only one vote on a political issue broke flatly with tradition and opposed Party policy. This was the rejection of Labour nuclear weapons policy in 1959 when, with only fifty hostile votes, the conference supported a seven point motion mingling official policy with the demands of the Campaign for Nuclear Disarmament—except the proposal for unilateral British renunciation of atomic weapons. Although Mr Cousins himself would have preferred a thorough-going unilateralist approach it is far from certain that such a policy would have won such heavy support. Ironically enough, while political commentators were discussing the gravity of the TGWU's challenge to the Party leadership, Mr Cousins was (with dubious accuracy) reassuring hesitant delegates who feared that the Party might be fatally split on the eve of an election, that the seven points of the motion were all contained in previous statements made on behalf of the Labour Party.

Mr Cousins is not wholly blameless if the TGWU is mis-understood, for the union is generally known by the face that its General Secretary presents to the world. His sincerity is unquestionable, but few men can speak with such passionate ambiguity. How far many of his utterances are simply muddled, and how far the inconsistency in them springs from his own more left-wing ideas intruding into his loyal exposition of his union's moderate position is not always clear. But he frequently manages to give the impression that his union is more to the left than in fact it is. Listeners to his celebrated speech on nuclear tests at the 1957 Party Conference believed he was attacking official policy; the union in fact supported it. The reader of the official report is left guessing about which side Mr Cousins was taking. The atmosphere of the union's conference has been similar. In 1959 some passages of Mr Cousins' speech on nationalization apparently challenged openly agreed party policy. Yet while he affirmed his belief in old-style nationalization more vigorously than has been customary at TGWU conferences, he also re-marked with a vagueness to which he is prone, in Macdonaldish terms, that 'nationalization is a good thing in the industries to which it is appropriate'. This speech, like so many, was all things to all Labour men. Amid the uproar few noticed that while the conference repeated its support for public ownership, it had agreed to reject five motions demanding that specified industries be added to the 'shopping list' for nationalization. Clearly the TGWU conference has not deserted moderation. However, during the early years of leading the union Mr Cousins (reacting to the 'totalitarian' approach of Arthur Deakin) has evidently not tried to cast the conference so consistently in his image. There seems little doubt that he could persuade his conference to accept more progressive policies if he made the attempt.

While future TGWU conferences might shift further left, in the short run the problem Mr Cousins and his union set the Party is not that they have gone into systematic opposition, but that their support can no longer be depended on as it was in Deakin's day. The old grouping of TGWU-NUGMW-NUM, which came to the aid of Party leaders for so many years could no longer be trusted to rally automatically.

Only a fraction of the political decisions the union must make are taken at the BDC. Except for the nomination of members of the Party Executive, all other questions are decided by the delegation to the Party Conference. Although over the years the BDC has sketched the broad outlines of policy, interpreting its decisions and dealing with new issues is still important. The powers of the delegation are circumscribed in practice by what the General Secretary or the General Executive Council say during the year, and by the votes of the previous month's delegation to the TUC, although these are not binding constitutionally. Its powers are substantial enough for its composition to be keenly debated. The union's 1945 conference decided to choose regional lay representatives by ballot within each region. This produced so long a ballot paper, and so small a poll was spread over a large number of candidates that in 1947 the union returned to the practice of letting each (lay) Regional Committee choose one or two delegates according to membership in the Region. In recent years eighteen lay regional delegates have gone to Conference, with two members and the Chairman of the General Executive Council (all laymen), three TGWU MPs, the General Secretary, Assistant General Secretary, Finance Officer, Administrative Officer, one of the four national officers, two organizers or Regional Secretaries, and one Trade Group Secretary, all taken in rotation. Rather more than half of the union's delegation of forty—it is entitled to 200 —are laymen.

This delegation meets for two or three hours on the eve of the Party Conference to discuss the union's vote on the issues which are to be debated, and whom to support in the NEC elections. Further meetings may be held during Conference to discuss new composite motions, to consider assurances which the Party leadership have given, or, very rarely, to decide how the vote shall be cast after hearing the debate. The General Secretary is usually the dominant personality—but this does not mean that he carries the day easily or inevitably. At times religious differences on educational policy have been so deep that the union has preferred to seek refuge in abstention. Arthur Deakin's determination to swing the TGWU behind German rearmament was strongly challenged by several delegates to the 1954 Conference. However, he was only defeated twice in delegation meetings—over the tied cottage issue and over the candidates the union should support in the election of the women's section of the NEC. The unilateralist and multilateralist approaches to nuclear disarmament were passionately debated by the delegation to the 1957 Conference, and the extent to which the union should oppose the statement of educational policy, *Learning to Live* led to a long discussion in 1958.

Nevertheless, when the General Secretary exerts himself, he usually appears to prevail. But he has never completely 'had the delegation in his pocket'. In the last resort the delegation has a lay majority which owes a Deakin or a Cousins nothing, while some of Arthur Deakin's most outspoken critics were officials. Once the decision is made the Chairman—not the General Secretary—is responsible for casting the union's vote.

## 2 *The National Union of Mineworkers*

Once the dominant union in the Party, the Miners now come second, with 687,000 votes.[1] The union took its present name only in 1944, when it succeeded the Miners' Federation of Great Britain. In many ways it still remains a federation of regional unions based on the coalfields. There are fifteen Area Unions, and two groups of local unions of colliery tradesmen, a Cokemen's Area, and a Colliery Officials' and Staffs' Area, which have been added since nationalization. Two Power Groups include the colliery membership of the TGWU, National Union of Enginemen, Firemen & Electrical Workers and NUGMW on behalf of whom the NUM negotiates with the National Coal Board.

The Annual Conference of Delegates is the main organ for making national policy decisions. With under 200 delegates the ACD is comparatively small, representing the Areas in the proportion of one delegate to every 5,000 members, with a maximum of twenty, usually elected by branch block vote. The national President, Vice-President, and Secretary attend but do not vote. Decisions are made by area block vote. Since

[1] Unions are listed in order of political affiliation. Both the AEU and the NUGMW have larger memberships than the NUM. Information is derived from Annual Conference Reports, the NUM Rule Book, Minutes of the National Executive Committee, and discussions with members and officials at Area and National level.

each Area can submit only three motions and two amendments
the agenda is short. It is circulated six weeks before the conference, to allow Areas to consult their members. Some issues
will already have been decided by an Area Annual Conference.
Several Areas summon special Area Conferences to consider the
agenda, while others hold a referendum after the Area Executive
has made recommendations.[1] Area delegations are not always
fully mandated, for they may request a free hand to decide in
the light of the debate—particularly on motions so worded that
they might be exploited in an undesirable sense.

With an agenda of only forty or so resolutions the Miners are
one of the few unions which complete their conference business.
Only three or four of these motions are directly political—of
which one is usually a pious declaration of devotion to the
Labour Party[2] and a fiery denunciation of its enemies. Nevertheless, the record over the post-war years is one of almost
consistent orthodoxy. The exceptions derive almost entirely
from the Miners' tradition of internationalism and working-
class solidarity—combined with left-wing leadership of several
Area Unions.

During the 1930's even Will Lawther and Sam Watson, who
later became pillars of orthodoxy, had run afoul of the Party
leadership by their support of the Popular Front. It was no
surprise, therefore, when the 1945 conference supported Communist affiliation to the Labour Party by 418 votes to 164,[3]
although this policy was reversed by a vote of the membership
in the following year. When the TUC broke away from the
WFTU the conference decisively refused to urge the TUC to
return. Since then, however, it has normally been willing to
accept mildly-worded motions favouring a rapprochement

---

[1] The Scottish Area submitted to financial vote the questions of withdrawal
from the WFTU, in 1949, of British participation in the Korean war, and of the
Hungarian revolution in 1956. R. Page Arnot, *A History of the Scottish Miners*,
London: Allen & Unwin, 1955, pp. 340–4 and *The Scottish Miner*, February,
March, November 1957.

[2] It might seem a waste of time for a Miners' conference to pledge loyalty in
this way but it gives the leadership a chance to attack the Communists: 'I hope if
this is adopted . . . that we shall never again witness the spectacle of miners'
leaders appearing on platforms against Labour candidates . . . it will be your duty
to appear on (Labour's) side and to support it to the utmost extent of the financial
and moral power you have got'.

[3] Thousands omitted.

between the ICFTU and the WFTU. It also supports motions which call for the extension of trade with Communist countries, so long as they are innocuously worded, and do not demand the removal of all strategic controls.[1]

More than in most unions the drafting of a motion and the way in which it is advocated make all the difference between success and failure. Militant Areas like Scotland often try to word resolutions so innocently that they will command wide, and unsuspecting, support in the coalfields. Then, at conference, they try to give them an unexpected gloss. They may even push a moderate motion through the conference in the hope that it can be used to justify a more advanced position at the TUC or the Labour Party Conference. This can produce complicated decisions. In 1953 the Yorkshire Area spokesman, Mr J. A. Hall asked that a motion on nuclear weapons be 'returned to the districts'.

'for the simple reason that never before have I known at any miners' conference a decision to be taken which will mean that an interpretation will be made, whichever way we think about it, that we are in favour of devastation.'

The decision on German rearmament was even more intricate. In 1952 the NUM National Executive proposed a resolution expressing 'appreciation of the job done by the Labour Government, and calling all members to work to demonstrate their loyalty to the policy of the Labour Movement, and to work for the defeat of the Conservative Government'. Derbyshire Area pledged support for the Labour and Trade Union Movement and proposed that the best way to defeat the Conservatives was 'a vigorous Socialist policy', including nationalization of banking, engineering, shipbuilding and chemicals, a reduction in arms expenditure and self-government for the colonies. The Executive demanded that the Derbyshire resolution be taken as an amendment to their own, although—whatever the intention —there was no real connection. After a long procedural wrangle

[1] One word in a motion on East-West trade may make all the difference, since the essence of such resolutions are the qualifying phrases. The 1952 Labour Party Conference accepted an ETU resolution urging the government to 'pursue a policy of developing trading relations with all nations', but in 1953 it rejected a motion referring to 'American imposed restrictions on East-West trade' in addition to calling for its expansion.

they were discussed separately, and eventually the Derbyshire resolution was heavily defeated. The Executive used the same tactic in 1954. A Derbyshire resolution flatly condemned the rearmament of Germany, while Yorkshire submitted a motion reiterating at length the Miners' appreciation of the Labour Party, and supporting 'its full programme, "Challenge to Britain", and the National and International defence decisions taken by the Parliamentary Labour Party and the National Executive Committee of the Labour Party'. It is doubtful whether the rank and file understood that their approval of this resolution would be interpreted as an endorsement of German rearmament. But the resolutions were taken as alternatives—as they were, strictly speaking—and the Yorkshire resolution was voted by 470 to 223. The left had been outgeneralled.

Every attempt to commit the NUM conference to left wing policies during the Bevanite period and since has been unsuccessful.[1] Mr Bevan is a sponsored candidate of the National Union of Mineworkers, and many of his supporters thought that his membership of the union, combined with its one-time left-wing tradition, might swing the Miners' vote behind his campaign for the Treasurership, despite the strong personal animosity between Mr Bevan and both Sir William Lawther and Mr Sam Watson. However, both the 1954 and 1955 conferences supported Mr Gaitskell; only in 1956 did Mr Bevan win the NUM vote, in preference to Mr George Brown.[2]

The Miners send the largest delegation to the Labour Party Conference; 120 strong—the only full delegation sent by a large union. The NUM Executive attend *en bloc* as delegates from their Areas, and the remainder are lay members of Area Executives and rank-and-file delegates elected by branch ballots within the Areas. No single personality dominates the dele-

---

[1] Although the Derbyshire Area resolution for further nationalization referred to was defeated, the 1956 conference carried an almost identical pledge to extend public ownership. However, the crucial phrase in the 1952 resolution had been a demand for 'a cut in arms expenditure' which, if carried, would have committed the NUM to oppose the Labour Party's rearmament policy.

[2] The NUM nominates a candidate for the following year, although its decision is taken as a mandate to vote in the autumn. Thus in 1954 Mr Gaitskell was nominated for 1955, but the union voted for him at the 1954 Conference. It nominated him in 1955, but he was not a candidate in 1956. Mr Bevan beat Mr Brown (whose candidature had not been announced when several Areas made their choice) by an overwhelming majority in 1956.

gation meetings, since the Area Secretaries, fully skilled in advocacy and procedure, are attending—although Mr Sam Watson (who represents the union on the Party NEC) is heard with great respect. The group of moderate leaders usually exercises collective control, but the interpretation of motions passed at the union's conference is often discussed at great length. In 1954 the conference had voted that:

'In view of the threatened economic crisis and the possibility of cut-throat competition from Germany and Japan in world markets, this Conference of the NUM considers the time opportune for the holding of conferences and discussions on the possibility of establishing international trade union unity as the best means of protecting the interests of the workers of all countries.'

If this meant anything it supported discussions between the ICFTU and the WFTU. However, according to the Scottish Area, the National President ruled at the TUC delegation meeting that as the motion had not mentioned ICFTU and WFTU by name, the union was not bound to support a resolution reading:

'This Congress instructs the General Council to use its influence within the ICFTU to bring about discussion with the WFTU with a view to reaching agreement on a common programme of economic demands.'

At the Labour Party Conference and the TUC there were stormy meetings over the application of the union's mandate on German rearmament.[1] But these are exceptions. Dissension

---

[1] Cf., *The Scottish Miner*, November 1954 and the *Daily Worker*, September 7, 1954. The Scottish Area Conference carried a resolution of protest (*The Scottish Miner*, December 1954). The NUM NEC reaffirmed that the decision had been correctly taken and represented union policy. (Minutes and Proceedings 1954, pp. 635 and 697).

The NUM vote had been solicited throughout the summer by the *Daily Worker* (June 25, July 8, July 16, September 2). It later ran a series of articles recording the discontent of working miners with the Union's decision, and alleged 'Had the leaders represented the feelings of the overwhelming mass of the men in the pits, today's result would have recorded the opposition of the TUC' (September 9, 1954).

At the 1955 TUC some members of the NUM delegation were so incensed at the decision to support the General Council on the 40-hour week that Congress was interrupted for several moments by the noise and two delegates all but came to blows. See Mr Ernest Jones' explanation, *Report of Congress*, p. 400.

within the delegation is inevitable when the conference has voted a motion like 'This Conference of the National Union of Mineworkers demands that the production and use of the hydrogen bomb be outlawed by all the nations of the world'—more of an exclamation than a policy. Yet if the Miners' vote normally favours the orthodox policies at the Party Conference, this is in keeping with the moderation of its own conference.

### 3 The Amalgamated Engineering Union[1]

'It's democracy gone mad', confessed an AEU leader, referring to his union's constitution. Its drafters set out deliberately to put the maximum control of policy into the hands of the members, and to prevent the undue influence of paid officials. This elaborate system of government, includes a strict 'separation of powers' between the National Committee (the annual conference), the Executive Council of full-time officials, and the Appeals Court. There is also a Quinquennial Rules Revision Conference.

The AEU's 2,500 branches are grouped into districts, which in turn are grouped into twenty-six geographical divisions. As unable as the other large unions to provide direct branch representation at its conference, the AEU has established a National Committee of fifty-two delegates in the belief that they are more capable of making policy decisions and deliberating usefully than a mass meeting some hundreds strong. The Committee is constituted through a doubly indirect system of representation. Branches elect District Committees by ballot. Each District Committee sends two delegates to the Divisional Committee, which in turn sends two delegates to the National Committee. They are joined by six or seven non-voting women delegates from the Annual Conference of Women Shop-Stewards' Representatives on District Committees. While power is put into lay hands, there is little evidence that the National Committee is any more responsive to the mood of the rank-and-file member than other union conferences.[2]

---

[1] Sources: AEU Rule Book; National Committee minutes; Reports of the Appeals Court; *AEU Journal*; AEU Research Department. The AEU has 673,000 votes.

[2] The AEU constitution is accounted exceptionally democratic because of the wide powers vested in the conference. Yet indirect elections (and these are twice

Any branch may initiate a resolution for the National Committee, which it sends to its District Committee. Districts forward resolutions they think suitable to the Divisional Committee. Before the Divisional Committee discusses the resolutions they are sent to the Executive, which indicates whether it considers they should be considered by the National Committee or belong more properly to one of the sectional conferences. The Divisional Committees then decide which resolutions shall go forward to the National Committee. The agenda is crowded. In 1957 it contained 361 resolutions, and in 1958 384, plus a few in both cases from the Youth Conference and from the Women's Conference. After all allowance for duplication this overtaxes even a ten-day conference. Sometimes nearly half the motions are left undiscussed. No amount of exhortation from the Executive produces a decline in the number submitted.

About a third of the agenda could be called 'political'. Unlike most unions the AEU spaces discussion of political issues throughout the conference rather than at the end, and consequently it deals with more political business, and in a rather more seemly manner, than some other unions. The 1954 meeting symbolically discussed the hydrogen bomb before its annual wage-claim.

In no large union is political policy-making more complicated by the struggle against the Communists. Since the war they have always held at least two seats on the Executive, and several times they have come within striking distance of winning control. The basic support for Communist or fellow-travelling motions in the National Committee varies between fifteen and eighteen, but most of the remaining delegates are either left-wing or feel bound to give that impression. The non-Communists on the Executive must constantly fight to deprive the Communists of the chance to claim they are the only authentic militants. Resolutions before the National Committee are often mere pawns in this struggle, their fate having little relation to their intrinsic merits. Thus the Executive and

removed from the membership) are normally considered undemocratic in other contexts by the Left. The system has shown itself peculiarly vulnerable to the action of organized minorities.

National Committeemen join to support harmlessly demagogic or extreme motions such as this piece of overheated militancy to maintain their left-wing record:

'This National Committee instructs Executive Council to take immediate steps through all channels of influence, viz., TUC, Labour Party Conference, etc., to get the reimposition/reintroduction of price controls and subsidies on all basic commodities. Further, that a national joint demonstration be arranged at an appropriately early date in support of this decision.'

Although the Committee voted that motion unanimously in 1956 and specifically reaffirmed it in 1957 and 1958 it is doubtful whether a single delegate believed that any demonstration would be held or that the Labour Party would adopt such a policy—and at bottom many delegates believed it to be misconceived. But in paying lip-service to such resolutions the non-communists can save their strength for the important battles— major industrial issues, and success in the frequent elections to important union posts.

The support for Communist policies has fluctuated. In 1944 a motion favouring Communist affiliation to Labour passed by twenty-seven votes to twenty-one, and unlike other unions the decision was not reversed in 1945 or 1946. Although it supported withdrawal from the WFTU, the National Committee soon supported Communist demands for a reconciliation between the WFTU and the ICFTU. However, the Executive loyally rallied support for Ernest Bevin's foreign policies. When the Communists tried to blame Bevin for the deterioration in international relations in 1947 the Committee amended the motion (by thirty votes to eighteen) into a vote of confidence. More surprisingly it rejected a demand for an end of aid to 'the reactionary Greek Government', and expressed support for Bevin's policy. Attacks on the Marshall Plan and the government's 'failure to fight monopolies' were as firmly rejected. Again, in 1950, extreme resolutions on further nationalization, workers' control of industry, the use of troops to break strikes and the abolition of the atomic bomb were all amended to read more moderately. Part of the price of such victories in 1948 was the voting of a demand for 'immediate' nationalization of the steel industry—quite plainly a Parliamentary and administrative impossibility at the time.

With the defeat of the Labour Government the pressure to be loyal was less intense, and the Executive was less prepared to commit its strength on purely political matters. While the Communists had been almost wholly isolated in opposing the Marshall Plan, the division between them and the democratic left was blurred from 1951 until the Hungarian revolution. Several foreign policy resolutions adopted by the National Committee contained distinctively Communist ingredients. The National Committee supported every Bevanite policy, usually unanimously. It was so incensed in 1955 at the decision to rearm Germany that many militants were determined to launch a national campaign to make the Party change its mind. Mr Ben Gardner, then General Secretary, warned them:

'If this resolution goes through it means elected officials of this union being on the platform with permanent national officials of the Communist party, mobilizing a campaign in opposition to the declared policy of the Labour Party Conference. The first probability would be that those individuals would be expelled from the Labour Party, the next that our union might be disaffiliated from the Labour Party'.

The Executive carried its point by only thirty votes to twenty-two.

With the gradual weakening of the Communist position, the AEU has been moving slowly to a more moderate line particularly under the leadership of Mr 'Bill' Carron. Not surprisingly the 1958 meeting condemned the Labour Party's statement on public ownership, *Industry and Society*, the spirit of which was radically at odds with nationalization motions voted at previous meetings. Even so the vote was narrow enough (twenty-eight to twenty-four) to show that the National Committee's attitude was gradually changing.

The conference still invariably supports unanimously most demands for the extension of east-west trade, cuts in arms expenditure, and the withdrawal of American troops from Britain, but it often refuses to adopt extreme positions on

K

questions where the challenge to the Labour leadership is more serious. During the debate on atomic weapons it has always demanded international control and inspection, and has rejected Communist attempts to divorce nuclear from conventional disarmament. During the later debate over unilateral nuclear disarmament, the issue was not even brought directly before the conference, and the motions voted were quite orthodox restatements of the Labour-TUC line. Although earlier National Committees called regularly for the period of National Service to be cut, demands that it be abolished were all rejected until the Party itself had accepted abolition. While motions favouring nationalization (notably of engineering) are carried unanimously, demands for outright expropriation receive short shrift. Such distinctions are often vital when the AEU delegation has to decide its vote at the Party Conference.

The AEU sends a delegation of the non-Communist members of its Executive, with two members from each Division—one a Divisional Councillor, one elected by ballot. Although there is keen competition for places (with ten to forty candidates for every place), only about eight per cent of the membership vote. The AEU MPs attend but do not vote. Normally the delegation must accept National Committee decisions as mandatory. As in other unions the question arises from time to time of how far the mandate applies. In 1954 the delegation debated for two hours whether circumstances had changed sufficiently to allow a switch in the vote on German rearmament, before unanimously deciding to maintain its opposition. Interpreting a mandate is often delicate when there is a choice between extreme motions on foreign affairs or economic policy, or the NEC's orthodox line. The delegation's decision on which resolution is nearest to National Committee policy may turn on such terms as 'without compensation', 'unilateral', 'immediate', or 'international agreement'. Sometimes the resolutions passed by the National Committee are so different that they provide almost no guidance. Although Jack Tanner, Ben Gardner, and Bill Carron have all been influential, none has always carried the day. More often than most leaders, the AEU's President has to go to the rostrum to support policies of which he disapproves.

The AEU delegation has caused more controversy than most. The trouble began in 1954, when the TUC delegation decided that it did not want to vote for Arthur Deakin for the General Council. The AEU Executive was speedily led to understand by the general unions that if the AEU withdrew its support for Mr Deakin, the AEU would disappear from the General Council. The AEU Executive overruled the delegation, insisting that it had the right to commit the union on a purely 'executive' matter. After a long, angry meeting of the TUC delegation the aggrieved members complained to the Appeal Court. The Executive argued that while the rules were silent on the precise issues, they provided that 'The Executive Council shall, previous to any National Meeting of the British Trades Union Congress or Party, call together the officials and delegates appointed to represent the Union at the meeting named'. They did not say that once convoked the delegation must be consulted. The Executive was empowered however, to act, 'with the best interests of the Union as the primary consideration'. The Appeal Court ruled against the Executive.[1]

Although a lawyer's interpretation of the rules might differ from the Appeal Court's finding, it was generally thought that the issue was settled and that the ruling also applied to Labour Party delegations. But the Executive dug in its heels. In 1955 it nominated Mr Gaitskell as Party Treasurer. At another angry meeting before the Conference a majority of delegates voted to support Mr Bevan; the Executive insisted on exercising its 'right' to vote for Mr Gaitskell. The issue again went to the Appeal Court, which again refused to uphold the Executive. After taking legal advice the Executive again refused to accept the decision, and further insisted that the rules gave the delegation no rights at all. Only by grace and favour had the Executive consulted it in the past.

---

[1] The heat of the meeting may be judged by Mr Ben Gardner's reply to a complaining branch: 'with regard to the reference in your letter to the No. 20 Division Delegate being told to "go to hell" we would further explain that this is a gross understatement of the position, and to that extent is untrue. . . . Bro Dinning, however, persisted in his protestations even to the extent of drawing the unwelcome attention of others to this disagreement between AEU delegates. He was persistent in expressing the demand that we should have found out from somewhere where he was staying and informed him of the meeting. It was because of the hysterical scene he was making that he was told to go elsewhere.'

Agitation among the Bevanites rose to a pitch where there was dark talk of the time when a recalcitrant Executive had been evicted from the union's Head Office in a pitched battle. The following year the Executive refused to accept a motion for the National Committee agenda proposing the nomination of Mr Bevan for the Treasurership—an act which some observers had considered impossible up to then—on the grounds that the rules forbade the National Committee to interfere in an essentially 'executive' question. The Executive then nominated Mr Charles Pannell, one of the union's Members of Parliament for the Treasurership. Although it claimed to have nominated Mr Pannell because 'the job required someone with a knowledge of finance', this looked suspiciously like an attempt to avoid having to support Mr Bevan by 'wasting' the AEU vote on a 'favourite son'. The storm broke at the 1956 National Committee. After an angry discussion the Committee rejected the resolution nominating Mr Bevan by 27:24, and accepted the refusal to put on the agenda a resolution withdrawing Mr Pannell's nomination by 38:14. Later it carried by 37:15 votes a motion deploring the Executive's 'denying to the elected delegates to the Labour Party Conference the right to decide the manner in which the AEU vote should be cast in the selection of the Labour Party Executive'. Since the lay delegates to the 1956 Party Conference still refused to support Mr Pannell, the Executive again decreed how the vote should be cast after another acrimonious debate. Recriminations rumbled on for a few months, then slipped into the background as the contest for the Treasurership was settled.

The AEU case is remarkable just because it is an almost unique example of a union Executive committing itself completely on an industrial issue. Behind the political battle there was the continuing struggle for power between the National Committee and the Executive. Partly the Executive believed itself justified because the Party leadership conceivably hung on their vote. Nothing less would have persuaded union leaders to take so great a risk on a political matter. Although their intransigence was stigmatized as typical of the unscrupulousness of union leaders, the AEU's vote at Conference is usually very close to National Committee policy, and the delegation's views are respected on questions where the National Committee has made no clear decision. On only one other vote since the war has the AEU seemed to vote at Conference in contradiction to National Committee policy—it was hard to reconcile the union's support for Labour's 1957 proposals for public owner-ship (*Industry and Society*) with the National Committee's consistent support for sweeping programmes of nationalization.[1] Against the suggestions that the Executive deforms National Committee decisions must be set the attempt by a majority of rank and file delegates to the 1956 Conference to commit the AEU to the immediate abolition of conscription in preference to a reduction in the period of National Service—despite the fact that the 1956 National Committee had rejected abolition in favour of reduction. Only the flat insistence of the President secured respect for union policy. Normally the differences between Conference voting and National Committee decisions are largely the result of the difficulty that faces any left-wing union, of having to choose between orthodoxy and extremism. In the last resort, when the issue is squarely fought the AEU usually sides with the orthodoxy—but so, too, has the National Committee.

## 4 *National Union of General & Municipal Workers*[2]

'Yes, I suppose we *are* a right-wing union', agreed an official of the NUGMW, as if surprised at the thought. In fact this union, with 650,000 votes at the Party Conference has supported the Party leadership even more faithfully than the TGWU, without ever being quite so controversial. In Mr (now Sir) Tom Williamson, General Secretary since 1946, it has had a less colourful leader than either Mr Deakin or Mr Cousins. The critics are also partly disarmed by the union's annual Congress. The Congress of 400–500 delegates is the union's chief policy-making body. As in the TGWU direct branch representation is out of the question. Accordingly, while branches can nominate delegates they are elected by ballots within each District, at the

---

[1] The National Committee did not formally reject *Industry and Society* until 1958, after it had been accepted by the Labour Party Conference.

[2] Sources: Annual Reports and Reports of Congress; the NUGMW Rule Book; H. A. Clegg. *General Union*; interviews with officials and members.

rate of one for every 2,000 members. The General Secretary, National Officers, District Secretaries, one-third of the organizers in rotation, and the General Council,[1] also attend with the right to speak but not to vote. Each delegate has one vote.

Congress spends most of its four days on industrial business and the annual report. Branches, District Committees, and the Executive can all submit resolutions, and the agenda of between 100 and 150 resolutions, is not always completed. Political matters must wait until the end, when time for debate is short. The longest purely political debate since the war, on German rearmament, included thirteen speakers. Here, by contrast, is the record of discussion of industrial and industrio-political motions at three recent Congresses:

| Year | Number of Motions | Formally Moved | Formally Seconded | No Discussion | No Executive Speaker | No Reply by Mover [‡] |
|------|------|------|------|------|------|------|
| 1956 | 16  | 9 | 11 | 14 | 10 | 15 |
| 1957 | 14  | 5 | 8  | 10 | 7  | 8  |
| 1958 | 19* | 5 | 10 | 13 | 5  | 15 |

\* Includes two foreign policy motions discussed jointly.
‡ Movers reply only when there has been opposition.

The motions debated in 1958 (higher pensions, repeal of the Rent Act, nationalization, economic planning, defence, UNO and world peace) were among the most important—while all three Congresses were admittedly relatively uncontroversial. Yet it is an exceptional year in which more than two or three issues are thoroughly discussed.

Really important questions are usually debated under Executive Special Motions. Clad in impeccable sentiments they seem to the casual observer to do no more than extol the unexceptionable virtues of (say) 'Peace'. In fact they help the Executive outwit the opposition. Tucked away in these long motions are phrases like 'effective and permanent inspection', 'securing inter-

---

[1] The General Council comprises one representative from each District plus extra delegates from the four largest districts, the Chairman, General Secretary, General Treasurer, and the District Secretaries. The detailed administration is in the hands of the National Executive which comprises one representative from each district and an equal number of full-time officials.

national agreement' on atomic weapons (rejecting unilateralism by implication), or some such key formula which is directly linked to a current controversy in the Movement. It is hard for loyal Labour Party supporters to oppose such motions solely because they object to half a dozen words.[1] While, as one observer has noted, Special Motions are an 'opportunity for the delegates to display their fervour in a good cause', they also provide a most useful source of reference to the TUC and Party Conference delegations.[2] However, the Executive has also used Special Motions to initiate debates on such issues as the Free Trade Area which might never have been discussed on branch initiative.

Throughout the years Congress has invariably been moderate. It was never so impressed by the Russian war effort that it would tolerate British communism. It has not so much as paid lip service to a 'Socialist foreign policy'. Communist or fellow-travelling speeches are almost unknown, while many of the motions which echo the current Communist line in near-identical terms at other union conferences are never even submitted for the agenda. Proposals to adopt 'progressive' policies on nationalization, colonial affairs, wages, defence, are invariably defeated. There was little wonder that the decision of the 1959 Congress to support unilateral nuclear disarmament amazed the union as much as the outside world. It was the sort of 'accident' on which many union decisions turn: a vote by 150 votes to 126, with seventy-five delegates either sunning themselves, drinking tea, or on their way home (according to who was making the excuses) and the Executive so sure of victory that it failed to put up its biggest guns. Yet, although the vote cannot legitimately be challenged, it is fair to call it a surprising aberration.[3] For normally the NUGMW Executive is exceptionally skilled in handling Congress, without ever holding a tight rein. There are few clashes of personality; debates are rarely heated, and the floor seems unusually ready to accept the platform's arguments. Its decisions were so indisputably right wing, and its rejection of 'progressive' policies has been so overwhelming that the Left has never been

---

[1] Special Motions cannot be amended.       [2] *General Union*, p. 59.
[3] A special Congress was later persuaded to reverse this decision, 194:31.

able to heap the reproaches on the NUGMW leadership which it poured on the TGWU between 1951 and 1955.

These policies have to be interpreted for the Party Conference. The union sends about sixty delegates, although entitled to 130. These include the entire National Executive Committee (half lay, half official), lay members elected by District Committees, and several national officers. While it has a lay majority the proportion of full time officials in the delegation is one of the highest in the movement. But the delegation's importance seems in any case secondary; voting is effectively controlled by the National Executive Committee, which is responsible for policy on all matters where Congress has given no mandate. The district delegates have apparently no function but to report back what happened. Most important decisions are taken before the TUC, and revised in terms of the Party Conference agenda a month later. Although the balance of power within the NUGMW Executive is not clear, an alliance of the General Secretary and one or two of his senior officials almost invariably carries the day. The union has voted at most once against the Labour Party leadership since the war, although its leaders have not always been enthusiastic about parts of the Party's programme. In so doing, however, they are faithfully reflecting Congress which, until 1959, had not adopted one resolution deviating from Party policy since 1945.

## 5 Union of Shop, Distributive & Allied Workers

USDAW has existed as such only since 1946, when it emerged from an amalgamation of the National Union of Distributive & Allied Workers, and the National Amalgamated Union of Shop Assistants, Warehousemen and Clerks. It is the largest union with direct branch representation at its Annual Delegate Meeting. Every branch has at least one delegate, with an extra delegate for every full 500 members after the first. In practice complete branch representation is never achieved. Only 595 of the 1,800 branches sent delegates to the 1959 conference, representing seventy-seven per cent of the membership. Their 775 delegates, with the Executive and Divisional Councillors, all officials, and the union's Members of Parliament (who could speak but not vote) brought the total strength of the meeting to 1,027. USDAW is also the only one of the 'big six' which decides by branch block vote—each branch having two voting cards, for industrial and political membership.[1]

Time presses even more heavily on the USDAW conference than others. The agenda usually includes over 150 resolutions, plus amendments. Although compositing cuts the number to half, and twenty to twenty-five more resolutions are withdrawn in the course of the conference, between forty and fifty motions are debated in the three days. The Annual Delegate Meeting also has to find time for a welcome from the Mayor and the Trades Council, fraternal greetings from foreign trade unionists, and the discussion of the annual report. Invariably, on the final afternoon as the President (Mr Walter Padley) remarked in 1958, 'almost every five minutes that goes by twenty or thirty people disappear from the conference' and it closes early.

Although so little time is available, the discussion of the 'general industrial and political policy' section of the agenda occupies about one-third of the conference. The union's membership is so diverse that many delegates welcome the discussion of political issues, about which they have views, rather than discuss the wages of junior roundsmen. Yet, although a few important issues are thrashed out at length, most matters are rushed through with little or no discussion, presumably because there is no disagreement.

The Annual Delegate Meeting is one of the few union conferences which is erratic enough to be interesting. Few others have had such a genuine fight against the Communists. At one time during the war the Communists were strongly entrenched on the Executive of NUDAW, and the union supported affiliation of the Communist Party to the Labour Party in 1945 —although it reversed the decision by ballot in 1946. But the Communists were strong enough not only to affect the union's industrial policies, but to commit the union to some of their views on foreign policy. As late as 1948 one of the USDAW delegation to the Labour Party Conference protested at the Labour Party's attitude to the Prague coup. Mr. Walter

[1] Sources: USDAW Rule Book; *The New Dawn*; Annual Reports and ADM Reports; interviews with officials and members of the union. USDAW has 334,000 votes.

Padley, elected President in 1948, attacked the ably-led Communist minority with the ferocious eloquence that he had learned as a member of the ILP. His General Secretary, Alan Birch, has been as solidly anti-Communist in a less dramatic fashion. But the fight to rout the Communists would never have been so successful without the determined organizing of anti-Communist factions by Labour supporters, who often beat the Communists at their own tactic of organizing 'slates' of candidates and preparing resolutions. Slowly the swing against the Communists gathered strength, although they remained influential for several years. At almost every conference the Party came directly under attack. In 1953 the meeting recorded its 'disgust' at the Prague trials; in 1956 it suggested that the disclosures of the 20th Congress of the Soviet Communist Party were an indictment of the mendacity of British communism, and suggested that the Russians might repudiate the British Communist Party as a contribution to international peace. The 1957 conference condemned all who had condoned Soviet repression in Hungary by remaining in the Communist Party, and in 1958 the union strongly attacked Yugoslav persecution of Social Democrats. Nevertheless, many USDAW decisions have been influenced either by the Communists or by the Executive's tactics in organizing opposition to them—particularly up to about 1955. In 1951 USDAW was the only non-Communist union which supported demands for investigation of allegations of germ warfare in Korea.

The union rarely 'votes the ticket'. From 1951 to 1955 it supported the Bevanites on the rearmament programme, nationalization, German rearmament—all the Bevanite issues but one: Mr Bevan. It was prepared to see him as Treasurer in 1954, but not as Leader in 1955. In 1956, however, it preferred him to Mr George Brown. Right back to the days of NUDAW the union has traditionally opposed conscription. Although it did not press the issue for some years it was almost the first union to take up the demand for the abolition of conscription after the outbreak of the cold war. But it is not neatly 'ILP-pacifist', for the conference has also rejected abolitionist or unilateralist views on nuclear weapons decisively.

USDAW is clearly moving to the right. While in the early

fifties the conference took the left-wing line on almost every issue it has acted more moderately in recent years. At one time demands for more nationalization were passed almost as a formality; in 1958 a call for the extension of public ownership to the major industries during the life of the next Labour government was carried by only 77,000 to 66,000 votes—with 111,000 votes not cast. Although Mr Birch argued that Labour physically could not carry through such a programme in addition to its existing commitments during its next term of office, and denied the Executive was 'retreating from the principles of our Movement', the listlessness of the discussion, and the absence of protest at the Executive's support of *Industry & Society* showed that the views of the rank and file were changing as well as those of their leaders.

No union meeting has a wider variety of opinion. Most conferences produce a boring succession of speeches in which the only argument is between the more and the less extreme. But the USDAW Annual Delegate Meeting includes pacifists like George Craddock, thoroughgoing anti-Communists like Walter Padley, a greatly diminished group of Communists, ably led by Alec Cohen, orthodox spokesmen like Alfred Robens, several ex-Communists who resigned over Hungary, and even, for some years, Joe Emden, an unorthodox Conservative who received a jovial hearing. No other major union has had a declared Conservative delegate since the war.

While USDAW could send over sixty delegates to the Labour Party Conference, its delegation numbers only thirty-four. Eighteen members (not more than four of whom may be full-time officials) elected by national ballot, the (lay) Executive Council, the President and General Secretary and the Parliamentary Panel. Although the Executive Council can recommend the line to be taken, 'the decisions for support or otherwise shall only be taken by the elected delegates, and representatives of the Union who shall have full power to determine the Union's vote . . . on all matters on which there is no direct mandate from the ADM'. The USDAW Executive nominates for the Party Executive, but the delegation decides how the vote shall be cast.

The USDAW delegation must take many of the decisions,

often after prolonged debate, because like the AEU it has had to choose between the moderation of the Labour leadership and the extremism of some of the left-wing opposition. Its attempts to avoid the choice and take an independent line sometimes enfuriates the two extremes and embarrass its own representatives.[1] Yet, while it is not easy for USDAW delegations to reflect the attitudes of this rather idiosyncratic Annual Delegate Meeting, its record at the Labour Party Conference is on the whole compatible with the Meeting's line.

## 6 The National Union of Railwaymen[2]

'Look around this building, at the packed ranks of the delegates here and the crowded platform. Within these four walls we have the spearhead of the Socialist Movement. Do not blunt that spearhead by departing from the principles of Socialism. Take [this document] back; I say to you, take it back and re-examine it. . . . Inject into it the rich red blood of Socialist objectives and swing the electorate solidly behind you.'[3]

Moving the rejection of *Industry and Society* in these terms Jim Campbell caught the self-conscious devotion to 'old-fashioned Socialism' which flavours the discussions of the NUR. The smallest (and most suspiciously secretive) of the 'Big Six', the National Union of Railwaymen still holds almost 300,000 votes. It may be no coincidence that, like the AEU, it is both left wing and has a small Annual General Meeting—of President, General Secretary, and seventy-seven delegates elected by districts on the single transferable vote.

On most key issues since the war the NUR has sided with the left-wing opposition. In 1943 it voted decisively for 'Progressive Unity', and clung to the policy until after 1946. Later it opposed the direction of labour and, from 1951, fought the wage freeze. Since 1951 Annual General Meetings have almost

[1] Thus, at the 1952 TUC, USDAW was surprised to find that the General Council was accepting its composite resolution on wages and the cost of living. Right-wing unions announced that they would support the USDAW resolution in preference to a militant ETU motion. USDAW accordingly voted for the ETU resolution as well as its own.
[2] Sources: NUR Rule Book, *The Railway Review*, Annual Reports. Interviews with union officials.
[3] *Report of the Labour Party Conference*, 1957, p. 132. The least communicative of unions, the NUR does not make full reports of its conferences public.

always been ready to support 'international trade union unity'—a reconciliation between the ICFTU and the WFTU—and have called for the lifting of 'trade bans' affecting Eastern Europe and China. Throughout the rearmament controversy in 1951-2 the NUR took the Bevanite line; it was one of the first unions to demand the withdrawal of foreign troops from Korea. Throughout these years the AGM worked within a framework of extreme-left Socialist shibboleths which in 1952 took it so far as to 'repudiate the approval by the Tory government of the American policy to extend the conflict in the Far East, including open war with China'. While the General Secretary, Mr J. B. Figgins, was not a Communist he frequently took positions on international issues which coincided with the Communist line.

Under his successors, Mr Jim Campbell and Mr Sidney Greene, the NUR has never been so immoderate. It backed every Bevanite cause by large majorities except, in 1955, Mr. Bevan himself. Its vote of seventy-eight to two against re-arming Germany was among the most decisive in the movement. It was quite in keeping with the AGM's line that the NUR was the only one of the Big Six to attack *Industry and Society* at the 1957 Conference. But AGMs have always rejected both extreme demands for expropriation of industries and the most 'advanced' positions on nuclear policy. The 1958 Conference wobbled towards the demands of the Campaign for Nuclear Disarmament in calling (by forty-six votes to thirty-one) for a British lead in refusing to set up missile bases, stopping hydrogen bomber patrols, and halting atomic stockpiling. But it rejected a call for unilateral disarmament by thirty-nine votes to eleven. Despite the gathering strength of the unilateralist movement the 1959 AGM not only voted by fifty-one to twenty-five against uni-lateralism, but reversed the decision of the previous conference. Mr Greene and his President, Mr Charles Evans, seem in the process of leading the AGM back from its most advanced commitments to left-wing Socialism.

But, with its overcharged agendas, the AGM makes relatively few political decisions. Those it does take are 'final and con-clusive and shall be accepted by all members of the Union'. All other political decisions are dealt with by an Executive sub-committee, whose recommendations, once approved by the lay

Executive, bind the NUR's delegates to the Party Conference as formally as the decisions of the Annual General Meeting, subject only to appeal to the next AGM. The Political Sub-Committee meets on the eve of Conference, with the union's Members of Parliament as advisers to consider all resolutions 'in the light of union policy' and to 'recommend whether the delegates should support, oppose, or have a free hand'. The delegation comprises the President, General Secretary, Assistant General Secretary, a member of the Executive and twelve lay members chosen by the single transferable vote. But its discretion is apparently confined to snap votes and references back. Few delegations are more tightly controlled than that of the NUR.

When forced to choose between extremism and orthodoxy the NUR shares the embarrassments of the AEU and USDAW. Until the past year or so it has been less ready than they to back the NEC, an attitude which is in accordance with the consistent militancy of the Annual General Meeting. Protests that mandates have been broken are rare. Apparently there has been only one appeal in recent years—against the Executive's decision to support Mr Gaitskell in 1955—and this was rejected at the 1956 AGM.

\* \* \* \*

These six unions have chosen radically different procedures for taking political decisions. Yet their experience is remarkably similar. The simple recital of the motions voted shows how far loyalty to the Labour Party and most of its policies is common ground. Conservative delegates are almost unknown. Policies which arouse furious debate outside may be taken as read within these conferences. Renowned for its 'moderation', the NUGMW congress nevertheless condemns Conservative Budgets, the Rent Act, Suez, or block grants to local authorities without a dissenting voice or a word of discussion. When the AEU and NUM vote their annual protestation of loyalty to Labour even the Communists must pay lip service.

Whether a union's conference is 'right' or 'left' the attitude to dissenters is broadly similar: left-wing dissent is respectable, right-wing opposition is not. Throughout the movement 'talking left' is listened to tolerantly. Under cover of such tolerance not only do genuine Socialists call for a return to the spirit of Keir Hardie, but Communists freely try to commit their union to supporting their policies at the Labour Party Conference. Only the most extreme attacks on a Labour Government or attempts to justify the crushing of the Hungarian Revolution provoke delegates to impatience with speakers from the far left. No one thinks of protesting when Mr Ted Hill declaims that 'The Tory Government have decided to declare war on the trade unions of this country in a more vicious way than any former Government. . . . This Tory Government is the most class-biased in living memory', though some might think his 'living memory' strangely short.

But delegates' patience is rapidly tried by the expression of views which are noticeably to the right of their own platform. It is doubtful whether Sir Thomas Williamson would get a hearing for his views on nationalization if he were a delegate to certain left-wing conferences, while in most unions a speaker who suggested that living standards had risen under the Conservatives would have run the risk of being shouted down even at the peak of full employment. No one would guess the strength of the working class Conservative vote from reading union conference reports.

Such inhibitions, combined with the system of choosing delegates in some unions, and the activities of organized factions in others, may mean that even questions which divide the Labour Party are scarcely discussed. At various times the AEU National Committee has unanimously favoured nationalization of the building industry, opposed differential rents, demanded the raising of all restrictions (armaments apparently included) on trade with Communist countries and calling on the next Labour Government to take 'immediate steps to introduce legislation to municipalize rented houses in such a way as to provide full security of tenure and rent control at pre-Rent Act valuation'. All these policies would be rejected by many Labour supporters.

Moreover, although every union conference produces hard-fought debates, many are dangerously one-sided. It is only where the platform or lay delegates put the opposing arguments that there is a chance that half-truths, misconceptions or misstatements are corrected. Despite the experience of trade agreements with Communist countries conference after conference still discusses expansion of east-west trade as if it were genuinely likely to solve Britain's economic problems, as if it made no difference whether the motion specified whether arms were to be included or not. The engineers may indeed believe to a man that American rocket bases in Britain are an obstacle to world peace, but there was no true discussion before the National Committee voted. Many unions have decided on matters as controversial as hydrogen weapons and wider nationalization after hearing only one side of the argument. Whatever the final decision it would have a greater claim to be representative if it were reached after a full and genuine debate. But of the six union conferences we have discussed only the USDAW ADM includes spokesmen of almost every viewpoint.

While the unions are constantly under pressure to take decisions 'democratically' the experience of these six unions shows just how difficult it is. Like all voluntary associations which attempt to form policies democratically, the unions suffer grave institutional limitations. Some of these are commonplace to sociologists or political scientists, but the repeated attacks from both right and left in recent years on the 'representativeness' of union decisions suggests that the extent of these inherent limitations is still not understood. We have already seen how far apathy prevents union decisions being a full expression of members' views, and how limited are so many union conference debates. Now we shall look in turn at the successive limitations which confront any union in the attempt to make sure that the vote which is finally cast at the Labour Party Conference genuinely represents the membership.

### The Frequency of Conferences

Although the classic place for trade unions to form their policies is the annual conference, many unions in fact meet only every two or three years. Some, such as the British Iron, Steel & Kindred Trades' Association, and the National Society of Metal Mechanics, have no policy conference at all.[1] 'What

---

[1] V. L. Allen gives details of the frequency and powers of union conferences, in *Power in Trade Unions*, pp. 72 ff.

right has Harry Douglass (of BISAKTA) to get up there and say that we support German rearmament?' demanded an indignant steel worker. 'He's never asked us'. During the Bevanite controversy the unions which met biennially also came under attack. 'How can Arthur Deakin make out he's got a mandate? He hasn't had a conference for eighteen months', grumbled a left-wing trade unionist. It may indeed be more difficult for unions which meet so infrequently to be fully in touch with their rank and file on political questions. However, if they are less acquainted with their members' wishes this has no consistent effect on their voting at the Party Conference; the group splits about evenly between left and right-wing unions.

Infrequent meetings obviously make it difficult for the members to contribute effectively to the formation of their union's policy. None of the unions which meets every three years discusses any significant amount of political business, while few of those which meet every two years can give much time. Some, such as the National Union of Boot and Shoe Operatives, almost wholly ignore political resolutions. Obviously two years' accumulation of industrial business must be dealt with first. Though some unions which meet biennially such as the TGWU, find time for politics, they still work under grave limitations. Many of the ephemeral issues discussed at a 1959 biennial conference would be quite dead before the 1960 Party Conference; other decisions would be hopelessly dated, while many matters that came up in 1960 would never have been thought of in 1959.[1] The most a biennial conference can do is to lay down the broad lines of political policy, inevitably leaving wide discretion to its executive and its delegations to interpret them. Unfortunately, through their preoccupation with matters of more immediate interest, or trivia like the repayment of postwar credits, the membership often fail even to do this much.

A union's political affiliation demands more attention to political policy than such infrequent conferences allow. Yet the frequency with which unions meet depends on their industrial

----

[1] In the year that these unions meet they are in only a slightly less favourable position to make meaningful decisions than unions which meet every year.

L

needs. Some introduced biennial or triennial conferences to enable their members to control long-term policy without becoming bogged down in petty day-to-day controversies. The Plumbing Trades' Union, usually on the left, claimed in adopting a biennial conference, 'The BDC will be a policy-making body, thus providing us with the opportunity to review the immediate past and keep abreast of developments in this fast-moving age'.[1] This may be true of industrial matters; it is not so true of political questions. However, although the NUGMW changed from a biennial to an annual Congress at the end of the war, most of the unions still meeting less frequently show little sign of changing their habits. The TGWU, National Union of Public Employees and Typographical Association conferences have all voted several times not to meet every year.[2] It may be desirable to form policies freshly each year for the TUC and the Labour Party Conference, but political issues are not important enough for any union to switch to an annual meeting on these grounds alone. Conferences are expensive; they involve the staff in heavy preparatory work, and they take the officials away from organizing. All these arguments weigh heavily. Though the executives who employ them doubtless also prefer not to have to face their members more often than is necessary, the feeble support for annual conferences among their militant members suggests that they, too, are content with the system, even though it does limit their union's political representativeness.

## Annual Conferences and the Making of Policy

From USDAW at Easter the conference season runs through to the Fire Brigades' Union in August, with the TUC at the beginning of September, and the Labour Party a month later. But the cycle really starts months before. The delegates have scarcely arrived home from the Labour Party Conference before they must submit resolutions for the union conferences which are held at Easter. Since branches must have time to discuss the conference agenda and propose amendments, most resolutions

[1] *Plumbing Trades Union Journal*, December 1947.
[2] *Minutes of the 1951 BDC. Minutes of Second Rules Revision Conference*, 1956. *Report of the Delegate Meeting*, 1950, pp. 30–4.

on the agendas of trade union conferences reflect the preoccu-
pations of the militants between December and March.

Most unions permit the submission of emergency resolutions
at the conference itself but, with agendas invariably over-
crowded, Standing Orders Committees are always reluctant to
let pass more than one or two. Sometimes (as in the NUGMW)
the Executive submits special political motions just before the
opening of the conference—but these cannot be numerous—and
the branches complain if they are submitted too late for full
discussion. They are in any case only palliatives. A union's
political decisions cannot be more up-to-date than its own
conference—which means that they are almost always six
months old when the Labour Party Conference meets, and that
they may reflect the political situation ten months previously.

Those months may be important. The pound was devalued
in the summer of 1949; in 1950 the Korean war broke out; in
1954 the proposed European Defence Community collapsed
after every union conference had made its decision on German
rearmament. In 1955 resolutions drafted when Mr Bevan was on
the verge of expulsion were discussed at conferences held in
the shadow of the election; the mandates had to be considered
in a profoundly altered industrial climate months later. In 1957
there was a balance of payments crisis; in 1958 a shift in Cyprus
policy, and in 1959 the Party's support of a non-nuclear club
was announced after many unions had met.

Decisions on nationalization, social services, housing, and
education date relatively little. But, nationalization apart, they
are relatively little discussed at union conferences. Other
decisions may be hopelessly out of date when they arise at the
Party Conference. 'Cut the call up' resolutions voted at Whit-
suntide in 1950 made little sense when the Party met in September. When the Communist-led unions decided that anger
over Hungary had died down enough for them to resume their
campaign for joint action between the WFTU and the ICFTU,
their calculations were brusquely destroyed by the execution
of Imre Nagy. Sometimes events make a resolution so obviously
inapplicable that it has to be cast aside as no longer binding.
More often the wording still covers the facts of the new situation, although had it been debated by the union conference in

the changed circumstances its decision might have been quite different.[1]

When the Party was issuing policy statements for discussion at Conference the time lag between union conferences and the Party Conference was more serious than ever. Most of the statements were published too late for branches to take note of them in forming their resolutions for union conferences, too late even for many of the conferences. Not one affiliated union discussed even half the policy statements, and most debated none. Although *Industry and Society, National Superannuation*, and *Public Enterprise* were discussed in several unions, there is no trace that any union directly considered *Economic Aid, The Smaller Territories, Personal Freedom*, or (the NUAW excepted), *Prosper the Plough*. Union delegations to Conference often had little more than the vaguest guidance from earlier union decisions. When Mr Frank Cousins declared that to accept the continued existence of Public Schools would be 'going back on Socialism',[2] he may indeed have spoken for the members of the TGWU—but the union had made no recent decision on the issue. Some unions claimed to have supported documents like *The Plural Society* because their conference had voted in general terms for colonies to have the widest possible self-government. Although every union had a policy of sorts on the extension of nationalization, only the handful of organizations which had discussed *Industry and Society* at their 1957 conferences could have had any clear policy to guide their delegations on the controversial proposal that the State should buy shares in private industry.

The unions cannot be blamed for the limitations imposed by the calendar. They must meet in time to prepare their policies for the TUC. Since large conferences are out of the question during the holiday season, they are forced to meet between late spring and early summer,[3] and must in consequence, run the risk

---

[1] 'Changed circumstances' is not exclusively a right-wing cry. In 1951 the Yorkshire Area NUM put down a resolution to support Labour foreign policy. Scottish Area came to the conference prepared to vote against it, but 'in the light of the explanation given by Mr Jones, and because of the new developments (a truce in Korea), the Scottish delegation is prepared to accept it'. *Report*, p. 130.

[2] *Report of the Labour Party Conference*, 1958, p. 101.

[3] Suggestions that unions should hold referenda are impracticable since the final text of the resolutions is not known in time.

of being unduly dated. The constituencies, which can brief their delegates on the eve of the Conference, have no such problems.

## How much Politics?

Crowded agendas are the bane of every union conference.[1] Even the AEU, with its small National Committee meeting for ten days, has not been able to cope with all the business.[2] Unions with larger conferences would find a ten-day meeting prohibitively expensive. Even unions which have set up trade-group or sectional meetings to lighten the burden on their main conference are troubled with overloaded agendas. Some organizations regularly finish their business—but only by drastically limiting the number of resolutions that may be admitted.[3] In others the Standing Orders Committee has to persuade branches to withdraw, remit, or composite their resolutions, since if every resolution goes on the agenda many will never be reached.

Purely political issues rarely have priority. Sometimes they may not be discussed until the entire industrial agenda is completed. Under such rules the Clerical & Administrative Workers' Union's 1954 conference was unable to deal with German rearmament, industrial de-rating, education, colonial affairs, five-power meetings, the Rent Act, admission of China to the United Nations, east-west trade, disarmament, or the South-East Asia Treaty Organization. In the CAWU, as in the Union of Post Office Workers, and the Association of Engineering & Shipbuilding Draughtsmen, standing orders may be suspended to take resolutions out of order, but obviously only a few resolutions can be promoted out of turn, and demands to suspend standing orders are often rejected.

All too often political issues are discussed at the end of conference when delegates are racing through the agenda, speakers

---

[1] The NUTGW BDC in 1955 had 300 resolutions on its agenda; the AUBTW Agenda for the 1955 NDC contained 328 resolutions. The 1954 NUAW BDC agenda listed more than 500 resolutions; and the 1955 ADC of the Boilermakers' had 169 resolutions. It lasted five days and dealt with seventy-nine resolutions.

[2] The National Committee costs about £5,000, and the USDAW ADM costs about £5,800, although it lasts only three days.

[3] The United Textile Factory Workers' Association, and the NUM both finish their conference agenda because their constituent unions can submit only a small number of motions.

are limited to three minutes, and debate is discouraged. For example, during one morning, the 1955 conference of the AESD:

accepted the Standing Orders Committee's recomendation that speakers be limited to five minutes for movers, two for others;

considered a resolution on *The Draughtsman*, with seven amendments;

held a long private session on officials' salaries;

discussed a resolution and amendment calling for more progressive policies in the Labour Party;

made nominations for the General Council of the TUC, Standing Orders Committee of the TUC and the National Executive Committee of the Labour Party;

passed a composite resolution on racial discrimination;

deplored old age pension rates (five amendments);

considered the voting powers of Trades Councils at the TUC;

declined to urge that English and Welsh workers might have facilities similar to those contained in the Education (Scotland) Act, 1918;

expressed itself perturbed at the school building programme and the supply of teachers;

debated changing the name of the Association;

disposed of a resolution, with six amendments, on the rates of branch honoraria;

went to lunch.[1]

Some unions, like the AEU and USDAW, make determined attempts to spread their political debates through the whole conference. Others set a morning or a whole day aside for political matters. The Amalgamated Society of Woodworkers hears a Parliamentary Report from one of its MPs, followed by questions and the discussion of a few political motions. Even this allocation is not universally popular. 'We waste far too much damn time on politics', confided a member of the ASW's General Council. One of the most political unions, the ETU, devotes slightly over one-third of its conference time (equivalent to one and one half days) to political resolutions. This is an

[1] *Report of the RCC*, pp. 370–417.

allocation which the most loyal Labour trade unionists would not be willing to exceed. Only the London Typographical Society is small and compact enough to hold a separate political conference—and this attracts only about forty members out of 9,000—compared with about 500 attending the Annual General Meeting.[1]

The most that can be fairly expected of the unions, as they come to the Party Conference, is that their conferences will have taken decisions on the major issues, so far as they had arisen by then. In general, most large unions will have directly applicable decisions on about one-third of the questions that come before the Party Conference, partially-relevant decisions on about a further third, and no appropriate decision on the remainder. They usually find time to make policy on matters that affect their industrial interests, but union conferences give their delegations far less guidance on party organization, local government, agriculture, many aspects of housing policy, commonwealth relations, education, the distributive system, and some of the social services. Year after year many union conferences reaffirm their faith in nationalization, or they vote such motions as:

'This National Committee declares its opposition to the policies being operated by the Tory Government. The blundering intervention in Egypt which has brought with it such drastic economic consequences is now followed by a threatened increase in rent. Working people will not shoulder these burdens and we reject any suggestion of sinking differences for the so-called good of the Nation. We call for a great united campaign from all sections of the Labour Movement to remove the Tory Government from office and secure a General Election.'[2]

But they almost wholly neglect a problem like the comprehensive school. Given that union conference debates reflect the interests of the branches—which are given to follow fashion and sudden enthusiasms in the way we have already seen—it seems inevitable that unions will come to Conference patchily and imperfectly prepared. By no system of expedients can union conferences lasting from three to five days, dealing with both

[1] *London Typographical Journal*, April 1954.
[2] *Minutes and Proceedings of the National Committee*, 1957, p. 270.

industrial and political questions, discuss thoroughly all the items which will occupy the Labour Party Conference lasting five days. Sheer shortage of time limits the effectiveness of union policy-making.

### Executives and Policy-Making

In unions with no annual conference the influence of the Executive on political decisions is obviously considerable; it is almost as great in unions which meet less than once a year. But even in unions with annual conferences the Executive often has a wide discretion. In the National Society of Operative Printers & Assistants (Natsopa), whose conference discusses almost no political business, the rules provide that 'Natsopa's line of policy is one for the Executive Committee of the Society. The EC takes cognizance of resolutions properly passed at the appropriate meetings held in accordance with the constitution laid down in the Society's rules'. The left-wing Amalgamated Union of Foundry Workers' rules provide that 'The Council shall consider resolutions from branches with a view to instructing representatives respecting their votes'. The NUR and NUGMW Executives have very wide powers to decide political policy. The extent to which such powers are used varies considerably. The NUR's and the Association of Engineering & Shipbuilding Draughtsmen's Political Sub-Committee go through the Party Conference agenda making almost all the major decisions left open by their annual conferences. In other unions, such as the Typographical Association, the Executive usually instructs the delegation on only one or two major issues.[1] Most executives of unions with under 50,000 members decide only the big questions: 'It's simply not worth our time spending hours going over the agenda, when you know quite well that the composites will be completely different. And anyway we've only got 15,000 votes.'

In some of the smallest unions neither the conference nor the Executive actively makes policy. The National Union of Scale-makers, with 2,500 members scattered about the country, cannot afford to deal with the Party Conference agenda at its

---

[1] In 1954 the Executive mandated the delegation on only one issue—German rearmament. *The Typographical Circular*, November 1954.

monthly executive meetings. The tiny vote of such a union is usually cast with far less discussion than that of a constituency with the same membership. These unions preserve a continuity of policy if the same delegate attends Conference for several years, but if the delegate changes they may endorse quite contradictory points of view over several years, or they may give inconsistent votes at the TUC or the Labour Party Conference. Many small unions almost always support the National Executive, partly out of general confidence in the leadership. 'We don't always have very strong views on some of the things that come up, and then we generally vote for the NEC, because it's their job to know, after all'. This attitude, sometimes found in larger unions, also reflects a natural fellow-feeling for another Executive. Fortunately these haphazard or unthinking votes add up to very little.

Executive determination of political policy has some practical advantages. Decisions can be taken just before the Conference, on the basis of the so-called 'Final Agenda' (though not the composite resolutions). They cannot become seriously dated, and an Executive does not have to waste time discussing issues which will not be raised. An Executive Committee can also co-ordinate industrial and political decisions. The Typographical Association's leaders argued (successfully) on a proposal that the Executive should have the power to instruct the delegation how to vote:

'We wish to ensure that in future there shall be some defined policy that is a TA policy, in relation to the important motions. . . . [The existing rule] leaves the decision on the votes on all issues to the delegates who are representing you at the conferences. That is not any criticism of the many able men who have represented you at these conferences in the past. We do think, however, that if you go there representing an Association, then you should have some instructions issued to them beforehand instead of decisions being left to them when they get there and hear what is said at these conferences.'[1]

Yet there are serious objections to Executives deciding how their union's vote shall be cast at the Party Conference.

[1] *Report of the Delegate Meeting*, 1953, pp. 72-5.

Many militants feel that even a lay Executive Council's views are too 'official', too divorced from the wishes of the rank-and-file.

Naturally Executives disagree: 'I can't understand all this business about being unrepresentative', a General Secretary complained. 'I talk to the government, I help settle strikes, I negotiate wage increases. Nobody says I'm not representative *then*. But the minute it comes to politics someone says I'm "unrepresentative", that I don't know what my members want'. Other leaders argue that 'The rules put on us the responsibility for seeing that conference decisions are carried out, and for taking action where conference has been silent. We cannot turn the job over to a delegation which has no responsibility to the members'.

These arguments have some substance. At times Executives, which are elected by the members, have a greater claim to speak for the whole union than a small and often unrepresentative delegation. Yet Executives are elected for their industrial abilities. A man's skill as a negotiator or his courageous militancy do not necessarily fit him to represent the union politically. In left-wing unions particularly the cry frequently goes up, 'Don't think about his politics—vote for the best trade unionist'. Many a Communist has been elected in such conditions. Having made such a plea, how can it be claimed that he is fitted to take 'representative' decisions on foreign policy? Delegates to the Party Conference must either be members of the Labour Party or eligible for membership. Short of deliberate fraud, and the presence of a few fellow-travellers, the union's vote is in pro-Labour hands if the delegation decides how it shall be cast. But Executive Committees may be of any political complexion. Through the mandates they issue, members of anti-Labour parties can have a say in Labour Party policy. Some fifteen unions have been sporadically or continuously under such influence since the war. In many others there is little check that the views of the Executive on political issues are similar to those of their rank and file. Finally, it is difficult to reconcile the extensive role of many union Executive Committees in the determining of Conference voting, with the clear understanding in the Party Constitution that—inconvenient though it may be

—there should be the widest possible participation in the forming of the Party's policy.

## Mandating

How far mandating is compatible with the idea that the Labour Party Conference is a deliberative body has never been satisfactorily discussed within the Labour Party. Most unions and local Parties mandate on some questions, although some delegates are tied hand and foot, while others are bound only on a handful of questions. Almost every union considers a directly applicable motion voted by its conference to be binding on the delegation. Breaking mandate is a serious matter. The problems that mandating raises—and the passion that breaking mandate can stir—were amply revealed in the most hotly-debated case since the war, the Amalgamated Society of Woodworkers' vote on German rearmament.

The 1954 Annual Delegate Conference of the ASW voted by a large majority against rearming Germany, stating specifically 'we request that Conference instruct the Society representatives to the TUC and the Labour Party Conference to secure the reversal of this tragic decision'.[1] There was a long debate, in which both the Society's Members of Parliament and Mr George Brinham (their member on the Party's NEC), argued the official case. The ASW delegation to the TUC duly opposed rearmament, but a month later its delegation at the Party Conference decided, by a large majority, to support the National Executive—thus assuring its victory.

Protests poured in. Many appeared in the *Daily Worker* before they had reached the union's office. It was alleged that Mr Brinham had forced the delegation to support rearmament because he had been threatened with the loss of his seat on the NEC if the vote went the other way. After protracted recrimination the issue came before the Annual Delegate Conference where, although the debate centred on the breach of mandate on German rearmament, it raised a longstanding controversy about the power of the conference to lay down union policy.

[1] Sources for this incident: *Report of the Annual Delegate Conference* 1954 *and* 1955, *The Woodworkers' Journal*, November 1954, *The New Statesman*, July 14, 1956, and the *Daily Worker*, October-November 1954. The final vote was 108:79 for the Executive.

The Executive argued, against the conference laying down mandates, that the delegation taking the decision had been representative—including nine lay members elected by general ballot, five (lay) members of the General Council, three (official) members of the Executive Council, and the General Secretary, with the two union MPs present but not voting. It was wholly unrealistic to mandate absolutely on international issues, for circumstances had changed even during the four weeks between the TUC and the Labour Party. It was quite proper to reconsider the vote; 'The principle which has pervaded our Society's history and constitution is the belief in the wisdom of a flexible representative authority, as against an inflexible mandated authority'. This was the rule at the union's Annual Delegate Conference, its local Management Committees, and on other bodies within the union. It should apply equally to the Labour Party Conference. Society delegates must have the power to interpret decisions in the light of the circumstances of the time.

The opposition, pointing to the rule that 'in cases *where policy has not been decided by the Annual Delegate Conference*, the Society delegation shall consider such resolutions, and the majority decision shall be binding on all delegates', contended that delegates had no discretion where the conference had clearly laid down policy. But the nub of the problem was revealed in a speaker's fear that:

'The people who are in control of the policy and administration will naturally be the people who will be able to stretch the elastic the way they want to go, and we who represent the rank-and-file of our Movement, will no longer have control of the machine. Conference cannot be a policy-making body if we allow circumstances which change from time to time to determine the decisions of individual delegations.'

If mandates are to be open to constant 'interpretation' the discussion of political issues at conferences loses much of its point, and the rank and file feel cheated of their influence on Party policy. Yet, another delegate countered,

'If . . . you tie down your delegate in May to a decision in September . . ., then the decisions of this Conference, so far as the affairs of the country are concerned will become abortive.

You might just as well as the General Secretary to have cards sent to the [Labour Party] Conference instead of sending delegates, and save money.'

The purist line that all conference decisions must be maintained intact is obviously untenable. Yet the point at which a mandate may legitimately be broken is likely to be controversial. Had circumstances changed enough in 1954, when the European Defence Community proposals had collapsed, and with M. Mendès-France awaiting the opening of the London conference even as the Labour Party Conference convened? In the Transport Salaried Staffs' Association and the NUM delegates argued that these events justified their switching to opposition to the official line. In the AEU and the ASW the same events were used to justify changing to support of the NEC. This vote raised a special problem; was it legitimate for a union which opposed rearmament, to switch to supporting it because it believed that the survival of the leadership was more important? The issue was never raised at the Woodworkers' conference, although some ASW delegates to the Party Conference must have had it in mind. In the end the ASW Annual Delegate Conference affirmed the right of the ADC to be the Society's policy-making organ, but endorsed its delegation's decision.

'Changed circumstances' is a dangerous weapon in the hands of an unscrupulous leader, who has disapproved of his union conference's decision. If made too frequently it isolates the ordinary member still further from any effective voice in policy-making. Such abuses are, in practice, extremely rare. It is much less frequently recognized that if circumstances genuinely have changed, holding a mandate may misrepresent the members just as greatly as breaking mandate with insufficient cause. The instance of the TGWU and German rearmament is a clear case in point. The delegation chairman ruled that a pair of three-year-old conference decisions, rejecting violently-worded opposition to German rearmament mandated the delegation to support the NEC.[1] He would never have accepted such decisions

[1] For one curious interpretation of a mandate see p. 202.

as binding had it not served his purpose. Similarly, it was ludicrous to claim that resolutions passed by union conferences during the Battle of Stalingrad in favour of Communist affiliation to the Labour Party, did not need reconsideration when the Cold War was breaking out. In such cases, no one can tell what the membership really thought, but it was apparent that clinging to an outdated mandate in drastically altered circumstances can give a union's decisions a spurious legitimacy.

Finally, unions must re-examine their mandates in the light of the Conference agenda. As Mr Attlee has remarked:

'generally speaking the circulated agenda becomes transformed in the course of business by consultation between groups in order to obtain support for essentials rather than the wording, so that the delegate may find that in the result he has to interpret his instructions, and the light in which he interprets them is that of the discussion.'[1]

The *Final Agenda* circulated to organizations before Conference contains four to five hundred resolutions and amendments, many of them repetitive (in 1955 twenty-one resolutions dealt solely with the length of National Service). In the weeks before Conference the National Executive persuades many organizations to withdraw or combine resolutions. The major issues are dealt with at group meetings of the interested organizations and NEC spokesmen, on the Saturday before Conference opens. These meetings usually produce one or several resolutions, normally including one which is acceptable to the Party leadership. About half the agenda is boiled down to about twenty composite resolutions (which may not be debated even then). The drafting of these composites leads frequently to discussion or reversal of mandates. Indeed, the Conference Arrangements Committee's genius for persuading organizations to put forward a composite resolution which contains some completely unacceptable phrase has often stood the Party machine in good stead.

Connoisseurs of committeemanship will appreciate the skill of the NEC representative in 1955, of whom a delegate complained 'He might have helped the delegates to sort out the

[1] *The Labour Party in Perspective*, p. 79.

resolutions. But it seems he just let them argue around the point for most of the time, and then decided to drop nearly all the resolutions except that from Govan (calling for nationalization without compensation)'. It was the most extreme pro-nationalization motion on the agenda. On another occasion a delegate came away from the meeting saying happily 'He's given us everything we asked for', convinced that he had struck a blow for Socialism. He never did realize how successfully he had been hoodwinked. As Mr Bevan remarked with feeling:

'. . . composite resolutions are apt to be clumsy instruments. There is no other way of getting things before the conference, but in our own experience over and over again we have found that when we are composited we find ourselves in strange company, and we find that we are having to vote for things with which we disagree in order to vote for the things with which we agree.'[1]

Yet there must be some boiling down of the resolutions, and it is hard to see how this can be done without distorting the intentions of some of the sponsors.[2]

Union delegates must still compare the motions on the Party Conference agenda with those voted by their own conferences. At the extreme this has meant deciding whether a 300-word motion voted by a union conference implies support of an eleven-point resolution on a slightly different theme at the Party Conference.[3] All too often the unions' own motions, which have passed through the same hazardous compositing process, simply will not stand up to this kind of exegesis. In 1957 the crucial debate at the Party Conference turned on whether a Labour Government should *unilaterally* refuse to test, manufacture or

---

[1] *Report of the Labour Party Conference*, 1957, p. 180.

[2] For another complaint about the way delegates hoping to forward a nationalization motion were outwitted see *Report of the Annual Delegate Meeting of the Amalgamated Union of Foundry Workers*, 1949, p. 167. On one occasion it was alleged that the Committee successfully encouraged the Group Meeting to nominate the most antagonistic mover of a nationalization resolution.

[3] The Plumbing Trades Union delegation to the 1958 TUC were 'quite unable to agree on the interpretation' of a motion voted on nuclear weapons and rocket bases by their 1958 Biennial Delegate Conference. (*PTU Journal*, December, 1958 and *Report of the BDC*, pp. 42–3.)

On the other hand, the Plasterers' delegation would have little difficulty in following a mandate to 'support all motions against the manufacture and testing of H-Bombs'. (*Quarterly Report*, September 1957).

use nuclear weapons. The TGWU delegation, turning for guidance to their own conference's 'mandate' found it referred to 'the immediate cessation of H-Bomb tests by all powers; total abolition of the H-Bomb on a universal basis, both in manufacture and stocks; directions of all researches into nuclear energy along peaceful lines. . . .' It was pious, but it was scarcely helpful. Understandably the delegates sharply disagreed on the line this implied. In the end Mr Cousins made a speech which Conference took to favour unilateralism but voted against it. The following year at least three trade union delegations were completely unable to agree on the interpretation of their conference's policy on nuclear weapons. Such problems arise in most years.

Although the compositing process often throws mandates into the melting pot, Mr Attlee's remarks on the problem of mandating seem unduly complacent. He argued:

'It might be thought that [the instruction] of delegates meant that speeches and discussions would be ineffectual, the issues having been decided previously. This happens no doubt on some subjects, but [the process of compositing leads delegates to interpret their instructions in the light of the discussion]. Frequently, too, the issues which emerge at the Conference arise out of the Annual Report or from some circumstances which were not envisaged at the time of instructions of delegates. There is, therefore, an opportunity for the Conference to be swayed by argument, and in practice, this often occurs.'[1]

In fact, there has been only a handful of 'snap' votes and references back on important issues since the war, and almost all could have been foreseen.[2] The larger unions re-examine their mandates within their delegation meetings rather than in the conference hall—where the dispersion of the larger delegations makes reconsideration physically difficult.

Sometimes an exceptionally divided or uninformed delegation agrees to decide 'in the light of the debate'. But normally the large unions decide their vote on every major issue before the

---

[1] *The Labour Party in Perspective*, p. 79.

[2] The most important references back, on expulsion of dissident members, and the affiliation of the Communist Party to the Labour Party were all well advertised.

Conference has even begun. At no time are they open to any public persuasion. Exceptions, such as the TGWU's reconsideration of its H-Bomb policy during a lunch-break in 1957, and a plea from Mr Robens, for USDAW, that the platform should 'help people like Frank Cousins and other unions here' by giving assurances before the vote, are rare.

The NEC still needs to woo the constituency parties and the small unions, while sometimes a union makes its support conditional on receiving specific assurances during a debate. In 1957 some unions felt that they must have a public statement that the Labour Party's plans to invest in private industry did not preclude further 'old-style' nationalization before they could reconcile support for *Industry and Society* with their mandates.[1] But precisely because it knows in advance what support it can count on the NEC faces Conference either assured of victory or with a shrewd idea of how much ballast must be thrown overboard to win over the wavering votes.

Far more frequently than is ever imagined or admitted the real decision lies with the delegations. Union leaders often insist that their delegations simply follow mandates on almost every issue. But the decision to hold a mandate is often as important and debatable as the decision to reject one. Since union delegations, executives, and conferences are often agreed on many issues, mandates are challenged more rarely than could be justified.

The handful of executive-controlled unions excepted, therefore, the delegations' influence is considerable. While the 'representativeness' of union decisions is inevitably limited, the way in which the delegation is made up may go far towards giving the voting a semblance of conforming to the members' wishes—even though the wide discretion confided to the delegation makes it impossible to associate a significant proportion of members directly with the decisions taken.

## *The Delegations*

Only a handful of unions—the largest being the Transport Salaried Staffs' Association—elect all their delegation. Normally

[1] Cf., Mr Carron's speech, *Report of the Labour Party Conference*, 1957, p. 137. See also the *Post*, January 25, 1958.

M

delegations are chosen to represent lay members, Executive and officials. The members have a say only in the choice of their rank and file representatives—if that. Some unions choose their lay delegates by national or regional ballots, others save expense by selecting them at the annual conference. Some unions (notably the TGWU) put the selection in the hands of their regional committees—the members have no direct say in the composition of the delegation, and their indirect influence must be negligible.

Most unions require that their delegates be members in good standing for between one and five years; limit the number of consecutive years anyone may serve on the delegation; and prohibit any lay member from serving on the TUC and Labour Party delegations in the same year. A few demand that delegates be members of the Labour Party, but most require simply that they pay the political levy and be eligible for Party membership.

There is usually even less interest in electing conference delegates than is customary in trade union elections; even where there is a second ballot the successful delegate can rarely claim the support of more than one in ten eligible members.[1] Informed voting is almost impossible. Most unions forbid canvassing or campaigning; in the NUR, where candidates can advertise in *The Railway Review*, they use slogans like 'Able, efficient, conscientious' without a word about policy.

Often elections are held before anyone can know what issues the delegates will have to decide.[2] A handful of active members may know the candidates' views through annual conference or work on district committees, but even a conscientious lay member is unlikely to have heard of more than one or two candidates, much less know with any accuracy what they stand for. Industrial experience (usually indicated on the ballot), and reputation, often count more than being 'right' or 'left'. Although religious factions or organized political minorities sometimes run 'slates'

---

[1] The AEU's experience is typical. 176 of nearly 400 branches of the Boilermakers' Society took no part in the election of delegates to the 1959 Conference (*Monthly Report*, March 1959). In the Patternmakers' Association thirty-six of 133 branches cast no votes in 1958 and the most successful candidate had only 709 votes (*Monthly Report*, June 1958).

[2] Several unions call for nominations in November for the following October: the National Union of Printing, Bookbinding & Paper Workers chose its delegation to the 1959 Party Conference in May 1958.

of candidates, it is almost impossible for an ordinary rank-and-filer deliberately to choose a delegation which matches his political colour.[1]

Whether chosen by district committees or directly elected the typical union delegate is a man (women delegates are few) in his mid-forties, holding branch office, a zealous trade unionist, but not necessarily much interested in politics. He is neither a puppet nor a man of straw, although the intricacies of Conference procedure are sometimes beyond him. While Conference is a welcome late holiday for him and his wife, he is earnest and conscientious enough at the delegation meetings. Usually he believes far more in the power of resolutions to transform a situation than the officials, and is extremely conscious of being a spokesman for the 'ordinary' member. Yet it is largely a triumph of fortune over the system if the votes he casts really represent those members.[2]

Some unions (chiefly the TGWU and NUGMW) are criticized for including so many officials in their delegations. If officials are elected—as in the Transport Salaried Staffs' Association—there can be little complaint. More often they attend ex-officio or are nominated by the Executive. No one would seriously contest the need for the General Secretary to attend—some unions make attendance at Conference one of his official duties. Whether a union needs to take along organizers, finance and administrative officers is far more questionable. 'We are just seeing that every section of the union is represented', say defenders of the practice. Yet the officials are represented out of all proportion to their numbers or the importance of the situation. The Labour Party Conference rarely discusses issues so complicated that specialist officials are needed, while the General Secretary alone can assure respect for mandates, and tell lay delegates the background to the decisions. Officials are elected for their industrial ability; an organizer has no special interests at stake which merit his inclusion.

There is always the danger that a caucus of officials may

---

[1] These considerations are only slightly mitigated when elections are held by region.

[2] Although some Constituency Labour Parties carefully select their delegate, many are only too pleased to send someone who can pay his own fare, or who has the leisure to go, without looking too closely at his political views.

outwit or outvote the lay delegates, thwarting the members' true wishes. This sometimes happens. But the claim of rank-and-file delegates to represent the members better than the officials is far from safely established. During the long wrangle between the AEU delegation and its Executive Council there was no evidence which side really spoke for the ordinary member. Over-representation of the officials has achieved just the open discussion in some unions that it is alleged to prevent. A determined General Secretary, exploiting procedural devices in collusion with his Chairman, can run rings around lay delegates, whose committeemanship and knowledge of union procedure and policies are inferior to his. Officials, who know all the General Secretary's wiles, and who also know how to sway committees, may lead (or constitute) the opposition. Just as some of the fiercest attacks on the platform at the USDAW and Amal-gamated Society of Woodworkers' Conferences are led by full-time officials, so, in several unions, the officials rather than the rank-and-file have prevented the General Secretary dominating the delegation.

The smallest unions have no such embarrassments. They leave attendance at Conference to the General Secretary (plus a member of the Executive and a rank-and-filer if there are enough places). Some General Secretaries, unwilling to sit through the same debates twice, let another member of the Executive attend the Conference, and go only to the TUC. The Packing Case Makers alone elect their single delegate—who is usually a member of the Executive. Other small unions feel their vote to be so insignificant that organizing a proper election is not worth the trouble. Whatever the means of selection, it contributes little to making the ordinary member feel that there is any real link between him and the decisions made in his name.

## Leadership and Executive Power

Although the possibilities and limitations of leadership in large organizations are trite enough, they are still widely mis-understood by commentators on the movement. The Bevanite controversy was bedevilled by a popular stereotype of the trade union leader, incarnate in Arthur Deakin, impatient with democratic flummery, ruthless in squashing dissenters, personally decreeing how 800,000 votes should be cast. 'It is very nearly true to say', Mr John Freeman complained, 'that the policy of the Labour Party at the moment can be determined by four men meeting in a private room. . . .'[1] The description of one union leader in action, reported to McKenzie by a senior union official, is in keeping with this crude picture: The Party Conference delegation 'becomes like another conference with X (a prominent union official) in the chair using his particular talents so that he can play ducks and drakes with the delegates. 'X' can be very deaf at times, and if he doesn't want to hear an amendment at times he won't. . . .'[2] Since the Bevanite controversy the increasing tendency to personalize industrial disputes in terms of the humours of men like Mr Frank Cousins has reinforced the idea that union 'bosses' wield effective personal power with little restraint.

The picture is not wholly untrue. Some unions have been immensely influenced by a single man—Bryn Roberts of the National Union of Public Employees, W. J. Brown and the infant Civil Service Clerical Association, George Isaacs and Natsopa, or Ernest Bevin and the TGWU. Some General Secretaries really do make political policy. One explained: 'Nobody else is really interested, so it's all left to me'. This can happen even in larger organizations: In 1954 the President of the National Union of Agricultural Workers, Mr Gooch, voted on the Labour Party Executive against rearming Germany. Since the union had made no decision, his opposition aroused attacks in the Press and within the union. At once he sought, and received, the support of his union's Executive. Subsequently the NUAW Biennial Delegate Conference voted unanimously against German rearmament. Meanwhile, Mr Harold Collison, the General Secretary, continued to support rearmament on the General Council of the TUC. Since the NUAW had supported the NEC on every other major issue since the war, and its BDC had been just as systematically moderate, it seems highly unlikely that the conference would have unanimously opposed rearmament if Mr Gooch had supported the Party as usual.

[1] Speech at Brighton, September 12, 1953.
[2] *British Political Parties*, p. 492.

The best-documented instance of an Executive's power on political issues is the Electrical Trades Union. In recent years a majority of the ETU Executive have been Communists or sympathizers. The Communists' aim has been to bring the ETU's policies as close to the Communist line as is compatible with remaining within the Labour Party—as they are quite entitled to do. The ETU Executive has the advantage of being able to count on the support of the many Communist delegates to the annual Policy Conference, and of facing an inept and divided opposition of ex-Communists, left-wing Socialists, Trotskyists and other splinter groups, whose tactics are no match for those of Mr Frank Foulkes and Mr Frank Haxell. Nevertheless, the ETU Executive knows that it cannot impose its will on every political issue. How much less can a less secure Executive.

For several years after capturing control in 1944 the Communists were cautiously consolidating their position. In 1945 the Executive Council supported affiliation of the Communist Party to the Labour Party, but the non-Communists were still able to force a ballot of the membership in 1946, and the Executive was defeated. Accordingly the ETU voted against 'Progressive Unity' in 1946—but abstained on the ground that it lacked a mandate in the vote to amend the Party Constitution in such a way that the Communists were permanently barred from affiliation.[1]

At the 1946 TUC the union's non-Communist President, Mr Bussey, made a heated reply to criticisms by Mr Attlee that the union was proposing a Communist-inspired foreign policy motion. But by a three to two majority the union's 1947 conference refused to endorse the Executive's approval of Mr Bussey's speech.[2] But in 1950 *Electron* was publishing the May Day manifestoes of the ICFTU and WFTU side by side,[3] and the Policy Conference was persuaded to support both ICFTU and the WFTU rather than show a preference for either.[4] Since

[1] *Electrical Trades Journal*, July 1946.
[2] *Report of the Policy Conference*, 1947, pp. 166–75.
[3] *Electron*, May 1950.
[4] *Report of the Policy Conference*, 1951, p. 84. This result was achieved from a skilful use of standing orders. Conference voted first (190 to 103) a motion preferring ICFTU to WFTU, but then amended it (169 to 103) to support both. Had the agenda been taken in different order the conference would have opposed WFTU and supported ICFTU only.

then meeting after meeting has urged that ICFTU and the WFTU should unite or negotiate.[1]

In recent years the ETU Executive has been confident of having its way on every question where the positions of Communists and of the extreme left-wing of the Labour Party are similar. The occasions in the past decade when the two have diverged have been relatively rare, and not all have been discussed. But when such differences do occur the Executive has learned to be prudent. What will happen at the Policy Conference often depends on the explicitness with which motions take the Communist line. The 1952 conference refused (158:142 with 16 abstaining) to agree that *any* member might represent the ETU at *any* body to which the union was affiliated. This amounted to a claim that the union's Communist President and General Secretary should be allowed to attend the Party Conference as delegates and that Communists should be delegates to Constituency Labour Parties.[2] This demand was rejected again by the 1953 Conference (165:151),[3] but in later years it has been smuggled through in the guise of a call for 'the removal of bans and proscriptions' with little difficulty.[4]

The union's 1950 Conference voted that 'all available means must be used to ensure peace. . . .' intending, apparently, to express support for a five-power pact. But the Executive took this as ground for affiliation to the British Peace Committee (proscribed by the Labour Party as a Communist Front in the same year), and circulated the Stockholm Appeal to shop stewards. Vigorous protests from branches led to a Special Delegate Conference refusing (by 332 votes to 178), to endorse a proposal that the union affiliate to the British Peace Committee and that the Stockholm Appeal be circulated.[5]

---

[1] *Report of the Policy Conference*, 1953, pp. 504–8; 1955, pp. 485–95; 1956, pp. 505–11; 1957, pp. 49–51; 1958, pp. 98–9.

[2] *Report of the Policy Conference*, 1952, pp. 526–38.

[3] *Report of the Policy Conference*, 1953, pp. 352–73.

[4] *Report of the Policy Conference*, 1956, pp. 484–90. Mr Haxell and Mr Foulkes attend the Labour Party Conference to advise their delegations, although they cannot sit as delegates. Mr Horner, General Secretary of the Fire Brigades Union, also attended Conference as a visitor when he was a member of the Communist Party. The Communist members of the NUM National Executive attend the NUM delegation meetings. This is quite compatible with the Labour Party's Constitution.

[5] *Report of the Policy Conference*, 1951, pp. 101–2.

In many ways *Electron* reads like other left-wing Labour periodicals. It gives much more space to Party policy statements than many orthodox journals—but it also gives glowing reports of life in the peoples' democracies and reviews with unfailing praise books issued by a fellow-travelling publishing house. At no time in the last decade has it openly advocated a policy contrary to the Communist line. While it does not openly recruit support for Communism, it comes fairly close at times; the April 1955 issue said:

'British monopoly capitalism, along with its counterparts and the NATO and SEATO pacts, is prepared to plunge the world into universal destruction. And it is to be aided and abetted by the Parliamentary Labour Party.

But the last word has not been spoken. There is an alternative road, the path to Socialism, and the brotherhood of man, which increasing numbers of the peoples of the world have chosen to take, not least the *members* of the British trade union and labour movement.'[1]

Criticisms of *Electron* receive almost no support.

In November 1956 all that *Electron* could say was:

'The tragic series of events in Hungary over the past few weeks have aroused the sympathy and compassion of the whole British people. In signifying our deep concern over the happenings in that country we can, at the same time, express our conviction that the working people of Hungary can and will overcome the grave difficulties which they are experiencing and march united towards a better life in the future.'[2]

Only in December did the Executive Council feel it expedient to 'regret the mistakes of the Hungarian and Soviet governments, which had created the situation in which the Hungarian government requested Soviet intervention'.[3] But the leadership could not contain the members' anger quite so simply. At the 1957 conference the Executive decided for prudence's sake to discuss Hungary in private session. After an angry debate delegates condemned the Executive's attitude (177:154 with

[1] Emphasis theirs.          [2] *Electron*, November 1956.
[3] The *Manchester Guardian*, June 4, 1957.

49 abstentions), and recorded its hostility to 'the brutal attack of the Soviet armed forces on the Hungarian people' by a show of hands.[1]

On several other issues the Executive has more success. It has won the backing of its conference on several international questions on which Communists and left-wing Socialists do not see eye-to-eye, notably on atomic weapons policy and on Germany. Sometimes it owes success primarily to motions which are worded with such complexity and with such skill in skirting the dangerous key jargon phrases (such as 'free elections under international control') that the conference either did not understand them or the opposition found great difficulty in explaining its dissent.

Although the ETU Executive cannot be sure of putting across specifically Communist policy unless it is wrapped up in complicated verbiage they are not unduly worried. The occasional defeats on political questions will not shake them so long as their industrial stewardship appears successful. Indeed, the leadership is skilful enough to strengthen itself by the way it accepts defeat—just as it knows how to use Press criticism to whip up solidarity. Mr Frank Foulkes, replying to the Hungary debate, declared: 'I think the Executive, in a majority, are of the opinion that you are wrong and ill-advised, but I am sure they will unhesitatingly carry out the decision and wishes of the majority of the conference'.[2]

The ETU is an extreme case, unmatched by Arthur Deakin at his most autocratic. Normally, as Mr Attlee said, 'The trade union leader, like the political leader, only has a certain amount of power. He derives it from his supporters, and he cannot flout their wishes'. A union leader has far wider discretion on political than on major industrial questions. The scope for autocracy therefore seems greater. Yet, just because political issues are usually less important to him, he is less likely to commit his power and prestige to getting his way. In unions torn by political and religious factions, the leadership finds it morally impossible to fight for its views on every resolution. It is usually

---

[1] The *Manchester Guardian*, June 5, 1957. The ETU's report of this conference contains no mention either of the debate or the resolution voted.
[2] *Report of the Policy Conference*, 1957, p. 109.

ready to give way on some to ensure victory on those it considers really important.

The years 1951 to 1955 were a rare exception. Several union leaders, considering that the controversies over the rearmament programme, nationalization, or the European Defence Community, involved the whole future of the Party, committed their strength at Conference and within their own organizations to an unprecedented degree. Their efforts were not necessarily inimical to forming 'representatives' policies. Had they decided on tactical grounds not to oppose resolutions, this would not have removed the barrier preventing 'representative' decisions being made. It would simply have abdicated leadership to a group of activists on the floor of their conferences—by definition untypical members. The silent delegates are led nonetheless.

Even some orthodox trade unionists exaggerate the power of Executives. They argue that some unions are 'left-wing' only because they lack leadership: 'Look at them! They've got no guts. They're followers, not leaders . . . scared to death of standing up to their own rank-and-file'. In fact every union leader has to be a 'follower' at times—although he wisely rarely admits it. 'If I hadn't known what they wanted, and what they would take, and got in with it first, I wouldn't be where I am now', said a general secretary with a touch of cynicism. There are some decisions which every leader knows he could not persuade his union to make, so he never makes the attempt. A General Secretary privately confessed 'We have nothing at all to hope for from nationalizing (our industry)—but obviously I can't go to our conference and say that'. Amid the welter of publicity whenever a leader seems to flout his members' wishes, the silent vetoes which his union's traditional policies and prejudices impose on him are easily forgotten.

The leadership may be divided. The United Patternmakers' Association at one time had the staidly orthodox Mr Wilfred Beard as General Secretary, but Mr Ellis Smith—who is much further left—as President. The political outlook of Mr Walter Padley is not invariably the same as that of Mr Alan Birch while the splits between Communist, left-Socialist and orthodox Labour within the AEU and NUM Executives are common knowledge. In other unions personal rivalries crystallize into political opposition. Even Arthur Deakin, whose Labour Party delegations could be distressingly docile, could not always 'play ducks and drakes' with them. The unions where allegations of executive autocracy have been loudest—the NUGMW, TGWU, and ETU—have conferences which noticeably lack effective opposition. What is termed 'dictation by the Executive' may really amount to like-mindedness.

Within the conference or delegation 'leadership' may mean that one member is better informed than others, or that he is more skilled in argument or procedure. Such abilities are usually more developed among full-time officials than among lay members. The borderline between legitimate and excessive use of the union's machinery to command support for Executive policies is inevitably hazy—but the cries of 'foul' rising from the defeated are not the best indication that it has been crossed. Every union Executive possesses immense procedural and tactical advantages at every level in the policy-making process, which it will use whatever its political hue to command support for its policies. There is no evidence that 'right-wing' leaders abuse these advantages more than those on the left. When USDAW and the NUR supported first Mr Bevan, then Mr Gaitskell, and then Mr Bevan again for the Treasureship of the Labour Party, who could tell whether any or all of these decisions was improper?

The influence of personalities on a union's political decisions is circumscribed by more than the shifting balance of forces within it. Rarely does the advent of a new leader bring an abrupt change of policy. He inherits a complex of traditional attitudes and policies which he can alter only slowly. He has probably worked his way up the union hierarchy, absorbing these policies as part of its structure and tradition. Such 'sacred cow' policies may outlast a succession of leaders, for they are far more difficult to reverse than others. Thus the NUM conference is often influenced by a traditionally strong sentiment of the solidarity of the working class throughout the world; the NUR and the Union of Post Office Workers cling to their support of workers' control of industry, and the old NUDAW bequeathed to USDAW a tradition of hostility to conscription. Other unions have socialist principles written into their rules, and 'rethinking' of their views on nationalization must be cautious.

Changes in political attitudes are usually gradual. The transformation of some of the sceptical craft unions of 1900 into the 'progressive' organizations of today was slow, while the general unions and their forerunners have not always had today's reputation for moderation. Industrial history and occupational composition as well as leadership have had their effect. It may be significant that the Blastfurnacemen and the British Iron, Steel & Kindred Trades' Association take almost identical political lines, while many engineering unions have a common leftish slant, and that there is a strong similarity of outlook among several of the printing craft unions. Certain Area Unions of the NUM (such as South Wales) have a long tradition of industrial and political militancy, while others (such as Durham) have always been moderate. No single simple explanation proves satisfactory. The English Bakers are often more advanced than their Scottish counterparts, and the three railway unions (TSSA, ASLEF and NUR) take quite different lines on political issues. The political militancy of the NUR may not be unconnected with its industrial expansionism. While it is tempting to attribute the moderation of the Blastfurnacemen and the National Union of Boot & Shoe Operatives to their long history of negotiated settlements, the cotton unions have always been conservative despite their bitter early industrial history. The agreement between Tom Williamson and Arthur Deakin on so many political issues may have amounted to a two-man conspiracy, but it also expressed a community of industrial interest.

How much this inherited background of tradition, taboos, prejudices, and enthusiasms counts is still far from clear, but it obviously limits the power of the trade union leader. While the interaction of all these influences requires more detailed study before generalizations about 'leadership' become really profitable, it is clear that a leader's power is both dynamic and ephemeral—possibly varying from one conference to another, depending on the clash of personalities, the proximity of union elections, and events quite outside his control. The stereotype of the trade union boss arbitrarily wielding his power is a crude distortion of a leader's real strength—even if many general secretaries do dictate their union's line to a far greater extent than they normally admit to enquiring research workers.

## Representative Trade Union Democracy

'The Labour Movement is in danger of dying a death of three million cuts—the block votes of four men. Their vote was not representative of the working trade unionist.'[1]

From 1951 to 1956 the gravest charge against the right-wing union leaders, made in such heated and categorical terms as these, was that they were betraying the wishes of their members. In Mr Bevan's famous phrase:

'You have only got to look at the voting papers for the election of the Executive this week to see how, in the industrial section, you have a travesty of the democratic vote. We are not going to be bullied or intimidated by individual trade union leaders—a handful of them.[2]

The attack does not always come from the indignant left:

'The ordinary London bus driver and conductor did not want the stoppage. . . . To call the garage delegates at Wednesday's conference "representatives of the Men" is absurd. . . . This strike is . . . being launched because Mr Cousins, and still more those immediately below him, feel that it is the professed obligation of trade union enthusiasts to make a demonstration. . . .'[3]

Such categorical statements amount to a claim to omniscience, to a special revelation of the wishes of the ordinary member. This belief that they speak for the rank and filer at the workbench, for the lay-member rather than a group of discredited officials, which constantly reappears in left-wing movements, was a particular article of faith among the Bevanites. It swelled into the myth of the three or four men in a smoke-filled room forming the sole barrier to the adoption of a 'full-blooded Socialist' policy. Never was this conviction more clearly revealed than in Mr Bevan's superb comment on his election to the Party

[1] Mrs Barbara Castle's speech at Brighton, September 12, 1953.
[2] Speech at Scarborough, September 29, 1951.
[3] *The Economist*, May 3, 1958.

Treasurership, 'I consider that, in some respects, the block vote has adjusted itself to the point of view of the rank and file'.[1]

The Bevanites (and later the supporters of nuclear disarmament) went beyond the claim to be the guardians of the ark of the Socialist covenant and to have the support of a majority of shop stewards and branch committeemen (which many of their opponents would have conceded to them), to say that they were the voice of the working trade unionist. Yet they scarcely ever went beyond flat assertion. It is easy for enthusiasts, moving within the overheated atmosphere of a leftist movement, to exaggerate their support. A small group of militants making speeches, putting motions through branches and local parties, writing to *Tribune* (and even to the *Daily Worker*) can soon form an impressive stage army. While the Bevanites always saw clearly enough the falsity of Communist claims to be the authentic voice of the worker, they were understandably unreceptive to suggestions that their own position was in some ways similar. In fact, so far as public opinion polls could cast light on their claims they usually suggested that the right-wing leadership was defending views closer to those held by trade unionists or by Labour voters in general than were the Bevanites. The 'average' Labour voter would have found even some of Arthur Deakin's ideas 'left-wing'. Those who sought in the polls for confirmation that the electorate wanted a more Socialist party looked in vain.

The trade union leadership was always bound to see in the Bevanites' claim to speak for the silent majority something more serious than a political rallying cry. Nothing strikes more surely at a leader's authority than the assertion that he does not speak for his members. Although the Bevanites attacked principally on political issues, the implications of their allegations obviously went wider. Some leaders saw in such attacks an attempt to undermine the whole idea of leadership in the movement, which threatened not only their standing at the Party Conference, but their industrial stewardship. This was a challenge they could not ignore. Any leader prefers to feel that he is fully backed by his members. Opposing the Plan for Engineering, Arthur Deakin proudly announced, 'I do want to put the point of view of my union, as recently affirmed by

[1] The *Manchester Guardian*, October 3, 1956.

over 800 rank and file delegates, and to indicate how firmly opposed to this proposal are the 100,000 people that we represent in the engineering and shipbuilding trades'.[1] In the same way Mr Jack Tanner carefully argued, in supporting a policy of Communist Party affiliation to the Labour Party, 'I hope you will take my word for it that the policy and the mandate that the Union is carrying to this Conference has been adopted entirely in accordance with the very democratic constitution of the AEU'.[2] Privately trade union leaders are well aware how imperfect a 'representative' decision can be.

Our argument has tended to show how difficult it is to realize the ideal of forming policy right up from a union's 'grass roots' in a truly representative fashion—rather than to conclude gloomily that unions misrepresent their members. Such are these limitations that union decisions are not surprisingly unrepresentative from time to time, even without any improper intervention by the leadership. The editor of *The Post*—one of the most thoughtful trade union journals—wrote, with this problem in mind:

'We read that at the TUC or the Labour Party Conference, the engineers or the postal workers voted in favour of this union or against that. We read that one union is reactionary, that another follows the Communist Party line. These judgments are obviously based on the speeches made by the leaders of the union concerned. What is almost impossible to ascertain is the extent to which the pronouncements and actions of the spokesmen in fact reflect the views of the men and women who make up the membership of the unions. Is Arthur Deakin speaking in the name of 1,300,000 members of the TGWU, expressing the democratic will of the majority when he stands "four square for moderation"? Does Mr Stevens of the Electrical Trades Union represent the bulk of his 200,000 members when he expresses a more advanced point of view? The answer from both quarters would probably be a stout "yes", but it is an answer which those who know the impediments to democratic expression would receive with considerable reserve.'[3]

[1] *Report of the Labour Party Conference,* 1952, p. 124.
[2] *Report of the Labour Party Conference,* 1946, p. 172.
[3] *The Post,* September 24, 1953.

Mr Jack Tanner said much the same (but how different from his confidence of 1946) to the Building Trade Workers in 1954:

'I know in my own organization—and I do not doubt that in this as in most other trade unions—resolutions are passed at branch level, shall we say without a full knowledge of all the facts. . . . Possibly even at the national conferences you have not a complete understanding of the situation. . . . I know perfectly well that resolutions do not get the discussion . . . that they should get. . . .

'I see that you have on your agenda about thirty resolutions dealing with world peace, and about half of them are resolutions opposing German rearmament. Well, probably you will adopt one of them like other unions have done, but I doubt whether the average member, the average trade unionist, has given full consideration to this matter.'[1]

In relating the change in the ETU vote on Communist affiliation to the Labour Party we have already seen an example of how difficult making 'representative' decisions can be. The National Union of Vehicle Builders Executive, which recommended its Conference delegation to support Progressive Unity in 1946 suffered an identical set-back. On an 'exceedingly good' turnout, its members voted by 'slightly over two to one' against affiliation.[2] The Tobacco Workers' Union provides another revealing illustration. In 1955 its Executive rejected an offer of six shillings per week rise in wages. Before the issue could be put to a general ballot the annual conference intervened. Only three of some twenty speakers favoured acceptance, and a 'fifteen bob or nothing' resolution passed by a two-to-one majority. The ballot paper sent to members bore the Executive's and the Conference's recommendation to reject the offer. It was decisively accepted. In all good faith the ADM and the EC had misjudged their members' feeling.[3]

In 1952 this union's conference voted by five to one to set up a political fund, but the subsequent ballot confirmed the decision by only 3,983 votes to 3,625.[4] The members of the Scottish

[1] *Report of the National Delegate Conference*, 1954, p. 114.
[2] *Quarterly Report*, July 1946.
[3] *The Tobacco Worker*, July/August 1954.
[4] *The Tobacco Worker*, July/August 1952, January/February 1955.

Typographical Association have four times rejected the setting up of a political fund, against their conference's advice. A member of the Executive gloomily admitted:

'One disturbing aspect about such a result is the fact that it is a complete denial of the delegates' decision, and the thought not unnaturally arises as to whether many of the other decisions taken by the same method may not also be placed in the same category.'[1]

Although political questions are rarely taken to a ballot, it is unlikely that these examples are unique. Short of a ballot there is no sure indication that representatives have gone too far to the right or left for their members.

The link between the ordinary member and the votes cast in his name at the Party Conference is so tenuous and complicated that critics outside the Party might fairly conclude that it is little more than good fortune if trade union leaders speak for the majority of their members. But the critics within the Party reckon to believe in the possibility of making representative decisions—and they would hesitate to dismiss their friends in the same condemnation as their enemies. All too often they have preferred to dismiss the decisions with which they agree and accept without question one which favours them. Among this confusion only one test seems helpful. Imperfect though they are, the decisions of trade union conferences, like those of any freely-elected body of representatives, must be taken as expressing the views of the membership until the contrary is shown.

In most unions the pattern of decisions over the years has amounted to a discernible political line—so much so that their vote can be predicted with confidence. While a union's delegation to the Party Conference may be given only a handful of direct mandates, it is still legitimate to talk of their 'representing' the membership if the decisions they take at the Party Conference are consistent with the pattern revealed at their union's conference. Although exceptions can be found in most unions, the description of the six large unions with which we opened this chapter showed how remarkably consistent con-

[1] *Annual Report of the Scottish Typographical Association*, 1954, p. 12.

N

ference and delegation decisions usually are. Perhaps this is merely a demonstration that one group dominates both—but the very suggestion concedes much of the argument it sets out to dispute. Executives can cheat their conference on this or that decision, and use every resource of procedure and demagogy, but unless the delegates are fraudulently elected, or a Communist Executive confronts a predominantly Communist conference no leadership can hope systematically to defraud the membership, warp decisions, and commit the union's whole influence in a perverse direction. Who, having met delegates to a TGWU or USDAW conference, can really believe that they are stooges? To deny that these conferences are as representative as is possible within the trade union movement raises as many problems as it explains.

This must be the rule of thumb for looking at political decisions. If there is harmony between the voting at a union's conference, and the votes cast by its delegation at the Party Conference, the decision must be accepted as 'representative'. Within the existing structure of trade unionism it is hard to see how the membership could be brought into any more true participation in the decisions made at the Party Conference, or how 'representation' could be made more real.

# CHAPTER V

# CALLING THE TUNE?—
# THE LABOUR PARTY CONFERENCE

'The day is passing when the power of the trade unions could
be used as a bulldozer to crush and obliterate difficulties
within the party.'

SIR CHARLES GEDDES*

'The trade unions' influence upon the Party is due to two
reasons: (1) money, lots of it, and (2) votes, many of them.
This money will be spent and these votes cast in the direction
which will further trade union policy. . . .'

SIR CHARLES GEDDES*

HERE is the focal point of the Labour Party's year, the culmina-
tion of a succession of Party and union meetings from Easter
to September. In the Party's own words 'Conference' is

'the final authority of the Labour Party . . . a Parliament of the
Movement . . . [It] lays down the policy of the Party, and
issues instructions which must be carried out by the Executive,
the affiliated organizations, and its representatives in Parliament and on local authorities.'[1]

This is the traditional view of Conference's power, held by
hundreds of the eager militants who flock there every year. But
in recent years a new orthodoxy, accepting R. T. McKenzie's
conclusions, has assigned a much less imposing role to Conference:

'Labour Party literature appears to imply that the Conference has
a decisive voice in the affairs of the Party, but in fact it does not.
By an adroit use of the internal Party mechanisms the Conference is kept carefully in control, and on the rare occasions
when the Conference gets out of control it usually succeeds in
doing little more than demonstrate its own impotence.'[2]

* (a) *Tribune*, November 2, 1951.
  (b) *The National & English Review*, December 1954.

[1] C. R. Attlee. *The Labour Party in Perspective and Twelve Years After*, Gollancz,
1948, p. 93.
[2] *British Political Parties*, p. 488.

Perhaps McKenzie is a little sweeping, a trifle too impressed by the ineffectiveness of Conference during the post-war Labour government and the first years of the Bevanite crisis, but his main thesis seems established: Conference has always had much less power, and the Parliamentary leaders much more, than the Party's founders envisaged.

This is already little short of heresy in many Labour circles, but McKenzie goes further. Conference, he argues, is simply an 'opportunity for the ardent partisans who belong to the mass organization to meet together to debate questions of national or party policy, and to offer advice on these matters to the leaders of the Party in Parliament', although it would be 'political suicide' for the leadership to disregard completely the wishes of its most militant and hard-working supporters. Discovering that Labour Conferences have had little success in tying down the leadership to unwanted precise commitments, he suggests that the role of Conference in the Party's affairs is very similar to the place of the annual Conservative conference in the life of the Conservative Party.[1]

Yet to show that Conference can rarely force policies on a reluctant leadership is far from proving that it resembles its Conservative counterpart or is unimportant. The cold-blooded analysis of the occasions when the NEC has been tied to unwelcome commitments at Conference cannot but make the proceedings look futile—for no rational Party leadership is going to risk defeat on the floor of Conference. On the one hand the leaders are watched by opponents who are delighted to exploit fresh evidence of the Party's lack of unity and discipline. On the other, they know that their own position within the Party could be fatally undermined by a major defeat. It is true that from 1951 to 1955 the NEC deliberately dug in its heels, courting defeat, on a series of issues which it saw as part of the struggle for the succession to Mr Attlee, and that in 1959 it was obliged to defend a nuclear weapons policy which allowed no compromise with the advocates of nuclear disarmament. But normally the NEC is careful to prepare its victories. It makes sure that its fate is no longer in the balance long before Conference meets, making promises and concessions if need be. The effect

[1] *British Political Parties*, p. 488.

of Conference on the Party extends beyond its five days of purple oratory to the policy statements which are produced because Conference expects them, the assurances which are made to win support, the meetings with the TUC during the summer, none of which would have the same urgency but for the ineluctable approach of Conference.

In the last resort Conference remains important because the 'ardent partisans' who flock there believe it is important. Rejecting or ignoring McKenzie's judgment they, unlike Conservative militants, cling to the tradition that this is where the Party's policy is formed. There is scarcely an issue in the Party which is not discussed in terms of the next annual Conference, even if it be months ahead. Labour must work within a tradition which requires every issue to be aired in public—and in the end the heads must be counted. The whole ethos of the Conservative conference is different. The fact that (unlike the Conservative leaders) the Labour leaders must meet their followers head on, and show not only that they control the Party but that they have it in hand by a comfortable majority, sets them problems which rarely trouble their Conservative counterparts. So long as the old mystique remains the authority of Labour leaders will always be more committed than is that of the Conservative leaders at their conference. And so long as the Conference arouses such continuing passion and so profoundly influences the Party's morale, the role of the unions with their millions of decisive votes cannot but be vital, and controversial in itself.

In recent years there has been greater awareness of the constitutional issues that Conference raises. As McKenzie points out, 'It would be quite unconstitutional if either parliamentary party allowed itself to be controlled and directed by its own mass party organization'.[1] Since earliest days most sections of the Party have accepted that Conference cannot bind the Parliamentary Party hand and foot in questions of detail or tactics. As Mr Bevan once argued in a celebrated reply to a demand for the abolition of the tied cottage:

'It is quite impossible for a conference of 1,100 even if it were constitutionally proper, to determine the order in which the

[1] *British Political Parties*, p. 488.

Parliamentary Labour Party and the government introduce legislation.'[1]

Even left-wing opinion has been changing. Mrs Barbara Castle admitted in 1958 that the 1957 Conference's motion on Cyprus 'would not, of course, be constitutionally binding on a Labour government'. However, while 'detail and tactics' can be stretched to a surprising extent, no responsible Party leader would dare challenge openly the power of Conference to lay down principle. As Mr Bevan added:

'It is for the Conference to lay down the policies of the Parliamentary Party, and for the Parliamentary Party to interpret those policies in the light of the Parliamentary system.'[1]

More recently Mr Gaitskell confirmed categorically that a decision of the Party Conference in favour of unilateral disarmament would be binding on a Labour government. Not only for the sake of its own authority, but to avoid a conflict between its responsibility to the electorate through Parliament and its responsibility to the Party membership, the leaders must try to keep the Parliamentary Party and Conference in step. So long as the Party continues to believe that Conference decides policy this potential clash of loyalties will remain.

It is less often realized that the tradition that Conference 'issues instructions which must be carried out by . . . the affiliated organizations' can embarrass the unions as much as the Party.

Their position was never made more clearly than in a reply by Mr Sam Watson for the NEC, on a motion about strike action:

'If 1,000 delegates here believe that they can give directions to 700,000 miners or to a million transport workers, or a million municipal workers or 500,000 people on the railways or a big union like the AEU, they had better think what the constitutions of the unions are in relation to a problem like this. . . . Before there can be a strike in the National Union of Mineworkers the

---

[1] *Report of the Labour Party Conference*, 1948 (hereafter *Report*), p. 214. For Mr Gaitskell's views see *The Times*, July 13, 1959.

constitution itself lays down very clearly that we must have the consent of the Union's National Executive Committee.'

'I will make my personal position perfectly clear: before I would be disloyal to a decision properly reached after having been discussed and voted upon by my own members, in favour of another resolution in the case of which we have not had the same opportunity, I would sooner resign my position on the National Executive of the party.'[1]

Sir William Lawther said more tersely:

'We think it would be absolutely wrong at this time of day, after we have made a complete investigation into the whole of the methods and decided on policy, that somebody from Coventry should come and tell us how to do our own business.'[2]

Arthur Deakin also told the 1953 Conference:

'This Conference will not, I am sure, misunderstand me when I say for the TUC that we have a day-to-day job to do looking after the interests of our members. We cannot always accept the theories launched upon us. I have in mind some of the ideas projected within the political movement. . . .'[3]

When the 1955 Conference was asked to adopt a resolution on the right to strike Sir Tom O'Brien urged rejection:

'It is rather noteworthy that the resolutions which created the composite resolution were tabled by constituency parties and not one trade union. . . . When the trade union movement wishes for support, as it will do from time to time, it will not hesitate to come to the National Executive, without waiting for a national conference. Let me remind you again—this is the national Conference of the Labour Party, not the Trades Union Congress.'[4]

These were men of the right, but the left spoke in similar terms throughout the long debate on the wage freeze.

The clearest statement of the clash of loyalties, and the choice that unions must make, arose from Bevanite attacks on several

[1] *Report*, 1955, p. 135.        [2] *Report*, 1953, p. 100.
[3] *Report*, 1953, p. 125.        [4] *Report*, 1955, p. 132.

trade unionists who accepted posts on the Iron and Steel Board which was charged with supervizing the denationalization of the steel industry. Mr W. B. Beard, General Secretary of the United Patternmakers' Association wrote:

'This attempt to hitch the trade union movement, holus bolus to [the Bevanite] star, displays a thorough lack of knowledge of trade unionism. . . . Trade unions, whilst they may have direct representation in Parliament, which to many is a distinct advantage, and through their Political Funds have affiliation to the Labour Party (and many have not) are, nevertheless, primarily industrial units, whose organization is based not upon political and religious convictions, but upon the industry or craftsmanship of the individual members, many of whom have other political affiliations and have contracted out of the political fund. . . . A trade union has to deal with its industrial conditions in the best interests of its membership, no matter what Government is in power. . . . Failure to do so spells disaster and disunity for the trade union movement.'[1]

Trade unions can accept Conference decisions on such purely political questions as the abolition of public schools or the municipalization of housing no matter how loud their opposition has been. They can usually accept distasteful decisions on minor industrial questions with no more than a restrained protest. But on wages policy, the right to strike, the more critical aspects of economic policy, and possibly nationalization, they cannot accept an adverse Conference decision. A General Secretary who had helped draft the Party's plans to nationalize his industry privately admitted that his union's conference might not accept it. 'Of course, in that case we should have no choice but to fight the Party.'

It is partly this potential clash of loyalties which leads to attempts to take certain questions out of the hands of Con-

[1] United Patternmakers' Association *Monthly Report*, February 1953.

A motion 'regretting' the action of four members of the General Council who accepted appointments on the Iron and Steel Board and calling for the resignation of any of its members who accepted such appointments in the future received 2,877,000 votes at the 1953 TUC.

Mr Beard's remarks on this issue contrast strangely with his declaration of faith in the movement quoted on p. 345.

ference. Replying to a demand in 1953 that the engineering industry should be nationalized, Mr Morgan Phillips said: 'It is under discussion with the Confederation [of Shipbuilding & Engineering Unions] and the TUC, and clearly in a matter of industrial policy it is vital that the trade union and political wings of the movement should go in harmony. . . .' At the same conference Mr Harry Douglass urged, 'Do not attempt in this party to take the TUC and wrap them in the cotton wool of legislation. . . . Listen to the views of the TUC men'.[1]

In short, discussion of some major economic issues may be so embarrassing that they are better not discussed at all. By tacit agreement the trade union movement itself is not directly debated at Conference. But some leaders go on to imply that Conference has no business deciding any question which vitally interests the unions. There is a union sphere of influence in which the Party should not intrude. Arthur Deakin put it bluntly enough:

'My advice to those people who have come to this rostrum and said, "Give us incentives" is this. The questions of wages and conditions of employment are questions for the trade unions, and the sooner some of our people on the political side appreciate that and leave the job to the unions, the better for production.'[2]

In office or in opposition the Labour Party must have policies on the economic problems of the day.[3] The unions know that if Conference makes no decision (and even an NEC victory can involve irritating concessions and precedents), they can negotiate directly with the Cabinet or the NEC, either through the TUC or individually. Taking such questions out of Conference leaves the unions greater freedom of manoeuvre, lets them gain their demands more discreetly, and avoids any public exhibition

[1] Report, 1953, p. 133.

[2] Report, 1947, p. 144. Mr Deakin also said, 'The position of the trade unions in relation to political parties—and this includes the Labour Party—is that they should leave industrial policy to the unions to determine'. The Record, October-November 1954.

[3] Mr Sam Watson said, in reply to a resolution on the right to strike: 'This Conference has not the right to deal with (strikes) and it would be a sorry day for this Movement if we as a political party were trying to take upon ourselves the fundamental right that belongs to the trade unions and is embedded in their constitutions and rules. We feel that this matter should go to the TUC'. Report, 1955, p. 135.

of their conflict of loyalties. Here, their interest often coincides with the National Executive's desire that the parliamentary leadership shall not be burdened with too many and precise commitments.

While union leaders believe that they should have their way on industrial matters, they are always loath to recognize that the local parties should have a comparable sphere of influence. Suggestions that such matters as discipline and organization might be left to their votes to decide are always firmly rejected.[1]

Even in foreign affairs many union leaders think that experience of Communists within their own ranks, and their skill in negotiating with employers give them a special competence and 'realism' that the intellectuals lack. At one time Sir Tom O'Brien seemed to think that the unions were specially qualified to rule on any issue that might arise:

'Must we assume that the trade union movement exists exclusively to protect the industrial interests and meet the inddustrial needs of the workers . . .? Is that the limitation of the political responsibilities and the functions of the trade unions? Can the trade unions, the Trades Union Congress, and its General Council contract out of the political responsibilities that confront all the citizens, the whole community?'[2]

Jack Tanner thought that German rearmament so gravely affected the unions that a special conference of union executives should be called—quite independent of the Labour Party.[3] He carried the claim that 'the unions know best' to its extreme by telling the 1954 Party Conference—which, as usual, followed the TUC—that 'no greater disservice could be possible than if

---

[1] Mr Deakin's reply to suggestions that the unions should abstain on the expulsion of Mr Zilliacus and Mr Solley also illustrated his conception of a mandate: 'Our people are entitled through their trade union, through its affiliation with the Labour Party, to express their views on those things which they think of importance to our Movement. . . . It has been said that as far as the trade unions are concerned, the question can properly be posed whether or not we have a mandate. Our mandate is consistently to support the foreign policy of this Government. If Mr Zilliacus and Mr Solley continue to challenge the democratically recorded decisions of Conference, then our mandate is perfectly clear'. Report, 1949, pp. 124–5.

[2] Report, 1953, p. 165.

[3] Report of the National Delegate Conference, 1954, p. 114.

any one of us or any group among us pushes any difference of opinion to the point where a cleavage opens up between the Congress and the Party'.[1] This would leave the Conference a mere annual echo of the TUC. Such attempts to claim the political direction of the Movement for the unions are rare. Although they expect Labour to respect their industrial demands, in return most unions have usually been ready to leave the initiative in other questions to the Party. Their exceptional intervention in 1952–5 sprang from a conviction that the inertia of the political leadership was in danger of letting the whole direction of the Party fall by default to the Bevanites.

These disastrous years showed how dangerous it is for big unions to use their massive votes to impose their political views. If they seek to reinforce orthodox policy or discipline they risk provoking violent internal disruption; if they join the dissidents their huge votes can scarcely avoid turning dissent into rebellion. In either case they offer the spectacle of a political party under union domination. Unless they are prepared to leave the political leaders some elbow room the alliance between the unions and the Party could not long remain either tolerable or workable.

Yet so long as they hold eight votes in every ten at Conference the unions' role is bound to be controversial. Unfortunately for Labour it is also invariably misunderstood, as much within the Party as outside. Out of the Bevanite quarrel sprang the four-men-in-a-smoke-filled-room theory, which served for a time as revealed truth about how the unions forced the Party to the right. Sufficient of this explanation still lingers for it still to be worth an examination. However the discovery that Frank Cousins' TGWU is not Arthur Deakin's, which revealed some of the inadequacies of the old orthodoxy, seems in the course of producing another—quite incompatible— authoritative explanation of how the unions use their votes at Conference. What has always been lacking has been a thorough examination of the way the unions really behave at Conference. As we shall see, the misunderstandings are reinforced and perpetuated from the moment that the Conference process starts.

[1] *Report*, 1954, p. 90.

## The Agenda

Year after year the Party Conference Agenda breathes militancy and extremism in every line. The number and tone of the fire-eating motions, suggesting a united rank and file fighting for socialist progress impress even 'responsible' newspapers. Just as regularly the Conference will eventually mysteriously rebuff them. Little wonder that the militants feel that they have been cheated.

Only about one union in four—compared with three in four constituencies—send in a resolution. Conference means much less to the unions than to the eager constituency militants. Unions which want support from the wider movement turn first to the Trades Union Congress. Not only does the TUC take decisions in the names of more members than the Labour Party, it can win concessions from both political parties. Within the Party the bigger unions have often had their say on policy long before the issues come to conference. Inevitably the leadership seeks to win over a potential majority before it launches a policy, and on industrial questions it consults the TUC or the interested unions. On other matters the big unions have their say through their representatives on the NEC. As a result some unions rarely think of contributing resolutions to the agenda.

Understandably, the most assiduous contributors to the agenda are the dissident left-wing unions (such as the ETU, Fire Brigades' Union, Foundry Workers, Draughtsmen, and Vehicle Builders). Their resolutions tend to increase the impression of solid left-wing feeling that is left by the constituencies. By contrast, almost half the affiliated unions have not submitted a single motion since the war—including several large organizations.[1] Most of the small unions show not the slightest interest in initiating policy—surprisingly, since a resolution on the agenda gives even the most insignificant organization a chance of being heard.

Some unions (notable the NUM and NUGMW) put down 'loyal' resolutions endorsing some aspect of official policy. At first sight these are little contribution to the work of Conference. However, they sometimes serve to emphasize to the outside

---

[1] Notably the British Iron, Steel & Kindred Trades' Association and the National Union of Dyers, Bleachers & Textile Workers.

TABLE 24

NUMBER OF RESOLUTIONS AND AMENDMENTS SUBMITTED
BY UNIONS FOR PARTY CONFERENCES 1945–1958

| Short Title of Union | Number of Resolutions/ Amendments |
|---|---|
| Constructional Engineers | 21 |
| Agricultural Workers | 19 |
| AEU | 15 |
| Draughtsmen | 12 |
| ETU | 12 |
| Foundry Workers | 12 |
| NUR | 12 |
| Vehicle Builders | 11 |
| USDAW | 11 |
| Fire Brigades' Union | 10 |
| NUM | 10 |
| Cine, Television Technicians | 9 |
| NUGMW | 9 |
| TGWU | 8 |
| Tailors & Garment Workers | 8 |
| Transport Salaried Staffs | 7 |
| Plumbing Trades Union | 6 |
| Woodworkers | 6 |
| Health Service Employees | 6 |
| ASSET | 6 |
| 29 other unions | 51 |
| 39 other unions | 0 |

world the unions' solidarity with the Party on specific issues, where it might be doubted.[1] They are also better tactics than the sterile rejection of 'progressive' motions, on which so many unions relied during the Bevanite struggle, which made the divisions in the Party more bitter than ever by encouraging the impression that the unions were hopelessly conservative and negative. The NEC, too, feels less embattled when accepting a motion instead of opposing everything that the floor suggests —sometimes it even inspires a union resolution.

A high proportion of union resolutions reflect their industrial interests—taking the term broadly to include the Musicians Union's concern with cultural standards, the Cine & Television Technicians' campaign to save the British film industry, and the desire of the National League of the Blind or the Confederation

---

[1] This has noticeably been true of several resolutions opposing Conservative transport policy or denationalization of road haulage.

of Health Service Employees to discuss the social services. Many of these were simply 'log-rolling' proposals which, in its comradely way, the Conference usually accepts. Although the unions —chiefly those on the left—do put down motions on wider issues, notably on defence and foreign affairs, they leave the initiative on internal Party matters to the constituencies and rarely submit motions on education, the Commonwealth and colonies, housing, agriculture or local government. In fact the agenda shows in a striking fashion how limited is the unions' interest in using Conference to make policy.

## The Debate

Conference debates often reflect the militancy of the agenda, since sponsors of 'composited' resolutions are usually favoured by the chair. The constituencies take up about thirty-four per cent of Conference's time, while the unions have only fifteen per cent. This is a meagre allocation compared with their votes, generous in relation to the number of organizations affiliated. (CLPs outnumber unions 8:1.)

Again the unions speeches are concentrated on industrial matters, foreign policy and defence.

Few unions are as single-minded as the National Union of Agricultural Workers, which scarcely ever speaks on non-rural problems; several actually speak more on such issues as defence and colonial and foreign affairs than on strictly industrial issues.[1] All except USDAW are on the extreme left wing. Almost half the unions have not spoken once at Conference since the war, although only the National Union of Public Employees is of any size. All the 'Big Six' speak frequently—but 'frequently' is a relative term. Since 1945 the unions have made an average of twenty-six speeches per conference.[2] Even leaders like Frank Cousins, who have only to crook their finger to catch the chairman's eye, can make their views known on no more than two or three subjects in any year.

This allocation of time produces an unhappy familiar type of debate. Up to the rostrum come the constituency militants

---

[1] Chiefly the Fire Brigades' Union, Constructional Engineering Union, National Union of Vehicle Builders, the ETU and USDAW.

[2] Speeches from the floor in open session.

TABLE 25

NUMBER AND SUBJECT OF TRADE UNION SPEECHES
AT THE PARTY CONFERENCE 1945–1958

| Short Title of Union | Number of Speeches on Industrial Topics | Non-Industrial Topics |
|---|---|---|
| USDAW | 16 | 24 |
| NUM | 20 | 18 |
| AEU | 18 | 15 |
| TGWU | 21 | 12 |
| Agricultural Workers | 26 | 1 |
| NUGMW | 14 | 7 |
| NUR | 14 | 6 |
| Foundry Workers | 8 | 5 |
| Constructional Engineers | 4 | 9 |
| Draughtsmen | 8 | 3 |
| Transport Salaried Staffs | 6 | 4 |
| Vehicle Builders | 1 | 8 |
| ETU | 3 | 6 |
| Textile Factory Workers | 6 | 2 |
| Loco. Engineers & Firemen | 2 | 6 |
| Fire Brigades' Union | 2 | 6 |
| Clerical & Admin. W. | 2 | 6 |
| 27 other unions | 39 | 17 |
| 44 other unions | 0 | 0 |
| TOTAL | 210 | 155 |

demanding red-blooded socialism, joined by speakers from the handful of extreme-left unions. Sometimes there is no union speaker at all, and often during the Bevanite controversy only the NEC spokesman sounded a moderate note. The militants feel that they have had the best of the argument. Then comes the vote. A silent, overwhelming majority crushes 'red-blooded socialism' flat yet again. Trade union delegates, complain the activists, spend most of Conference in the tea room, saying nothing, and contributing nothing but an uninformed, imperious wave of a voting card. Of course the militants would be no happier if the unions always monopolized debates to explain their views.[1] There is so little time that the 'silent millions' of trade unionists must remain silent—yet they cannot but look

[1] Mr Ben Gardner remarked, with some irritation, 'The parrot cry of "block vote" might be countered by a union retort of "block grants". Besides, the unions might well have something to say about the "block resolutions" from the constituency parties which monopolize the time of the Standing Orders Committee and often of the Conference itself.' *AEU Journal*, November 1955.

grossly unfair to the enthusiasts, cannot but convey an impression of insensitive trade union power, impatient of argument, beating down socialism by brute force, whenever the Party is bitterly divided.

## The Delegations

Even the delegations swell the misunderstanding. In 1958 the unions sent only 627 of the 1,125 delegates they were allowed—about as many as the local parties. Almost every large union except the Miners sends an under-sized delegation. In 1956 the ETU sent five members, although entitled to twenty-eight; the TGWU forty-one instead of 250; the National Union of Vehicle Builders, four instead of seven; National Union of Public Employees five (twenty); the NUR, nineteen (fifty-nine) and the AEU thirty-three (127).

Some unions keep their delegations small because any increase would lower the proportion of full-time officials. Some object on grounds of expense. Others see little point: 'Why should we take along a mass meeting? We wouldn't vote any differently', demanded a left-wing official.[1] If every organization was at full strength there would be almost 2,000 delegates—and officials, Members of Parliament, agents, and the Press. Although it is already more a mass meeting than a deliberative assembly, the addition of another 600 delegates would make a change of kind rather than degree. Even now Conference is so large that it can meet at only a handful of resorts. As Ben Gardner put the problem, a shade complacently: 'We would never be guilty of forcing the Labour Party to copy the ludicrous and undemocratic Tory habit of a main hall for the favoured, and overflow meetings addressed by loudspeaker, for the second-class supporters.'[2]

The unions' self-denial is not counted unto them for righteousness. Their votes already decided, union delegates can slip from their places for a stroll down the front, or sleep comfortably through the debate. When votes are taken the small union

---

[1] Cf., Mr Frank Foulkes of the ETU, 'Hands do not count at Congress, and we feel that if we send a good negotiating team, that is the best method of having this Organization represented at any national body'. *Report of the Policy Conference*, 1951, pp. 180–1.

[2] *AEU Journal*, November 1955.

delegations may be smaller than ever, while the constituency delegate must be in his seat if he wants his vote to be counted. This causes a familiar, unhappy end to important debates. The speeches over, the chairman calls for a show of hands. He takes the 'for' and 'against'. The hands shooting up for the motion may far outnumber those against. 'Lost', declares the chairman. 'Card vote', cries a delegate. In due course the figures show that the motion has been overwhelmingly lost. It is next to impossible for such voting not to appear grossly unfair. The distortion is sometimes so marked that chairmen prefer to call directly for a card vote to avoid embarrassment and ill-will. This discrepancy would never exist if the unions were at full strength and in their places, but the militants do not stop to think that they would be no happier to see 200 TGWU and 130 NUGMW hands raised in a solid phalanx. Albeit accidentally, the unions throughout give a misleading impression of their voting, particularly of their support for left-wing causes.

## The Voting

At almost every period in the Party's history someone has been worried about a cleavage on policy matters between the unions and the political wing. Many observers have voiced their disquiet in terms like these:

'Looking into the future he foresees a growing cleavage between the constituency parties led by the left-wing enthusiasts, and trade unions, led by rather dull-witted and conventional trade union officials. The keenest of the young trade unionists are in revolt against the block vote and the dictatorship of the well-established officers of the big trade unions.'[1]

That was Beatrice Webb, reporting Sir Oswald Mosley (then a Labour Member of Parliament) in 1930, but the same words could have been written a quarter of a century later. It was argued during the early fifties that the unions (or their leaders) were a solid conservative block, while the constituencies were fighting united for socialism. This notion that the Party was split on policy received the widest support. *The Seaman* concluded after the 1952 Party Conference:

[1] Quoted in *British Political Parties*, p. 506.

o

'There is evidence of a serious divergence between the trade unions and the constituency parties.'[1]

Sir William Lawther was just as convinced:

'It is no good keeping up the fake that there is no division among us. There is. The opinion of the trade unions is that the Bevanite activities are a deliberate attempt to undermine the leadership in the same way as Hitler and the Communists did. There is no difference between them. Their goal is the same— the glorification of power.'[2]

Arthur Deakin felt the same. At the 1952 Conference he said: 'I want to say a word about the division of opinion which exists within the ranks of the Party'.
A delegate: 'There is division in the unions.'
Mr. Deakin: 'There is no division of opinion in the unions.'[3]
The left-wing unions naturally did not see the issue in such black and white terms. Mr E. J. Hill of the Boilermakers' told his members:

'At the Labour Party Conference the political side of the Movement naturally got the support of those Trade Unions who were in the minority at the TUC.'[4]

The Fire Brigades' Union reported that:

'It was not the "Bevanites" v. The Rest, but the forward-looking constituency parties and the progressive unions against the right wing and the block vote of a few large unions.'[5]

Naturally enough Conservatives happily agreed that:

'The influence of these extreme intellectuals who now dominate the Party's political wing is now brought into direct conflict within the trade unions who represent the industrial wing of the Socialist movement. . . .'[6]

Not everyone accepted this explanation. Mr Cyril Hamnett, Administrative Officer of USDAW, wrote after the 1953 Conference:

[1] *The Seamen*, October-November 1952.
[2] The *Daily Telegraph*, January 29, 1953.      [3] *Report*, 1952, p. 126.
[4] *Monthly Report*, October 1952.      [5] *The Firefighter*, November 1954.
[6] *Notes on Current Politics*, October 20, 1952.

'Most of the debates emphasized the fact that on policy matters "Left" and "Right" are not clear-cut terms which divide constituency parties and trade unions into clearly marked boxes, but that some trade unions can be more left than some constituency parties on some questions, and on in infinite variations. That again is an important reason why there will be no split between the industrial wings of the Movement.'[1]

Miss Ellen McCullough, Education and Political Officer of the TGWU, reported in 1952 that 'on no single occasion did all or most of the constituencies vote one way and all or most of the unions the other'.[2] *The Times'* Labour Correspondent, who had no cause to whistle in the dark, wrote, 'The trade unions command an overwhelming vote at the annual Labour Party Conference, but in the main policy-making is left to the political leaders, and on controversial issues the unions seldom vote as a block'.[3] R. T. McKenzie, who sceptically quotes a senior Party official's claim that on no important issue in the fifteen years to 1953 had a majority of union votes opposed a majority of the constituency parties, nevertheless advances only once exception—the controversy over the rearmament programme in 1952.[4] Mr B. C. Roberts, Mrs Eirene White, and Professor G. D. H. Cole all remarked on the absence of solidarity in the union vote.[5] But they went unheeded. By 1955, the dogma—inherited from quieter times—was solidly established: the local parties and the unions are seeking quite different ends, and a solid trade union block vote is all that stands between Labour and Socialism.

The suggestion that the unions invariably acted as a homogeneous group could scarcely survive in its purest form the spectacle of the TGWU under Mr Frank Cousins—exasperating Transport House, dismaying the old guard of the General Council, delighting left-wingers who would have booed the very mention of the 'T and G' only a few years before. Yet even Mr Cousins might be simply an aberration, while the old beliefs

---

[1] *The New Dawn*, October 10, 1953 and October 25, 1952.
[2] *The Record*, October 1952.    [3] *The Times*, January 31, 1950.
[4] *British Political Parties*, p. 502.
[5] B. C. Roberts, Trade Unions and Party Politics, *Cambridge Journal*, April 1953. Eirene White, M.P., *Fabian Journal*, December 1953. G. D. H. Cole, The Labour Party and the Trade Unions. *Political Quarterly*, January-March 1953.

about the unions' behaviour in the Bevanite crisis remain as entrenched as ever. It is still important, therefore, to try to see the general pattern of the post-war years as a whole.

For all the categorical assertions about voting at Conference, discovering the attitudes of all affiliated organizations is not easy. Some unions consider that not even their own members have a right to know how they voted.[1] Nevertheless, articles, speeches, reports and interviews do furnish a fairly complete picture. It is also safe to assume that many unions vote consistently—that the ETU's position will be as close to Communist policy as is possible within the Labour Party, that the British Iron, Steel & Kindred Trades' Association will maintain its invariable support of the platform. Such aberrations as the ETU's opposition to 'Progressive Unity', the Union of Post Office Workers' support of workers' control, and the National Union of Agricultural Workers' hostility to German rearmament are normally so widely publicized that the dangers of error are small.

Yet few unions 'vote the ticket' for or against the National Executive. The NEC can count invariably on a small group of unions, none of which is known to have voted against it since the war.[2] This group of right-wing organizations is not always as happy as its loyalty suggests. Although the British Iron, Steel & Kindred Trades' Association bravely supports renationalization of steel in public, its real views may be gauged by the way it commended the policy to its members:

'It would be unnatural for this union with its roots so deep in the Labour Movement and giving strong support to the Labour Party to find itself at odds with the Party. Hugh Gaitskell can rest assured that this union will not falter in its support of official policy. There will be no dividing of the ways to delight our political opponents. The support will not, of course, be blind and unquestioning, nor would the Party have it so.'[3]

Although the Party has gradually swung away from many left-wing policies, it still works within a tradition which makes

[1] See pp. 258-9.
[2] NUGMW, National Union of Seamen, National Union of Boot & Shoe Operatives, United Textile Factory Workers' Association, British Iron, Steel & Kindred Trades' Association, and the National Union of Blastfurnacemen, etc.
[3] *Man and Metal*, December 1958.

the public expression of right-wing dissent far from easy. Accordingly the leadership is often further from the Party's true Right than the public debate reveals. A larger group of unions disagrees with the NEC from time to time, but almost always gives its support.[1]

On the extreme Left is a group of about a dozen unions, some led by Communists, others by social democrats, which normally vote and speak alike, but which split sharply on Communist affiliation to the Labour Party, Hungary, and the unilateral renunciation of nuclear weapons.[2] The moderate Left is less sharply defined.[3] During the Bevanite controversy these unions voted fairly consistently against the National Executive. The collapse of Bevanism dispersed them, some into consistent opposition (the Association of Engineering & Shipbuilding Draughtsmen and ASSET), and some into regular support of the new leadership (USDAW, and the AEU).

Some unions, like the Woodworkers, Patternmakers and the Locomotive Engineers & Firemen hover between orthodoxy and dissent. Often they are classified carelessly as 'right-wing' unions. Yet—for example—the Union of Post Office Workers opposed the proposal that the Deputy-Leader of the Party should be ex-officio a member of the NEC, and in 1955 it opposed official policy on control of profits and prices and the revision of the cost-of-living index. While the UPW supported German rearmament, its delegation was so split on another Bevanite issue—the scale of the post-Korean war rearmament programme—that it was forced to abstain. Its delegations have, in recent years, supported *Industry and Society* only after assurances that old-fashioned nationalization had not been abandoned, joined the left in the demand that public schools be abolished, and while they support official policy on nuclear weapons their demands that arms expenditure be cut are in

[1] National Union of Dyers, Bleachers & Textile Workers, National Society of Pottery Workers, Prudential Staff Union, National Association of Theatrical & Kine Employees and the Scottish Bakers' Union.

[2] ETU, National Union of Vehicle Builders, Constructional Engineering Union, Amalgamated Union of Foundry Workers, National Society of Metal Mechanics, United Society of Boilermakers Shipbuilders & Structural Workers, Chemical Workers' Union, Tobacco Workers' Union, Fire Brigades' Union.

[3] The most important unions are AEU, NUR, USDAW, with National Union of Furniture Trade Operatives, Plumbing Trades Union, Association of Engineering & Shipbuilding Draughtsmen, National Union of Tailors & Garment Workers.

advance of official policy. The UPW clings to its traditional policy of workers' control, and wants wider political rights for civil servants than Labour will concede.

The 'Left' and 'Right' which make up successive minorities and majorities at Conference may vary widely from one vote to the next. The political attitudes of the unions range almost continuously from the ETU on the most extreme left to the Textile Factory Workers on the far right. Up to 1956, 2·8 million union votes regularly supported the NEC, 1·8 million were solidly on the left, and one million were unpredictable. While the union vote therefore fell heavily in favour of the NEC, unless all the floaters backed the left, the movement was never homogeneous. Since 1956 the blocks of left- and right-wing union votes have been even less cohesive.

For a more precise picture of what happens in practice there is the evidence of Conference votes. The unions are large enough for the identification of almost all their votes to be physically possible. Unfortunately no public record is made of how the CLPs vote, and it is out of the question to gather the information directly from all 618 of them. But their attitude can be deduced indirectly. If we can establish that after subtracting the known trade union votes from the total votes cast against the platform the residue is less than half the votes held by the local parties, we may legitimately infer that the Constituency Labour Parties were not, on balance, opposed to the official policy.[1] Only if a majority of union votes is cast for one side of the question and a majority of constituency votes is cast for the other, can it be said that there was a split between unions and local parties.

Post-war Conferences fall conveniently into three main periods: the years of Labour government, the Bevanite controversy and the struggle for the succession, and the return to policy-making under Mr Gaitskell. They reveal the changing and widely different motivations in the various elements in the Party.

---

[1] For example:—Assume a conference at which the constituencies hold 1,000,000 votes. A resolution receives 2,000,000 votes. If it can be established that more than 1,500,000 trade union votes were cast for it, then it follows that it received fewer than half (500,000) the constituency votes.

*Labour in Power*

The Labour Party had decided the main outline of its post-war policy at the 1944 Conference. When the Party met in 1945, as the war-time coalition was breaking up, the main issue was the Party's relations with the Communist Party. Ever since Russia's war effort had rehabilitated British Communists from the ignominy they had earned in 1939, the demand for 'Progressive Unity' had been swelling. The 1943 Conference rejected the opening of negotiations with a view to affiliation of the Communist Party to the Labour Party. Since then an increasing number of union conferences had recorded their support for a closer relationship. Now the Conference Arrangements Committee refused to admit a resolution favouring the opening of talks, under the Three-Year Rule preventing reopening of a debate on a question for three years after a Conference decision. The vote to refer back their report gave Conference a chance to express its view on the substantive issue. Progressive Unity was defeated by 1,314,000 votes to 1,219,000. Four of the 'Big Six'—the Miners, Engineers, NUR and the National Union of Distributive & Allied Workers—favoured talks. They were joined by the Foundry Workers, and (probably) the Firemen, Building Trade Workers, and some smaller unions. The *known* union contribution to the minority was at the very least 1,030,000, leaving no more than 189,000 to come from the 541,000 CLP votes.[1]

Alarmed and surprised the NEC campaigned throughout the following year, asking organizations to revise their mandates —some of which went back to pre-war Popular Front days. In 1946 it was the AEU President, Mr Jack Tanner who moved that:

'One of the great needs of this country is to unify the ranks of the Labour Movement so that we are unitedly able to carry through the programme set out in "Let Us Face the Future". . . . With this in view, this Conference accepts the application of the Communist Party for affiliation to this Party. . . .'[2]

---

[1] 'CLP' includes, throughout, the votes of the City Labour Parties and the County Federations.

[2] *Report*, 1946, p. 72.

He was seconded by the Fire Brigades' Union, and supported by the NUR, which was still bound by its 1944 Conference decision. The Miners, Vehicle Builders, NUDAW and the ETU, had all withdrawn their support, but out of the 468,000 votes cast for the minority, 411,000 came from the unions whose support was announced, and the Foundry Workers and Building Trade Workers contributed 37,000 more.[1]

The Executive's proposed constitutional amendment to preclude Communist Party affiliation was carried by 2,413,000 to 667,000 votes. Again, the unions made up almost the whole of the minority—the increase being mainly attributable to NUDAW. As Mr Herbert Morrison told the Conference, 'There is no doubt what is the attitude of the Constituency Parties at this Conference. They have "had some", and they are great experts on Communist associations.'[2] This was probably the last occasion when the Constituency Labour Parties were held up as models of enlightenment to the unions. It was worth remembering when Mr Gaitskell spoke a few years later of 'Communist inspired' constituency delegates[3] that in 1945 almost every vote for affiliation with the Communists came from the unions. All but one of these unions had adopted such policies with Executive approval, thanks to the general goodwill towards Russia—and the effort of Communist Party members.

The gravest tensions within the Party during the immediately post-war conferences sprang from the division of Europe into two camps, and the vanishing of the dream that 'Left speaks to Left' successfully. Throughout these years there ran a nostalgic demand for a 'return to a socialist foreign policy', rarely precisely defined, but believing that the United States was as likely

---

[1] Cf., *The Electrical Trades Journal*, July 1946. *The Quarterly Journal of the NUVB*, July 1946.

The National Union of Foundry Workers' conference voted twenty-five to eight for Progressive Unity in the summer of 1945. It is not clear whether the union had voted for affiliation in 1945, but it should have done so in 1946.

The National Delegate Conference of the AUBTW voted (44:3) for affiliation in 1945, and 20:16 in 1946. Though the NDC could not bind the Executive, its spokesmen appeared to favour affiliation. *Report*, 1945, p. 191, and *Report*, 1946, p. 226.

[2] *Report*, 1946, p. 172.

[3] 'I was told by some observers that about one-sixth of the CLP delegates appear to be Communist inspired or Communist. This may well be too high. But if it should be one-tenth or even one-twentieth, it is a most shocking state of affairs. . . .' *The Times*, October 6, 1952.

a danger to peace as the USSR, turning hopefully to the notion of a Third Force, or to neutralism, as an alternative to membership of either power block, and supposing that however unthinkable Popular Fronts might be in Britain, foreign communists could safely be treated as good democrats.

The first disquiet was aroused by events in the liberated countries. In 1945 there were protests at the 'reinstatement of the old ruling classes in Greece, Poland [*sic*], Italy and Belgium'—which were defeated by an overwhelming majority of unions and constituencies alike. By 1946 the deterioration of relations with Russia, and the Government's support of the campaign against the Communists in Greece, brought a motion 'regretting the Government's apparent continuance of a traditionally Conservative Party policy of power politics abroad'. 'The rank and file members are profoundly distressed at the attitude of Bevin. They are asking "What does Ernest Bevin think he is doing?" ', cried a constituency delegate. 'It is not possible for a Socialist Government to have national unity with capitalist parties on foreign policy', affirmed Mr Koni Zilliacus. But the resolution was withdrawn without debate, while a demand for the severing of diplomatic and economic relations with Franco Spain was overwhelmingly defeated.

In 1947 Bevin defended his policies in person. 'A Foreign Secretary', he declared, 'has the right to know whether he has the support of his Party behind him', and he commented bitterly on those by whom he had been 'stabbed in the back'. With every vote implicitly a question of confidence, there was no doubt about the outcome. An attack on policy in Greece, demanding withdrawal of British troops, was rejected without a card vote, while references to 'subservience to capitalist America' were swept aside. Other debates revealed a similar frame of mind. Protests at the proscription of the British-Soviet Society, a Communist front, were defeated without a card vote. Supported by the pacifists, and by some neutralists, a demand that conscription be speedily abolished won only 571,000 votes. Although pacifism is traditionally stronger in the local parties than in the 'unsentimental' unions, it was Mr Walter Padley who told Conference that 'When Keir Hardie declared that conscription was the badge of the serf, he was not old fashioned. He understood the free force of democratic Socialism. . . .' The known opposition of USDAW and the Associated Society of Locomotive Engineers & Firemen meant that 275,000 at least of the minority votes came from the unions; there were probably many more. Finally, a resolution demanding a reduction of military commitments abroad and cuts in the armed forces 'in view of the manpower and production problems' was rejected by 2,357,000 to 1,109,000 votes. This time some of the extreme-left unions joined the anti-conscription group, and the resolution should have had the Engineers' and NUR's support. At least 850,000 trade union votes should have been cast against the platform, which had the support of a clear majority of the local parties.

During the following year 'the political activities of Mr J. Platts-Mills, MP' led to his expulsion from the Party. A motion to suspend Conference's standing orders to hear his appeal was rejected by 2,563,000 votes to 1,403,000—with 1,481,000 votes not cast.[1] The high abstention rate was not surprising: Conference was not told the grounds of Mr Platts-Mills' expulsion, though the final decision had obviously turned on his organizing of the so-called Nenni-Telegram.[2] How the two wings of the party voted is not wholly clear—although at least 1,500,000 votes were either not cast, or did not heed the Executive's plea not to establish a dangerous precedent.[3] This was far from the automatic rubber-stamping of Executive disciplinary action that is sometimes alleged against the unions.

Mr Zilliacus returned to the attack against Bevin's foreign policies in 1948. This time he was moving an amendment to a resolution approving the Marshall Plan, which *inter alia* advocated 'instructing the Service Departments to frame their estimates and make their strategic dispositions on the assumption that Britain need not prepare for self-defence against either

[1] There are always some votes not cast, because delegates are out of the hall when the vote is taken, or have mislaid their voting card, or have not attended the Conference.

[2] This was an encouraging message to the Nenni socialists, who were at that time collaborating with the Italian Communist Party.

[3] The Conference has never accepted a motion to suspend Standing Orders to hear an expelled member. If it did so now, Mr Morgan Phillips suggested, it might have to hear Mr Alfred Edwards, who had been expelled for right wing deviations.

the USA or the USSR'.[1] His highly personal formulation of a 'socialist foreign policy' was rejected by 4,097,000 to 224,000 votes (mainly from the left-wing unions). It commanded almost no support in the constituencies—though the 1,150,000 abstaining votes showed many to be unconvinced by Bevin's massive statement of his case. As the cold war sharpened the abstainers were to diminish. Once again the demands for withdrawal from Greece, protesting at 'the grim spectacle of seeing the life crushed out of Greek democracy' were swept aside, along with criticisms of the zonal system and denazification in Germany.

During the following year both Mr Zilliacus and Mr L. J. Solley were expelled from the Party for adopting an attitude 'more in sympathy with Communist international policy than with the policy of the Labour Party'. Asked to hear their appeals, Conference refused by 3,023,000 to 1,993,000, then voted by 4,721,000 votes to 714,000 against referring back the NEC's report of its action. Abstentions were negligible. The delegate for Mr Zilliacus' constituency bitterly declared 'You may kill Labour Parties everywhere, you will be no better off for it. . . . You have to have common sense and decency even in the way you treat Constituency Labour Parties. . . .'[2] Mr Sidney Silverman argued that 'If this matter were left to a vote of the Constituency Labour Parties . . . alone the reference back would be overwhelmingly defeated'.[2] He was convinced that the disquiet of many members of the PLP found a sympathetic echo in the country—erroneously. The voting on the motion to lift standing orders cannot accurately be established—but it was moved by Mr Sandy of USDAW, and seconded by Mr Jack Stanley of the Constructional Engineering Union. The voting on the expulsions was clearer. Apart from USDAW's opposition, which was probable but not finally ascertainable, at least 249,000 union votes are *known* to have been cast against expulsion. To these should probably be added several small unions and two of the Socialist societies. Taking the minimum of 249,000 votes, the remaining 465,000 minority votes were slightly more than half the total CLP vote of 869,000. If full information were avail-

[1] Mr Zilliacus' motion covered two pages of the agenda in much this vein.
[2] *Report*, 1949, pp. 120–4.

able, it seems certain that the constituencies split either evenly, or slightly in favour of the NEC.

Bevin's foreign policy came under attack for the last time in 1949, in a motion demanding a series of initiatives—such as the ending of all trading embargoes with Eastern Europe—in order to halt the 'increasing danger of war'. Though moved by Mr Harold Davies it was seconded by the Foundry Workers, and openly backed by the ETU. Surprisingly, although both the NUR and the AEU found the proposal far too extreme, it had the support of USDAW.[1] At least 580,000 of these opposition votes are known to have come from the unions. The pro-Bevin vote of 4,861,000 was swelled by a decisive majority of local parties.

Not all contentious issues came before Conference, nor did the resolutions debated always express clearly the opposition view. Yet as long as Bevin remained Foreign Secretary there seemed little chance of his winning less than a sweeping victory no matter what the subject or the drafting.

This impression of the unions' role is confirmed by the record of the TUC. While Party Conferences were brushing aside protests on policy in Greece, successive TUCs showed much sharper antagonism. The 1945 Congress voted its disquiet at the handling of Greek affairs (principally on trade union questions) without taking a card vote. The next Congress referred back as too mild a strongly worded report on the Greek situation and by 3,951,000 votes to 2,984,000 demanded that the Government bring pressure to bear to obtain restoration of trade union rights. In 1948 Congress again demanded an end to 'persecution' in Greece and asked the Government to help restore democracy there—although, like the Party Conference, it rejected demands for withdrawal of British troops.

Similarly, resettlement of Polish troops in Britain, unchallenged at the Party Conference, was accepted at the TUC by only 3,300,000 to 2,416,000 votes—with the TGWU in opposition. The Congress also wanted to 'get tough' with Spain. In 1946 a motion expressing disquiet at the foreign policy pursued in Greece and Spain, and the deterioration of relations with the USSR gained 2,444,000 votes—although 3,557,000 voted

[1] *The New Dawn*, October 14, 1950.

against. But by 4,534,000 votes to 1,391,000 the Congress demanded that economic and diplomatic relations with Spain be broken. In 1947 a minority of 3,025,000 votes still favoured breaking off economic relations with Spain and recognizing the Republican Government in exile.

After the Prague coup and Russian refusal to join the Marshall Plan the tide flowed rapidly against the far Left. A demand that Britain withdraw from the European Recovery Programme found no seconder. In 1949 a challenge to the TUC's withdrawal from the Communist-led World Federation of Trade Unions was overwhelmingly defeated—though over a million votes favoured continued affiliation. In 1950, when the General Council submitted its report on Korea and atomic weapons—which only the Communists opposed, only 525,000 votes were cast against it. When the dispute over Spain was aired for the last time in 1951 a protest at the arrival of a Spanish ambassador in London received 2,608,000 votes. A demand that restrictions on trade with Communist countries be removed and that German and Japanese rearmament be abandoned also won substantial minority support (1,795,000 votes).

No other question arose as consistently at both Conference and Congress. In 1948, when both discussed wages, profits and prices, the orthodox line triumphed easily—although the minority at the TUC gathered 2,818,000 votes. Thereafter Conference never debated wage restraint alone; it was always one of several elements in motions on economic policy. But it remained the key debate at every Congress until 1955. While the General Council's shifting line won every time, its 'victory' in 1950, when Congress rejected a resolution opposing the wage freeze by 3,949,000 votes to 3,727,000, was tantamount to a moral defeat.

As early as 1947 militants who suspected the government of being lukewarm on the nationalization of steel were campaigning for the industry to be taken over during the Parliamentary session in course. Conference rejected these demands without a card vote, but at Congress the minority of 2,360,000 votes showed that many 'hard-headed trade unionists' could make quite impossible demands on Parliamentary time and ministerial resources. Demands that the Party adopt a 'national wages policy', which came before the 1947 Conference, were rejected without a card vote. By contrast, the 1946 Congress defeated (by 3,522,000 votes to 2,657,000) a proposal that the General Council prepare a report on a national wages policy. Against National Executive advice the 1947 Party Conference demanded the immediate introduction of equal pay by 2,310,000 votes to 598,000—with 750,000 votes not cast. Many unions were bound by long-standing mandates, and even one or both of the general unions refused the NEC its customary support. The local parties were much more able to heed the platform's plea that 'the time is not yet ripe'. In the same year Congress adopted the same demand by a simple show of hands, while in 1950 it again rejected General Council advice and voted for immediate equal pay by 4,490,000 votes to 2,367,000.

The remaining issues were secondary. In 1947 even Mr Bevan's persuasive powers did not deter Conference from demanding that the tied cottage be abolished immediately, by the tiny margin of 1,558,000 votes to 1,555,000. The normally loyal National Union of Agricultural Workers seconded the motion, and the TGWU (which has a sizeable rural membership) joined them in voting against the platform. This was in no sense a trade union-constituency party split; although some left-wingers would vote for anything which 'dished' the landlords, it is likely that most of the country CLPs voted against the platform, and the urban parties were more ready to listen to Mr Bevan's arguments about the Parliamentary timetable. When a similar motion deploring the Government's failure to act came before the 1949 Conference even more unions voted against the National Executive—which preferred to concede defeat rather than take a card vote.

Some enthusiasts became alarmed during 1947–8 at signs that fascist activities might be beginning again in Britain. While Harold Laski persuaded sponsors of a motion at the 1948 Conference that the NEC had the situation in hand, the 1947 TUC referred back a report by the General Council, couched in similar terms, as not being sufficiently strong, by 4,857,000 votes to 2,360,000.

Finally the widespread realization that nationalization had not brought the expected millenium led to a confused and troubled debate in 1950 on the workers' control of industry, and the administration of the nationalized industries. If the debate was full of rather muddled disquiet, the chairman's questionable acceptance of a previous question motion on the four separate motions simultaneously—one of the most blatant examples of NEC manipulation since the war—made the vote completely meaningless. Although it is unlikely that the constituencies and the unions were opposed on this essentially industrial question it was impossible to tell how the vote split. Although other questions were discussed, and some—such as the Ireland Act— raised a storm in the PLP without reaching Conference, none stirred more than a numerically insignificant minority, and certainly there was little division between CLPs and unions.

The backgrounds to Congress and Conference were so dissimilar during these years that their votes can be compared only cautiously and approximately. The General Council was preoccupied with resisting Communist attempts to take over the leadership of the movement. On such crucial issues as wage restraint it fought pitched battles; on peripheral questions, such as Greece or Spain, it was good tactics to 'talk left' and accept extreme resolutions, in order to keep goodwill for more important battles. The leadership could not move too far or too fast. Voting on foreign policy matters was often profoundly influenced by such tactical considerations: it might have differed markedly had anything vital been at stake. The falling support for extremist views from 1948 onwards was partly a genuine reflection of changing attitudes within the movement, but also the discrediting of the Communists enabled leaders who had consolidated their positions to turn and fight motions they would have had to let pass in the immediate post-war period.

By contrast every vote at the Party Conference was a vote of confidence in the Labour Government. Bevin particularly would not concede defeats on lesser issues just to send delegates home happy. Personality also counted; at Congress, able leaders put the Communist case in person. At Conference they had to rely on less talented fellow-travellers—and they had to contend with Bevin himself. Such was Bevin's authority that the hostile resolution on Greece on which he spoke at the 1945 Conference was swept aside into a vote of thanks at the end of his speech. Although Bevin's confidence in facing Conference was often attributed to his certainty that he commanded the massive and loyal support of the unions, and his most vocal critics were 'intellectuals', he carried most of the constituencies too. His critics in the Parliamentary Party never really convinced the rank-and-file.

During the years of Labour government the unions did remain massively loyal, in domestic as in foreign affairs. Nevertheless, most of the votes cast in opposition to the government's policies came from the unions. Outside Conference, the government was much more frequently embarrassed by the unions' inability to maintain a wage freeze, or their hostility to the Control of Engagements Order than by the actions of the local militants. During this period the unions were further to the left than usual—perhaps even slightly to the left of the local parties. For all the doubts that the constituencies may have had—and for all the noisy activity of dissident Members of Parliament—they remained overwhelmingly loyal.

### The Bevanite Years

Though revolt had been rumbling through the Party from the moment an expanded and accelerated rearmament programme was announced in January 1951, the Bevanite controversy really burst into the open with the resignation of Mr Bevan, and two other ministers, over the imposition of charges on the National Health Service in the 1951 Budget. Through the summer the dissidents kept up a running assault on the official leadership and on trade union leaders in such *Tribune* pamphlets as *One Way Only* and *Going our Way?* The trade unionists were so incensed that they were as eager as the Bevanites for a show-down at Conference. Instead, the election intervened and the cracks had to be papered over in the interests of electoral unity. It was only in 1952, at the acrimonious Morecambe Conference that the controversy could be brought before the whole Party. Thereafter, in a series of battles over policy and the party leadership, it became an article of the Bevanites' faith that they were the authentic voice of the rank and file in constituency and trade union alike.

Conference never did discuss the Health Service charges, but the 1951 TUC did. The General Council only just succeeded in rallying Congress to support the Government by 3,775,000 votes to 3,272,000 (with the NUR's 392,000 inadvertently not cast for the minority). Such a vote might well have spelled defeat at the Party Conference. Some of the NEC's most constant supporters had joined the opposition. On the first of the Bevanite issues the unions were almost evenly divided.

The crucial debate at Morecambe was the attack on the scale of the rearmament programme. Mr Walter Padley, who put the moderate case that the proposed level of expenditure was beyond the capacity of the economy, remarked, 'The abiding power of this Movement . . . depends upon a recognition of the unity of interest between the trade unions and the constituency parties, and on the issue before Conference this morning there is certainly not a division of that kind at all'.[1] He was right.[2] The NEC carried the day by 3,644,000 votes to 2,288,000—with 237,000 votes not cast. At least 1,811,000 trade union votes were committed to opposing the Executive, and the Union of Post Office Workers (147,000 votes) abstained. Accordingly the constituencies gave a maximum of 477,000 of their 1,164,000 votes to the left-wing challengers.[3]

The TUC was not comparable. The main motion dragged in references to germ warfare, multilateral disarmament, and aid to underdeveloped countries. USDAW proposed an amendment limiting the motion to criticism of the scale of expenditure on economic grounds. The opposition was completely split. The orthodox and far-left unions united against the USDAW amendment (which won only 1,272,000 votes), and then the moderate left and orthodox unions joined forces against the substantive motion (which won 1,801,000 votes). The true

[1] *Report*, 1952, p. 142.
[2] *British Political Parties*, p. 503, McKenzie suggests this was the only post-war example, up to 1953, where the conference clearly split on union-constituency lines.
[3] The unions pledged to oppose the rearmament programme were: AEU (587,000 votes); USDAW (317,000); NUR (317,000); ETU (120,000); Tailors & Garment Workers (98,000); Boilermakers (46,000); NUPE (45,000); Vehicle Builders (36,000); Plumbing Trades Union (33,000); Draughtsmen (30,000); Metal Mechanics (26,000); Sheet Metal Workers & Braziers (25,000); Constructional Engineers (19,000); Plasterers (16,000); Fire Brigades' Union (16,000); Foundry Workers (16,000); Furniture Trade Operatives (16,000); Patternmakers (14,000); 9 unions (36,000).

P

opposition of about 2,300,000 votes—was comparable with the unions' Party Conference vote.

A motion calling for a campaign against the government and supporting 'the trade union movement where it is forced into industrial action to defend the living standards of its members' provoked an acrimonious debate. This ambiguous phrase in an immoderate, but otherwise acceptable, resolution might have passed unnoticed in quieter times. In the bitterly suspicious atmosphere of this Conference, it appeared to many union leaders to be an attempt to commit them to use the strike weapon for industrial purposes. Its source—the perennially far-left Salford West CLP—and the angry barracking of Arthur Deakin by constituency militants, confirmed their suspicions. But Jack Tanner emphasized that the AEU had no similar fears, and sufficient other unions agreed with him to contribute at least 985,000 of the 1,728,000 votes the motion received (against 3,986,000).[1] Possibly the angry atmosphere stirred a slight majority to support the resolution, part from conviction, part from irritation with Arthur Deakin's taunt that 'You are the fellows who would squeal the most if it came to a strike for any purpose at all, much less for political action'. Even this is not fully established.

The nationalization controversy did not break out fully in 1952. There was no dissent when Mr Deakin proposed the renationalization of road haulage. However, an extremist demand that on renationalization no 'further compensation' should be paid and that 'all profits made . . . during denationalization, should be expropriated', was rejected by 2,386,000 votes to 1,652,000, with 2,121,000 not cast. Most unions were mandated against expropriation—which has never had much support in the Party. The high abstention rate, and the sizeable minority may have been a demonstration of hostility to de-nationalization of road haulage and steel, but no detailed examination of the voting can be made. Even a union as far to the left as the Association of Engineering & Shipbuilding Draughts-men felt unable to join the minority. Yet, since there were only 1,164,000 CLP votes, the minority must have included at least

---

[1] Union support included: AEU, ETU, AUFW, FBU, NUVB, USBISS and some smaller unions.

490,000 union votes. Since this was more than the hard-core extreme-left vote, one or more large moderate left union must have cast an eccentric vote. In this case the union support might have been as high as 850,000–1,000,000. But this issue was not specifically Bevanite.

The nationalization debate was really fought out in 1953 on a series of motions proposing either sweeping nationalization, or the taking over of single industries. They were unusually clear-cut, and the debate was straightforward. Nevertheless, the voting—in which every motion was rejected—was far from clear. The nationalizing minority ranged from 1,395,000 votes for 'socialization of the essential industries' to 2,022,000 for taking over the aircraft industry. The Confederation of Ship-building & Engineering Unions' plan to nationalize the engineering industry received more votes than the proposal to take over the machine tools industry—which was part of the plan. Unions holding 1,781,000 votes were committed to an extension of nationalization. Clearly all this support did not materialize.

It was rumoured that both USDAW and the NUR had defected from the nationalizers' camp—although they had unequivocally demanded more nationalization at the Douglas TUC only a month before.[1] Yet the debate itself showed that the demand for extended nationalization did not come only from the 'intellectuals' in the constituencies. It was R. W. Casasola of the Foundry Workers who moved the adoption of the CSEU plan, seconded by Jack Tanner of the AEU—which also announced its support for the machine tools resolution. The motion to take the aircraft industry into public ownership was moved by Mr George Cornes of the Draughtsmen—many of whose members work in the industry. The Patternmakers added

[1] The promised union support included: AEU (627,000 votes); USDAW (330,000); NUR (323,000); ETU (120,000); AUFW (50,000); USBISS (46,000); NUPE (45,000); NUVB (40,000); AESD (32,000); PTU (33,000); NUSMWB (26,000); NSMM (25,000); CEU (20,000); FBU (15,000); NAOP (15,000); Small unions, 20,000.

Though it was suggested (*Fabian Journal*, December 1953) that USDAW and NUR had backed down, the NUR had seconded the reference back of the General Council's report on nationalization, as too mild. Walter Padley supporting the reference back said: 'I come to the rostrum as an unrepentant advocate of an immediate extension of public ownership, and I speak under direct mandate from the last annual conference of my union'. *Report of TUC*, 1953, pp. 387–8.

their firm support, and the Typographical Association gave its qualified backing to the CSEU plan. Neither union could be called left wing. Even had both the NUR and USDAW defected, the union support for more nationalization was at least 1,130,000 votes. It seems probable that a majority of the constituency votes favoured the NEC. It is quite out of the question that they backed the Bevanites by a large majority.

If confirmation were needed that a powerful minority of unions supported more extensive nationalization it lay in the reception of the General Council's proposals to make only minor extensions of public ownership. Unions which felt that these proposals were too mild made up the appreciable 2,640,000 vote minority.[1]

One other major issue—not associated with Mr Bevan— came before Conference. The NUR proposed that the principle of workers' control be introduced into the nationalized in-dustries. It was rejected by 4,658,000 to 1,488,000 votes.[2] Since the NUR, ETU, AEU, and Union of Post Office Workers were sure to give their votes—totalling 1,224,000—there is no need to examine the smaller union votes to show that industrial democracy raised no enthusiasm in the local parties.

The 1954 Conference, the most bitter of all, met in intrigue and recrimination. It was dominated by the German rearmament debate, which had been raging through constituencies, unions, and the political weeklies since the beginning of the year. In September the TUC had supported the official line by only 4,077,000 votes to 3,622,000, a majority which was almost certain to spell defeat at Scarborough. Delegations met in long, stormy sessions through a weekend of constant lobbying and manoeuvring. The Amalgamated Society of Woodworkers' delegation switched its vote, and for technical reasons two cotton unions also changed to back the NEC.[3] The Amalgamated Union of Building Trade Workers, opposed to German rearmament at the TUC, decided to abstain in the course of the debate. It was

---

[1] The 1952 TUC had pushed a reluctant General Council into preparing proposals for the extension of public ownership, by 4,542,000 votes to 4,210,000.
[2] It was defeated without a card vote at the 1953 TUC.
[3] The Weavers and the Beamers, Twisters & Drawers had opposed German rearmament at the TUC, but the United Textile Factory Workers' Association, of which they are members, voted *en bloc* for rearmament at the Party Conference.

probably the only time since the war that the National Executive has faced Conference without knowing in advance what the outcome of the debate would be. By 3,270,000 votes to 3,022,000 —thanks, in fact, to the ASW—the platform snatched victory.

No fewer than 2,091,000 trade union votes were cast with the minority.[1] With them went Poale Zion, the Socialist Medical Association, the National Association of Labour Teachers and (probably) the Royal Arsenal Cooperative Society,[2] a further 34,000 votes. The CLPs and Federations must therefore have split about 900,000 to 280,000, with 125,000 votes uncast. There could be no doubt that a trade union majority confronted a constituency majority—although the third of constituency votes which either abstained or supported the NEC was surprisingly high. Yet, how real was it to talk of a 'split' between the local Parties and the unions when the unions were themselves so deeply divided? The official line 'triumphed' by fifty-three per cent to forty-seven per cent at the TUC, by fifty-four per cent to forty-six per cent at the Party Conference. Further, although the Bevanites had tended to claim that the issue was 'theirs', the opposition included such staunch anti-Bevanites as Mr Gooch and Mr Hugh Dalton.

The real measure of the Party's bitter demoralization was its discussion of the remaining foreign policy motions. In the debate on the South-East Asia Treaty Organization Mr Harold Davies, for Leek CLP, opposed 'any commitment in Asia and the Pacific that has as its purpose the encirclement of China'. The Fire Brigades' Union, a trifle less tendentiously, would support a regional pact in South-East Asia only if China and Japan were included. Neither made a reasonable formulation of the case against SEATO; both were soundly rejected, but the former won 2,570,000 votes, and the second 1,572,000. Why one drew so

[1] Of the seventy-seven unions on which there is information, thirty-four voted against the NEC, thirty voted for it, two abstained, eleven were not represented at Conference. The unions opposing the NEC were AEU (621,000 votes); NUR (328,000); USDAW (328,000); ETU (120,000); NUTGW (84,000); NUAW (71,000); AUFW (50,000); NSP (47,000); USBISS (46,000); NUVB (40,000); Natsopa (34,000); PTU (32,000); AESD (29,000); NUSMWB (26,000); NSMM (26,000); NUPBPW (25,000); NUFTO (19,000); CEU (18,000); FBU (16,000); AUOBCAW (16,000); NAOP (15,000); small unions (55,000).

[2] The Cooperative Congress opposed German rearmament. It was reported (Daily Worker, September 22, 1954) that Royal Arsenal Cooperative Society delegates had been advised to oppose rearmament.

much more support is not at all clear. Some delegates may have
suspected the second motion's obviously Communist origin, and
they may have been deterred by its proposal to give China and
Japan a perpetual veto on the creation of regional pacts. But
perhaps they were stirred by Mr Harold Davies' cry: 'We are
fighting for a different foreign policy from the Conservatives at
the next election. . . . The purpose of this Conference is to
clarify its position and tie the Executive down to Socialist
principles in foreign policy.' Here was a motion that had been
discussed at scarcely any union conferences. By now some
delegations were so bitter that they had ceased to vote on the
merits of the issues and were 'voting the ticket'. It seems likely
that a slight majority of the local party votes supported the
FBU, and practically certain that about 700–800,000 backed
Mr Davies.

The same problem arose over the call for American troops to
be withdrawn from Britain. The more militant supporters of
'a Socialist foreign policy' had been campaigning for withdrawal
of American troops for years, but it was never a Bevanite
demand. Normally it would have won almost no support. Now,
after an angry and confused debate on six foreign policy resolutions it received 1,822,000 votes. Obviously many of these
must have been union votes—possibly as many as 1,200,000 if
the AEU gave its expected support. The CLPs were probably
almost evenly divided. Again, another muddled resolution
involving control of profits and prices, revision of the cost of
living index, and the reduction of arms expenditure, received
2,132,000 votes (against 3,758,000). This time a clear majority
of constituency parties supported the platform, while the AEU,
USDAW, the Union of Post Office Workers and the inveterate
left-wing unions joined the minority.

Finally, the Conference was asked to disapprove of the NEC's
proscription of the Trotskyist periodical, *Socialist Outlook*. The
reference back (moved by Miss Jennie Lee) was seconded by
Mr Jack Stanley of the Constructional Engineers, and was
known to have the support of the AEU and USDAW. Despite
the inevitable complaints about block votes stamping out
freedom, a majority of constituencies had enough acquaintance
with the Revolutionary Communist Party to give the NEC

their support. The minority of 1,596,000 came predominantly from the unions—well under 400,000 came from local parties.[1]

Dominated by the open competition of Mr Gaitskell, Mr Morrison and Mr Bevan for the leadership, the 1955 Conference was nevertheless not as tense. It was the first of the H-Bomb Conferences, but the issue raised little passion as yet. From the beginning it was clear that the local parties were more susceptible to demands to stop making or stocking nuclear weapons than the unions, who have always felt more keenly the advantages of negotiating from strength. This Conference had three motions to consider. Wycombe CLP opposed manufacture of the H-Bomb and condemned its use. Mr Zilliacus, restored to membership, if not to grace, moved one of his familiar manifesto-resolutions, declaring *inter alia*, that manufacturing the Bomb was economically wasteful, that Britain should not be committed to going to war by the United States 'if the US Administration fails to come to terms with us on how to make peace', and that more research into the effects of nuclear tests was needed. Finally, the AEU proposed (and the Foundry Workers seconded), that the H-Bomb should be banned through negotiation in the United Nations.

The first resolution, clearly appealing to the pacifists, abolitionists, and Communists, was lost by 5,300,000 votes to 1,174,000. The NUR was one of the few large unions at this time favouring banning the Bomb. Neither the AEU nor USDAW supported the Left, but a slight minority of local parties favoured abolition. Mr Zilliacus' proposals, rejected by 4,630,000 votes to 1,995,000 also seemed to have won a small majority of the local parties. Finally, the NEC accepted the AEU motion. Significantly, the TUC had already anticipated the Party's change of course by proposing the suspension of tests.

Congress also anticipated Conference over National Service. It agreed to an immediate reduction in the period of service,

[1] The Conference also dealt with the composition of foreign delegations, the establishment of a National Agency service, and the eligibility of delegates for election to the NEC. All these touched directly on constituency rights. They had never been discussed in the unions, and it seems probable that the constituencies made up almost all the minority on the first and third of these, and split about evenly on the second.

while the Party, adopting a similar resolution rejected a demand
for immediate abolition, by 4,900,000 votes to 1,337,000. Many
union conferences had agreed to support immediate reduction
after debates where abolition had been rejected. Therefore,
while the left-wing and anti-conscription unions gave the
resolution their support, the Constituency Labour Parties, who
were less tied, split about evenly.

Conference had also to consider the fag end of the German
rearmament controversy, raised by an amendment moved by
the Fire Brigades' Union to a 'loyal' foreign policy motion
proposed by the Miners. This demand for the preventing of
'the rebirth of German militarism' was defeated by 4,968,000
votes to 1,669,000. Some unions were unsure how far their
former mandates still applied, but the AEU and the majority
of left-wing unions felt bound to support the amendment, which
was supported surprisingly well, considering it coincided with
Communist Party policy. The constituencies split almost
evenly.

## The New Leadership

As long as the succession to Mr Attlee remained in doubt every
disagreement in the Party had widened into an angry quarrel.
Once the struggle for power was settled, and Mr Bevan
reconciled to the new leadership, the first three Conferences of
the Gaitskell era were very different from the five preceding
years. Now the Party's humiliating failure in the 1955 election,
and the weariness with wrangling and bitterness damped down
the differences that remained. One by one the most able leaders
of Bevanism made their peace, until in 1957 Mr Bevan himself
stood clasping Mr Gaitskell's hand on the platform at Brighton.
When Mr Bevan, replying to demands that Britain renounce
the Hydrogen Bomb, snapped 'You call that statesmanship?
I call it an emotional spasm',[1] the disintegration of the Left
seemed complete.

While the opposition was scattered and leaderless, the
National Executive could face Conference with more confidence
than at any time since the war. For years it had been simply
demanding the rejection of the demands made by the Left, the

[1] *Report*, 1957, p. 181.

very picture of immobilism. Now it was presenting three major
policy statements a year—which took up a large slice of conference time. The opposition (to whom it apparently never
occurred to submit alternative policy statements as resolutions)
was in the unfavourable position of picking away at occasional
paragraphs or demanding outright rejection—which would leave
the Party with no policy at all. The Executive had greater
advantages than ever—simultaneous discussion of a policy statement and six dissimilar resolutions can never be quite coherent.
It was scarcely surprising that only one amendment in the
whole nine debates came within half a million votes of success.

The National Executive's success was partly the result of a
renewed determination to drum up support. In 1950 the NEC
was alleged to have issued *Challenge to Britain* without consulting either the AEU or the Confederation of Shipbuilding
and Engineering Unions.[1] Now there were protracted discussions between the NEC's Study Groups and both the unions
and the Economic Committee of the TUC. These Groups included not only both orthodox and ex-Bevanite members, but
the leadership made special efforts to convince unions like the
AEU which had sided with the Bevanites.

Most union objections were overcome long before the
documents reached the floor of Conference—indeed the real
debate on Labour's economic aims entirely preceded publication. Despite the apparent agreement on *National Superannuation*—Labour's pension policy—at the 1957 Conference,
the NEC's main problem had been to coax the TUC away from
its long-standing insistence on flat-rate benefits to accepting
graded pensions. It was also understood that when the draft of
*Personal Freedom* came before the NEC trade union members
demanded that the references to the unions be pruned down to a
hymn of praise which revealed no suggestion that unions could
use their power to infringe liberty.

Yet there was still opposition. Although the most vocal
critics came from a small, perennially militant group of Constituency Labour Parties, there were dissenting unions too.
'The rank and file of both our movements are becoming vigilant
and looking for a real Socialist lead', argued Mr A. E. Sumbler

[1] *AEU Journal*, January 1950.

of the AEU. Despite its general drift to the right the AEU declared that *Personal Freedom* was 'not sufficiently forthright, and . . . those entrusted with the task of drafting this document appear to have been hampered by a desire not to give offence'. Although the AEU did not press its demand for the withdrawal of *Personal Freedom*, it joined most other left-wing unions in backing the Draughtsmen's demand that greater safeguards be introduced before the dismissal of 'security risks'. Although the motion was lost by 3,478,000 votes to 2,625,000 the minority contained 2,127,000 trade union votes.

The discussion of differential rents, during the debate on *Homes for the Future* shows how disagreements run through both wings. Differential rents are a Tory device to 'sow dissension among the different sections of the working class', Miss Howell of Perry Barr CLP announced, with the approval of the Boiler-makers' spokesman and the support of the AEU. On the contrary, 'they are a practical expression of "From each according to his ability, to each according to his need" ' declared the delegate of South-East Leeds CLP, and Mr H. Solomons announced USDAW's flat opposition because 'in the distributive trades we have some of the lowest paid workers in the country, and we do not see why it should be made impossible for our members to obtain council accommodation merely because their incomes are too low. . . .'[1]

Again, in 1957, it was Mr Campbell of the NUR who moved the rejection of the Party's proposals for public ownership, *Industry and Society* in the name of 'red-blooded Socialism'. Every other member of the Big Six came to the rostrum to support the new policy; even the normally far-left Amalgamated Union of Foundry Workers surprisingly added its approval.

---

[1] *Report*, 1956, pp. 98ff.
Conference had a diluted impression of union opposition. Thus, the Amalgamated Union of Building Trade Workers' journal thought that in *Homes for the Future* 'the main problem has been ignored' (*Building Worker*, August 1956), while *Industry and Society* was attacked three times—including an Executive resolution, as 'a most depressing document. Hesitant, vague, full of generalities' (*Building Worker*, September 1956). It was remarked of *Personal Freedom* that 'the trouble is not so much its platitudes but that when in power Labour does not practice what it now preaches' (*Building Worker*, August 1956). More expected critics denounced *Industry and Society* as 'little less than utter confusion' (*Electron*, September 1957) and 'ineffectual and unnoticed' (*Railway Review*, November 21, 1958).

For all this well stage-managed mustering of the potentates of the industrial wing, Mr Campbell's amendment received 1,442,000 votes (against 5,383,000), and *Industry and Society* was adopted by 5,309,000 votes to 1,276,000. Although some constituency militants felt that Keir Hardie had been irremediably betrayed and Mr Herbert Morrison had found that 'This document is confusing. It is too clever by half', about half the constituencies were coaxed into supporting it. The NUR amendment attracted about 865,000 union votes. Another demand for a 'shopping list' of industries to be included received only 630,000 votes, of which at least 250,000 came from the unions. Even the minority for rejecting *Industry and Society* included 700,000 union votes.

There was only one other major disagreement, over *Learning to Live*, the statement on educational policy. For the second time since the war the TGWU openly opposed the platform.[1] Mr Frank Cousins argued that the call for the abolition of public schools restated 'a simple, basic Socialist principle of the integration of the whole education system for our benefit'. As Mr Cousins talked darkly of his opponents 'going back on Socialism', the NEC must have thought nostalgically of Arthur Deakin. One of the union's senior officials took an almost naïve pleasure at being among the rebels: 'This year at least the platform has not been able to count automatically on the support of the TGWU'. Few unions had recent mandates. Determining how their votes were split was therefore exceptionally difficult. The amendment was lost by only 3,067,000 votes to 3,544,000, while *Learning to Live* was accepted by 5,176,000 votes to 1,436,000. The unions contributed at least 2,400,000 votes to the minority wanting to abolish public schools, and probably as many as 2,556,000. How many of them were willing to reject the document altogether because of their disappointment at this inadequacy is much less clear—for even many vigorous opponents of public schools hesitated to leave the Party with no policy.

There were other, minor, disagreements, such as Mr John Lawrence's appeal against his expulsion from the Party for his

---

[1] In 1946 Arthur Deakin moved a demand for the immediate adoption of the forty hour week which was rejected by the NEC.

activities in Holborn & St. Pancras. The 1957 conference rejected by 4,101,000 votes to 2,531,000 a motion to hear him—
the appreciable minority was more a measure of Conference's
liberalism than of its approval. About two million of those votes
came from the unions. When an attempt was made to refer back
the NEC's report of its expulsion of six members of the St.
Pancras Borough Council breakaway group, it won a derisory
476,000 votes. Since this included the votes of such unions as
the ETU, the Foundry Workers, and several smaller organizations, there was little doubt that the local parties had overwhelmingly supported the NEC.

Few issues have so exposed the weakness of making certain
types of policy at Conference. It is all but impossible to formulate
an atomic policy in the hundred words or so of a Conference
resolution. Moreover, unilateral disarmament was not a policy
in itself, it was a mere fraction of a policy. It could not be
separated from the complete recasting of defence and international policy which would inevitably follow. Yet the nuclear
disarmers were not only trying to persuade Conference to adopt
this morsel of a policy, but to mandate a future Labour government to it regardless of events at the time, in utter ignorance of
what the circumstances would be. In part the unilateralists
were taking the familiar course of demanding a policy which
was pure, clear-cut, and apparently simple. But they were also
unable to present Conference with a coherent formulation of the
international policy for Britain after nuclear disarmament because their unity scarcely extended beyond their single demand.
A more ambitious motion would be too confusing for Conference and would put them at the mercy of the leadership.

Here was an issue which not only stirred many sincerely
troubled members of the Party but awakened all the nostalgic
longing for a Socialist foreign policy, for the precise objective,
the stirring demonstration. Out came all the old beliefs about
the effect of moral gestures, and that strange revelation of
nationalistic pride—the exalted estimate of British influence
on world opinion. Yet although this was a far graver issue than
either German rearmament the debate never reached the depths
of rancid bitterness touched in 1954. The supporters of nuclear
disarmament avoided the Bevanites fatal error. By wooing the

unions instead of insulting them it also prevented the debate turning into a constituencies-union wrangle which would have reopened the old sores. Moreover, although the Left recovered its unity the new movement was not involved in a struggle for personal power—for Mr Bevan was now among the angels, assaulting his former supporters with brutal frankness: 'Do it now, you say. . . . It is not in your hands to do it. All you can do is pass a resolution.'

But for all the unilateralists' tact they rallied union support slowly. At first only a handful of far-left non-Communist unions such as the Constructional Engineers and the Draughtsmen were willing to support them. Several normally left-wing unions were influenced by the sudden switch of the Communists to supporting the British Hydrogen Bomb in 1957. The 1957 Conference[1] offered the rare spectacle of the ETU and other Communist-led unions defending the NEC against 'irresponsible' unilateralists. When the issue became really heated in 1959 Communist influence helped several Executives rally their conferences to the official line. But in general, drawing from their industrial experience, the unions have been sceptical that abandoning British nuclear weapons was likely to persuade other nations to follow the example. They have always been less sentimental about using power than many members of the local parties.

Consequently the unions' support for unilateral disarmament was exceptionally low in 1957 and 1958—a mere 200,000 to 300,000 according to the terms of the motion. In fact the Left recruited much more union support for the rejection of missile sites. Here their opposition had the support of such moderate unions as the Dyers, Bleachers & Textile Workers and the Printers & Bookbinders, while Communist influence was naturally cast with the Left on both this issue and the question

[1] In 1957 the Conference voted on a demand that (*inter alia*) a Labour Government refuse to make, test, or use nuclear weapons. This was lost 781,000:5,836,000 votes.

In 1958 it voted on:
  (*a*) a demand for total nuclear disarmament (proposed by the Fire Brigades' Union). Lost 890,000:5,611,000 votes.
  (*b*) opposition to rocket sites and Hydrogen Bomber patrols. Lost 1,926,000: 5,349,000 votes.
  (*c*) demand that a Labour Government get international agreement within one year to stop making, testing, or using nuclear weapons, or do so unilaterally if agreement was not reached. Lost 1,005,000:5,538,000 votes.

of Hydrogen Bomber patrols. Among the constituencies, too, the support for the campaign for nuclear disarmament in the early stages has been exaggerated. The derisory votes obtained by the Left in 1957 and 1958 suggested that the local parties were divided fairly evenly. It was probably only in 1959 that the campaign really caught their imagination to an extent equivalent to the reaction to German rearmament.

## II

Reconstructing the exact pattern of voting over so many years is obviously delicate. A single inaccurate report of a union's vote could upset the whole calculation of how constituencies and unions divided on a given issue. But the general pattern is clear. It points several lessons which are often forgotten within the Labour Party. For example, the stereotyped image of the unions as a sort of orthodox lump of suet pudding clogging the Party's progress is a potentially disastrous oversimplification. As *Tribune* once remarked, surprisingly enough:

'It has always been a myth that the local parties are on one side, and the trade unions are on the other in two solid blocks.'[1]

*Tribune* was right, although few would have agreed at the time those words were written—in 1954. It took the behaviour of the TGWU under Mr Cousins to put paid to the old myth that monolithic union support for official policy was the invariable law of Party life. Yet while it was striking to see a union which had for years been the very symbol of loyalty to the leadership cast as chief rebel, more important is the fact that since the war there has always been a substantial left-wing minority in the trade union movement. At any given time two or three of the six largest unions have been voting against important sections of official policy. The unions have never been as thoroughly unprogressive—nor the local parties as fanatically left-wing—as popular legend decreed.[2] Obviously the con-

---

[1] *Tribune*, September 3, 1954.

[2] Support for left-wing candidates in elections to the Party Executive cannot safely be used to 'prove' the constituencies' views on policy. The link between voting in NEC elections and policy has never been direct enough for the slogan 'A vote for Bevan is a vote against rearming Germany' to make sense. Obviously considerations of policy contributed to the Bevanites' first success in

stituencies are on balance to the left of the unions, but the overlap is considerable. This overlap is one reason why the two wings have held together through all the Party's internal upheavals.

However, the constituencies are so divided and unpredictable that beyond any doubt the leadership would be forced to move to the left if it could not count on the support of several large unions. Left-wingers are, therefore, partly right in complaining that 'the unions are the brake on the wheels of the Party'. But this is another oversimplification. It begs the whole question about the direction that Party policy should take.

If the only possible line of advance for Labour were towards traditional red-blooded Socialism, then the balance of union power has undoubtedly been a brake. No movement with the immense entrenched interests of the unions will ever be the revolutionary force the extreme Left looks for. But are the unions the only brake? Since 1956 Mr Gaitskell has been trying to show the Party an alternative direction that it might take while remaining true to its ideals, replacing traditional slogans and war cries with new policies. He has had to respect the unions' susceptibilities, of course. But few who read the series of Party policy statements in all their embarrassing ambivalence, designed less to mislead the public than to disguise the change of direction from the zealots, could doubt that the real brake was not the unions this time but the fundamentalists in both movements.

It could be argued that at Conference what count are votes, that the largely ineffective trade union left-wing minority is simply an interesting curiosity of little practical consequence. Yet the fact that the two movements do not react as homogeneous blocks is of capital importance in Labour policy making. It is because the unions are not monolithic that the opponents of official policy can hope first to build on the left-wing union

1952. But some constituencies voted for left-wingers to balance the trade unionists, others supported the Bevanites because they claimed to be the champions of local party rights. It is not uncommon to find constituency delegates who combine a readiness to be talked into supporting the platform on specific issues with voting for left-wing candidates for the NEC. Celebrity and skill at keeping in the public eye and journalistic ability—all of which the Bevanites possessed—all played their part. So did the skilful concentrating of support on a Bevanite 'ticket' through circulars to local parties. Such considerations, coupled with the wish to get rid of a jaded team, tarnished with defeat, all combine to explain the Bevanites' victories in the early fifties.

minority, then to rally sufficient union support to carry the Party or to force the leadership to change ground. Perhaps this is more important in a negative way, by setting limits which the leadership knows cannot be transgressed without tipping the balance against it. But Aneurin Bevan's whole campaign made sense only on the assumption that the unions could be split, that sufficient of their votes were 'redeemable' to bring him victory. With time and more tact he could well have succeeded. The advocates of unilateral nuclear disarmament have also assumed that a sufficient number of union votes could be persuaded to move left to commit the Party to a new policy.

There has always been a strong enough left-wing union minority for talk about a 'split' between the two movements on questions of policy to be unrealistic. It would be strange if there were not issues on which the majority of constituencies opposed a majority of unions. But these are rare: German rearmament, and SEATO caused such a division but the rearmament programme and nationalization did not. There may have been splits over the expulsion of Mr Zilliacus, expropriation of re-nationalized industries, composition of overseas delegations, eligibility for the NEC and Mr Zilliacus' foreign policy motion in 1955, but the exact votes cannot be established.[1] It is also probable that a majority of the local parties opposed the successive official positions on nuclear weapons. But in every case except German rearmament, about forty per cent of the constituency votes have been cast for the platform. On almost as many occasions the dissident minority has been almost wholly composed of union votes.

What is really important for Labour is that despite differences of emphasis, and sharp isolated disagreements, there has been no consistent cleavage over policy. Every great issue which has divided the Party since the war has also divided the trade union movement. Not a single issue roused the constituencies without causing controversy in the unions—but several stormy disagreements within the trade union movement (wage restraint, industrial democracy, direction of labour, association with the

---

[1] The method of analysis we have followed means that whenever information about union votes is not complete we shall tend to exaggerate any division between unions and parties. The argument is, therefore, based on the least favourable hypothesis.

WFTU) scarcely ruffled the local parties. In all these analyses of the divisions within the Labour Party it is also easy to forget that even at times of blackest controversy there remained considerable undisputed common ground.

In bewailing its defeats the Left has always been too ready to attribute its defeat to the unions' obscurantism, too little aware of the importance of the 'machine'. For example there is the success of the Conference Arrangements Committee in encouraging the production of composite motions which sink themselves. In 1955 the agenda contained two motions for further nationalization, selected from many. One demanded outright expropriation, the other called for automation to lead to the nationalization of 'all industry'. Another motion demanded that 'unlimited funds' be spent on automation, while a fourth spoke of the United States 'coming to terms' with Britain on foreign policy. Repeatedly moderate left-wing unions and constituencies have chosen to support the NEC rather than vote for motions which are mischievous, meaningless, impossibly extreme or utterly incapable of realization. Although the Left has been more wide-awake in the past few years, every Conference brings its crop of self-defeating motions.

The order and timing of debates (effectively controlled by the Conference Arrangements Committee) are more tactically important than is sometimes realized. Delegates spend a happy hour on Monday lambasting the wicked Tories, in blissful ignorance that the price of their pleasure is a hurried debate at the end of the week. By that time speakers will have been cut to three minutes, and a reasoned presentation of their case will be impossible. The simultaneous debating of six resolutions (in the pious name of getting through as much of the agenda as possible) is ideally calculated to confuse delegates to the maximum. At other times the discussion of Executive policy statements, to which organizations submit amendments, gives the NEC a tactical and moral advantage.

Despite drastic limitation of speeches from the floor, there is never any limit on the speakers for the NEC (although General Council spokesmen are limited). Again, unlike the TUC and almost every union conference, there is no right of reply. The Chairman is not an impartial arbiter; his discretion

Q

is invariably exercised in the Executive's favour. The Conference is probably the most tightly dominated by the platform of any in the Labour Movement—yet, despite periodic mutterings of protest, all attempts at reform have failed.

Unless they are strictly mandated constituency delegates are often susceptible to arguments that the TUC must be consulted, or that resolutions are impracticable or unconstitutional. The Executive can often cajole them by a sympathetic reply into supporting remitting of a resolution—a mover who refuses to remit is considered churlishly uncooperative and is often rebuffed. The compositing process throws many mandates open to reconsideration. Realizing this, some local Parties go to the desperate lengths of issuing sweeping instructions such as 'Support *any* resolution which will extend nationalization', 'Vote for *any* anti-Bomb resolution'.

The fixed image of the constituency militant, at one time graven on trade union leaders' minds, was the counterpart of the caricature of the 'trade union boss' common in many CLPs. A rank and file trade unionist wrote in 1954:

'Trade union delegates seemed to be used to taking decisions and having to operate them, thereby developing a sense of responsibility. Constituency delegates appear to be persons imbued with an enthusiasm but inexperienced in having to operate proposed changes. . . . There seemed an air of irresponsibility on one side of the Conference as opposed to the steadying influence on the other.'[1]

F. G. Moxley, the left-wing editor of the *Railway Review*, remarked on:

'the poverty of ideas among the most virulent rank and filers, their mistaken assumption that shouting into the microphone was good enough speaking. . . .'[2]

The Natsopa delegation to the 1950 Conference felt:

'it is important to note that any suggestion of fellow-travellers or left-wing propaganda always comes from the individual membership delegates.'[3]

[1] *The Building Worker*, November 1954.
[2] *The Railway Review*, October 2, 1953.    [3] *Natsopa Journal*, November 1950.

Mr Shinwell had no doubt either. He concluded in 1952:

'Thank heaven for the Trade Union Movement at this time. Thank heaven for what is often called the block vote. It is keeping the Party steady. . . .'[1]

Some union leaders found it useful to exploit the Shinwell line of argument in public, to emphasize the leadership's dependence on their goodwill. But many have been genuinely misled about the constituencies' voting. Some of them gauge the character and temper of the local parties from the wild, muddle-headed, and frequently inept speeches made by lay constituency delegates at the Conference. Union conferences have their wild men, whose importance their leaders appreciate by second nature, but they do not always make such a calculation at the Party Conference. They pride themselves that the silent majority of their own members 'will not fall for a lot of hot air', but assume that constituency delegates do. Although most union conference agendas are crammed with leftish resolutions which will inevitably be rejected, the militancy of the Labour Party's agenda arouses instant misgiving.

While the Party Conference has its hotheads, any serious observation shows how few these are. In 1955, for example, Conference heard Mr J. Crawford of the National Union of Boot & Shoe Operatives on productivity and automation, and Sir Alfred Roberts, of the United Textile Factory Workers' Association, on social insurance. Both took a line which the left found completely unacceptable (Mr Bevan's views on insurance were in direct opposition to Sir Alfred's); both were thoughtfully heard and warmly applauded. This is the normal mood of Conference when it is addressed moderately as an intelligent body. Delegates reacted naturally enough to the diatribes of the militant minority of right-wing leaders, who thought that the constituencies should be fought, not led. Such personal bitterness should never have been taken for a policy split.

Although the Conference provides little real ground for misgiving to the trade unionists, the mistrust is nonetheless real. They are often more critical of a proposal before Conference than they would be if it was before Congress. This may be

[1] *Report*, 1952, p. 106.

because they accept the fight against the Communists at the TUC as natural, but when they find views expressed at the Conference coinciding with the Communist Party line, they think at once of disloyalty and infiltration. Some distrust power which is outside their direct control. A union leader knows the limits of his authority and influence at his own conference; at the Party Conference he never feels as confident even if he has a large block vote. He may not speak; someone else will have the last word. During the Bevanite controversy several leaders of important unions quite lost their sureness of touch at Conference. Sir Lincoln Evans, Arthur Deakin, Sir Tom O'Brien and Sir William Lawther seemed unable to discriminate, or to sense the undercurrents and nuances that would have been apparent to them in their own unions. It might be no coincidence that none of them had sat on the NEC.

Underlying these attitudes is a general suspicion of the constituencies—intellectuals who do not understand the working class movement or, worse, dissident members of their own unions who challenge their right to speak for the rank-and-file. Only such suspicion makes this statement by Arthur Deakin understandable:

'The trade unions have done their utmost to create the measure of understanding with the political Labour Party that will enable us to go forth as a united force. If you want to maintain that do not drive us into the position of breaking with the Party on such an issue. . . .'[1]

He was speaking to a motion moved by the AEU and seconded by the Foundry Workers, favouring the 'Confed' plan for the engineering industry. It was supported by almost every union in the CSEU except his own and the NUGMW. The TUC had made no directly parallel decision. At the moment Deakin came to the rostrum no constituency speaker had spoken directly on the motion. At the subsequent vote a majority of the CLP representatives voted on the same side as he did. It was Labour's misfortune in 1951 and later that the chief protagonists in its quarrels so imperfectly understood the forces they were fighting.

Yet during the Bevanite crisis the depth of feeling within the

[1] *Report*, 1953, p. 124.

Labour Party was often over-estimated. Both the NEC and the Parliamentary Party were bitterly split, while many of the constituency militants passionately supported Mr Bevan. Yet the Party was never really as shaken to its roots as some observers claimed. The Socialist League controversy of the thirties had been far more bitter in many areas. The Party was still agreed on many fundamentals. It was caught up in a struggle for power and a series of running revolts rather than any systematic doctrinally coherent challenge. But if the whole membership had taken the quarrel as seriously as the chief combatants the Party could scarcely have avoided splitting irrevocably. It was saved by the ample cushion of apathy in all sections of the movement. The closing of the ranks at general elections, a real if transitory unity, would not have been so readily realized if the bitterness had been as deep and as widespread as was often supposed.

So many people had a vested interest in the belief that the Party was split on policy. The Conservative and Communist Press automatically dubbed every difference of opinion a 'revolt'. Some militant right-wing union leaders preferred the leadership to believe that the Party was divided, and look to them for support. The Bevanites made the fatal tactical error of attacking their union opponents so indiscriminately that they frightened many moderate union leaders into believing that they were flatly anti-union. At other times—until Mr Bevan set out to win union votes for his campaign for the Treasurership—they seemed indifferent to the unions, preferring to pose as the champions of the local Parties. They were bound to emphasize the importance of policy disagreements to refute the charge that 'Bevanism' was simply a cloak for Mr Bevan's personal ambition. By insisting on the fervent unity of the local militants, and saying little about their union support the Bevanites fostered the impression that the Party was split right down the middle. Of course, when it was not launching thunderbolts at the Bevanites, Transport House repeatedly denied there was any split. But who would believe them?[1]

[1] The Parliamentary Report for the 1951 session—covering the ministerial resignations, says simply 'There have, of course, been differences of opinion, yet, today, the Party is united, vigorous and as determined as ever to build a Socialist Britain'. *Report of the Labour Party Conference*, 1951, p. 56.

Yet there was a split—over power rather than policy and therefore more difficult to resolve than disagreements over policy. It crystallized around the block vote. There is little doubt that this was a consistent and near-absolute split, which questioned the whole basis of the unions' and the Party's relations.

## That Block Vote

The 'block vote', so contentious in the fifties, was admitted without debate at the inaugural meeting of the Labour Representation Committee. At the TUC it had begun to succeed a system of one-man, one-vote in 1894. Although today unions are encouraged to cast their entire vote *en bloc* for one side of the question by giving each delegation a single voting card, the block vote still rests on custom and practice, not on formal rule. When it was adopted in 1900 the unions to all practical intents and purposes *were* the Labour Party: it was never conceived of as a means of permitting one wing to dominate the other. When the Party was framing its Constitution in 1918, despite disquiet behind the scenes there was little open discussion of the block vote. The problem really developed only after the Divisional Labour Parties established themselves between the wars. It has burst out intermittently ever since.

While block voting is not mandatory, unions rarely split their vote.[1] Although the Woodworkers used to divide their vote among their seven-man delegation, this dispersion of the union's power was so unpopular that once the Annual Delegate Conference established itself as the union's policy-making body after 1945, there was general agreement to begin block voting. If unions are deeply divided they normally prefer abstention to splitting their vote.

The block vote is used in the TUC, the CSEU and many union conferences—although the AEU and NUR are among the numerous exceptions—in unions of every size, type and political nuance, and it is rarely questioned. Its defenders can legitimately claim that it is a traditional and integral part of representative trade union government, and that it has nothing

---

[1] Mrs Webb reported that the Miners gave Sidney Webb 400 of their 600 votes in the NEC elections, Beatrice Webb *Diaries, 1912–1924*, p. 182.

to do with union domination of the Party. But since many unions never employ it, block-voting is clearly a matter of choice rather than necessity. Workable alternatives do exist.

Trade union opinion is not completely complacent about the block vote. For example, Natsopa's Governing Council has supported it only because they say there is no acceptable alternative,[1] and the ETU Policy Conference has demanded a fairer voting system.[2] But in most unions such complaints have found no noticeable support.[3] The President of ASSET, a left-wing union, said candidly:

'Many delegates complained of the larger unions using their block votes to force their own policy on conference, but under the constitution they were quite in order, and I wished many times that I could have used a voting card bearing a higher number than three.'[4]

Most union leaders would probably agree with Mr Attlee that:

'the main objection is generally less against the method of voting than against the results of voting. Those who make the loudest song about the block vote are significantly silent when it happens to be cast with their own views.'[5]

The gibe was partly justified. During 1954 and 1955 left-wingers varied their attitude to the AEU, NUR and USDAW purely according to whether or not these unions supported Mr Bevan. Some were profoundly convinced that the rank and file favoured left-wing policies that they genuinely believed that a left-wing decision was by definition representative, while a right-wing vote was *ipso facto* undemocratic—but many were simply bad losers. Happily maintaining that the block vote controversy was a product of envy the Party's moderate wing remained outwardly complacent. The decline of criticism of the voting system once the struggle for the leadership ended gave this judgment credence. Yet the block vote poses a problem for

[1] *Natsopa Journal*, August and September 1954.
[2] *Report of the Proceedings of the Policy Conference*, 1955, p. 217.
[3] For other comments on the block vote see: *Report of the (NUGMW) Congress*, 1954, p. 216. *Woodworkers' Journal*, January 1956. *The Stereotyper*, November 1955.
[4] *ASSET*, November 1953.     [5] *The Labour Party in Perspective*, p. 102.

every section of the movement, not simply its perpetual oppositionists.

In 1956—the last year for which the Party released full statistics—the constituencies and federations held 1,150,000 votes. The unions had 5,630,000. The average local party delegate held a puny 2,000 votes; only South Lewisham had as many as 8,000. But the eighty-seven unions' strength was distributed as follows:

|  | Votes |
|---|---|
| 9 sent no delegate | — |
| 32 held 8,000 votes or less | 109,000 |
| 26 held 9,000 to 49,000 votes | 611,000 |
| 8 held 50,000 to 99,000 votes | 561,000 |
| 12 held 100,000 or more votes | 4,349,000 |
|  | 5,630,000 |

Almost half the unions either did not attend or cast no more votes than the largest CLP. Even the seventy-five unions with under 100,000 votes had only slightly more votes than the local parties. But the real problem is the strength of the twelve largest unions, and particularly of the six which controlled 3,689,000 votes—more than half the total vote. What were then the three right wing unions (2,328,000 votes) were nowhere near matched by the three left-wing unions (1,361,000). Commentators are fond of remarking that these six organizations could defy all the rest of the Party. But they never do. Far more serious than such hypothetical alliances is the effective power of one or two individual votes.

The TGWU alone has held from thirteen per cent to fifteen per cent of the votes at every Conference since the war. By a wave of its card this one union can cancel out the votes of nine-tenths of the local parties. The five next largest unions all hold from a quarter to more than a half of the total constituency votes. Can it seriously be claimed that a comparison of these unions' efforts with the contributions of the local parties would show these relative strengths to be fully justified?

The constituencies have a legitimate grievance. Their membership has almost doubled since the war; so have their votes.

But the unions have kept pace—due mainly to the lucky intervention of the 1946 Act, without which the problem of the block vote would have been radically modified. At the 1945 Conference the unions held eighty-one per cent of the votes; in 1958 they had eighty-three per cent. Although the constituencies are unquestionably stronger than in 1945, for all their efforts they have actually lost ground at Conference. The customary reaction in recent years has been to abuse the TGWU either for its power or its votes. Yet the TGWU's decisions have probably been as representative as those of most small unions and local parties—although it has the misfortune of being so large that its defects are more embarrassingly evident. The fault lies in the Party Constitution which allowed such a lack of balance to develop.

How serious this lack of balance can be is revealed in the fifty-six card votes taken between 1945 and 1958. No fewer than thirteen of these decisions would have been altered if the TGWU vote had been cast the other way. The number of decisions other unions could have swayed was NUM (eight), NUGMW (four), UTFWA, UPW, ASW (two), AEU (? two), NUBSO and TSSA (one.) One other vote may have turned on the decision of either the TGWU, NUGMW, or NUM or (less probably) the NUR or AEU. Since the left-wing unions usually voted with the minority the 'marginal' unions were normally on the right. The NUR and USDAW therefore scarcely ever carry the day, while the AEU may have done so no more than twice. The tied cottage was the only issue in all fourteen conferences on which a CLP could have cast a decisive vote. On only one other question—Progressive Unity in 1945 —could any organization with under 100,000 votes have altered the decision. By contrast the TGWU was decisive in almost one vote in four.

These votes cannot but be enervating to the rest of the Party. The general secretary of a union with about 40,000 votes, which usually supports official policy, put the feeling in these terms: 'It all seems so futile. It doesn't matter a damn how we cast our vote, we know quite well that it can't possibly affect the issue'. Leaders of smaller unions excuse their sketchy procedure for deciding their policy by saying, 'We've only got X votes. The big unions make all the decisions. It isn't really worth it.'[1] The leadership might be shaken to hear how many staunchly right-wing constituency delegates resent the voting system as bitterly as the Left, feeling that whatever the merits of the case the big unions will carry the day, deciding in a caucus which has not even waited to hear the debate. This hostility exists to some extent independently of the policies which the big unions favour. Of course the Conference would be intolerably unstable if decisions were continually turning on the decision of a small union. The real difficulty is not that the small unions are too rarely decisive, but that so frequently a big union is. The figures we have quoted obviously understate the influence that the few large organizations must have among a mass of small unions and parties. It is to these large concentrations of power that the leadership will obviously turn in attempting to ensure adequate support for its policies at Conference.

It is scarcely surprising that the Right has complacently accepted the Party's lopsided distribution of voting power, and that demands for reform have been practically a left-wing monopoly. For years the consistent support of several large unions for official policies ensured their acceptance at Conference. The block vote seemed a simple, ideal system of managing a potentially anarchic Party. Yet it has never been an immutable law of the Party's existence that large blocks of moderate union votes should protect the leadership from the demands of the Left, and keep the Party's policies roughly in tune with what the electorate might accept. Any such comfortable illusion should have been shattered by the example of the TGWU in recent years.

In Mr Cousins' first three years as General Secretary of the TGWU the union in fact voted to reject official policy only once. Nevertheless, the sure old triumvirate of TGWU–NUGMW–NUM, which had lasted since the war, was shattered. The steady shift of the AEU and USDAW towards more moderate policies both mitigated and partly concealed the consequences of this defection, and enabled the NEC to win as much support from the six large unions as it did during the

---

[1] A delegate complained at the AESD's 1951 conference that no union could effectively influence Labour Party policy. *Report of the R.C. Conference*, 1951, p. 120.

Bevanite crisis. Yet, where one union had proved unreliable others might follow. It was at all events evident that the million votes of the AEU and USDAW made a much less stable basis of support for the leadership than the million of the TGWU had done.

The consequences of a radical shift in the political attitudes of one or more large unions could be considerable. If the balance of the big block votes tilted decisively the Party would have to find new leaders or the Party leaders would have to accept a far greater degree of positive union dictation of policy than has been known in recent years. In short the present leadership might come to feel about the block vote much as the Bevanites did in 1954. Alternatively the political complexion of the unions might change in such a way that the large votes of the left- and right-wing unions neutralized each other, throwing Conference decisions open to the smaller organizations. If that happened consistent leadership could become impossible. It would be a situation such as Sidney Webb had in mind in remarking, 'If the block vote of the trade unions were eliminated it would be impracticable to continue to vest the control of policy in the Labour Party Conference'.[1] The block vote may some day harass the leadership as much as it once oppressed the militants. No section of the Party has much cause for complacency.

What, then, of reform? Two main approaches are proposed: abolition of the block vote, and redistribution of voting power. The most popular proposal is that unions should divide their votes according either to the division of opinion at their annual conferences, or in a referendum or in their delegation. This system would represent the opinion of the minority, which is at present not expressed, while breaking up the large votes into less massive units. The claim that decisions would become more 'representative' is of doubtful validity. There is no time to submit to the membership resolutions which are formulated only on the eve of Conference. The lapses of time between union and Party conferences, and differences between the motions voted there and those debated at Conference, make any claim that the vote of a union conference could simply be translated, in the same proportions, to the Party Conference completely arbitrary.

[1] Quoted in *British Political Parties*, p. 506.

Dividing the delegation vote is more a workable solution. Yet it may be no less invidious than the present system, so often attacked as letting individuals hold too much personal power. At present delegations must be persuaded by their leaders, and there is scope for discussion at delegation meetings. But the divided delegation vote means that the individual delegate, chosen more or less democratically, has arbitrary discretion over as many as 50,000 votes (unless organizations were forced to send full delegations), without the least responsibility to the membership, and with no certainty that such a vote would be 'representative'.

Resting on no standing order, the block vote can be renounced at will by any organization. The unions dislike advertising their differences; the block vote expresses their solidarity. Whether this solidarity is really necessary when a union is not facing the 'enemy' but is engaged in policy-making is more doubtful. More practically, the block vote enables unions to bring the whole of their power to bear, while the split vote dissipates their influence. Under the present distribution of voting power at Conference, reform could only come from the unions themselves. This is in itself unlikely enough, but reformers rarely realize that any new voting systems they propose could be frustrated. The unions cannot be made to divide their vote. No rule could prevent them from insisting that their delegates vote *en bloc* for majority delegation decisions (which would effectively re-create the block vote). If the system of one-man-one-vote were introduced the unions would simply send their full delegations and insist that delegates abide by majority decisions. The voting would be no different, but Conference would be more expensive, more unwieldy than ever. The end of the block vote could only come by a voluntary abdication by the unions themselves.

Radical reformers would like to redistribute voting power. Unions might be given one vote for two thousand members instead of one per thousand; there might be a weighted system giving no organization more than 50,000 votes; or unions might be represented through the CLPs to which they were affiliated. These activists have often criticized the unions because leaders ignore their membership in taking political decisions. Anyone acquainted with the tenuous nature of trade union affiliation in the constituencies might wonder whether this *Victory for Socialism* plan did not propose to exploit the situation. It is argued that if union leaders oppose such reform they are implicitly admitting that they are unrepresentative of their local membership. This is not so. The sum of the views of the branches expressed through the Labour Party does not necessarily correspond to the decision made at a union's own annual conference, which is conscious that its own interests are directly at stake. Without an opportunity for national leaders to have their say spokesmen for the union in the constituencies may be quite unrepresentative of the ordinary members.

Others think that a separate constituency party conference would be a solution. Such proposals were put forward both in 1937 and 1955 by local parties who were irked by Transport House discipline. The real case for the local parties having their own conference is that at present they have no responsibility, since they never feel that their vote counts. A conference would give them the chance to show that they are not hotheads and wild men. But if a conference of local parties led to a constituency block vote, a clash between the two wings would be almost inevitable—as most left-wingers have realized. Despite the strong arguments for giving the CLPs a talking-shop it seems too dangerous a luxury.

Yet the present voting system is far from ideal. A union's or a local party's vote represents simply the number of members for whom it pays affiliation fees. In the extreme case votes can be bought at ninepence each. The distribution of voting power takes not the least account of the devoted efforts of the activists on the doorsteps and in the committee rooms; neither can it measure the electoral advantages of the Labour sympathy of the majority of official trade unionism. Finding a new system would not be easy. Proposals to double the CLP vote or to halve the union vote are just as arbitrary as the present system, even though a new Party Constitution would doubtless function well with such provisions. Were the Constitution being written today surely no one would create a situation where two organizations outvote seven hundred. It would almost certainly limit the number of votes any organization might hold, and see that there was a higher minimum vote. Members of the large unions often refuse to accept the need for such a change. They argue, 'Why shouldn't we be free to bring our whole weight to bear?' Yet the TGWU and NUGMW know quite well how intolerable they would find the Confederation of Shipbuilding and Engineering Unions if the AEU affiliated on its full membership, instead of limiting it.[1] Limiting the maximum vote would not be 'fairer'—it is obviously quite arbitrary—but it would be healthier for the Party as a whole.

Such constitution-making is harmless—but futile: reform requires the consent of the unions themselves. History has rarely recorded such an act of self-abnegation. Mr Charles Geddes put such plans in perspective at the 1955 Conference:

'We are now talking of the block vote as though it were an evil thing or at least, if not evil in itself, used by evilly-minded people. This has now developed into an attack, through this new word, upon two particular organizations in the trade union movement. But it is not an attack upon two unions; it is an attack upon the whole trade union movement, because the use of the card vote is part of the normal democratic machinery of the trade union movement of this country. If in this Conference, and outside this Conference, attacks continue upon that part of the democratic instrument of trade unionism it may lead in course of time to an undermining of the faith and interest of the trade unions in the leaders of the trade union movement.

'The trade union movement is a massive strong organization. When it fights, it fights hard. It is fighting now on behalf of its membership in the industrial field. It would be a sad day indeed for the Labour Movement of this country if it turns its energies on to other enemies. It would be surprising, I think, what a solid front it would present.'[2]

The applause which rose to Mr Geddes from almost every union delegate was the clearest demonstration that retaining the block vote is dissociated from specific considerations of policy. Any attack on the block vote will be taken as a general attack on the trade union movement itself.

[1] The AEU holds 500,000 of the 1,250,000 votes within the CSEU. The Conederation's constitution provides that the AEU shall not affiliate on a higher number—its full United Kingdom membership is over 900,000.
[2] *Report*, 1955, pp. 155–6.

In the past the unions' chief concern has not been so much to win this or that vote, or to force their policies on the Party, as to ensure that they hold the decisive mass of votes at Conference. So long as the unions can feel that they are the arbiters of Conference they will retain their confidence in it. It is just as vital to them that effective power does not fall into the hands of men or organizations who neither know nor understand their policies, traditions and problems. For all their dissensions on policy, they are all but unanimous on this. It is clear that in no foreseeable circumstances would they tolerate any constitutional revision that gave the constituencies greater power—however much it could be justified objectively. Nor will they voluntarily limit their strength within Conference to placate either the militants or the leadership; they will insist on their 'rights'. The ending of the block vote or the redistribution of voting power would almost certainly entail dissolution of the union-Party alliance. However unsatisfactory the position may be, this is a fact with which Labour must live and come to terms.

The problem of the block vote should not be put out of perspective. All too often the unions' influence on Party policy is credited simply to their voting power. But the private conversations between the General Council and the NEC, or directly between the TUC and the Parliamentary Labour Party or a Labour government, establish a second circuit quite independent of Conference. Within these meetings, while the General Council takes account of its left wing the advice it offers is primarily that of its majority. It is rather as if, once decisions were taken at Congress the General Council casts a block vote for orthodoxy during the talks with the Party.

The intimate relationship between the two movements leads even many members of the Labour Party to forget that at the same time as the unions are within the Party they are a semi-external and independent pressure group. For although Conference discussed *Plan for Progress*—the statement of economic policy—it was clear that the real debate had been the private discussions between union and Party leaders that preceded publication, and that the real problems which will arise between the unions and future Labour governments will be thrashed out in similar private meetings. Whatever its colour any government must now hold such talks with the TUC; with its special traditions and sympathies Labour is always under moral pressure to be particularly attentive. While the unions' domination of Conference obviously consolidates their influence, so long as the 'honourable and open alliance' which was so painstakingly constructed in 1900 endures, any Labour leadership will have to find a *modus vivendi* with the unions. Blaming the block vote for the Party's failure to adopt 'progressive' policies, or for its susceptibility to union economic demands, is a dangerously incomplete analysis of the problems of power within the Party, and its difficulties of living in harmony with the unions.

Yet the block vote can still be a major problem to the Party. Whether it remains tolerable depends largely on the unions themselves. The manner in which they use their power can make an enormous difference to relations between the two movements and to Party morale. It is clearly important that the unions' voting should remain as reasonably predictable as in the past. Small unions which cannot affect the issue can afford the luxury of hesitation and capriciousness; large unions, whose weight could tilt the whole balance of Conference, cannot. Although the TGWU's havering over nuclear weapons in the 1957 Conference debate was in many ways to its credit, the task of the leadership would be gravely complicated if hesitant or erratic decisions were frequent. The Party's leaders must have a clear conception of the forces with which they must come to terms before they are launched into a debate at Conference in the full glare of publicity for all the world to see.

If there was one lesson that the battles of the early fifties should have taught the unions about the block vote it is that in the hands of truculent and demagogic leaders whose ill-chosen phrases give the impression that they hold arbitrary and personal power, the block vote can be disastrous for Party unity and morale. It was bad enough for Sir William Lawther to be casting 660,000 votes; it was doubly galling for the militants to hear him say:

'. . . we shall determine our own action, and please remember what we might be fighting when a lot of you are running in the other direction. Consequently so far as we are concerned . . .

this Conference has no right whatever to lay down a mandate as to how the unions in any given situation will act. Not only have you no mandate, but even if you had one we would not accept it. . . . You have the happy assurance that the block vote and the money that is provided will be used in the direction that we think is in the interests of our membership and the people we represent, rather than any mad hares that may exercise themselves on this course. . . .'[1]

Ordinary constituency delegates, knowing Arthur Deakin only through his appearances at Conference and his intermittent thunderbolts against the Bevanites, ignorant of the workings of the TGWU, understandably believed that he kept 800,000 votes in his pocket and used them as he pleased. His public personality matched the stereotype of the trade union boss. A trade unionist from the Parliamentary Party or the leader of a small union might assume the role of the candid friend at Conference. This is a dangerous game for leaders of the bigger unions. Invariably they appear determined to dominate the Party, and their interventions are more resented than heeded. They risk turning any debate into another clash between unions and constituencies. So long as the block vote is a problem the Party must pray for less choleric union leaders, who will speak softly while carrying the big stick.

*Accountability*

'Unrepresentative?' snorted the General Secretary. 'How can I be "unrepresentative". This is a *democratic* union. I've got to answer to my members'. It was a common reply—but less than frank.

Accountability is the least satisfactory aspect of the unions' participation in Conference. Many unions never tell their members of the decisions made in their name. Most of the bigger unions print delegation reports in their Executive minutes, but almost no one reads them. Many active members have never seen a copy. The union's journal is usually the chief means of communication. Most print a conference report—a summary of decisions combined with a smiling photograph of the union

---

[1] *Report*, 1952, p. 79.

R

delegation 'on the front', and assurances that the Party has demonstrated its unshakable unity and its will to progress, that the Tories have taken a decisive beating, and that the union was in the limelight. Apart from a pious attention to the union's own contribution, these accounts usually give members less information than they found in their *Daily Mirror*. The member who wonders which way his union voted often has to read between the lines with the skill of a student of *Pravda*.

A few unions, like the Union of Post Office Workers and the Association of Engineering & Shipbuilding Draughtsmen, submit reports to their conferences. Others report how their delegations voted on the major issues—which is all that is wanted. Usually inquisitive members may persuade their Executive to tell them how the union voted, but not every union keeps a record of its voting, and requests for information must rely on very fallible memories. ('German rearmament? Let's see . . . No . . . George, do *you* remember? Did we vote for or against?' or, 'Well, I'm sorry, but our delegate's emigrating to Australia, and I don't think he ever told us which way he voted. . . . No, I don't really know whether he was a Bevanite or not.') A few unions require delegates to report back to District Committees, but direct reporting to branches is usually impracticable.

Some unions show the greatest reluctance to releasing information. A member who wanted to know how Natsopa had voted on nuclear weapons motions was told by the editor of *Natsopa Journal* that there was 'insufficient space'—a common excuse.[1] Asked by one of its branches to release information about how delegates had voted the Executive of the National Association of Operative Plasterers refused, giving no reason.[2] The United Patternmakers' Association's *Monthly Report* has printed several protests from members that the delegation report gave no useful information, but to little avail.[3] The National Society of Painters' Executive simply 'noted' a branch resolution asking for information about TUC and Party Conference voting.[4] Even the normally informative Union of Post

---

[1] *Natsopa Journal*, January 1958. *Typographical Circular*, November 1954.
[2] *Quarterly Report*, March 1956.
[3] *Monthly Report*, August 1954; February 1956; April 1956; November 1957.
[4] *NSP Journal*, May 1956.

Office Workers refused to disclose how it had voted in the NEC elections—and was upheld by its Annual General Meeting.[1] Another union told the author: 'We do not make this information available to our own members, so obviously we cannot divulge it to someone outside the organization'.

Sometimes this attitude can cause misunderstandings. The London District of the National Union of Sheet Metal Workers & Braziers once grumbled darkly that the union's delegates— who never said how they had voted—were suspected of invariably supporting the NEC. In fact they had fairly consistently supported the moderate left.[2] While the information given to members has been increasing steadily, there is usually not sufficient information available for an ordinary member to make a proper assessment of his delegation's actions.

The lack of information partly explains why complaints about Conference votes are rare. If the delegation has been deeply split the minority may carry the struggle to the union's next conference. Sometimes there are angry arguments about broken mandates. Such cases are rare, either because there is little cause for complaint, or because few people are interested. There was the attempt to censure the President of USDAW by militants who believed that he should have supported a motion on which he abstained, and the disavowal by the ETU Conference of its President's rejoinder to Mr Attlee's criticisms of the Communist inspiration of its resolutions.[3] Most of the other serious complaints date from the Bevanite period. The Clerical & Administrative Workers' Union's 1955 Conference carried a motion 'regretting the intrusion of the Executive Council into the affairs of the PLP'—a reference to Executive's support for the withdrawal of the Whip from Mr Bevan.[4] It also censured the Executive for supporting German rearmament—although the union's 1954 conference had been so little interested that it had not waived standing orders to discuss the issue.[5] In 1956 it again censured the Executive for continuing to support the rearmament of Germany, although the union's rules explicitly bind the union to follow Party decisions. The Amalgamated Union of

[1] *The Post*, July 6, 1957.
[2] *Fusion*, January 1952.     [3] See p. 182.
[4] The *Manchester Guardian*, April 11, 1955.
[5] The *Manchester Guardian*, April 9, 1955.

Building Trade Workers 1955 National Delegate Conference repudiated its delegation's abstention on the German re-armament issue at the 1954 Party Conference,[1] but the UPW, TGWU, and ASW conferences rejected similar attempts.[2] The AEU and NUR Executives also came under attack for their support of Mr Gaitskell for the Treasurership. A challenge by the moderates (a rare exception), was successful at the NUR 1957 Annual General Meeting, which carried an appeal against Executive support for a one-day strike in protest against the Rent Act.[3] By implication both USDAW and the AEU re-pudiated their delegations' support of *Industry and Society*.[4]

Attempts to reverse decisions are infrequent, and rarely successful. Even unions which provide full information about their activities are not wholly accountable—it is questionable whether a union can be. In any representative organization leaders take unpopular decisions, from time to time, in the hope that any discontent will die down by the next conference. This is particularly possible on political issues, on which fewer members feel strongly. But also, as one General Secretary blandly remarked about his vote on German rearmament, 'What's done's done. They can't take the vote back now. All they can do is say they didn't like it'. Members can lock the stable door, but there is rarely any opportunity for a union to correct its vote at a later Conference. Members of the AEU may not like *Industry and Society*, but now that it is Party policy there seems little they can do about it. There was a revealing incident at the 1958 meeting of USDAW. The conference had just narrowly adopted a demand for widespread nationalization under the next Labour government, against the Executive. 'That will commit the Union at the Labour Party Conference, I take it', asked a delegate. 'It depends', said Mr Padley. 'It depends, does it not, on the resolutions'.[5] Even on such recurring issues as nationalization motions may be differently worded at later Conferences, on nuclear weapons policy both the circum-stances and the motions may be quite different.

---

[1] *Report of the National Delegate Conference*, 1955, p. 283.
[2] *The Post*, July 16, 1955. *Report of the Annual Delegate Conference*, 1955 (ASW), p. 184. *Minutes and Proceedings of the 16th Biennial Delegate Conference* (TGWU), Minute 47.    [3] *The Railway Review*, July 5, 1957.
[4] See pp. 145 and 155.        [5] *Report of the ADM*, 1958, p. 115.

However annoyed the militants may feel they have little ground for complaint if the delegation's vote can be linked, even implausibly, with a previous decision of the union's conference. Although leaders have little room for manoeuvre on many industrial issues, they know that there is more leeway on political questions. Serious rank and file opposition would be mustered only by flagrant or persistent flouting of declared union policy. Most officials know better than to collide head-on. With the exception of such dramatic breaks as Mr J. H. Thomas' dismissal from the General Secretaryship of the NUR it is almost unknown in recent times for an official to get into serious trouble on political matters.

This does not mean that the opportunity is exploited. With a few exceptions, trade union leaders, delegations and executives adhere more faithfully to the spirit of conference decisions than their critics allow. But their reasons are probably social rather than constitutional. The system rests on a presumption that they will not abuse the discretion they have. There is a very human dislike of the unpleasant acrimony that may arise if the delegation is suspected of behaving unethically and committing a breach of trust. The structure of trade unionism makes it almost impossible that delegations—particularly of non-responsible rank and file members—should be made effectively accountable for their actions. In the last resort it is not constitutional safeguards that come to the member's aid, but the political morality of his elected representatives.

# CHAPTER VI

# THE UNIONS IN PARLIAMENT

'We are of the workers; they are our kin; we are part of them; their battle is our battle; what hurts them hurts us; where they gain we gain; and, remembering the heroism of their toilsome lives, we shall, as a Party, seek to create conditions in which their nobler aspirations . . . shall have free play.'

KEIR HARDIE*

'To devise ways and means of securing the return of an increased number of labour members to the next Parliament.' This was the key phrase in that motion of the 1899 TUC which led to the formation of the Labour Representation Committee; the Committee's very name was significant. For over thirty years the demand for Direct Labour Representation in the House of Commons had been slowly growing.[1] As early as 1874 the Miners had sent Alexander Macdonald and Thomas Burt to Parliament, the first working-class MPs. The idea of the unions supporting candidates had slowly spread. Henry Broadhurst of the Stonemasons was elected, and George Howell of the Bricklayers fought Stafford, in 1880. Joseph Arch received the backing of his Agricultural Labourers' Union, and Havelock Wilson, secretary of the Sailors and Firemen, had entered the House in 1892. By the time the Labour Party was formed the knot of Lib-Lab mining MPs had grown to five or six. The idea of achieving direct representation of labour in the House of Commons through trade union sponsorship was therefore deeply rooted long before the Party's birth. It has remained an important element in the unions' relations with the Labour Party ever since.

The Labour Representation Committee continued the practice of allowing socialist societies or affiliated unions to sponsor candidates. Within a few years the Railwaymen, Postmen,

* Quoted in H. Fyfe, *Keir Hardie*, Duckworth, 1935, p. 117.

[1] At the second meeting of the TUC, in 1869, the secretary of the Yorkshire Miners, John Normansell, read a paper on 'The best means to secure Direct Labour Representation in the Commons House of Parliament', proposing that it be financed through the TUC.

Engineers, Boilermakers, and the Coopers & Barge-builders were all sponsoring Parliamentary candidates. But the greatest expansion came after the First World War. Urged on by Arthur Henderson the unions sponsored more candidates than ever at the 1918 election, although many were now backed by the new Divisional Labour Parties.

Most Labour MPs were union nominees—naturally enough since the winnable seats were in heavily unionized areas. The unions had the funds: the Independent Labour Party and the DLPs had not. Sometimes the unions 'gave' a seat to an outsider—the Seaham miners nominated Sidney Webb, Ramsay MacDonald and Emmanuel Shinwell in turn. But in general what they had, they held, and the PLP was mostly a group of middle-aged trade unionists. Towards the close of the decade the position changed. The Trade Disputes Act of 1927 cut the unions' political income and the competition for seats was growing. In the Birmingham area one or two candidates unexpectedly stood down, and were replaced by men close to Sir Oswald Mosley—then a Labour MP. When nominations were called for some constituencies were known to sell themselves to the highest bidder.[1] Then came the 1931 debacle, and the inevitably intense competition for the few winnable seats. Transport House, the unions, the unfavoured constituency parties, and Party leaders who were looking for seats, were all unhappy at the thought of a free-for-all auction of nominations. The situation was ripe for a truce. The 1933 Conference accepted the 'Hastings Agreement' governing adoption of sponsored candidates, laying down the maximum contributions that might be paid to a local Party by a candidate or an affiliated organization. The agreement was an immediate improvement. In 1937 Mr Attlee found that it had 'reduced the danger of undesirable competition' although he admitted that 'the influence of trade unions is, perhaps, greatest in the sphere of Parliamentary candidates'.[2]

The effect of sponsorship had been changing steadily since the First World War. The number of union candidates had

[1] Until 1932 the Typographical Association paid West Bromwich DLP the agent's salary, full election expenses, and part of the running expenses of the constituency. A. E. Musson, *The Typographical Association*, OUP, 1954, p. 403.
[2] *The Labour Party in Perspective*, p. 105.

fallen in the 1922, 1923 and 1924 elections, partly because some unions had used their political funds to pay strike and unemployment benefits. Already, in 1922 the trade unionist Clynes lost the leadership of the Party to the 'intellectual' MacDonald—despite the predominance of the trade unionists. Success in the 1922 and 1923 elections brought in more MPs who had no union backing—but the set-back in 1924 all but restored the proportion of union MPs in the Parliamentary Party. Even now, however, there were complaints that the 'bourgeois' element in Parliament was growing too rapidly.

Success in the 1929 election again cut the proportion of sponsored union MPs, and the non-unionists were more numerous than ever before. But the balance tilted yet again in 1931, when thirty-five of the tiny band of forty-six Labour MPs (including twenty-six miners) had union backing. Once again the non-unionists increased their strength in 1935, and sponsored candidates were slightly over half the PLP. Right up to the close of the Second World War the Labour Party in Parliament remained predominantly working class and trade union in spirit and composition—but only in 1924 and 1931 had the rise in the strength of the middle-class group been checked.

The strength of the various unions was also changing. Financially distressed by the 1922 lockout, disillusioned with political action, the Engineers showed scant interest in sending men into Parliament for another two decades. The cotton unions were slowly waning as a Parliamentary force, while the strength of the general unions was steadily growing. By 1945 the change was unmistakeable. Into the House came a flood of middle class Members, often straight from the services, with little experience of the trade union movement. Throughout the 1945 Parliament the influence of the trade union MPs steadily declined, although they still included most of the veterans. According to the precedents the proportion of trade union MPs should have risen after the set-backs of the 1950, 1951 and 1955 elections. Instead it remained steady. Numerically the unions' weakness was clear. In the 258-strong Parliamentary Labour Party of 1959 there were ninety-two trade union MPs—five less than there had been among the 191 Labour MPs in the 1923 Parliament.

## TABLE 26

### TRADE UNION SPONSORED CANDIDATES 1929-1959*

| | 1929 | 1931 | 1935 | 1945 | 1950 | 1951 | 1955 | 1959 |
|---|---|---|---|---|---|---|---|---|
| National Union of Mineworkers | 42 | 43 | 38 | 34 | 37 | 37 | 35 | 31 |
| Transport & General Workers' Union | 17 | 16 | 11 | 18 | 19 | 17 | 16 | 19 |
| National Union of Railwaymen | 11 | 10 | 12 | 13 | 12 | 10 | 11 | 9 |
| National Union of General & Municipal Workers | 8 | 11 | 11 | 10 | 9 | 7 | 4 | 6 |
| Transport Salaried Staffs' Association | 8 | 7 | 10 | 9 | 11 | 11 | 10 | 8 |
| Union of Shop, Distributive & Allied Workers | 6 | 5 | 9 | 8 | 9 | 10 | 10 | 10 |
| United Textile Factory Workers' Association | 6 | 8 | 6 | 3 | 3 | 3 | 2 | 2 |
| Associated Society of Woodworkers | 6 | 5 | 4 | 4 | 3 | 3 | 2 | 3 |
| Union of Post Office Workers | 6 | 5 | 3 | 1 | 3 | 4 | 2 | 2 |
| National Union of Boot & Shoe Operatives | 5 | 5 | 3 | 4 | 2 | 1 | — | — |
| United Society of Boilermakers, etc. | 3 | 4 | 2 | — | — | — | — | — |
| British Iron, Steel & Kindred Trades Association | 5 | 3 | 2 | 2 | 2 | 2 | 2 | 2 |
| National Union of Agricultural Workers | 3 | 4 | — | 3 | 2 | 2 | 3 | 4 |
| Amalgamated Engineering Union | 3 | 3 | 3 | 4 | 10 | 13 | 12 | 15 |
| Associated Society of Locomotive Engineers & Firemen | 1 | — | 1 | 1 | 2 | 3 | 3 | 3 |
| Electrical Trades Union | — | — | — | 1 | 2 | 3 | 2 | 4 |
| Others | 7 | 13 | 15 | 9 | 11 | 10 | 13 | 11 |
| TOTAL | 137 | 142 | 130 | 124 | 137 | 136 | 127 | 129 |

\* Based on Labour Party Conference reports modified by examination of union accounts.

The relative strength of the unions in the House is still changing. The TGWU has held its ground, while the AEU, which has become interested in Parliamentary representation again has strengthened its group of MPs. The Miners, so long impregnable, are slowly waning, the NUGMW, which had ten

MPs in 1945 fell to four in 1957, while the Boot & Shoe Operatives and the cotton unions have all but vanished from Westminster. Although more unions than ever are trying to send their members to Parliament, the large unions still have almost all the successes.

The crude figures of the numbers of sponsored candidates do not tell the whole story. Working class candidates are sometimes sponsored by the Cooperative Party or by constituency parties. Nor are the terms 'working class' and 'trade unionist' necessarily synonymous. If anything the number of Labour candidates and Members of Parliament who are members of trade unions is actually increasing. In 1955 over seventy per cent of Labour candidates were members of trade unions—eighty more than in 1945, when the numbers were unusually low because of the war.[1] This is not so surprising since membership of the appropriate union or professional association is a condition of Party membership. Although a few white-collar non-unionists have been adopted most selection conferences expect intending candidates to produce a membership card.

The steady rise in the number of trade unionist candidates is not quite as healthy as it appears. Many are professional men, who are more likely than their predecessors to join a union for political or sentimental reasons. This explains why so many more candidates now come from the Clerical & Administrative Workers' Union, the general unions, USDAW and ASSET (which has attracted a number of left-wing MPs whose connection with the engineering industry—ASSET's primary field of recruitment—is tenuous at best). Many more are teachers, clerks and journalists—whose claim to be an authentic part of the movement would be disputed by some militants. The manual workers are losing ground. The Miners and some of the craft unions have today almost no hope of winning a nomination unless their candidate is sponsored. These are the unions which have showed the greatest alarm about nominations in recent years.

In some ways the change in the social composition of the Parliamentary Labour Party is even more alarming for the

---

[1] Sources: *The Times House of Commons, Labour Party's Election Who's Who*, union journals, and direct communication with almost all unions affected.

TABLE 27

TRADE UNION SPONSORED MEMBERS OF PARLIAMENT 1929–1959*

| | 1929 | 1931 | 1935 | 1945 | 1950 | 1951 | 1955 | 1959 |
|---|---|---|---|---|---|---|---|---|
| National Union of Mineworkers | 42 | 26 | 32 | 34 | 37 | 36 | 34 | 31 |
| Transport & General Workers' Union | 13 | 1 | 7 | 17 | 16 | 14 | 14 | 14 |
| National Union of Railwaymen | 8 | — | 5 | 12 | 10 | 9 | 8 | 5 |
| Transport Salaried Staffs' Association | 7 | — | 6 | 9 | 7 | 7 | 5 | 5 |
| National Union of General & Municipal Workers | 6 | 2 | 6 | 10 | 6 | 6 | 4 | 4 |
| Associated Society of Woodworkers | 6 | 1 | 2 | 3 | 3 | 3 | 2 | 1 |
| Union of Shop, Distributive & Allied Workers | 4 | 1 | 6 | 8 | 8 | 9 | 9 | 9 |
| British Iron, Steel & Kindred Trades Association | 4 | 1 | 1 | 2 | 2 | 2 | 2 | 2 |
| United Textile Factory Workers' Association | 4 | — | — | 3 | 2 | 1 | 1 | 1 |
| Amalgamated Engineering Union | 3 | 2 | 3 | 4 | 8 | 8 | 6 | 8 |
| National Union of Boot & Shoe Operatives | 2 | — | — | 4 | 1 | 1 | — | — |
| Associated Society of Locomotive Engineers & Firemen | 1 | — | 1 | 2 | 2 | 2 | 2 | 3 |
| United Society of Boilermakers, etc. | 1 | 1 | 1 | — | — | — | — | — |
| Union of Post Office Workers | — | — | — | 1 | 1 | 2 | 1 | 2 |
| National Union of Agricultural Workers | — | — | — | 1 | 1 | 1 | 1 | 2 |
| Electrical Trades Union | — | — | — | 1 | 1 | 1 | — | — |
| Other | 13 | — | 8 | 9 | 6 | 6 | 6 | 5 |
| TOTAL | 114 | 35 | 78 | 120 | 111 | 108 | 95 | 92 |
| All Labour MPs | 287 | 46 | 154 | 393 | 315 | 295 | 277 | 258 |

* Based on Labour Party Conference reports modified by examination of union accounts.

unions than the bare figures suggest.[1] The proportions of trade union and working-class Labour candidates (thirty-eight to

[1] Cf., J. F. S. Ross, *Elections and Electors*, Chapter 26. M. I. Cole, *The General Election of 1945 and after*. Fabian Research Series, No. 102. H. G. Nicholas, *The British General Election of 1950*, pp. 53–4. D. E. Butler, *The British General Election of 1951*, Macmillan, 1952, pp. 41–4. D. E. Butler, *The British General Election of 1955*, Macmillan, 1955, pp. 40–3.

forty per cent)[1] and Members of Parliament (forty-eight to fifty per cent) are stationary. But, allowing for the decline in the size of the Parliamentary Labour Party since 1945, the proportion of working class Labour MPs who hold safe seats is slowly deteriorating, while the proportion who sit in marginal constituencies has risen. There are fewer working class candidates in marginal Conservative seats. At every level the working class and trade union element is being undermined.[2]

Meanwhile the background of the middle-class candidates is also changing. Before the war many successful middle-class candidates came into Parliament with a long experience of social service or work on public bodies which brought them into direct contact with the unions or with the working class. Since the war the number of candidates who have backgrounds of social or public service has been falling. In 1955 the Parliamentary Party contained about as many MPs with no such background as the far larger Party of 1945. Despite the frequent grumbling about 'people who haven't been in the Party five minutes', renegade Liberals, converts, and raw products of the Oxford Union are not often adopted in winnable seats. The interests of these middle-class candidates are more strikingly diverse than might be guessed from the complaints made about 'longhaired intellectuals' at union conferences. But a growing number know the trade union movement only through a white collar union, lecturing for the Workers' Educational Association, and service on a constituency General Management Committee. While they sympathize with the unions and respond to the unions' demands as Party solidarity and tradition require, in the eyes of many trade unionists they are no substitute for men who have thoroughly experienced the working-class movement, react instinctively with the unions—who are in fact workers themselves.

The unions' roots in the PLP are still deep. After the 1955 election at least 141 Labour MPs had held trade union office at some time, compared with 188 in 1945, 155 in 1950, and 145 in 1951. But the decline is most marked in the Parliamentary

[1] 'Trade union and working class' includes manual workers, sponsored union candidates, trade union officials, and white collar trade unionists known to have held union office for at least five years.
[2] See p. 272.

leadership. When Mr Attlee formed his ministry in 1945 he had to call on the experienced Parliamentarians, many of them working class and trade unionist. Successive ministerial changes weakened the unions' position, while the death of Ernest Bevin was a greater loss to them than simple statistics can ever tell. Only the Whips remained almost solidly trade unionist, perhaps because trade unionists are thought to know about discipline, but also because a Labour Prime Minister is under pressure to give the unions as many posts as efficiency allows. Among the junior ministers several trade unionists had no prospects of promotion, while some who were not working class could hope to hold office when Labour came to power again. The allocation of 'special responsibilities' when the Party passed into opposition revealed a similar trend. The problem is so marked that when Mr Crossman remarked to readers of the *Daily Mirror* in 1957 that among the trade union MPs 'only four suggest themselves for key jobs' there was a storm of protest, the trade union group solemnly recorded its disapproval—but no one said Mr Crossman was wrong. Everyone knew he had blurted out the truth. Even if a few lame ducks have to be carried the unions will probably have to hold more than four places in a future Labour Government—but a majority of its members will not be of working class origin.

The unions may eventually restore their position in the PLP, by now there is a 'missing generation' of trade union MPs. Unless a senior trade unionist is coopted into Parliament in the way that Bevin left the TGWU to join the War Cabinet and the Labour Government. The decline of the unions' representation in the Parliamentary leadership is bound to continue. While the fall in the numbers of really able men entering the House is a problem going far beyond the Labour Movement, it is more serious for the unions. While there is little danger that Party leaders will forget the unions' wishes, fewer and fewer of them will know the unions from direct experience. Many see the unions as an external force to be conciliated, with which the Party must live. Without a trade unionist of stature who can interpret the unions to the Party and the Party to the unions the problems of keeping the two wings of the Movement in harmony are likely to deepen.

There is little wonder that manual trade unionists particularly are worried. Mr Fred Lee, an AEU MP, warned:

'If this tendency continues we shall find that the Parliamentary Party has become a middle-class organization which strives desperately to prove its connections with the working class by displaying its few remaining trade union products with all the enthusiasm of a child with an unusual toy.'[1]

Mr George Porter, a former Woodworkers' MP, told his union:

'My experience has been that at Selection Conference after Selection Conference those candidates who are being selected have in many instances, no connection with the trade union movement . . . I would say there is a danger of no trade union representation in the House of Commons.'[2]

Labour's growth into a national party inevitably ended the unions' early near monopoly of seats. But while they accept that the Party must have middle-class MPs many trade unionists feel that the trend has gone too far—and they are afraid that it is unlikely to stop. Even the Miners, who thought themselves so securely entrenched twenty years ago, now fear that they will be winkled out of their strongholds one by one. Whatever advantages there have been in bringing all classes into the Parliamentary Labour Party, this is a far cry from the hopes of the men who saw in the Labour Representation Committee their long-awaited means of sending working men to Westminster.

## Causes of a Decline

It is not hard to see why the unions are losing ground. In only one respect can they feel that fate has been unkind; they may have been hampered unduly by the two redistributions of seats since the war. In 1948 several of their seats (chiefly in the over-represented London area) disappeared altogether, some trade union safe seats became marginal, and several marginal seats held by non-unionists became safer. When the tide ran against Labour in 1950, 1951, and 1955 it swept out a few more

---

[1] *AEU Journal*, January 1954.
[2] *Report of the ADC*, 1955, p. 40. Cf., *The New Dawn*, July 18, 1953.

sponsored MPs than was to be expected. Then, as the number of seats that Labour could win was falling, and the competition from former MPs for nominations was increasing, it was harder than ever for the unions to send new men into the House. In 1954 redistribution again led to the defeat or retirement of several more trade unionists. To some degree these periodic reshuffles have hindered the re-establishment of the 'normal' pre-war pattern, by which the unions' relative strength in Parliament increased when the Party suffered an electoral set-back.

The unions' unimaginative approach to winning nominations has not helped them. They compete furiously for Labour seats, but they are often remarkably casual in seeking nominations to less hopeful constituencies. Some critics attack them for being selfish in trying to put their money only into safe seats, yet it is unfair to ignore the financial support that they give the Party in other ways. Such complaints would only be justified if the unions were giving so much money to maintaining safe seats that they could spare too little for the rest of the Party.

They have never wholly shunned the forlorn rural constituencies or Conservative suburbia. The Association of Engineering & Shipbuilding Draughtsmen's conference insisted, against its Executive's advice, on sponsoring candidates in unpromising constituencies. 'We have a moral responsibility to the Labour Party', a delegate urged. 'We should not leave to the very weak organizations in the constituencies the responsibility of fighting those elections'. Another delegate argued, 'It is a paradox of the whole history of the Labour and trade union movement to suggest that a trade union has not got the responsibility of undertaking pioneering work in constituencies which have to be won for Labour'.[1] Following a decision of its annual conference the Transport Salaried Staffs' Association supported Mr Tom Bradley for some years in the 'backward and rural constituency' of Rutland and Stamford. The NUGMW maintained candidates at Sheffield (Hallam) and West Derbyshire in 1950 without any hope of winning. The NUR fought the Inverness by-election in 1954, although the seat was not even marginal. The TGWU, which sponsored Mr H. White at Maidstone in several elections,

[1] *Report of the RCC*, 1945, pp. 349-50.

the Typographical Association which fought Mr Churchill at Woodford in 1950, and NUM (Somerset) who regularly contest a seat in the county, had no illusions about the outcome. They were not alone. The Building Workers, the Seamen, and the Foundry Workers, have all sponsored candidates in safe Conservative seats.

Nevertheless, the unions do pay much less attention to winning nominations in non-Labour seats. They suffered heavily from following this policy before the 1945 election. Although all but four of their candidates were elected, the unions simply did not nominate sufficient candidates for them to hold their position within the PLP. Had they tried to win the nominations in many of the Conservative seats which were captured by Labour they could have had them almost for the asking. In later elections they were just as cautious. Although there was little hope of winning Conservative seats in 1950 and 1951, even in 1955 only about ten trade union candidates stood in marginal Conservative seats. No matter how well Labour had done in any of these elections the unions' representation within the Parliamentary Party would have been little or no better. Unless they take their chance in far more unpromising constituencies—instead of furiously disputing the nominations only in clearly winnable seats—they have little chance of ever regaining their former position.[1]

The unions' ability to win nominations has also been affected by the increased strength of the local Parties. They had 431,000 members in 1936, 645,000 in 1946, and 934,000 in 1957. Inflated though these figures are, they indicate a real improvement in the constituencies' finances. More and more Parties can afford the luxury of independence in their choice of Parliamentary candidates—while from about 1950 to at least 1957 the financial inducements to accept a sponsored candidate looked less attractive than before the war.

[1] This is a long-standing weakness. In 1945 there were twenty-one working-class/trade union candidates (sponsored or not) in seats which the Conservatives won by under 5,000 votes, compared with seventy-two middle and upper class candidates. In 1950 there were thirty and sixty-eight respectively; in 1951 twenty-six and sixty-six; and in 1955, twenty-six and seventy-two. Had Labour won more seats at any of these elections the strength of the unions in the PLP would have been weakened. This holds true even if more sophisticated criteria are used for assessing what is a marginal seat.

How far Labour nominations are influenced by financial considerations is not fully clear. Wilfrid Fienburgh once alleged bluntly: 'The Labour Party is the only Party in Britain in which you can buy a seat'.[1] Another Labour writer admitted that 'It is most difficult for a member of the Labour Party to reach the benches of the House of Commons unless he is financially supported either by an organization or from his own resources'.[2] Many trade unionists are convinced that nominations can be bought. 'We have indicated that we are not going to buy seats', said a member of the AESD Executive. 'That is done in some instances, but we are not going to be a party to it.'[3] Explaining why the National Union of Vehicle Builders had failed to win nominations one of its leaders remarked that 'Many organizations paid more than did the NUVB to the constituency party to ensure that a man got a seat'.[4] A member of the Typographical Association Executive told his conference:

'Imagine your position if you go along with a lower offer than other trade union representatives who are on the short list of candidates. That is the position. There is fierce competititon for the safe seats. . . . If you are not prepared to foot the bill, then you will not get your man accepted.'[5]

On the other hand experienced Party officials say that the influence of finance has been exaggerated. In the nature of the case acceptable evidence is hard to obtain. For obvious reasons candidates are sometimes all too ready to allege that nominations have been bought. The Party is always buzzing with misinformed and malignant gossip about how nominations were won or lost. Some constituencies are venal, but few are as irresponsible as the local party cited by R. T. McKenzie, which almost chose a sponsored candidate in his absence without anyone present knowing him.[6] The financial strain of the 1950 and 1951 elections tempted some Parties to look for a paying candidate for the next election. At least one Regional Organizer

[1] The Future of Labour's Organization, *Fabian Journal*, November 1955.
[2] C. Ford, *The Labour Organiser*, October 1955.
[3] *Report of the RCC*, 1951, p. 174.
[4] *Report of the Annual Delegate Conference*, 1955, p. 113.
[5] *Report of the Delegate Meeting*, 1950, p. 65.
[6] *British Political Parties*, p. 556.

S

advised constituencies not to hurry the selection of their candidate—knowing that some were so weak financially that they
would feel unable to choose on merit. Nevertheless some
constituencies succumbed. A Constituency Labour Party in the
Home Counties, which had been irritated by a trade unionist's
flaunting of his financial backing during 1950 adopted him
shortly after the 1951 election.

It is also whispered that unions offer more than the Hastings
Agreement rate to win nominations. One senior trade union
official (whose union would have strongly disapproved)
certainly did offer a substantial donation to constituency funds
over the Hastings Agreement scale. He was nominated and
fought the seat unsuccessfully. Although he made a similar
offer before the next selection conference he was not re-
nominated. Such cases are rare.

In a few constituencies the agent is the weakest link. Labour
agents are still notoriously underpaid; many spend much of
their time running football pools to raise their own salaries. The
irregularity with which they are paid can be even more de-
moralizing than the poor wages. General Management Committees may not be influenced by financial considerations, but
to an agent in a struggling constituency, a union maintenance
grant represents an assured source of a large slice of his salary.
Many agencies are sustained simply by the continuance of
sponsorship grants. The agents are sometimes well placed for
successful intrigue. 'I haven't any particular preference', said a
Borough Party agent, 'but I expect my two candidates to bring
in at least £500 per year'. This was no idle boast. There had
been one or more sponsored candidates in the Borough ever
since 1931. In a northern constituency, where a union contributed to the agent's salary, the sitting Member died. Determined that the next candidate would come from the same union,
the agent took the initiative and urged the union's Executive
Council to send a good man quickly. The newcomer was taken
around the wards, introduced to the Women's Section, and spoke
to trade union branches before the other contenders were in the
field. He won the nomination handsomely. In another constituency the agent successfully resisted attempts by a Trotskyist executive to get rid of the sitting MP, knowing that his

job would not long survive the cutting off of union funds. It would be unfair to suggest that many party agents act in such a way, but so long as the livelihood of a large number of agents depends on the CLP nominating—and retaining—a candidate who can bring money, some agents will be influenced. The spread of Transport House grants to support agencies in marginal constituencies may remove or limit the danger.

Quite frequently a local Party decides that its next candidate *must* be sponsored—but finally chooses one with no money because he impressed them. A GMC member recalled, 'We had a sponsored candidate in 1951, and this time we decided we wanted to have one without ties. So we chose this chap. He's a shocker—but at least he's ours, and we don't have to kowtow to anyone'. Party officials claim that such cases are frequent.

Two MPs disputed the nomination for a redistributed seat in a northern city in 1955. The first candidate made it quite clear that there was no question of a financial contribution. After the second, the ageing nominee of a craft union, had spoken, a delegate from his union arose and asked: 'What financial support can Mr ——— promise the constituency?' There was a shocked hush—later described as a 'silent boo'—throughout the room. The first candidate was adopted. Another constituency secretary recalled quite frankly, 'We used to have a union candidate. Now we run a football pool'.

It is often suggested within the Labour Party that only money could explain the election of some of the miners. This is understandable but inaccurate. The NUM does use its money as a lever from time to time. In one northern selection conference in 1956 the NUM spokesman said flatly, 'Choose this lawyer if you like—but don't think that you can kick us about and then turn round and ask us for money five minutes later. Don't forget, that it's the Miners that pay your affiliation fees'.

But such cases are rare today. It is unlikely that lodges would disaffiliate from a CLP just because they lost a nomination. The miners pay only small maintenance grants, and modest election expenses. A grasping Party would probably benefit substantially from choosing a candidate from another union. The Miners' hold on their seats has been due less to their money than to their ability to swing the support of their own delegates, and miners (and their wives) representing other organizations, behind their candidate.

Since the war particularly the unions have had to compete with the Cooperative Party and with unsponsored candidates who contribute to constituency funds. Many Labour Members of Parliament gave £50 to £100 per year to their Party's funds, while a few rich candidates paid as much as the Hastings Agreement rate.[1] Although only a handful could match what the unions were offering, they reduced the temptation to adopt union candidates. At one selection conference in North London the issue was put in terms as crude as these: 'Mr Smith, you can see our problem. We are a poor Party. Up to now we have had a trade unionist, and we've just managed to get by. We can't really afford to be without that money. Now, if we adopted you, how far do you think you could help?' Other Parties bluntly demanded £100 per year. There were repeated squabbles between local Parties and MPs who agreed to make an annual grant and then refused once they were elected. However, such competition limited the worst dangers of sponsorship. At most selection conferences in winnable seats several of the short-listed candidates are partly or wholly sponsored. Financial backing can buy a place on the short list, only rarely does it decisively favour a single candidate at the selection conference, although this is small comfort to the candidate with no backing.

Opinion within the Party may be changing. As we have seen the pressure for sponsorship grants to be raised comes almost exclusively from the local Parties, but some members of the

---

[1] The Party never revealed the extent of self-sponsorship. The Assistant National Agent, Miss Sarah Barker, wrote, of candidates' donations: 'Most of these grants are modest and only a very small number of candidates contribute anything like the maximum permitted under the Hastings Agreement . . .' *The Labour Organiser*, January 1956.

The 1946 Report of the Lancashire & Cheshire Regional Council revealed that in the two-member boroughs of Blackburn, Oldham and Bolton, one of the two seats was supported by the candidate himself; so were Ashton-under-Lyme, Rochdale, Birkenhead, Accrington, Bury and Crewe. It is understood that Mr Charles Royle received support from the Meat Traders at West Salford until they disagreed in 1949. Poale Zion (The Jewish Socialist Labour Party) is said to have financed Liverpool, Walton in 1950. A seat in Cumberland was personally financed for a short time. The North West was probably untypical at this period. There were known to be two personally-financed seats in Yorkshire, one in East Anglia, and one in the West Country. In a number of other instances—notably the National Union of Teachers' candidates—constituencies are subsidized by other organizations.

political wing are beginning to look on sponsorship as an anachronism. The Wilson Committee commented firmly:

'We are disturbed at the number of candidates who, out of their own pockets, are required to make annual contributions towards Constituency Party finances. Quite apart from the undesirability of this practice, on general grounds, the dependence of CLP finances on such a source of income has a detrimental effect on organization. We recommend that early steps be taken to end this practice and that it shall be an instruction to NEC representatives at Selection Conferences, that any attempt to extract a financial pledge from a possible candidate shall invalidate the conference.'[1]

Although the realities of power within the Party made it unthinkable that the Committee should have said so, there is little difference between constituencies being influenced by candidates' personal donations and their letting a union's contribution determine their choice. During 1957 the NEC decided that finance must not be mentioned at selection conferences, and forbade unsponsored candidates to give more than £50 per year to constituency funds—twice the maximum permitted in the Conservative Party.[2] Regional Organizers had already been insisting unofficially that money must not be mentioned for several years, but the new rule reinforced the slowly-developing hostility to letting money overtly influence the choice of candidates. Some union officials complain that in certain constituencies sponsorship harms their chances of winning the nomination. Nevertheless, even now selection conferences do not completely ignore financial considerations. They are usually well-acquainted with the terms that the unions offer —for no amount of rule-making can prevent a candidate's local backers from letting it be known how much their union will pay before the conference takes place.

It may well be that sponsorship payments are a fraternal and disinterested gesture from a union to a constituency where one of its members is standing. Yet undeniably such a system lends

[1] *Report*, para. 68.
[2] *Report of the Labour Party Conference*, 1957, p. 13. They may contribute no more than their personal expenses at general elections.

itself to corruption. Labour Party officials do not deny that some constituencies are venal—although some veteran officials put the proportion at no more than three in a hundred. The Party has not yet matched the Conservatives' success in banishing financial considerations from selection conferences.[1] Even if a scandal can be avoided, the importance of finance in swinging nominations has declined, and seems likely to decline still further—to the detriment of the unions' representation in Parliament.

The fate of sponsorship may be beyond the unions' control; other reasons for their lack of success are not. The most humiliating by far are the nominations lost because the unions' delegates to CLPs do not turn out to support their own candidates. There are few seats outside the mining areas where a single union has sufficient delegates to carry the nomination, but there are many which can be won by a union which acts as a determined minority. Local members are particularly well-placed to persuade Executive Committees to include their union's candidate on the short list. The branch can provide a friendly questioner at selection conferences. But time and again trade union Executives charge their rank and file with disloyalty or laziness. Mr A. S. Moody, MP told the 1955 Conference of the Amalgamated Society of Woodworkers:

'I went before a selection conference at Carlisle. There was one joiner present. Bro. Marshall lost a good seat which ought to have been ours by one vote. The joiners were very badly represented at that Selection Conference.'

Another delegate agreed that:

'If it comes about without first activizing our branches to take their part locally there is no point in increasing the Parliamentary panel . . . I had that experience on two occasions; no members of our Society affiliated to the local constituency Party,

---

[1] Cf., 'The circular letter from the Battersea Labour Party & Trades Council stating that nominations in connection with the Battersea Borough Council Election, May 10, 1956, must be accompanied by a sum of £6 (six pounds) towards election expenses for the candidates (such fee being refunded only if the nominee is not selected as a candidate) was read . . .' *Quarterly Report of the National Association of Operative Plasterers*, March 1956.

so that my chances of being adopted as a Parliamentary candidate were very slim indeed.'[1]

Mr Paxton of the Seamen complained that 'a little while ago he had been at a seaport town at a selection conference, to find to his horror that there was only one man in that conference who was a seaman'.[2] A railway union's nominee once went to a selection conference in a large railway city and received no votes at all.

Sometimes a union brings off a coup. In one such case branch affiliations flooded in to the local Party after the seat fell vacant. Delegates were appointed. At the conference the agent, accustomed to patchy attendances, saw to his astonishment that all the numerous delegates from this one union were present. Some looked about them with the uneasy curiosity of men attending their first Party meeting. They knew how to vote. Their candidate was selected. But this is the exception. The failure of delegates to support their own candidate more often makes the difference between success and failure. Many delegates to Constituency Labour Parties are 'Party-minded' rather than 'union-minded'. They are unwilling to back their own union's candidate solely from solidarity as their leaders expect. Although some trade union leaders try to put the blame on the 'long haired constituency members who crowd out the workers' they know quite well that many of the candidates they complain about the most bitterly were chosen by overwhelmingly working-class selection conferences. Although occasional selection conferences during the Bevanite controversy took on an overtly anti-union tone, questions of policy are far less responsible for the unions' failure than their inability to find candidates who win their own members' enthusiasm and interest, and who have the qualities the local Parties are looking for.

## Choosing the Panel

There has scarcely been a time in the history of the Labour Party when trade union candidates were not a matter for

[1] *Report of the Annual Delegate Conference*, 1955, p. 38 and 1954, p. 53.
[2] *Report of the Annual General Meeting*, 1954, p. 42.

derisory comment. It seems to be one of those things that is never quite what it has been. Nevertheless, even within the trade union movement it is readily admitted that there has been a deterioration since the war. Their leaders say vaguely 'We must do something about it'. Some of the faults may lie in the qualifications that the unions set for their panels and the way they choose their candidates.[1]

Selecting Parliamentary panels has often been a rather haphazard affair, varying considerably between unions, but usually similar to the procedures used for choosing permanent officials. Most unions rely on a general ballot of the membership. On grounds of efficiency or economy others prefer to choose candidates by ballot at their annual conference, and a few form their panel through selection committees. Some unions have no selection procedure at all; they may agree to sponsor an outstanding member or official when they have the chance. The National Union of Furniture Trade Operatives, which has lacked an MP for many years, vaguely hopes that some day a member will be adopted by a constituency, so that the union can then sponsor him.

In unions with a panel the formal qualifications are usually modest, analogous to those demanded for other offices. Candidates must hold 'clean cards' and have been members for periods varying between one year (Union of Post Office Workers) and seven (AEU). There is no minimum age except that implied by the membership qualification, and most unions impose retiring ages. Most refuse to let candidates join the panel if they

[1] NUM Durham uses an extraordinary two-vote system, apparently to avoid the stalemate that would result if every lodge supported its 'favourite son'. Voters choose two candidates, in the first ballot. If no one receives an absolute majority a second ballot is held, and the candidate with most votes is nominated. The correct tactic in such an election is to vote for the favourite candidate and the one thought least likely to succeed. Unfortunately if several lodges make the same tactical choice the weakest candidate may be elected. Extraordinary tales are told of the consequence of this system. One Party official insists that in a Durham constituency the miners once found to their horror that they had selected a candidate whose abilities were beyond a joke. Loyal to their mandates, they nevertheless adopted him. The poor man, to whom the election was a shock, and the reactions a humiliation, collapsed and was taken to hospital. This was the opportunity for a tactical withdrawal, and a chastened group of lodges selected another candidate. The attempt to select a single candidate sometimes breaks down on religious differences—notably at Sedgfield where bitter opposition between backers of a Methodist and a Roman Catholic NUM candidate gave another union the nomination.

are over fifty-five, and retire them at sixty unless they are in the House. They stop paying maintenance grants to the constituencies when their Members of Parliament reach sixty-five, although the constituency may still renominate the sitting Member on its own responsibility. By contrast—impressed by the example of Ernest Bevin—the TGWU has refused to make candidates retire at sixty and MPs at seventy.

Formal qualifications are less important than custom and practice. Aneurin Bevan was elected NUM MP for Ebbw Vale at thirty-two, and Walter Padley became Member for Ogmore at thirty-four, but while Dr J. F. S. Ross has estimated that in 1951 the average age on first election of Labour MPs was forty-three years three months, the average age of the sponsored candidates was forty-five years four months.[1] Among the larger unions the figures were: NUM forty-six years, four months; TGWU forty-eight years, eight months; NUR forty-four years, seven months; and USDAW forty-three years, six months. Although the average trade union MP is only four years older than his non-union colleague when he enters the House, this small difference hides the real problem of the candidates who stay on the panel year after year without being selected. In most unions a high proportion of these unsuccessful members are over fifty.

Recruiting younger candidates is far from simple. Nothing impresses members more than a 'record of service to the Movement'. They are always suspicious of ambitious young men, who may be using the union organization to further their own fortunes. History has provided plenty of defections to foster such prejudices—although John Burns, Frank Hodges, and J. H. Thomas were among many apostates with impressive records. Quite apart from the hostility to careerists it takes time to make an impression even on the unions' militants. The budding candidate must either have attended the union's conference for several years or served on a District Committee. He must have at least a district reputation, and possibly be nationally known if candidates are chosen by general ballot—and these are not won overnight. Small wonder that members selected for the

---

[1] The calculation attributed to Dr Ross is found in *Elections and Electors*, p. 393. The remaining calculations are the author's.

panel usually have between fifteen and thirty years of union membership behind them.

Though the perennial cry for younger blood is perhaps not to be taken too seriously, there is little doubt that unions which have formed panels exclusively of ageing members have hindered their chances. The least successful have been those which combine a small panel with a general ballot—younger men are sometimes elected if the panel is large enough. Some cling resolutely to panels of two or three candidates, although the successful unions are usually those which maintain a larger panel than they can support, allowing their Executive to choose which candidates to nominate for vacant seats, leaving the perennially unsuccessful men to one side.

Despite the clear 'democratic' advantages of selecting candidates by ballot it is doubtful whether it has served the unions well. Whenever the system is questioned members argue, 'If we're fit to choose officials, why can't we also choose the panel?' The problems are quite different. Members are more likely to have a precise idea of what makes an able official than of the sort of man who will make a good Member of Parliament. In selecting a panel they have little opportunity to assess the candidates' merits. In unions where competition is keen— there have been thirty-eight candidates for a single vacancy on the Woodworkers' panel—not all the contenders will be known even to active members. Usually unions forbid canvassing or advertising for support, although a few, like the National Union of Tailors & Garment Workers, print a brief statement of each candidate's industrial and political record. Only the National Union of Vehicle Builders publishes election addresses from the candidates. It is far more difficult to cast an informed vote than during the election of union officials, or during a general election where party preference counts more than personality. Voters can go to see and hear Parliamentary candidates; they usually have no such chance in a union. Accordingly they are forced to rely chiefly on the candidate's record. This may show an impressive list of offices held in the branch and in local politics, but it may be no guide to suitability for Parliament.

Most unions reconstitute their panels after each general election (although sitting MPs are not normally subject to re-election). If the panel is elected it is almost impossible to get rid of poor candidates once they are on the panel; few members become aware of their unsuitability and they benefit from the general tendency to re-elect office-holders. The leader of one union which has loudly complained that it wins no nominations admitted, 'There's not one of our candidates has a cat-in-hell's chance. Quite frankly none of them are any——good. But what can we do? They get put back on the panel time after time'. Several unions have switched from general ballots to conference ballots, hoping for more informed voting, but the improvement has rarely been considerable.

Since the war more unions have realized that selection by ballot was not improving their chances. Significantly, the AEU, whose democratic zeal for elections outstrips any other large union, switched to selecting candidates through weekend schools. Aspiring candidates are interviewed, make speeches, and write essays, under the eyes of the union's MPs. The average age of the panel has fallen. Several of the largest unions, among them the TGWU and the NUGMW, rely on interviews by Executive sub-committees without formal tests, and several others combine branch nominations with Executive selection. The British Iron, Steel & Kindred Trades' Association allows its branches to nominate, and selects by a combined examination and interview. The Draughtsmen, who have only sponsored candidates since the war, tried hard to combine expert selection with rank and file participation. After several years of selection by committee at the annual conference, and demands for election by general ballot, they turned to a combination of tests and committee selection, subject to ratification by the conference. The members' participation is now negligible.

The NUR, which once chose its panel by its customary procedure of examinations combined with a general ballot, also found that too many candidates were elderly, with no appeal in the constituencies. It decided to put on its panel members who had been accepted for the Labour Party's List B of individual candidates—for which the backing of a constituency is necessary. The union Executive would sponsor him if he was adopted for a winnable seat. The union hopes to find candidates who have proved their acceptability to the political wing—although at the price of limiting its own freedom of choice. The National Union of Seamen tried sending candidates to Ruskin College, in the hope that they would subsequently enter union service, and be better equipped to meet the competition at selection conferences.[1] There have been beginnings of schemes to train and help prospective candidates in other unions, notably the NUM (Midlands) but none has had the chance to prove itself.

Whatever democratic theory may say, selection has some clear advantages over election—particularly if branch nomination is retained to preserve some rank and file interest. (A man who cannot carry his branch is unlikely to carry a selection conference.) Committees have the chance to make more intelligent choices than ordinary members. They can see whether candidates' records are really so illustrious, and consider the terms on which they are willing to stand.[2] They can weed out the semi-literates, the inarticulate and the politically uninformed and match the candidate against selection conference standards and make sure that the union will not be disgraced. Although some unions shrug off the nominations that they have lost, bad candidates have sometimes impaired their chances for years afterwards. As constituency Executive Committees run through the long list of would-be candidates in search of six names to place before the selection conference, a member may remark 'The NU*** has got a man in. But we tried one of *them* last time. We can give him a miss'. Sometimes branch delegates to local parties have been so ashamed of their union's candidate that they have been reluctant to propose a member of their panel again.

The theoretical advantages of committee selection are not always realized. The NUGMW's selected panel has won few nominations while USDAW, which elects its panel, has been successful. There are dangers in committee selection. For all its faults, the ballot has produced some unorthodox candidates. Within USDAW it has led to the choice of such contrasted personalities as Alfred Robens, a pillar of orthodoxy, George Craddock, a pacifist left-winger and Walter Padley, a militant

---

[1] One member of the union who has been through this process has since been adopted. Finding jobs in the movement for such ex-students in practice raises considerable difficulties.

[2] Several unions have been saddled with candidates who refused to accept nominations outside a small area, or who made other onerous reservations.

ex-ILPer. Selection committees will always be under the temptation to choose candidates whose views reflect those of the leadership. How far Executives choose 'reliable' men for their panels is not clear. NUGMW candidates are rarely left-wingers, while the ETU's nominees are rarely quite orthodox —but there are no prominent rebels within either union.[1] Covert discrimination could deprive the Party of able men.

Since the war the unions have realized that their candidates were not always what the constituencies wanted, although some trade unionists feel that the local Parties are too easily swayed by candidates with a meretricious appeal. 'These local Parties seem to fall at the feet of a man if he's an ex-Liberal, a public school boy, or a smooth-talking professional politician. They don't seem to care even if he's only been in the Movement five minutes', one militant complained. After all, as Mr J. B. Figgins once remarked, 'It is *our* Labour Party'.[2] Despite the 1944 Education Act there is no lack of talent within the movement. The unions' first problem is to find good candidates. If they are really concerned to build up their numbers in the House of Commons many will have to think again about selection procedures. Although more efficient methods are gradually being adopted it is doubtful whether enough has yet been done. Candidates must not only be found; they often need coaching and training too. The experiments in the AEU and the National Union of Seamen may be showing the way the rest of the movement will have to follow.

*Officials in Parliament*

The unions must not only take pains to find the right candidates if they want to remain a Parliamentary force—they must be ready to let them go into Parliament. While there are sufficient potential run-of-the-mill back benchers among the lay members, they must also find at least a handful of candidates of ministerial

---

[1] One of the ETU's candidates, Mr S. Goldberg (a member of the ETU Executive Council) is so far to the left that the Labour Party refused to endorse his nomination for Nottingham South, and refused to include his name on its List 'A' of members available for nomination as sponsored candidates. The Labour Party told the union it had reached its decisions 'due to his past political associations and it was felt that insufficient time had elapsed since he had broken those associations . . .' Cf., *Report of the Executive Council* (ETU), 1956, p. 3, and 1957, pp. 4–5.
[2] *Railway Review*, June 29, 1951.

calibre if they want the Party's highest councils to include their spokesmen. Their attitude towards officials entering Parliament is the greatest single obstacle to the unions' best men coming forward. This problem is almost as old as the movement. When John Hodge wanted to stand as a Liberal in Glasgow in 1894 his union, the Steel Smelters, decided that, 'we, in face of the fact of our funds being low and our General Secretary having sufficient work, cannot see our way clear to allow the General Secretary to enter Parliament as our representative; nor to allow him to contest the representation of any constituency'.[1] Later Hodge did go into Parliament, and many other union officials followed. At one time no fewer than eight of the Miners' Executive were in the House. The reaction soon set in. The Miners decided that no official of the Miners' Federation of Great Britain could go into Parliament. Even Arthur Henderson could not persuade them to make an exception for Frank Hodges, the MFGB Secretary, who went into Parliament in 1923 and was obliged to resign. Between the wars the restrictions spread until by 1945 they were so general that the Party sent a letter to all affiliated unions asking them to reconsider their policy. A few—notably the NUGMW—did so. Most made no change.

Some trade unionists seem to think that on becoming an official a man abdicates his civic rights and enters a priesthood. Replying to a request that certain officials should be allowed to stand for Parliament, Arthur Deakin said:

'When a man is appointed an officer of this Union he is asked a specific question—whether or not he proposes to devote his life's work to the industrial side or whether he has any ambition to enter the political field, and that is a consideration that must be borne in mind. In each case, any application that is made for inclusion in the Parliamentary panel is always related to that consideration and must of necessity be.'[2]

Since the time of J. H. Thomas the NUR has forbidden its officials even to accept nomination. Many other unions provide, in the words of the AEU Rules, that 'any General Officer may

---

[1] Sir Arthur Pugh, *Men of Steel*, p. 106. When Hodge later became Minister of Labour there were demands that he should relinquish his post as General Secretary for the time being, but he threatened to resign and was upheld.
[2] Quoted in V. L. Allen, *Trade Union Leadership*, p. 151.

be nominated, but if he is elected he shall cease to hold office in the union'.[1] Another group forbids some officials to go into the House, but allows others (usually its organizers) to do so. The rules are not always the best guide to a union's practice. The General Secretary and his Assistant are the only officials of the TGWU excluded from entering Parliament by rule, but the (lay) General Executive Council has made it quite clear that neither the National Officers nor the Regional Secretaries will be allowed to go on the panel. Similarly officials of the Transport Salaried Staffs' Association and the National Union of Tailors & Garment Workers may in theory be candidates, but senior officials are in practice refused permission.

For most senior posts the choice is clear. Either the official must be allowed to hold his post while in Parliament, or he must resign. Granting leave of absence while in Parliament with a guarantee of reinstatement is impracticable in the most senior positions, while reinstatement to any elective post might be constitutionally impossible. Feeling against letting officers hold their posts while in Parliament has hardened even since the war. The work of senior officials has increased, while the demands made by Parliament during the period of small Labour majorities—still not forgotten—reinforced the belief in 'one man, one job'. Although many union officials accept this principle, the real pressure comes from the rank and file—including many who complain at their union's failure to win nominations. Branch officials allege that when national officers are in Parliament they are not readily available, and correspondence is neglected. They sourly note the rise in administration costs if a deputy or extra clerical staff have to be taken on. The fact that the MP is drawing two salaries also rankles. 'We're paying him his full salary, why shouldn't we have his full attention?' they exclaim. Beneath such remarks lies the assumption that only the official, using the union for his personal advancement, benefits from such arrangements. Few rank and file members have a clear idea of the usefulness of having spokesmen in the House who have first-hand knowledge of the problems they speak about. Head offices understand rather better the limited effectiveness of MPs who can speak only from a brief.

[1] *AEU Rules*, 46(4).

In many unions the release of senior officials is out of the question. The General Secretary of one small union, who had had to give up his seat as a borough councillor, explained 'I couldn't think of going into Parliament. When I'm out of the office half the staff is out of action'. In the largest unions the work is clearly too heavy for an official to carry two jobs. But there is a range of second rank officials in large unions, and of top rank officials in smaller unions, who could be spared—although the possibilities vary appreciably between unions. The General Secretary of a union with over 100,000 members agreed, 'Yes I suppose I could cope with both jobs if the Executive wanted me to. But they don't think it's really worth it'. This group could provide the PLP with a handful of capable, experienced trade unionists of some standing, who could assume higher office. They would certainly have brighter hopes of being adopted than other union candidates.

Some unions have been willing to let their senior officials go into the House even in recent years, among them the Association of Cine & Television Technicians, the Chemical Workers' Union, the Post Office Engineering Union, and the National Association of Theatrical & Kine Employees. On the other hand, Natsopa, and the Inland Revenue Staff Federation, who have had their General Secretaries in the House, and the Associated Society of Locomotive Engineers & Firemen, whose Assistant General Secretary was an MP would probably not repeat the experience.[1] The NUGMW's policy of letting senior officials go into Parliament was short-lived.[2] Sending these officials into the House has always meant administrative inconvenience, delay, and expense. The unions which are willing to let their General Secretaries go into the House are of medium size and without other Parliamentary representation. They have been willing to make the sacrifices because it seemed important that they should have a Parliamentary spokesman. Conversely, restrictions on officials of other unions entering

---

[1] Cf., Attempts to refuse permission to Mr Douglas Houghton (General Secretary, Inland Revenue Staff Federation) to stand at the 1950 election. Although these were unsuccessful the Executive indicated that future General Secretaries would not be given the same privilege. *Taxes*, July 1950.

[2] For a full account of the controversy see H. A. Clegg, *General Union*, Part IV, Ch. 3.

Parliament are tighter than ever because their rank and file do not believe that representation is important enough to make the sacrifice worth while.

Organizers are a different problem. Strikes cannot be settled, or building sites organized from Westminster. With rare exceptions organizers cannot hold down two jobs. Most unions which are prepared to let them go into Parliament either grant leave of absence or promise reinstatement if they are defeated. Reinstatement is not a major problem in a union which employs many organizers, for the vacancies are frequent. Smaller unions, like the Tobacco Workers' Union, where vacancies are rare, understandably find it impossible to guarantee re-employment. A few unions have been strangely reluctant to commit themselves explicitly to reinstatement and prefer to work on simple understandings—which may not encourage organizers to throw up their posts and go into the House. With a few exceptions, the problem is not reinstatement, but the refusal of large unions (the NUM, AEU and NUR) to allow their junior officials to stand, and failure of some other unions (notably the NUGMW) to give them any encouragement.

Reinstatement is often a much greater problem for the defeated rank and filer; ageing manual workers, or craftsmen who have been away from the bench for ten years, are not good employment prospects. The unions have been very cautious. At one time the National Union of Teachers and the National Union of Boot & Shoe Operatives promised employment as organizers to defeated MPs, but experience showed that Westminster is not the best training school for union officials. Although the National Union of Dyers, Bleachers & Textile Workers retains such guarantees, other unions avoid them. USDAW says cautiously 'such member shall have his financial position considered by the Executive Council who shall be empowered to act as they may deem desirable'.[1] The AESD promise that if MPs are defeated they 'will place at his/her disposal every facility to find fresh employment'.[2] Unions in the nationalized industries have negotiated reinstatement agreements. The Typographical Association and BISAKTA,

[1] *Rules*, p. 72.
[2] *Proceedings of the RCC*, 1948, p. 206.

T

make money guarantees to defeated MPs. Other unions, while declaring that none of their defeated members will be allowed to suffer, have not even written USDAW's noncommital phrases into their rules. Proposals to give either officials or rank and filers more generous or sure guarantees often meet surprising hostility. When the Typographical Assocation was asked to increase its guarantee to defeated MPs to £350 for two years an Executive spokesman argued:

'When the seat was lost at Cambridge the Labour candidate went along and signed the book the same as any other member of the TA would have to do if he lost his job, so that he was not tied down to £200 at all. In this time of the welfare state, he is entitled to unemployment benefit. We cannot afford to denude our fund still further by carrying this item.'[1]

In successfully opposing a suggestion that the NUGMW 'take all adequate measures for the future of our Members if they are defeated' Mr A. G. S. Whipp, a Scottish official, said:

'If our young people in this organization require an assurance of security and that nothing will happen to them before they are prepared to accept political responsibility, then we do not want them. . . . Quite definitely this organization plays the same by all persons whom it asks to accept responsibility on its behalf, and I do not think there is any need for a motion of this particular type to be passed. After all, what we are asking from youth today is a spirit of adventure, a willingness to take a risk for the things they believe in, and let the financial provision, or whatever it may be, take care of itself and rely on the good sense of the members.'[2]

Even some normally generous unions are deterred by the cost, apparently believing they might have to support all their candidates after a 1931 scale debacle. Post-war experience of the problem is far more modest. Although the Party's representation fell from 393 in 1945 to 258 in 1959 only thirty-one sponsored MPs were defeated, or eliminated by the redistributions of 1948 and 1954. Of the twenty-nine for which there

[1] *Report of the Delegate Meeting*, 1950, p. 66.
[2] *Report of Congress* (NUGMW) 1953, p. 245.

is data, twelve were over retiring age, six were serving officials, four former officials were reinstated, two former officials went into business and another into industry, and four rank and filers returned to the British Transport Commission. Even if Labour suffered an electoral disaster the unions would not be forced to provide for more than twenty ex-MPs, some of whom would be retiring or not in need of help. Sure and generous guarantees need not be expensive. Some such promise would seem all the more desirable from the unions' point of view if they were to contest more marginal seats—which would mean accepting more defeats. It would still cost relatively little.

Little thought has been given to pensions. Officers are reasonably well provided for. Normally if they had under ten years' service on entering the House they receive no pension. The NUGMW is an exception. Full pension is payable only after eighteen years' service. An official's pension is frozen at the rate he earned on entering the House. Parliamentary service does not count. Unless he has been an official eighteen years, then, he will never receive full pension. Sir Thomas Williamson explained:

'I think that the National Executive will have to take the view that before officers are placed on the Parliamentary Panel they must have served an industrial apprenticeship. . . . This union cannot safeguard the pensions of young officers of thirty-five to forty years of age, who have been in office for perhaps three years, and want to go into Parliament for the next twenty-five years, and expect the union to give them a pension when they come out at sixty-five.'[1]

On this reckoning officers should not go into the House until they are fifty. There is small wonder that the few NUGMW officials now joining the panel are mostly elderly. But there is less provision for rank and filers, except in the few unions which grant their MPs officer-status. More than one working-class MP has lingered on in the House after his health had gone, or has had to retire to a shameful poverty that is no encouragement for new candidates to come forward.[2] Throughout the opposition

[1] *Report of Congress* (NUGMW) 1950, p. 298.
[2] A minimum of ten years as a Member of Parliament is necessary to qualify for a Parliamentary pension. Men who were elected in 1945 and could not return in 1955 received no pension.

to better pensions for union MPs runs the assumption that the union is being asked to give them unjustifiable special treatment. This is a one-sided picture. Taking expenses into consideration union officials and even rank and filers may not gain financially by being in the House; many have lost. Manual workers are usually unable to supplement their income while they are in the House. By entering Parliament officials almost always forfeit any prospect of promotion within their organization.

Pensions, reinstatement, fall-back pay may be simply the provisions required today to find sufficient good candidates—there is no lack of mediocre ones. Yet in most unions any attempt to give Members of Parliament more generous treatment meets heated opposition from the rank and file. It is more their opposition, rather than the hostility of the officials, which prevents the adoption of a more liberal attitude to officials entering Parliament. The militants' reluctance to make sacrifices to maintain their unions' position in the House of Commons reflects their assessment of the value of Parliamentary representation. This has probably never been lower.

## Unions in the House

In the early days the trade union MP's job was clear. He spoke for his union and for the working man. He pressed for legislation on industrial matters, opposed the employers' representatives in debate, carried matters on to the floor of the House when the union was unable to get a hearing in Whitehall, and brought matters before Ministers. All unions had a direct interest in the Trade Union Acts and in the struggle for recognition; most wanted better Factory Acts, abolition of sweated labour, and unemployment and national insurance benefits. The Lib-Lab, and subsequently the Labour MPs were an unquestionable part of their union's *industrial* action, even though the results were often dishearteningly meagre. Since many were working officials or Executive Committeemen the links between the union and its officials were often tight. Some unions exerted considerable pressure on their Parliamentary groups. The Miners' MPs voted according to their Executive's instructions for many years.[1] Later Sir Robert Young of the AEU declined a

[1] Beatrice Webb, *Diaries, 1912–24*, p. 207.

post in the wartime government because of opposition from his Executive. Mandating Members of Parliament to support the union's policies was not considered improper.

How the relationship between union MPs and their unions has changed over the years has never been adequately traced; manifestly it is far more tenuous now. Although some unions still cling to rules permitting them to 'mandate' or 'instruct' their MPs, these are empty relics. Since the Robinson and Brown cases it has been apparent that any attempt by a union to coerce its MPs would probably be a breach of privilege, which might call into question the whole sponsorship system.[1] Old habits linger among the rank and file of some unions, and conferences debate resolutions to 'mandate' their MPs to a course of action. Although few trade unionists seriously believe their representatives can be ordered around, the militants are irritated from time to time by their MPs taking a line opposed to union policy. The contradictory positions adopted over German rearmament by the USDAW MPs created some ill feeling.[2] The editor of the NUR *Railway Review* also demanded:

'We ask, with all due respect to the customary freedom allowed to our MPs, how long they are going to support policies which have been condemned not only by the bulk of the constituency

[1] Alderman Robinson was Political General Secretary of NUDAW. He was called on to vacate his seat because the Union was dissatisfied with his handling of constituency matters and his conduct as an individual. When he refused to resign the Union withdrew his retainer. This was held not to be a breach of privilege. (*H.C.* 85, Session 1943–4).

W. J. Brown was Parliamentary General Secretary of the CSCA. His political attitude, particularly over the repeal of the 1927 Act's restrictions on civil service unions affiliating to the TUC, was at variance with the Association's, and at times he appeared to identify the CSCA with such views. Eventually the CSCA terminated his contract. The Committee of Privileges observed that it might be a breach of privilege for a union to use the fact that a Member had an agreement with it to put pressure on him to follow a particular course. It would be improper to punish him financially because of his activities as a Member. But the termination of a financial relationship by a union in what it felt to be its own interest would not constitute a breach of privilege in itself. (*H.C.* 118, Session 1946–7).

Where the line may be drawn is still uncertain. There was considerable indignation in the PLP at the report—of questionable veracity—that Mr Bevan threatened to raise the issue of privilege if he lost his retainer from the NUM, should he be expelled from the PLP.

[2] *The New Dawn*, March 29, 1952. Messrs. Padley, Fernyhough and Craddock took one side; the remaining MPs took the other. Later Mr Craddock and Mr Fernyhough were deprived of the Labour whip, and the union had to suspend their allowances.

parties, but by the Union upon whose support they have relied and still rely?

'To whom, then, do our Members of Parliament owe their first allegiance; to those who enabled them to get into the House of Commons or to the Leadership of the Labour Party whose policy has been opposed. . . . We do not think that on every issue trade union MPs should necessarily consult the organization which supports them financially and politically. They are representatives, not delegates. But in the present instance the issue is of such vital importance and the views of our organization have been attacked so unequivocally, that we believe there is justification for our questions.'[1]

This relatively mild attack was immediately repudiated by the NUR Executive, while the NUR MPs retorted that they were bound by the 'higher law' of the decisions of the PLP, not by the Annual General Meeting of the NUR. Some unions' rules provide that their MPs receive their retainers only as long as they receive the Labour Whip. However much it might agree with an expelled MP, a union could not in fact continue to support him without courting disaffiliation from the Party.[2] Left-wing executives may not like such a position, but they have to accept its inevitability.

The slackening of the unions' control over their MPs came just as their role in the House was changing. Under Ernest Bevin the trade union movement was assimilated into the war-time alliance. Consulted on far more than narrowly industrial problems, they were even the channel for obtaining permits to buy alarm clocks. Even before the post-war Labour government had confirmed the new structure of consultation the unions could speak directly to ministries, instead of going through their MPs. As Arthur Deakin said in 1946, 'We have an open door in relation to all State Departments and are thus able to get our difficulties examined in such a way as would not have been possible with any other Party in Government'.[3] The Con-

---

[1] February 14, 1952 and March 21, 1952. A similar controversy broke out over German rearmament. See the issues of December 3 and December 31, 1954.

[2] USDAW warned its MPs that it would not be able to support them in 1955 unless they had regained the Labour Whip.

[3] Quoted in *Trade Union Leadership*, p. 150.

servatives preserved the system almost intact after 1951, although there was not the same familiarity of contacts with Conservative ministers as under the Labour Government. While the TUC might not convince the Conservatives on many major economic issues, there was less difference on the everyday technical level. But the unions' views were heard. 'If I want to talk to the Minister', said a leading trade unionist in 1957, 'I just pick up that telephone'. The trade union MPs task of ensuring that his union's case is heard by the Government has all but vanished.

The Trade Disputes Act of 1946 may prove to have been the last great battle for full recognition. The post-war Labour government enacted the social and industrial legislation so long awaited by the unions. Reforms which could be won only by political action were now fewer than ever. At least up to 1956 when the industrial climate deteriorated, the trade union MP seemed less and less useful. He belongs to an age when the unions had to fight for a hearing and governments had to be challenged repeatedly. The House of Commons is a far less suitable terrain in a period of negotiation and compromise. In the earlier period the unions' and Labour's tactics were often identical. Later it became evident that while, in peacetime, the Labour Opposition's primary duty was to combat the Conservatives, whatever government was in power the unions must still try to exact concessions. The House of Commons cannot be relied on to show either the tact and patience, or the willingness to compromise that are essential in industrial relations.

Meanwhile, where once the unions had looked to Parliament to protect them against the employers in their weakness, as their industrial strength grew they were increasingly reserved about Parliamentary intervention in certain fields, notably in the fundamental trade union function of wage negotiation. Arthur Deakin openly expressed this mood in 1953:

'. . . never be led into the mistake of supposing you are going to get an advantage by people asking questions in Parliament affecting your collective agreements, conditions of employment and those things which are more properly dealt with by the Union on the industrial level. . . .'[1]

[1] *Trade Union Leadership*, p. 147.

Once the spearhead of his union's industrial-political activity, the trade union MP now stands on the side-lines. While negotiations are in progress he may be asked not to 'rock the boat'. Arthur Deakin met members of the TGWU Parliamentary group before the debate on *Personal Income, Costs and Prices* in February 1948, and 'advised them, in view of the discussions going on between the TUC and the Government, not to take precipitate action. . . .'[1] At a celebrated meeting with the Trade Union Group of the PLP in 1954 Deakin belligerently stated that there were certain industrial matters which could not be dealt with in Parliament at all.[2] Often when Bills do come before the House on industrial questions, they contain agreed compromises which must not be upset.

This does not mean that the trade union MP is wholly irrelevant. He may be used to move amendments to the Finance Bill, or to measures affecting his industry. The NUM employed its MPs to great advantage during the committee stage of the Mines & Quarries Act, 1954. The Clerical & Administrative Workers' Union, the National Union of Agricultural Workers, USDAW and the National Federation of Professional Workers have tried to extend the Factory Acts to non-industrial premises. The National Union of Seamen, whose industry is tightly regulated by statute, the Tobacco Workers' Union, and the National Union of Furniture Trade Operatives (which is particularly affected by changes in credit policy) still believe that they need an MP.

Although trade union MPs are still useful sometimes, there is small wonder that unions are unwilling to send their best men into the House—or that Mr Fred Lee (AEU) could say:

'Those of us who find ourselves working on the political side of the union's activities are made to feel rather cut off from it. Apart from occasional meetings with, and communications from Executive Council, our contacts with our fellow members of the Union are of the most tenuous nature. The union's attitude to outstanding political questions of the day is determined without reference to the AEU Members of Parliament. Living

[1] *Trade Union Leadership*, p. 147.
[2] *Report to the GEC*, June 14, 1954.

as we do in the centre of these matters, it is not, I suggest, beyond the bounds of possibility that we may know a little about them.'[1]

The MPs still have a place in union life. Most unions publish Parliamentary reports which keep the MPs before the members, but give little real indication of their value. Some publicize concessions that their MPs have won—the TSSA publishes leaflets which hasten to give credit even where it is doubtfully due. Other unions use their MPs at summer schools and weekend conferences. Several give their panel little more than a pious paragraph in the annual report.

USDAW MPs attend their Annual Delegate Meeting as full delegates, showing by their contributions to debates that they are active in the union's work. The Amalgamated Society of Woodworkers and the National Union of Boot & Shoe Operatives set aside a special session at their conferences for a Parliamentary report. Since the war the National Union of Public Employees' MPs have progressed from speaking 'with the permission of conference' to being regular spokesmen on foreign policy. Two unions, BISAKTA and the NUM, put members of their Parliamentary group on their Executive, while the Building Workers and the Draughtsmen include their candidates on their Political Sub-Committees. But in several unions the Parliamentary panel becomes a rarely-debated and unread entry in the annual report. MPs have no part at all in the AEU and TGWU conferences. Few trade union Members of Parliament can hope to give rank and file members any impression that they are doing a useful job. Moreover, many have only a vicarious knowledge of the decisions their own union is taking. Even within their own unions many of them tend to become unknown, vaguely superannuated figures. For all the publicity their union gives them the TSSA MPs have found to their dismay how rapidly they are forgotten once they transfer from industrial to political work. In other unions the relegation to the shadows is often swifter.

Yet the day of the trade union MP is not over. It is true that leaders of some unrepresented unions are unable to suggest how

[1] *AEU Journal*, January 1954.

they have suffered from not having an MP, and many are content to rely on friendly Labour MPs who are not connected with their trade.[1] But the unions which are represented in the House still want to maintain their place, and others, feeling that well-meaning amateurs may not present their case adequately, still hope to win seats.[2] There is no real likelihood of the trade union MPs disappearing within the foreseeable future despite the constituencies' greater reluctance to adopt them. But the real problem, the cause of all the recent heart-searching goes back to the old desire for working-class representation. It is significant that the loudest complaints come from the Miners, who still have over thirty MPs, the envy of many of the smaller unions. There is not the remotest direct *industrial* need for so large a group. Making every allowance for illness, absence and ministerial promotion the Miners cannot possibly use more than ten of their group fully. If the remaining twenty were thought of as a fraternal aid to the Labour Party their gradual disappearance should have caused no heart-burning. But the real grievance is that the Labour Party is ceasing to be a *labour* party. The reason why the unions are so concerned to keep their strength in the House is that they want to ensure that the atmosphere and outlook of the Parliamentary party are constantly influenced from within by working-class thought and reactions.

Perhaps trade union thinking is changing. The members of the NUGMW's unofficial panel are all middle-class, while the TGWU has put Mr Anthony Greenwood on its panel.[3] Although represented in Parliament by Mr Ernest Thornton, the United Textile Factory Workers' Association called in Mr Harold Wilson to help produce the *Plan for Cotton*. These may be the straws in the wind. But if the unions are more ready to accept and use middle-class MPs, many militants still agree with the delegate to the NUGMW Congress who complained:

'Too many people who, in the past, considered that we were not sufficiently respectable to associate with, are jumping on the

---

[1] 'We could get help from plenty of Conservatives, but of course we don't ask them', one leader remarked.

[2] *NUFTO Record*, June 1952.

[3] The members of the Unofficial Panel in 1958–9 were Mr W. Coldrick (member Cooperative Union executive); Mr Gaitskell; Mr J. Johnson (teacher); Mr F. E. Jones (barrister); Mr F. Peart (teacher); and Mr G. Willis (bookseller).

wagon, to the exclusion of the ordinary trade union representative. Whilst we welcome the professional and middle classes in the Labour Movement . . . I believe that so far as the political side of the movement is concerned, the dominant part should be trade union representatives.'[1]

It was no coincidence that the unions started complaining loudly just at the time when their confidence in the official leadership was wavering, and they feared that the Bevanites might take control. Undistinguished though its members might be, a strong trade union group in the House has to be reckoned with when the Party is choosing a new leader. The trade union MP has become a means of protecting the unions against the non-unionists within the Parliamentary Labour Party, and for making sure that the unions' viewpoint is heard in the PLP's private discussions.[2] Working within the Party in Parliament these members of the industrial movement provide cement for a relationship which would otherwise be precarious. Trade union MPs not only advocate union policies, they are a constant personal reminder of the unions' values and enthusiasms. Without them the unions would look increasingly like an alien pressure group to Labour Members of Parliament, and decisions on policies interesting the unions would depend all too evidently on agreements between the Party and union leaderships. Deprived of its trade unionists, not only would the atmosphere of the Parliamentary Labour Party change, but the unions and the PLP would be in far greater danger of drifting slowly apart.[3]

## The Unions' Reply

The unions have not been ready to stand idly by while their representation dwindled. Some have turned in irritation to Transport House. Mr Percy Knight, whose National Union of

[1] *Report of Congress*, 1949, p. 217.
[2] V. L. Allen quotes (*Trade Union Leadership*, p. 148) the example of the Transport Bill in 1947. The TGWU wanted 'C' licence holders to be brought within the scheme of nationalization, but the Act omitted them. In a report to the General Executive Council Deakin wrote that 'there was a great deal of opposition from amongst those Labour Members who are not associated with the Trade Unions, in regard to this particular feature of the Bill'.
[3] See the significantly titled 'Trade Unions and the Labour Party: Should the Link Remain', by Mr Charles Geddes (former General Secretary of the Union of Post Office Workers), *The National & English Review*, December 1954.

Seamen has sponsored candidates in safe Conservative seats in the hope of progressing to winnable constituencies, told the National Executive that 'it was only common justice that the Party should make some special effort to see that any persons put forward by this union were given more than a fair crack'.[1] The National Union of Agricultural Workers, worried at the reduction of their representation to a single marginal seat, voted that 'more Labour seats with part rural votes be made available to NUAW candidates'.[2] The Building Trade Workers, without a seat since Mr George Hicks retired in 1950, and the London Typographical Society, also without representation since 1950, have both turned to the Party for help.[3]

The same demand broke out when the party was asking for higher affiliation fees in 1955. Both Mr Tomkins of the National Union of Furniture Trade Operatives, and the Miners' leader, Mr Ernest Jones, said flatly 'If the unions give more money to the Party they are entitled to a greater say'—a phrase which was understood to refer to Parliamentary candidates. Mr. Tomkins' union put down a resolution for the 1955 Conference that:

'This Conference, while recognizing that the selection of a Parliamentary candidate must rest with the Constituency Party notes with concern the diminishing number of Trade Union sponsored candidates at succeeding General Elections, and accordingly requests the Executive to consider this matter with the object of strengthening the Trades Union group of Labour Party Members of Parliament.'[4]

The Miners have made the loudest complaints. Since 1944 they have lost eleven of 'their' seats, and have regained only three. Their losses in South Wales have been particularly

---

[1] *Report of the AGM*, 1954, p. 42.

[2] *Report of the BDC, The Landworker*, July 1952.

[3] Some members resented relinquishing Woolwich to Ernest Bevin. 'We have always considered Woolwich as a building workers' seat.' The Executive decided that pressing the AUBTW's claim would not be 'politic'. *Report of the NDC*, 1950, p. 40 and *The Building Worker*, June 1952. *London Typographical Journal*, June 1953.

[4] The ETU has also protested at the failure of trade union candidates to win nominations. *Report of the Labour Party Conference*, 1958, p. 139.

And cf., *Quarterly Journal of the National Union of Sheet Metal Workers and Braziers*, October 1955.

serious. The rejection of NUM nominees at both Aberdare and
Morpeth in 1954 stung the union to angry protests. After the
Morpeth selection union officials complained first in the North
Region, then to Transport House. 'In Morpeth', they argued,
'we were paying eighty per cent of the Party's affiliation fees,
but because the local Party imposed a limit of five delegates to
a branch, our representation at the Selection Conference was
cut from 108 to 51.'[1] Even after the NEC confirmed the
nomination the Miners' Executive stonily 'noted' the candidature, and reaffirmed their 'grave concern' at the under-
representation of trade union branches on General Management
Committees which it blamed for the loss of several mining seats
and feared might lead to the loss of more. Pressure on the
Party's Organization Sub-Committee extracted only a promise
to 'consider the problem'.[2]

While they were smarting from such rebuffs the Miners
were little inclined to listen sympathetically to Mr Percy
Knight, who expressed the envy felt by several small unions:

'I have impressed upon the NEC . . . my view as to the un-
preparedness of many trade unions, starting with the Miners
who have forty members in the House of Commons, and coming
down to those who have two or three to give us a seat. I ask
them why it is they cannot somehow make an opportunity for
seamen in the House.'

Those who turned to other unions or to Transport House were
disappointed. As Percy Knight ruefully concluded, 'The bald

[1] This was not the complete picture. The Regional Office of the Labour Party
had warned the Area Union some time before the selection conference that their
proposed candidate might not be adopted. The Miners received the same warning
at Aberdare. In both cases the traditional solidarity of those miners who were
delegates of other organizations, and the miners' wives broke down, and they
refused to vote for the NUM candidate. At Morpeth the NUM nominee was said
to have received fifty-three votes. The NUM lodges had fifty-one votes. It was
reported that there were 135 miners and wives among the 152 members of the
General Management Committee.

[2] The Miners' indignation at the attitude of Transport House was stirred again
in February 1959 when Mr David Ginsburg, a Transport House official, won the
nomination for Dewsbury, a 'Miners' seat'. While they were still in full cry over
this it was announced that Mr Morgan Phillips intended to seek nomination in
North East Derbyshire—a 'Miners' seat' since 1918. Mr Phillips, who had been
acquainted in forthright terms of the unions' views of this wondrous display of
*lèse-majesté*, withdrew within forty-eight hours. But he tried again in September
1959, and was again rebuffed by the Miners.

fact is this: that the autonomy in the selection of a candidate is with the local CLP concerned . . . whether he be a man sponsored by a trade union or any other political organization, and they make up their own minds'.[1] Arthur Greenwood confirmed:

'The NEC, therefore, is really limited. If it is asked to put up names it will do so from a long waiting list that it has. Sometimes the NEC will suggest a name from that long list to the local Party so that it might perhaps be included in their list of candidates, but in the last resort it is the men on the spot who are mostly trade union representatives who decide the matter.'[2]

Mr Greenwood was unduly modest, but the power of Transport House is limited—even more now than when he spoke. Nowadays it will intervene to support a candidate only in the most pressing circumstances. Transport House helped Ernest Bevin and Mr Attlee (at Woolwich and at Walthamstow) in 1950, but party officials were clearly upset at having to persuade constituencies to accept Dr Edith Summerskill (then chairman of the NEC), when she was crowded out at Fulham just before the 1955 election. But one or two ex-Ministers, such as Mr. Creech Jones, obvious candidates for any help Transport House might give, had to trudge from one selection conference to another before they were re-elected. Normally even to be suspected of having Transport House backing is a handicap at a selection conference. Moreover, after the St. Helens selection conference of 1958 (where Mr Tom Driberg, the Chairman of the NEC, tried to win a 'trade union seat') the NEC decided that it would make no more nominations for selection at by-elections. Even before that Transport House never had the power to influence local Parties on the scale that some union leaders seemed to expect.

Some trade unionists have toyed with limiting competition in the constituencies. 'Trade union leaders ought to get together over matters such as this because it is no good them fighting one another', Arthur Greenwood told the Seamen.[2] Sometimes the unions already to do this, by declining to nominate in seats which other unions have held for some years. 'No, we're not

[1] Report of the AGM, 1953, pp. 46–8.
[2] Report of the AGM, 1953, p. 92.

going after Carlisle', said an NUR leader. 'It's really a TSSA seat and we'll be backing their man'. For all their complaints the Miners have benefited from this attitude more than most unions. 'Of course we're not nominating for Consett', said another railway leader. 'There's no point. Sam Watson's got that all sewn up'. Even here 'working class solidarity' often breaks down. When the Amalgamated Society of Woodworkers learned that Mr Sam Viant would not seek renomination at West Willesden (an ASW seat since 1923) at the end of the 1955 Parliament, they wrote to all possible competitors 'indicating to them that because of the interest in this division which has obtained for a great many years, it was the intention of this Society to again nominate a candidate for that Division'. In short the ASW wanted their man to have a clear run.[1] Four other unions sought the nomination—and none of them got it. Cooperation between unions for nominations in seats where none has an established position is far more rare. Some trade unionists have hoped to institute a pre-selection conference caucus of the unions affiliated to the local Party, to settle on one candidate for whom the unions would then vote *en bloc*. They see this as a reply to a so-called 'constituency members' block vote'. Mr J. Marshall, a Woodworkers' candidate, suggested:

'I object to the manoeuvres that sometimes went on prior to a Selection Conference, where there was a certain amount of ganging-up, so that no matter what effect you may have on a selection conference certain of the delegates have already taken a decision before the Conference. I believe we ought to act conjointly as trade unions on this matter.'[2]

Little attempt has been made to put such plans into effect, and it is doubtful whether they could be very successful. Few trade union delegates to Constituency Labour Parties are interested in winning nominations for other unions solely so that there shall be a trade unionist in the seat.

Meanwhile the unions cling more tenaciously than ever to 'their' seats, bitterly resenting competition from outsiders. A party agent, echoing this proprietary attitude, said scornfully of a trade union official who had sought nomination in his

[1] *Report of the ADC*, 1958, p. 26.        [2] *Report of the ADC*, 1954, p. 54.

constituency, 'Percy should have known better than to stick his nose in. He knew damn well it was an USDAW seat'. The cotton unions have resented the ingratitude of some Lancashire constituencies:

'Clitheroe, Blackburn and Preston Labour Parties, who for some years accepted our financial support and our candidates, have seen fit to choose their Parliamentary nominees elsewhere. This attitude of readiness to accept our financial support during long inter-election periods, and selection of candidates elsewhere when an election impends, has caused the Legislative Council great concern.'[1]

When Sir Hartley Shawcross resigned his seat at St. Helens in 1958, Lancashire miners' leaders claimed that the nomination should be theirs of right: St. Helens was a 'miners' seat'. Yet no miner had fought the constituency since the First World War, and the 1951 Census shows that under 5,000 out of a population of 109,000 were employed in mining and quarrying.

It was probably no coincidence that the demands by several unions that more seats be made available for their candidates, and the Miners' indignation at losing so many seats were followed by measures that limited the competition that the unions must face. The fixing at £50 per year of the maximum contribution that unsponsored candidates might make to their local Party clearly removed one source of financial competition.[2] Then, early in 1957, with no public explanation the Party abruptly terminated its agreement with the Cooperative Party governing the adoption of Labour & Cooperative candidates. Some trade unionists attributed many of their lost nominations to the unscrupulous rattling of Cooperative moneybags. The discontent which had been smouldering since Morpeth (won by a Cooperative candidate) in 1954 burst into the open when Wednesbury chose a Cooperative official in 1956 in preference to a trade union member of the NEC who was also an ex-MP.

When the negotiators met to draw up a fresh agreement the Labour Party's apparent aim was to make the Cooperative

---

[1] *Annual Report, UTFWA*, 1945.

[2] *Report of the Labour Party Conference*, 1957, p. 13 and p. 125. A constituency delegate suggested that the proposed maximum contribution by candidates should be a minimum.

Party accept a gradual reduction to six Members of Parliament, with the rather vague prospect of 'at least one senior post'. The Cooperators not only declared this proposal utterly unacceptable, but unsportingly recruited support by a series of embarrassing 'leaks' to the Press. Finally the two sides agreed on a 'freeze'—to the obvious displeasure both of Cooperative militants and the trade union members of the NEC, and the relief of many Transport House officials. The Cooperative Party would be allowed to sponsor its twenty sitting MPs and ten more candidates at the next general election. After each election the maximum number of candidates the Cooperative Party might sponsor would be reviewed. The most remarkable feature of the new agreement was the setting up of a National Organization Committee to decide whether a Constituency Labour Party can adopt a sponsored Cooperative nominee or not.[1] Although the unions got much less than they wanted, they will apparently have no further worries about the spread of Cooperative competition.

By such manoeuvres the unions may bolster their position on the short term. In any case there is no immediate likelihood that trade union MPs will disappear from the House of Commons. However irritated the unions may be at losing certain nominations, they are well aware that the working-class element in the Parliamentary Labour Party will remain substantial—in contrast with the almost total failure of the Conservatives to find working-class MPs. But unless they are prepared to take more positive action the unions have little hope of checking—let alone reversing—the gradual waning of their Parliamentary strength. Some trade unionists see no inconsistency in refusing to let their most able candidates go into the House of Commons and complaining that the PLP is becoming too 'intellectual'. Yet Constituency Labour Parties cannot be expected to accept candidates simply because they are good trade unionists, regardless of ability.

If the unions believe that Parliamentary representation is still valuable, their course is clear. They must make greater

[1] The full text is published in *Report of the Labour Party Conference*, 1958, pp. 254-5. For expressions of Cooperative discontent see the *Manchester Guardian*, February 16, 1957; March 27, 1958; April 5 and 7, 1958; May 28, 1958; July 11, 1958; March 5, 28 and 30, 1959.

V

efforts to find candidates and to prepare them for selection. They must be ready to let a few more of their officials go, and they must also try far harder to whip up support for their nominees among their own delegates to selection conferences. For all the pious tributes to the value of trade union MPs published in their journals, the unions have not really decided whether Parliamentary representation is worth these sacrifices today. With a real effort the unions could probably keep their strength in Parliament. But if Parliamentary representation is not worth such a price, the trade union MPs seem doomed to be a slowly dwindling anachronistic band.

# CHAPTER VII

# ELECTING THE NATIONAL
# EXECUTIVE COMMITTEE

'It is a travesty of democracy.'

MR ANEURIN BEVAN *

THE Labour Party's National Executive Committee, twenty-eight strong, comprises the Leader and Deputy Leader of the PLP, ex-officio,[1] the Treasurer and five women's representatives elected by the whole Annual Conference, one Socialist, Cooperative and Professional Societies' representative elected by those organizations, seven members elected by the Constituency Labour Parties and twelve by the trade unions.

Until 1937 the Executive was elected by the whole Conference, a system which the constituencies considered tantamount to election by the unions. Since 1937 the local Parties have elected their own representatives and (in formal terms) the unions theirs. Not every union agreed. The change would split the Party, warned Charles Dukes of the NUGMW. By 1952 some union leaders recalled his warning:

'When, in 1937, the Party altered its constitution to permit the constituency parties not only to nominate but also to elect their representatives on the National Executive, the late Charles Dukes warned the Conference of the dangerous course it was embarking upon. It has taken us fifteen years to recognize how right he was.'[2]

Dukes' fears sprang from the belief that the constituencies would elect one faction to the Executive, and the unions another. The laments of 1952 suggested that this was just what had happened. The Morecambe conference had been a triumph for the Bevanites, while members of the old guard, such as Mr

---

* *Tribune*, October 7, 1955.

[1] The Deputy Leader has sat ex-officio since 1953.

[2] *Man & Metal*, October 1952.

Morrison and Mr Dalton were swept away, to the chagrin of the moderate unions.[1] There are obvious advantages in an electoral system which ensures that members of the NEC have support in all sections of the Party. But this was no better achieved before 1937 than since. When the unions cast four votes to every one from the local parties the 'constituency representatives' had to find favour with the unions—but the unions had no need to choose candidates who were attractive to the local parties. Mr Dukes' fears really amounted to a belief that the Executive could only remain united through union domination.

Apart from the Bevanite years the election of the NEC has never aroused any interest in the unions. This is not surprising. Most candidates are almost unknown outside their unions, and open fights for places are rare. The largest unions all have 'their' place. Five of the 'Big Six' (TGWU, NUGMW, NUM, NUR, USDAW), the Transport Salaried Staffs' Association and the United Textile Factory Workers' Association have sat continuously since 1918.[2] The AEU, which was kept off the NEC from 1949 to 1955, normally has an equal claim to 'its' place. Thereafter the Amalgamated Society of Woodworkers and the British Iron, Steel & Kindred Trades' Association (BISAKTA) are the next most favoured. They have usually elected a member but have no permanent claim to a seat. Since the war the National Union of Agricultural Workers has been trying to establish its claim to a permanent place as the representative of rural interests. Finally, the National Union of Seamen has held a place for long periods although it is too small to have a right to one.

The small unions have only one real chance of joining the Executive—by filling a vacancy arising in the course of the year, either through the death of a member of the Executive or his promotion to the General Council. Since the war no outsider has joined the Executive by election. Both Mr Casasola of the Foundry Workers and Mr Mulley of the Clerical and Administrative Workers' Union owed their places on the Executive solely to their persistence in accepting repeated defeats as the

---

[1] Notably see: *Man & Metal*, October 1952. *NUGMW Journal*, November 1952.
[2] The NUR missed election in 1940. The NUGMW, USDAW and TGWU were represented by forerunners of the present amalgamated unions.

## TABLE 28

TRADE UNION REPRESENTATION ON THE NATIONAL EXECUTIVE COMMITTEE OF THE LABOUR PARTY

| Union | Year Beginning 1935 | 1936 | 1937 | 1938 | 1939 | 1940 | 1941 | 1942 | 1943 | 1944 | 1945 | 1946 | 1947 | 1948 | 1949 | 1950 | 1951 | 1952 | 1953 | 1954 | 1955 | 1956 | 1957 | 1958 | 1959 |
|---|---|---|---|---|---|---|---|---|---|---|---|---|---|---|---|---|---|---|---|---|---|---|---|---|---|
| Transport & General Workers' Union | x | x | x | x | x | x | x | x | x | x | x | x | x | x | x | x | x | x | x | x | x | x | x | x | x |
| National Union of General & Municipal Workers | x | x | x | x | x | x | x | x | x | x | x | x | x | x | x | x | x | x | x | x | x | x | x | x | x |
| National Union of Mineworkers | x | x | x | x | x | x | x | x | x | x | x | x | x | x | x | x | x | x | x | x | x | x | x | x | x |
| Union of Shop, Distributive & Allied Workers | x | x | x | x | x | x | x | x | x | x | x | x | x | x | x | x | x | x | x | x | x | x | x | x | x |
| United Textile Factory Workers' Association | x | x | x | x | x | x | x | x | x | x | x | x | x | x | x | x | x | x | x | x | x | x | x | x | x |
| Transport Salaried Staffs' Association | x | x | x | x | x | x | x | x | x | x | x | x | x | x | x | x | x | x | x | x | x | x | x | x | x |
| National Union of Railwaymen | x | x | x | x | x | x | x | x | x | x | x | x | x | x | x | x | x | x | x | x | x | x | $x^e$ | x | x |
| Amalgamated Engineering Union | x | o | x | x | x | o | x | x | x | x | x | x | x | x | $x^a$ | x | x | x | x | x | $x^c$ | x | x | x | x |
| British Iron, Steel & Kindred Trades Association | x | x | x | x | x | x | x | x | x | $x^b$ | $x^d$ | x | x | x | $x^a$ | x | x | x | x | x | x | x | x | x | x |
| Electrical Trades Union | – | o | – | – | – | o | – | o | o | o | o | o | o | o | o | o | o | o | o | o | o | o | o | o | o |
| National Union of Boot & Shoe Operatives | – | x | x | x | x | x | x | x | x | x | $x^d$ | x | x | x | x | x | x | x | x | x | x | x | x | x | x |
| National Union of Seamen | – | – | – | – | – | – | – | – | – | – | – | – | o | o | o | o | o | o | o | o | o | o | o | o | o |
| Amalgamated Society of Woodworkers | – | – | – | – | – | – | – | – | – | – | – | – | – | – | $x^a$ | $x^a$ | x | x | x | x | x | x | x | x | x |
| National Union of Agricultural Workers | x | x | x | x | x | x | x | x | x | x | x | x | x | x | x | x | x | x | x | x | x | x | x | x | x |
| Typographical Association | x | x | – | – | – | – | – | – | – | – | – | – | – | – | – | – | – | – | – | – | – | – | – | – | – |
| National Union of Vehicle Builders | x | x | – | x | x | x | x | x | – | – | – | – | – | – | – | – | – | – | – | – | – | – | – | – | – |
| Associated Society of Loco. Engineers & Firemen | – | – | – | – | – | x | o | o | o | $x^b$ | – | – | – | o | – | x | – | – | o | – | o | x | x | o | x |
| London Society of Compositors (now LTS) | x | – | – | – | – | – | – | – | – | $x^b$ | o | o | o | o | o | o | o | o | o | o | o | o | o | o | o |
| Prudential Staff Union | – | – | – | – | – | – | – | – | – | – | – | – | – | – | – | – | – | – | – | o | $x^c$ | o | o | o | o |
| Amalgamated Union of Foundry Workers | – | – | – | – | – | – | – | – | – | – | – | – | – | – | – | – | – | – | – | – | – | – | – | – | – |
| Clerical & Administrative Workers' Union | – | – | – | – | – | – | – | – | – | – | – | – | o | o | o | o | o | o | o | o | o | o | $x^e$ | o | o |
| United Society of Boilermakers, etc. | – | – | – | – | – | – | – | – | – | – | – | – | – | – | – | – | – | – | – | – | – | – | – | – | – |
| Asso. of Engineering & Shipbuilding Draughtsmen | – | – | – | – | – | – | – | – | – | – | – | – | o | o | o | o | o | o | o | o | o | o | o | o | o |
| Association of Cine & Television Technicians | – | – | – | – | – | – | – | – | – | – | – | – | – | – | – | – | – | – | – | – | – | – | – | – | – |
| Constructional Engineering Union | – | – | – | – | – | – | – | – | – | – | – | – | – | – | – | – | – | – | – | – | – | – | – | – | – |
| Plumbing Trades Union | – | – | – | – | – | – | – | – | – | – | – | – | o | – | o | – | o | o | o | o | o | o | o | o | o |
| National Federation of Building Trade Operatives | – | – | – | – | – | – | – | – | – | – | – | – | – | – | – | – | – | – | – | – | – | – | – | – | – |
| Union of Post Office Workers | – | – | – | – | – | – | – | – | – | – | o | – | – | – | – | – | – | – | – | – | – | – | – | – | – |
| National Amal. Union of Life Assurance Workers | – | – | – | – | – | – | – | – | – | – | – | – | – | – | – | – | – | – | – | – | – | – | – | o | o |
| National Union of Public Employees | – | – | – | – | – | – | – | – | – | – | – | – | – | – | – | – | – | – | – | – | – | – | – | o | – |
| ASSET | – | – | – | – | – | – | – | – | – | – | – | – | – | – | – | – | – | – | – | – | – | – | – | – | o |

x = member of NEC   o = unsuccessful candidate   – = no candidate

(a) AEU representative elected to General Council, ASW succeeded.
(b) BISAKTA representative died, PSU succeeded.
(c) TGWU representative elected to General Council, AUFW succeeded.
(d) NUBSO representative died, ETU succeeded.
(e) NUR representative died, CAWU succeeded.

highest placed unsuccessful candidate. Thus Mr Scrafton of the Prudential Staff Union, and Mr Mulley, came to the Executive through the death of a sitting member, the Woodworkers recovered their place on the Executive when Mr Openshaw of the AEU moved to the General Council in 1948, and Mr Casasola, after trying vainly at seven successive elections, filled the place vacated by Mr Cousins on his elevation to the General Council in 1956.

Once on the Executive members are rarely defeated. Mr Irwin remained until his retirement ten years later. Mr Casasola held his place until his retirement—although he would have been removed rapidly enough had not Mr Irwin's retirement allowed the TGWU to regain 'its' seat without displacing him. The AEU was unable to regain the seat it lost in 1949 until 1955, partly because several union leaders had little sympathy for the AEU candidate, but chiefly because there were no natural vacancies, and no smaller unions to be elbowed out. Two sitting members have been defeated since the war: Mr Scrafton and Mr Mulley. Both represented white collar unions, and Mr Mulley had the additional handicap of being a Member of Parliament. Mr Scrafton was removed to make way for the Agricultural Workers, while Mr Mulley's seat was required for the Boilermakers—apparently through an agreement among several unions belonging to the Confederation of Shipbuilding & Engineering Unions.

Apart from the occasional outsider, seats are allocated according to size and importance. The chief exceptions have been the National Union of Tailors and Garment Workers, which has never put up a candidate, the Union of Post Office Workers and the National Union of Public Employees which have made only sporadic attempts.[1] With re-election the rule, eight seats held permanently by certain unions, and three more almost as surely spoken for, there is a serious contest only if a smaller union's seat falls vacant. Accordingly it is usually easy to draw up an agreed ticket. Thus, as early as 1954 it was generally understood that the AEU would regain its seat on the

---

[1] Owing to a long-standing feud between Mr Bryn Roberts of NUPE and the two general unions, which has kept Mr Roberts off the General Council of the TUC, it is unlikely that NUPE would win a seat on the NEC during Mr Roberts' term of office.

retirement in 1955 of Mr Percy Knight of the National Union of Seamen. In 1958 only 350,000 votes separated the most successful candidates from the eleventh. The only real contest was between Mr Mulley and Mr McGarvey for twelfth place.

But graver allegations are sometimes made. It may have been no coincidence that, while the AEU supported the TGWU candidate for the Conference Arrangements Committee in 1955, rather than Mr Geoffrey Bing, the two general unions gave the AEU the votes they had refused it for the five previous years. Other critics alleged that there had been an even larger 'package deal' by which the general unions voted for Mr Tallon in return for AEU support for Mr Gaitskell as Treasurer. It was suggested in 1954 that right-wing leaders warned Mr George Brinham of the Woodworkers, 'Unless the ASW votes for German rearmament, you've had your seat on the Executive'.[1] The same leaders were said to have told USDAW that Mr Walter Padley would not be elected to the NEC unless the union voted for Mr George Brown for Treasurer. Such a threat would have shown little understanding either of USDAW's constitution or its internal politics. USDAW voted for Mr Bevan; Mr Padley was elected to the NEC.[2] It was stated categorically that right-wing leaders had warned Mr Irwin that unless he refused, for 'reasons of health', the Party Chairmanship (for which he was due by seniority), he would lose his place on the Executive. Although some of these allegations were quite false, and the truth is always hard to establish, no one who knows how much 'horse-trading' surrounds the elections would say they were inconceivable. True or not, they reveal the cynicism which the election arouses.

There is almost no open competition for nomination within the unions: the National Union of Mineworkers is the only union with a seat on the NEC which elects its nominee.[3] For a quarter of a century the seat has been occupied by Secretaries of the Durham Area, Mr Swan and Mr Sam Watson. There is

[1] Cf., *New Statesman*, July 14, 1956. For a clear case of 'horse-trading' see p. 147.

[2] The USDAW vote is decided by the delegation during the weekend before the opening of Conference. The suggestion that pressure had been put on USDAW was made in the *Sunday Times*, June 24, 1956, and the *Daily Herald*, June 30, 1956. Mr Padley had the support of at least one of the general unions.

[3] The NUM has elected its nominees only since 1953. The AESD, which has never sat on the NEC, also elects its nominee.

rarely a contest. Most unions nominate their second senior official—General Secretaries sit on the General Council.[1] Thus the TGWU member is normally the Assistant General Secretary,[2] the NUR sends its President, and the United Textile Factory Workers' Association sends the secretary of a constituent union. The AEU nominates the senior non-Communist member of its Executive. The Transport Salaried Staffs' Association has chosen either its Assistant General Secretary, Treasurer or President.[3] In the NUGMW the seat has been held by the Chairman or a National Industrial Officer. Until 1944 both BISAKTA and USDAW had Political Secretaries on the NEC, but the former is now represented by its Assistant General Secretary, and USDAW has had a former organizer, Mr Wilfrid Burke, MP, and then its President, Mr Walter Padley MP, as its representatives. The ETU, which has had a Communist President and General Secretary for most of the post-war years, has to nominate a National Officer. Other unions have not put up enough candidates for their policy to be evident.[4] The unsuccessful left-wing unions, whose candidates also fail to win places on the General Council, are more likely to put forward their General Secretary. Since the war Mr Scrafton is the only member of the NEC to have been elected while a General Secretary.

Since nomination to the NEC normally either goes with a specific office or is restricted to a tiny group there is little 'damn nonsense about merit', and not much about ideology. At one time it was argued that the left-wing unions had to appoint moderates to the NEC as the price of the support of the right-wing leaders. Even in Arthur Deakin's day this was hard to substantiate. Mr Irwin was well to the right of his union, but he came to the NEC by accident, and he really belonged to the pre-Communist period. The ETU's leaders might not have welcomed a progressive and able representative who could

[1] No one may belong to the General Council and the NEC simultaneously.

[2] Excepting 1947-9 when Mr Corrin, National Docks Officer, was on the NEC.

[3] In recent years its representatives have been F. Dalley, President, P. T. Heady, then W. J. P. Webber, AGS; J. Haworth, President, and R. J. Gunter, Treasurer and later President.

[4] Mr. Gooch is President of the NUAW, and Mr Casasola was President of AUFW. Mr McGarvey is Chairman of the Boilermakers' Executive Council and Mr Percy Knight was National Organizer in the National Union of Seamen.

have used his place on the NEC to build a following and challenge their own supremacy. Perhaps the right-wing leaders thought that the ETU's next candidate, Mr Scott, was too closely identified with his union's policies—but Mr Irwin's place was taken by R. W. Casasola, an extreme left-winger whose union (the Foundry Workers) was then under strong Communist influence.[1] He was succeeded, on retirement, by another militant left-winger, Mr D. McGarvey.

On several key issues during the Bevanite period Mr Wilfrid Burke of USDAW stood well to the right of his union. While his election was not originally a sop to the right his union may have thought twice about replacing him during 1953-5 by the fear that a more Bevanite candidate would be defeated. Some trade unionists also looked askance at his successor, Mr Walter Padley, but not because of Mr Padley's views. 'Will your union vote for Padley?' a member of the NEC was asked in 1956. He looked doubtful. 'Too left wing?' 'Hell no! That doesn't worry us. . . . But we've got enough MPs already. . . . Padley's a politician. . . . He's really nothing on the industrial side of the movement.' The NUR and the AEU, whose choice is almost automatic, have little chance to trim their sails and choose a candidate who will please the Right. It may be, however, that USDAW was deterred from replacing Mr Burke during

---

[1] The AUFW *Annual Report for* 1956 said that many had been 'shocked' at events in Hungary, but did not condemn Russian action. The AUFW voted a niggardly £100 to Hungarian relief, remarking that 'workers everywhere have been greatly disturbed and deeply moved by the tragic events in Hungary . . .' (*Foundry Workers' Journal*, December 1956). While on November 1 the Executive 'condemns the Tory act of aggression at Suez . . . which violates the most elementary principles on which the United Nations was established', it was only on November 27, after considering 'correspondence' that the NEC 'deplored the military intervention of the USSR' and called for withdrawal and free elections. Even then it went on to say that 'the only way to avoid such incidents as happened in Hungary and in Egypt, is by the withdrawal of all armed forces to their home bases'. In May 1957 the *Foundry Workers' Journal* devoted three pages to a defence of Soviet intervention by the Chairman of the Central Committee of the Transport and Heavy Engineering Union. While Mr Casasola was only one of the people taking these decisions, speaking personally to the 1957 ADM he said, 'There was not a Socialist in the world who was not shocked by the happenings in Hungary', but made no condemnation of the Russians—although he admitted, as Communists did, that there had been misgovernment in Hungary—and reserved his attacks for 'reactionaries' and 'Radio Free Europe'. Despite all this he was re-elected to the NEC with 3,619,000 votes in October 1957, *Report*, p. 7.

Mr Casasola was among a group whose participation in a joint meeting with Gaullist and Communist opponents of German rearmament in Paris was brought before the NEC, *The Times*, December 21, 1954.

1953–4 by the fear that a more militant candidate would be defeated.[1]

The election of the women's section of the NEC has aroused continuing discontent. 'End this rotten borough', the Left has cried, alleging that the five women members of the Executive are the creatures of the trade unions. Some of the constituency activists would like to see the women representatives elected by them alone; others prefer to merge the women's section into a twelve-seat constituency parties' section. Again it is hard to extract the truth from the mass of rumour and recrimination.

The unions have never packed the women's section with their own members. At no time since the war has there been more than one direct union nominee on the NEC; in 1958 there was none. Mrs Martin, an USDAW candidate, stood for years without success.[2] For several years there were so few women candidates—partly owing to the unions' attitude—that it was hard to tell whether union and constituency wishes clashed. In 1955, when there were only seven candidates for five places, Miss Alice Bacon, who had sometimes been termed the 'hatchet woman of the Right', won a majority of both union and constituency votes. So did Miss Margaret Herbison and Dr Edith Summerskill. However, Mrs Lena Jeger and Miss Jennie Lee, though unsuccessful, won constituency votes and appreciable union support both then and in 1956.

Other incidents showed how important it was to have the approval of the big unions. Mrs Braddock almost certainly lost her fleeting membership of the NEC by having aroused Arthur Deakin's hostility by intervening on behalf of unofficial dock strikers in Liverpool.[3] Mrs Eirene White declined nomination

[1] The number of Parliamentarians, or former Parliamentarians, on the trade union section has nonetheless been considerable. Three consecutive representatives of USDAW have been MPs (Robinson, Burke, Padley). Mr Mark Hewitson represented NUGMW on the NEC while in the House of Commons, and was succeeded by Mr Jack Cooper, a former MP. Mr E. G. Gooch of the NUAW has been a Member of Parliament since 1945, and Mr R. J. Gunter of TSSA has been an MP from 1945–50 (like his predecessor, Mr J. Haworth), and since 1959.

[2] Miss Ellen Wilkinson was backed by USDAW, and Mrs Braddock was associated with USDAW. Mrs Ayrton Gould was a member of the NUGMW's unofficial panel—but all of them belonged primarily to the political side of the movement.

[3] V. L. Allen, *Trade Union Leadership*, p. 146.

in 1951, believing that because she refused to take sides in the Bevanite quarrel the two general unions would remove her from the NEC as 'unreliable'. It is evident that from 1951 onwards a majority of union leaders wanted 'loyal' women on the NEC. This was completely within their rights—although it is doubtful whether their members realized what was afoot. The composition of the section during these years suggested that orthodoxy was preferred to ability. But the support of the trade union 'club' was just as necessary after the Deakin era. It was never more clearly revealed than when Mr Frank Cousins made amends to Mrs White by swinging the TGWU and several other unions behind her. Mrs Jean Mann, who apparently heard of Mr Cousins' intentions well before the Conference, resigned over a trifling difference and did not stand for re-election. Mrs Braddock, benefiting from a similar amnesty, came back to the NEC with union support. That the unions will use their full power in times of stress is abundantly clear; they are much less concerned to pack the women's section in normal times.[1]

But the classic case of the union-constituency split is the struggle for the Party Treasurership in 1954–6. Since the real stake was the leadership of the Party this battle still merits re-examination.

The Treasurership may be a strictly political position, or a technical post for which financial or economic experience would be an advantage, or a haven for elder statesmen. All these interpretations were used with little consistency by the partisans of the candidates. The conflict really began in 1953, when Mr Arthur Greenwood, the Party's ageing Treasurer, came under pressure to resign. Mr Herbert Morrison's candidature was announced. Belligerent right-wingers, thinking of Mr Morrison as the next Party leader, decided to avenge his dismissal from the NEC in 1952. But, deeply wounded by such 'ingratitude' Mr Greenwood refused to retire. And he won. Some trade unionists found Mr Morrison's ambition premature; others jibbed at what they deemed the callous rejection of a loyal servant. Left-wing, sentimental and anti-Morrison feeling rallied. Advised that

[1] But since 1955 the unions have taken every place on the Party's Conference Arrangements Committee.

the bitterness his insistence on standing would arouse might jeopardize his hopes of the leadership Mr Morrison withdrew. Whereupon the NEC proposed that the Deputy Leader should be an ex-officio member of the Executive—an expedient if inglorious solution.

But Arthur Greenwood died in 1954. Now many who had backed Morrison as a wise man whose counsel must not be lost argued that the job required an economist who could restore order to the Party's finances—Hugh Gaitskell. The Bevanites were at least consistent: to them the Treasurership crystallized a battle over policy.[1]

Mr Gaitskell and Mr Bevan fought for the Treasurership in 1954 and 1955. The unions and the local parties were never united. In their first encounter Mr Bevan was nominated by many constituencies and by five unions (NUR, ETU, ASSET, Fire Brigades' Union and the Foundry Workers). Union support accounted for 1,200,000 of his 2,032,000 votes, while the 1,305,000 constituency votes split slightly better than two to one in his favour.[2] But the following year, after his near-expulsion and the Party's electoral defeat he lost support everywhere. Both USDAW and the NUR deserted him for Gaitskell, while not a single union rallied to him. His union backing now was only 550,000 to 600,000 votes out of 1,225,000—but this time he won only half of the 1,184,000 constituency votes.

After Mr Gaitskell became Party Leader early in 1956 Mr Bevan still continued the fight. Now he was opposed by Mr George Brown (TGWU), not widely known either as an elder statesman or an economist, Mr Charles Pannell (AEU), and Mr David Rhydderch, Treasurer of the Clerical & Administrative Workers' Union. Many who refused to accept Mr Bevan as Party leader in 1955 now turned to him in the hope of

[1] Mr Bevan's supporters in the NUR, USDAW and the AEU argued that since their unions had supported Mr Bevan on the main policy differences since 1951 logic compelled them to support him for Treasurer.

[2] Mr Bevan was also understood to have the support of USDAW, NUPE, and the Cine Technicians.

An unofficial examination was made of the ballot in 1954. According to a leading Bevanite source the constituency vote split roughly Bevan fifty-five per cent; Gaitskell forty-five per cent. Since not all union votes are known this may be correct, but it appears to underestimate Mr Bevan's support among the local parties.

ending the Party's internal feuds. For the first time he had the support of his own union, the Miners, and of several smaller organizations like the Associated Society of Locomotive Engineers and Firemen, and he won back several more, notably USDAW and the NUR. He won. 'At last we've got one over on the block vote', a militant exclaimed as Mr Bevan's victory was announced. In a way he was right; for the first time since the war the combined votes of the general unions had been rebuffed. Yet of the 3,029,000 votes which brought him to the Treasurership, at the very minimum 1,980,000 were trade union block votes—and he may have won as many as 2,322,000 union votes.[1] While the overwhelming majority of local Party votes came back to him (his opponents shared under 100,000) Mr Bevan's support in the unions was always considerable, and finally decisive.

In all but a handful of left-wing unions the importance of policy in the struggle for the Treasurership was played down. Most unions still left both nomination and voting to their Executives. In all the 'Big Six' but the NUM the Executive decided nominations, and in all but the TGWU and USDAW it also decided how the delegation should vote.[2] In most smaller unions the machinery for deciding how the vote should be cast was sketchier still; either the Executive issued a mandate or the delegation was left a free hand. Since their votes were unlikely to decide the issue there was little agitation in these small unions about how they should be cast. Sometimes the procedure was questionable. At the 1955 Party Conference the General Secretary of the National Association of Operative Plasterers 'informed the delegates that we were more or less committed to vote for Hugh Gaitskell'. The other three delegates, including

[1] The unions which should have supported Mr Bevan were: NUM (678,000); USDAW (324,000); NUR (300,000); ETU (140,000); NUPE (100,000); Boilermakers (61,000); Foundry Workers (50,000); Painters (46,000); Vehicle Builders (39,000); Loco. Engineers & Firemen (29,000); Sheet Metal Workers & Braziers (27,000); Draughtsmen (26,000); Constructional Engineers (19,000); Scottish Bakers (16,000); Fire Brigades' Union (16,000); Patternmakers (14,000); Plasterers (15,000); 11 other unions 45,000.

The possible supporters were: Tailors & Garment Workers (88,000); Building Trade Workers (70,000); Plumbing Trades Union (37,000); Natsopa (37,000); Printing, Bookbinding, Paper Workers (30,000); Furniture Trade Operatives (23,000); Bakers (15,000) and London Typographical Society (12,000).

[2] It would be difficult for the TGWU or USDAW delegations to reject the candidate their Executive had nominated. For the AEU's experience see pp. 147–8.

a member of the union's Executive, wished to support Mr Bevan. None was aware that the Executive had issued a mandate.[1]

Some leaders viewed the upsurge of interest after 1954 with dismay. The AEU Executive felt that it should keep the right to decide the union's vote: 'It is strange', said Mr Openshaw, the President, 'that after all these years during which the Executive have nominated for the Treasurership and other posts, suddenly in the last two years there has been all this clamour that some-one else should have the right'.[2] Mr A. E. Tiffin insisted that the General Executive Council of the TGWU had the right 'by custom and practice' to make nominations. Not only were there practical difficulties in the way of a biennial conference making nominations for an annual election, but delegates to the union's conference were not competent to make such a decision. It should be left to the GEC, who knew more about the candi-dates, and would make proper decisions.

Some trade unionists became increasingly irritated as the battle continued. The National Union of Railwaymen justified its switch from Mr Bevan to Mr Gaitskell in 1955 in these terms:

'Our Executive Council feel that the decision having gone in Mr Gaitskell's favour (in 1954) the best interests of the Labour Party are now served by accepting it and avoiding bitterness within the Party.

'The battle for the Treasurership took place in 1954. What useful purpose can be served in reviving it year after year?'[3]

Mr Alan Birch, General Secretary of USDAW, resisted an attempt to nominate Mr Bevan at the union's 1956 conference, commending an amendment which deplored the 'tendency to make the annual election of the Treasurer a cockpit of ideo-logical strife'. He said:

'The question of election to the Treasurership has become distorted out of its true shape and significance. It has become so much fetish, and the old controversy with Mr Bevan, which might have had a meaning in 1951, is now almost solely kept

[1] *Quarterly Report*, December 1955.
[2] The *Manchester Guardian*, May 2, 1956.
[3] *Railway Review*, October 7, 1955.

alive by this Treasurership. If Mr Bevan would take his place in the ordinary election for the National Executive, no one would doubt he would be elected and the last justification for this artificial controversy would be removed.'[1]

Mr Bevan could easily have won a place on the constituency section—by displacing one of his friends—but he needed to show support in all sections of the Party, just as Mr Gaitskell, sensitive to the charge that he was afraid to stand for the constituency section, had needed to show he was not simply the nominee of a handful of right-wing union leaders.

The criticisms of Mr Bevan's campaign for the Treasurership revealed an odd conception of democratic socialism. The insistence that a decision between Mr Bevan and Mr Gaitskell was purely an 'executive matter' was utterly implausible at a time when it was so evidently a major policy issue. The Executives who decided their union's vote were really deciding for or against Mr Bevan's political views or his suitability to lead the Party—for by 1955 it must have been clear to every Executive what was at stake. What was this but a major policy decision? In suggesting that Mr Bevan's candidature was not just inconvenient but improper some union leaders were again assuming that the methods and values appropriate to industrial action are just as suitable in politics. Although Mr Bevan's supporters may have been a misguided group of activists, they did at least arouse unprecedented interest in this side of their union's political activities. For all their frequent laments about apathy many leaders thought this enthusiasm a mixed blessing. Yet it was only when the dispute broke out that most unions gave their members the least information about how they voted. Even now scarcely a union tells its members for whom their votes are cast in the election of the other members of the National Executive. In no realistic sense can union Executives or delegations be considered accountable to their members for their nominations or votes. It is in the deciding of the votes for members of the NEC that trade union 'representative democracy' is at its weakest.

The status of the union members of the NEC is controversial.

[1] *Report of the ADM*, 1956, pp. 16 ff.

Mr Percy Knight expressed the traditional view in answering critics of his support for the expulsion of Mr Bevan: 'The twelve trade union members of the National Executive represent no trade union. I do not sit there as a representative of the National Union of Seamen. I am chosen as one of the trade union members'.[1] The ETU Executive completely disagrees:

'The whole idea that members could accept nomination or sponsorship by an organization and then regard themselves as free agents with no responsibility to the organization to which they owed their position was completely untenable.'[2]

One of the most violent Bevanite attacks on the trade union members of the Executive sprang from their support of the 1951 Budget.[3] If they had been loyal to motions adopted by their own organizations, it was argued, almost every trade unionist on the Executive would have backed the Bevanites.[4] Later members of USDAW attacked Mr Wilfrid Burke for his support of German rearmament and the expulsion of Mr Bevan. But he easily turned their criticisms by appealing to his status as representative rather than delegate, and by invoking his union's generous tradition of free speech.[5] In the National Committee of the AEU a motion which would have mandated the union's representatives on 'all National Organizations' to vote in accord with union policy was narrowly defeated.[6] Its adoption would probably have meant the end of AEU representation on the NEC.

The argument that trade union members are simply delegates is untenable. They are trying to form a policy, not to defend one that has been adopted elsewhere. If the union members were delegates the domination of the Party by the largest organizations would be greater than ever. At present the trade unionists have a responsibility to speak for other unions with similar interests as well as to their own. The real problem is again

---

[1] The *Manchester Guardian*, May 4, 1955.
[2] *Report of the Policy Conference*, 1953, p. 14.
[3] *Going Our Way?* Tribune pamphlet, September 1951.
[4] Most of these union decisions had reflected on certain aspects of government policy, and did not directly reject the Budget.
[5] *Report of the ADM*, 1955, pp. 15–17.
[6] *Minutes and Proceedings of the National Committee*, 1953, p. 298.

accountability. Theoretically if members of the AEU consider the TGWU member of the Executive either incompetent or unrepresentative they can vote for someone else. If they make no changes, then they must be satisfied. Unfortunately it does not work like that. The most certain consequence of the AEU's refusal to vote for the TGWU would be the disappearance of the AEU from the NEC, while the remaining members of the 'club' would see that the TGWU kept its seat. Unions outside the 'club' have no hope of affecting the outcome, for the 'club' holds sufficient votes to overcome their disapproval. Even if they are aware of their delegate's unsuitability some unions cannot vary their nominee to meet the wishes of others. The NUR, for example, will send its President in almost any circumstances. Obviously electing such an agreed 'ticket' would be almost impossible if nomination or voting were submitted to the membership. Accordingly the member has no say at either stage. How the union is represented, and by whom, is not his concern.

Trade union members of the NEC are almost always their union's second string. They are not necessarily second-rate. Many later become General Secretaries. But the abler men often do not serve long enough to make either a reputation or a significant contribution to the work of the NEC. Those who permanently hold secondary posts are not necessarily less competent—Mr Sam Watson has been one of the ablest members of the NEC. In general, though, the standard of trade union representatives is not high—and little wonder when nomination is attached to a specific office. Holding subordinate office, they can rarely commit their own unions. They put a general trade union point of view, while the more important bargains are a matter for direct discussions with the TUC or their own General Secretary.

The work of the National Executive does not come within our present terms. Little has been published about its deliberations.[1] But it is clear that, as at the Conference, almost every issue which troubles the Party divides the trade union group. When the leadership has come under attack—usually

[1] Cf., McKenzie, *British Political Parties*, pp. 517 ff, for the fullest account. In an otherwise excellent *résumé* of the balance of power on the NEC McKenzie possibly draws too sharp a distinction between Parliamentarians and the trade union members. As we have seen there is always some overlap, which may be important.

from the constituency section—a majority of the trade unionists almost invariably rallies to its defence. But they are scarcely ever a monolithic group. During the Bevanite controversy the NEC did tend increasingly to split into blocks, but the trade union members were always divided. They were still divided on the final battle—the proposed expulsion of Mr Bevan. Almost all those crying loudest for blood were leading trade unionists—but only one was a member of the NEC. The opinions of the trade union members ranged from Mr Stafford (NUR) and Mr Gooch (NUAW),[1] who voted against expulsion to the member who bitterly attacked Mr Attlee's lethargy, waving his fork in anger, and exclaiming, 'We've got to smash Bevan—now. It's our last chance. If we don't break him now—in two years he'll be at the top. And then God help the Party'.

The work of trade union members of the NEC is little known within the Party. The constituency members have more flair for publicity than the trade unionists—and the advantage of being Parliamentary figures. They also undertake most of the representative functions at regional meetings and elsewhere. The trade unionists are far less in demand, and many have obligations to their own organizations at weekends. Even at Conference most trade union members of the Executive pass unnoticed by the keenest militants—unlike the constituency members. With the exception of Mr Watson, who winds up discussions on foreign affairs, the trade unionists are rarely chosen to reply to important debates.[2] Mr Irwin is not known to have spoken a word from the platform during his whole ten years on the Executive. On average trade unionists make four or five of the twenty-five NEC speeches in the course of a Conference. When unions move resolutions it is the General Secretary who takes the rostrum, though sometimes—particularly for a 'log rolling' resolution—the NEC representative is put up to reply to his own chief.[3]

[1] Five of the twelve trade union members were understood to have voted for Mr Attlee's proposal to give Mr Bevan, 'a final chance to toe the line'.
[2] Trade union members made eighteen of the sixty-eight speeches for the NEC at the Conferences of 1956–8. Mr Watson spoke six times. Seven members did not speak.
[3] See, for example, the exchange between Mr Alan Birch and Mr Walter Padley of USDAW, moving and replying to a resolution on the Shops Act, *Report of the Labour Party Conference*, 1957, pp. 161–2.

For all the valuable work they may do on committees and sub-committees at Transport House, the trade union members of the Executive make little impression on the rest of the Party. Even after the Bevanite controversy has ended the impression still lingers within the Party as a whole that they are slow and dull, concerned only with discipline, and out of touch with the rank and file.

# CHAPTER VIII

# THE NON-POLITICAL UNIONS

'The organized workers of the country are our friends, indeed it could not be otherwise.'

MR EMMANUEL SHINWELL*

ALTHOUGH the overwhelming majority of trade unionists are members of unions which engage in political action, many other unions claim to be in one sense or another non-political. While their total membership is relatively small, the unions without political funds far outnumber those affiliated to the Labour Party.[1]

Most important are the Civil Service unions. Before 1927 they could affiliate. The Civil Service Clerical Association, Inland Revenue Staff Federation and the Union of Post Office Workers all had political funds and ran Parliamentary candidates. After the Trade Disputes and Trade Unions Act, 1927, the CSCA and IRSF retired from party politics—although Mr W. J. Brown of the CSCA became a Member of Parliament, and the Postal Workers worked through a 'front organization', the Direct Parliamentary Representation Society, which sponsored Labour MPs but did not affiliate to the Party.[2] After 1946 only the UPW re-affiliated. Most other Civil Service unions have affiliated to the TUC but have no political fund,[3] while a few also remain outside the TUC.

There are also the unions of semi-professional workers—

---

* Speech to ETU conference, May 7, 1947.

[1] About half the unions affiliated to the TUC have some connection with the Labour Party. Although it is impossible to make an accurate count of the unions without political funds, there are about 500 organizations included in the Ministry of Labour's list of unions and professional organizations which are 'non-political'.

[2] The DPRS, formed in 1930, functioned through the UPW and its membership and officials were all members of the UPW. Its Annual General Meetings were held immediately before the UPW annual conference. Cf., *The Direct Parliamentary Representation Society—Its Origin, Constitution, and Aims.* DPRS 1934.

Oddly enough, the idea for the DPRS seems to have sprung from remarks made by Mr Churchill, one of the staunchest advocates of the 1927 Act, in the course of debate. Cf., 207 *H.C. Deb. 5s.* col. 68.

[3] The Post Office Engineering Union held an unsuccessful ballot in 1958.

some of them doubtful whether they want to be thought of as trade unions at all.[1] These include the National & Local Government Officers' Association, the National Union of Teachers, National Union of Bank Employees, Actors' Equity, the insurance staff associations, Association of Scientific Workers, National Union of Journalists, and the Medical Practitioners' Union, of which only the NUT and NALGO are outside the TUC—although NALGO associates with TUC committees and observes the Bridlington Agreement.[2]

Thirdly there are working-class unions which have never formed a political fund. The National Association of Colliery Overmen, Deputies & Shotfirers has resisted repeated attempts to set up a national political fund.[3] Such undoubtedly working-class unions as the National Amalgamated Stevedores & Dockers, United Road Transport Workers' Association, Amalgamated Society of Wire Drawers and Kindred Workers, Scottish Typographical Association, Iron, Steel & Metal Dressers' Trade Society, National Union of Hosiery Workers, Amalgamated Society of Leather Workers, and Amalgamated Society of Lithographic Printers have all affiliated to the TUC, but made no political affiliations.

In many of these unions the slightest mention of political issues rouses heated controversy. Even the TUC is too closely identified with the Labour Party for some to accept affiliation. This has been true of NALGO, one of the largest unions still outside the TUC. The Executive denied that TUC affiliation would be the thin edge of the wedge leading to the setting up of a political fund, but admitted that some of the TUC's objects 'are, or at any rate have been, characteristic of the Labour Party'. It concluded that though there is 'de facto support, because of the link represented by the National Council of

[1] Although they are all counted as such in Ministry of Labour and National Service Statistics.

[2] The Bridlington Agreement is intended to prevent 'poaching' of members and to define areas within which unions may recruit members. To these may be added unions like the British Air Line Pilots' Association, Navigation & Engineer Officers' Union, National Union of Cooperative Officials, Radio Officers' Union, National Union of Heating, Ventilating & Domestic Engineers & General Metal Workers, and the Electrical Power Engineers' Association.

[3] Its Durham, Northumberland and Yorkshire Areas have set up political funds since the war.

Labour',[1] individual unions were not called upon to contribute any practical degree of support for the Labour Party. It proposed that the Association should reaffirm its insistence on political neutrality before joining the TUC.[2] Even these assurances were insufficient. In 1948, 1955 and 1958, NALGO members voted against affiliating. Many may have voted on purely social grounds, but others believed that membership of the TUC compromised their political neutrality as public servants.

The National Union of Bank Employees also had to play down the TUC's political role when affiliation was discussed. It argued that a majority of affiliated unions had no political fund, that the Non-Manual Workers' Advisory Council was particularly free of 'political' unions, and that the TUC has very limited party political connections.[3] Once affiliated the Executives of such unions have to be moderate—or they would quickly be forced to withdraw. The National Union of Journalists' affiliation to the TUC, won with the greatest difficulty, has been repeatedly challenged by discontented members, and by the rival Institute of Journalists.[4] In 1950 its General Secretary, replying to allegations that the union was too political, revealed that the 1949 TUC delegation had abstained on the wage freeze issue because they feared their action might be attacked as political.[5] There was a significant incident at the 1957 TUC, during the vote on the extension of nationalization. Mr Tom Yates looked around the hall and announced, 'That seems to be unanimous'. In a moment Mr T. G. Edwards of the National Union of Bank Employees was at the rostrum to point out that 'there are certain unions, of which my own is one, which abstained from voting. If the declaration of unanimity goes into the Press it creates certain difficulties for unions such as mine'. Earlier in the same day Mr E. M. Thomas felt obliged to make

[1] The National Council of Labour, on which the Labour Party, the TUC and the Cooperative Movement are represented, has been principally used to issue manifestoes and pronouncements in the name of the whole movement on such subjects as Hungary and the Suez intervention. It meets rarely, and has had little influence on the course of Labour policies since the war.
[2] *The Question of Affiliation to the Trades Union Congress.* NALGO pamphlet.
[3] *NUBE and the TUC,* NUBE pamphlet.
[4] F. S. Mansfield, *Gentlemen, The Press,* pp. 319–320. C. J. Bundock, *The National Union of Journalists, passim.* Nine ballots were held between 1920 and 1941. Cf., for opposition methods, *The Journalist,* February 1950.
[5] *The Journalist,* February 1950; also November 1958.

a special statement at the end of the debate on wages on behalf of his own union, the Ministry of Labour Staff Association, and other civil service unions. Remarking that 'we have always regarded the TUC itself as an industrial instrument and not one tied to a political party (cries of "shame")', he asked that 'when announcing the vote . . . [you] would allow for the fact that there will be abstentions. We wish to abstain, and we trust that Congress will understand the peculiar position in which we find ourselves'. The leader of a non-political union wrote:

'Our delegates are instructed to vote according to the policy of our union adopted by the Biennial Conference. On matters upon which policy has not been declared they abstain from voting. To divorce politics from our work is impossible, but we can operate without "party politics" intervening, and by use of a good deal of common sense and, at times, a great deal of patience on my part, we manage to survive. How we do it is sometimes incredible to me, but it is done.'[1]

Another union's delegation, 'tend if possible to avoid voting on the purely political issues, but if they do vote they favour the General Council'.[1] The General Secretary of another non-manual union wrote:

'Not only do we keep clear of political affiliations in the party sense, but we definitely circumscribe our activities to the trade union activities on which our members united under our Constitution and Rules when they in fact became members. In other words, and unlike many, and perhaps most, other trade unions, we do not pursue any general political objectives. We withhold ourselves from participating in what may no doubt be activities and bodies worthy in themselves, but having objectives of a general political character.'[1]

The CSCA's TUC affiliation has been repeatedly criticized. In 1951 the Association's General Secretary complained:

'Our delegates to the Bridlington Congress . . . had to omit from the report . . . references to some parts of speeches of Mr Attlee and . . . Sir William Lawther, because they were appeals to the

[1] Private communication.

affiliated unions to work for the return of the Labour Party at the General Election. Had we published these references we should have been using our machinery for party political purposes. . . . If the TUC wishes to retain the support of unions which have decided to have no party political ties, it should make it possible for those unions to affiliate for industrial purposes without being dragged into party political activities.'[1]

*Red Tape* also commented on the White Paper on wages policy; 'Now being non-political, we cannot, as an Association, object to the policy of the Government, and are more or less helpless in regard to its natural consequence—the wage freeze'.[2] The 1953 CSCA conference narrowly rejected a motion disapproving the union's voting on German rearmament at the TUC.[3] Its 1957 conference decided that the Executive had 'made an error of judgment' in passing a motion expressing 'concern' at the Suez intervention—yet it almost immediately voted that 'Conference strongly opposes the Rents Bill, as this iniquitous measure will inflict hardship on thousands of our members. . . .'[4]

Like the CSCA the Inland Revenue Staff Federation had a political fund before 1927; unlike the CSCA it has not attempted to re-establish it since the war. Its delegations are left freer— they voted on the German rearmament issue—but the 1957 TUC delegation felt bound to abstain on 'motions with a party political flavour such as nationalization, the Rent Act, and the TGWU motion on wages and economic policy'.[5] The funds of the former Association of Officers of Taxes, held in trust since 1927, were spent in support of Mr L. J. Callaghan in 1945, and later Mr Douglas Houghton. Mr Houghton's double role as

---

[1] Mr L. C. White, the General Secretary, a member of the *Daily Worker*'s editorial board, must have derived a particular satisfaction from keeping the union politically neutral. *Red Tape*, March 1951.
[2] *Red Tape*, February 1950. The Association in fact fought the wage-freeze strenuously.
[3] *Red Tape*, July 1953. For attacks on affiliation to the TUC see conference reports in *Red Tape*, July 1950 and July 1957. Decision not to attend Women's TUC, *Red Tape*, July 1957 (carried); disaffiliation from the NCLC, *Red Tape*, July 1952 (not carried); disaffiliation from the Labour Research Department (not carried), *Red Tape*, July 1950.
[4] *Red Tape*, July 1957.
[5] *Taxes*, October 1957.

party politician and head of a non-political union aroused such
heated controversy that a less securely installed leader might
not have survived. Had Mr Houghton taken a more partisan
political line the attempts to force him to resign might well
have succeeded. When several members of the Executive sent
branches circulars asking financial support for Mr Houghton's
election campaign in 1951, the Executive was obliged to dis-
claim all responsibility.[1]

The Association of Scientific Workers is one of the few unions
with a political fund which is not affiliated to the Labour Party.
So much hostility was aroused by the fund that the Executive
had to announce that, while it might be spent in local government elections it was intended chiefly to pay for meetings with
Members of Parliament and promoting legislation on matters
of scientific interest. All this could just as well be paid for from
industrial funds. Although *The Scientific Worker* has reduced
the space given to political questions, the fellow-travelling views
of some AScW leaders causes constant wrangling. The union's
conferences have repeatedly debated motions attacking association with Communist bodies, or complaining that 'recruiting
and maintenance of membership are seriously prejudiced by
some officers and members', and demanding that the Executive
discourage 'the support of controversial party politics in Association meetings and publications'. The Executive has been
close to defeat several times.[2] Among members of other non-
political unions the AScW's experience is frequently quoted as
a classic example of the dangers of a divided union taking too
extreme a line. The Association would be far larger and
stronger, they argue, if it would concentrate on 'industrial'
issues.

This hostility applies *a fortiori* to more direct political commitment. Executives, although almost as predominantly Labour

[1] *Taxes*, January, February, July 1950 and October 1954.
[2] Cf., Motions on dissaffiliation from the World Federation of Scientific
Workers, in *The AScW Journal*, July 1956 and July 1957. The AScW affiliated to
the Labour Party in the twenties, and made a much debated intervention in the
General Strike, which caused such grave dissension that the Association was
forced to adopt a neutral attitude towards political issues. In 1939 political affiliation
was defeated, according to *The AScW Journal*, September 1957. However the
Executive's motion on Hungary of November 10, 1956 avoided all condemnation
of Russian action. *AScW Journal*, January 1957. See further criticism reported in
the *Manchester Guardian*, March 20, 1957. *The Observer*, May 22, 1955.

as in many more militant unions, recognize that affiliation to the Party is out of the question. It would lead at best to dissension, at worst to an irrevocable split. Active Conservatives and Liberals form an obstacle to political activities rarely understood by trade unionists from organizations where they hardly exist. They are constantly on the alert for bias in the union journal: they nag continually about TUC affiliation. Their conception of what is political often depends on which party is in power. Sometimes it assumes that anything with which the writer disagrees is biased:[1]

'A genuine non-political organization would surely have exerted its influence, and indeed taken the lead, in trying to get the TUC to face up to the fact that the only way to bring down prices and raise real wages is by spending less and earning more, by greater output—not by free-for-all scrambles for higher pay.'[2]

An uneasy balance—and some fine humbug—often result from the tug of war between the factions. Here was the Chairman of the CSCA:

'I do not want to be accused of entering into political controversy, but in a modern society living in a welfare state it is difficult to draw a line of demarcation between politics and economics and the conditions under which we live. Therefore anything I may say I hope will not be interpreted as advocating a Party political line. There can be no denying the fact that the recent budget not only contained calculated attacks upon the social services but introduced measures which have already, and must in the future continue, to increase the cost of living. . . .'[3]

But these unions are not cut off from politics. Many have either direct representation or appreciable influence within the House of Commons. Mr W. J. Brown was a spokesman for civil service causes for many years. Since the war the representation

---

[1] With some reason when *Red Tape* recommended 50 *Facts on Food* published by *Reynolds News* as containing, 'a good store of ammunition for the coming election', and an answer to 'the constant and vicious attacks by the anti-government Press'. January 1951.

[2] *Red Tape*, November 1951.

[3] *Red Tape*, July 1952.

of white collar unions in the House of Commons has swelled.[1] They can now be sure of finding either one of their own members or a knowledgeable member of an allied profession who can put their case. The most remarkable, and unique, example is the National Union of Teachers. The NUT has never recognized itself as a trade union. Though its conference discusses wage claims, and may decide to work to rule, or even threaten strikes, it still considers itself a professional association.[2] So by a lucky anomaly, it can pursue political activities without setting up a separate political fund. Though its membership is too vocal and divided for any partisan political activities, it was one of the first organizations to sponsor Parliamentary candidates; Sir James Yoxall (Conservative) and Mr Ernest Gray (Liberal) were elected in 1895. The NUT spreads its favours equally between the three parties, supporting up to four candidates from each, paying an annual allowance and part election expenses.[3] When the NUT first backed candidates it was seeking a voice in the House of Commons. Today the profession is adequately represented in both major parties, and the NUT's views are sure of a hearing in Whitehall. The union is embarrassed by the obligation of the Labour members of its panel to support the comprehensive school—against the NUT's own policy. No doubt the union would not inaugurate such a scheme today; it remains a unique survival. However the NUT offers no useful line of development for other non-political unions, which would have difficulty in finding sufficient Conservative candidates.

Even non-political unions have political activities, circumspect though they must be. Every union makes representations to Members of Parliament. Every union approaches government departments to represent its members, and tells the political parties its view on policies and legislation affecting it. It cannot

[1] Since the war there have been Mr Houghton and Mr Callaghan (IRSF); Mr Redhead (Society of Civil Servants); Mr L. J. Edwards (Post Office Engineering Union); the UPW MPs; several members of NALGO; Mr A. M. F. Palmer (Electrical Power Engineers' Association) and numerous members of the insurance unions, NUJ, and other professional organizations.

[2] It has taken counsel's opinion on this point.

[3] At present the NUT grants fifty per cent of election expenses up to £400, and an annual personal allowance of up to £250. The NUT MPs elected in 1955 were Mr Chuter Ede, T. G. Thomas and W. G. Cove, Labour; Mr J. C. Jennings and I. J. Pitman, Conservative.

fully represent its members without mixing in politics. If a government rejects its pay claim, or refuses to discuss matters with it, it must defend its members, even if the Opposition seizes its complaint to make political capital. 'Non-political' must really mean 'non-partisan'. While 'political' unions invariably ask Labour spokesmen to plead their cause, several non-political unions have sought Conservative help.

There are also the militant non-political unions. They really belong to the inter-war period, when some dozens of 'industrial' unions flourished and faded. The chief was the Nottinghamshire and District Miners' Industrial Union, formed by George Spencer after the General Strike. Similar unions were set up with the encouragement of the coal owners in most coalfields, despite bitter attacks from the Nottinghamshire Miners' Association and the rest of the Miners' Federation of Great Britain. Havelock Wilson, of the Seamen and Firemen's Union, who had refused to come out in the General Strike, lent Spencer funds, cars, and officials and issued a journal. The Seamen were expelled from the TUC and the Party, and Wilson launched a campaign to set up non-political unions, which commanded some support during the late 1920's, but died down after his death. Industrial unionism outlived the reaffiliation of Spencer's union to the Miners' Federation in 1937. It was reported in 1946 that the Federation of Independent Trade Unions, pledged to keep politics out of the trade union movement, included forty-five unions and had an affiliated membership of 400,000,[1] At the 1950 election the Federation, now claiming to represent over 100,000 workers, urged trade unionists to ignore the TUC election appeal and vote according to their consciences. It concluded, 'This Federation is convinced that party politics have no place in trade unionism'.[2] It is doubtful whether the Federation ever had any real existence; many of the unions associated with it have now disappeared. Almost all were on the fringe of trade unionism; several were breakaways. By 1951 there was little discernible organized movement for non-political trade unionism.

---

[1] The *Daily Telegraph*, August 31, 1946 and The *Manchester Guardian*, July 1, 1946.
[2] *The Times*, February 6, 1950.

The explanation of the apathy or hostility to politics of the non-political unions lies primarily in their history; little of which has yet been written. Some have grown up round a team of men with differing political views, whose early decision to avoid political disputes rapidly became a tradition. Others take their members from occupations where the traditions of political neutrality remain strong. Some, such as NALGO, have only recently come to think of themselves as part of the trade union movement at all. Few can look back on the bitter industrial struggles, or on the incomprehension of the established parties, which the political unions are fond of recalling. Others have recruited more active Conservatives than is normal, and other members have accepted them as officials. The Labour Party has come to appreciate and accept the special position of the civil service unions. It understands, with scorn, the 'lack of class-consciousness' or the 'snobbishness' which keep middle-class unions from taking an active part in politics.

But the truly working-class unions which have remained non-political are a different problem. Some, like the National Union of Hosiery Workers, have unsuccessfully tried to set up political funds. Others have never made the attempt. One union, which engaged in politics in the thirties, simply allowed its political fund to fall into disuse and disappear from the rule book.[1] Several of these unions have been captured by non-Labour groups.[2] Some profess a general sympathy for Labour and others keep a strict neutrality, both in their journals and their conferences. Their leaders find it hard to explain why. 'Our members have just never been politically-minded' they say. 'It never seemed worth while'; or 'Do you know, we've never really thought about it'.

'It never seemed worth while' comes naturally enough to a union which cannot measure up to the giants of the movement. Such unions show little interest in representation in the House of Commons, a pleasurable luxury whose absence they scarcely regret. Unlike the large organizations, they could never hope to carry weight in the Party's counsels. They can always turn

[1] The Amalgamated Society of Woodcutting Machinists.
[2] The National Amalgamated Stevedores & Dockers was long under extreme-left leadership.

to the TUC if they need the backing of the wider movement. When the Party is taking policy decisions which affect them, they feel they exert just as much influence through the TUC as if they were directly affiliated.

The confession that 'we've never really thought of it' is just as significant. Historians of the Labour movement have tended to argue that events at the turn of the century swept the unions irresistibly into party politics, then into the Labour Party. Incidents like the Taff Vale decision of 1901 unquestionably helped convert the unions. But the Party was no idle spectator. Several of the largest unions—notably the cotton workers and the miners—stood aloof. If the Party was to survive and prosper they had to be won over. So, through the first years of the century, the Party aided and encouraged the Socialists within these unions in the organization of cells, caucuses, and election 'tickets' to capture control. It was as much the work of groups of activists as the conviction fostered by external events which finally converted the laggards. Grateful though the Party was for the adherence of the smaller unions, their support was never as vital and the Party made far fewer attempts to campaign within them. It has never made a concerted effort to win over these smaller unions and the time is long since past when unions would tolerate the organization of factions within their ranks by a political party. On the one side there has been no sense of need; on the other, little missionary zeal.

It is true that the great mass of the movement is associated with the Labour Party. Yet many individual organizations have stood aside from this decision. The eighty-odd non-political unions within the Trades Union Congress cannot simply be branded as 'blacklegs', who sit back and let others have the expense and effort of winning political battles. Their attitude suggests that unions can both be 'in politics' and avoid political affiliation. The lessons of trade union experience seem to admit of more than one conclusion. By showing that they do not point irrevocably to affiliation with the Labour Party this group of unions is a standing challenge to one of the Movement's most cherished myths.

# CONCLUSION

'It is excellent to have a giant's strength, but tyrannous to
use it like a giant.'*

THE influence that the two wings of the Labour Movement
exercise over each other has always provoked a torrent of
commentaries, most of them contradictory, almost all extreme.
It was Aneurin Bevan, for example, who lamented during one
of his periods of disaffection that 'the outstanding fact is that the
Labour Party is dominated utterly by the trade unions'.[1] Yet it
was also he who complained bitterly in 1951 that 'When the
[Labour] government called for a bang on the rubber stamp
these trade union leaders rushed in to give it'.[2] Conservatives
are forever fond of reproaching Labour for its inability to resist
union demands—yet their spokesmen also cry, 'Our object is
to free the unions from the domination of the Socialists'.[3] At one
Conference Mr Emmanuel Shinwell was thanking the Deity
that the unions were 'keeping the Party steady';[4] at another he
complained that they were turning it into 'no more than the
rubber stamp of the TUC'.[5]

There are few sports so unfair as unearthing the incon-
sistencies of public men. Unfortunately such double-think has
become endemic in discussions of the unions' power within the
Party. Few commentators on the Party's affairs have not been
guilty of it at one time or another. Do the members of the
moderate wing who cried 'dictation' when the TGWU pressed
for more 'advanced' nuclear weapons policies forget how they
called the influence of the same union 'statesmanly' when it was
cast against the Bevanites? Has not the Left been as inconsistent? From 1948 it was claiming that the wage freeze was the
result of the union leaders' subservience to the Party; after 1951
it somersaulted into maintaining that the failure of the Party

---

* Chairman, NUGMW, 1949 Congress.

[1] *Tribune*, July 23, 1943—quotation taken from *What They Have Said*, Conservative Research Department, 1950.
[2] *Going Our Way? Tribune* pamphlet, 1951.
[3] Mr E. H. C. Leather, *Advance*, August 1950.
[4] *Report*, 1952, p. 105.
[5] *The Star*, September 28, 1956.

to adopt red-blooded Socialist policies was the consequence of these same leaders' 'domination' of the Party. During 1959 it suddenly discovered that the pressure of one of the great unions amounted to 'leadership'. For all these categorical pronouncements and contradictions, the issues are serious enough. Let us look more closely at the accusation that the unions dominate the Labour Party.

That the Party Constitution would permit the unions to run the Labour Party if they wished is beyond doubt. But it is a matter of fact that the Labour Party has never been purely and simply the political expression of trade unionism. The unions have usually been prepared to leave to the political leadership the initiating of policies which do not directly involve their own interests. It would be hard to find a single instance since the war of the unions successfully forcing their views on the Party on a non-industrial issue.

Almost invariably the initiative of policy and the opposition to it both spring initially from the political movement. If there is disagreement the unions simply take sides. If the issue is put to the test the unions have such massive voting power that they cannot but influence the final decisions. However, their strength is not all cast in one direction. They have not acted as a united force in a single one of the great policy struggles which have racked the Party in recent years. Although obviously their influence is cast on balance with either the official line or the opposition, the views they are defending are not specifically trade union policies. Nor, for all their voting strength, are the unions necessarily the arbiters of the situation. In recent years the balance of union strength has usually been thrown against left-wing policies—but therein lies only a partial explanation of the failure of the Left. It has not been without relevance that they also failed consistently to carry the Parliamentary Labour Party, that their constituency support was less substantial than they would have liked to think,[1] and that there was the abundant evidence of public opinion polls that the electorate did not share

---

[1] Had the constituencies been as determinedly to the left as was often claimed they would have seen to it that Parliamentary nominations went only to left-wingers. There have been sufficient new nominations since 1951 to change the whole balance of the Parliamentary Party. Yet, for all the exhortations of the left-wing Press the strength of the Left in the PLP seems to have changed little.

their enthusiasm for thoroughgoing left-wing programmes. Blaming the 'trade union knights' for their lack of success was an over-simplification of the problem of the Socialist Left, which is not just to commit the Party to 'Socialism', but to show how power can be won with such a platform. Political rebels may safely ignore the market for their ideas; political leaders can rarely afford such a luxury.

Sometimes, too, union pressure may seem to shift the Party to the left. Appearances may be deceptive. The struggle over nuclear weapons is a case in point. The real problem for the leadership arose because traditionally loyal unions defected. Among them was the TGWU which was sufficiently large to swamp the other dissidents and thereby to appear to lead the rebellion. In fact it joined the opposition belatedly, after a ferment in the political movement lasting over two years. Again it is an oversimplification to call this a case of union 'dictation'— although the incident reveals the difficulties which arise when the leader of any of the largest unions intervenes vigorously in a major controversy.

For all the understandable frustration of those who find union forces used against them the use of union power within the Party has never really amounted to outright dictation or consistently intolerable pressure. But this uneasy balance is no immutable law of its existence. It is the product of good fortune and common sense. Fortunately union leaders have usually been divided, or uninterested in dictating the Party line on non-industrial issues—or prudent enough to leave the brunt of the struggle to the contending factions. The wisest of them have always seen that while they hold considerable power, which they can never abstain from using, the alliance could be fatally endangered if they took the leadership of either camp when feeling is running high.

Most union leaders realize that the position of the political wing (rebels and leaders alike) becomes quite intolerable if people with no public responsibility insist on intervening with all their force in the complex affairs of the political movement. Such considerations apply just as much to the union leader who campaigns for a root-and-branch purge of those who dissent from the leadership to which he is loyal, as to one who

x

heads a revolt to force the Party to adopt left-wing policies. Any such attempt at dictation by the unions would be just as unconstitutional as would be control of the Party by the mass movement in the constituencies. Worse, it would allow opponents to depict Labour as the puppet of trade union bosses, a political satellite of the unions. This would not only be of no help to the Party's election chances but would be disastrous for the morale of the whole political movement.

Counselling moderation cannot but seem a feeble rejoinder to this problem of union power. But is there any other course? When controversies arise union leaders cannot help taking sides and using their votes. There is no way they can contract-out of bringing their weight to bear. The Party has to live with its constitution. Within this system the Party has no right to expect that the traditional pattern of union votes supporting the official leadership will be maintained. But whichever way the unions throw their influence it must surely be with tact and under-standing. Nowadays any spectacular commitment of union strength in either direction not only rouses antagonism on the losing side, it risks turning every difference into a squabble between the political and industrial movements. More than once in recent years, in seeking to intervene more 'positively' in the running of the Party, leaders of major unions have seemed oblivious of the dangers. For while there are plenty of examples in the Party's earlier history of massive deployments of union power, one of the lessons of recent years is surely, as Mr Geddes remarked, that the day of the bulldozers is past—or it ought to be.

It would probably not be seriously contested even within the Labour Party that the unions sometimes receive more than their due. But it would be unwise to conclude too swiftly that this is because they dominate the Party's formal organs. Labour is not alone in facing accusations of being 'soft' with the unions in recent years. Such charges were levelled consistently against the Conservatives while Sir Walter Monckton was Minister of Labour. The engineering employers insisted that it was only the Conservative government's lack of determination which prevented them from forcing a showdown with the unions during the engineering strike of 1957.[1] At least until 1958 *The Economist* repeatedly lamented the way that the Conservatives sold the pass by granting wage increases in the nationalized industries. The merits of these accusations need not concern us; nor does the discovery that both parties succumb to union pressure remove the problem. But the terms in which the Conservatives have been criticized, even though they have far more formal relationships with the unions than Labour, suggests that the forces at work are too complicated to be explained by the unions' implantation in the mechanisms of the Labour Party.

The real explanation lies largely in the millions of workers who are represented by the trade union movement. At times the unions' own vested interests cut across the real interests of their members—but it is easier to make the distinction in the calm of an ivory tower than to pursue a policy based on it. Both parties cannot help being profoundly aware that trade unionists and their immediate families make up about half the electorate. In such circumstances boldness comes more easily to leader-writers than to practising politicians.

It is scarcely surprising that the Conservatives tried so strongly to woo the unions away from Labour between 1951 and 1955, or that from 1948 to 1950 some Conservative trade unionists, curiously echoing the Communists in their attacks on the wage freeze, should have used its unpopularity to persuade trade unionists that there were drawbacks to being linked with Labour. So long as the ordinary voter tends to look upon himself primarily as a producer rather than as a consumer, the two political parties will continue to bid for union support in terms which may at times appear demagogic or unscrupulous.

With their nine million-odd members the unions cannot help but be among the most powerful groups influencing governments. In the past few years they have rarely been able to impose their demands against its will on either party. But they are one of the small number of groups which are strong enough to impose an effective veto on a small number of policies against which they are strongly united. The Conservatives are not immune. We have seen them drop the Industrial Charter, and

[1] See *Looking at Industrial Relations*, Engineering and Allied Employers' Federation, 1959.

the pledge to restore contracting-in, disown a Conservative backbencher who wanted to bring in a Bill limiting union prerogatives, and decline to adopt proposals to introduce a 'Companies Act' to restrain abuses of trade union power.[1] It is far from magnificent—but it is political war.

Such restraints bear more heavily on Labour than on the Conservatives. There are a number of questions on which the balance of political advantage and conviction may push the Conservatives to act where Labour dare not venture even if it would. It is hard enough for a Labour leader to admit publicly that the trade union movement is less than perfect; it seems almost unthinkable that Labour would be prepared to take remedial action, were it necessary, to curb abuses of trade union power. In these respects the Party is virtually crippled. This greater sensitivity is not due solely to the unions' power within the Party itself. It is doubtful whether Labour leaders ever pause to consider the state of Party funds before making a decision.[2] They rarely fear that the unions will use their commanding position at the Party Conference or on the NEC to reject their proposals, or that the trade union group of Members of Parliament will revolt.[3] Indeed, the unions have constantly sought to take the discussion of issues directly affecting them out of the Conference and the Parliamentary Party, so that they can be raised directly with the Party leadership.

The union pressure of which Labour leaders are constantly aware comes from the TUC itself, independent of the Labour Party and drawing much of its strength in negotiating with Labour from that independence. If the unions are going to disagree with Party policy or press the Party to move in a new direction, their influence will normally be felt here, in talks between the Party and representatives of the General Council and the interested unions. The fact that these TUC leaders are usually also prominent within the Party is less important than might be assumed. The Labour Party is bound to the unions not just by cash and card votes, but by personalities and doctrines, common experience and sentiment—and mutual advantage.

[1] *The Economist*, February 15 and 22, 1958, June 14, 1958, May 16, 1959.
[2] Although attempts to bring financial pressure are not wholly unknown.
[3] However, the docility of the trade union group should not be over-emphasized. It has always contained a proportion of active rebels.

Drawing more heavily on the votes of trade unionists and their families than the Conservatives, Labour feels less often than its rival that electoral advantage or doctrine counsel opposition to union demands. On these grounds alone it is scarcely surprising that Labour is so frequently receptive to union wishes—even though its concessions may stem more from solidarity than from conviction.

The room for manoeuvre left to Labour is therefore limited. One of the most delicate problems of the Labour Movement is the use that the Party makes of it. In older theories of the Movement the problem scarcely arose, partly because the Party was thought of as an emanation of the unions themselves, partly because it was assumed that there would be identity of views— but largely because for most of these years Labour was in opposition. Even in 1947 Mr Sam Viant, a Woodworkers' MP, happily told his members, 'It is impossible to draw a distinction between the interests of the members of the ASW and the interests of the working people I represent in Willesden'.[1] Yet any student of Labour Party history knows that the interests of the two wings do diverge at times. When they do the position of the TUC and the unions is clear enough:

'Our responsibility is primarily to the trade union movement, and the decisions taken by the trade unions under the guidance of the TUC, must have regard to the interests of the organized millions who look to the unions for the protection of their standards of life.'[2]

While the unions are responsible only to the section of members they represent, Labour's responsibilities are wider.

This problem of what is to be expected of the Party when the two movements disagree has never been fully faced. In the past commentators have tried to define spheres of interest or areas of autonomy as a way out of the difficulty. Mr Attlee laid down these principles in 1937:

[1] *Report of the ADC*, 1947, p. 157.

[2] *Labour*, November 1949. The General Secretary of Mr Viant's union also put the point clearly enough in emphasizing: 'The whole purpose of this conference, and the whole purpose of the trade union movement is to enhance the living standards and working conditions of its members'. *Report of the ADC*, 1953, p. 5.

X*

'It is useless and harmful to look on the trade unions purely as a revolutionary force to be subservient to the demands of political leaders. It is equally dangerous for the trade unions to regard politicians merely as an agency for obtaining particular advantages for organized Labour.'[1]

Frank Cousins put the same view more bluntly:

'I told you last year not to tell the unions how to do their job, and I am certainly not going to tell the Labour Party how to do its job.'[2]

Today scarcely anyone in the Labour Party seriously thinks of 'telling the unions how to do their job', or expects them to be 'a revolutionary force'. It is understood that the refusal to accept instructions from a political party is one of the marks of an independent trade union movement.

But is not the refusal to take orders from such outside interests as the trade unions one of the marks of an independent political party? The idea that the Labour Party should have the degree of freedom that the unions enjoy has never been so strongly developed within the Movement. This failure tends to limit the field of manoeuvre which the Party might otherwise have had in dealing with the unions. That is not to say that Labour slavishly follows their wishes. While its alliance with the unions sets up a group of things that the Party simple dare not do, the goodwill which it accumulates through its consistent support and sympathy allows a Labour government to take liberties with the unions such as only the Conservatives would think of taking with the farmers.

While in office Labour drew heavily on this store of goodwill with some courage, in obtaining union support for its economic policies, such as the wage freeze, and by dealing firmly with strikers (who admittedly were unofficial). It is hard to conceive of a Conservative government carrying through its economic programme during those years with as little industrial conflict, even though the unions' bargaining power and the precarious state of the economy would have ruled out a really tough line with the unions. Although the extent to which wages were

[1] *The Labour Party in Perspective*, p. 62.    [2] *Report*, 1956, p. 82.

effectively frozen may be contested, it is undeniable that many union leaders identified themselves with Party policy to a degree which undermined their authority in their unions. At local government level, too, it is not uncommon to hear trade union officials complain that it is harder to win concessions from Labour councils than from Conservative.

Nevertheless, for all the understanding of the Party's responsibilities to other sections of the community that union leaders have shown, these have never really been grasped at the lower levels—outside those who have had direct experience of the problem through local government. Few difficulties arise when the unions' own interests are not at stake. The real test comes on economic, social and fiscal questions. On such matters it is clear that belief that the Party is 'an agency for obtaining particular advantages for organized labour' is still deeply engrained in the minds of the rank and file. They still think that they have a 'right to tell the Labour Party how to do its job', whatever Mr Cousins may say. Few of them would see that there could be a distinction between the good of the community as a whole and the demands of the organized working class.

Consequently opinion within the Movement is rarely sympathetic to the leadership making the most of its room for manoeuvre. A minor instance is the freedom which many union leaders allow themselves in commenting on political questions. It is almost unthinkable that any Labour fraternal delegate to the TUC should dwell on the imperfections of the industrial movement with a frankness remotely approaching that adopted at times by TUC fraternal delegates to the Party Conference. Similarly it is traditional that the Party gives complete support to the union view in public discussion of industrial disputes while the Party is in opposition. The nearest it comes to criticism is silence. Even when reform is clearly needed Mr Gaitskell can only say, 'we can safely leave it to the unions to take the necessary action'. And so the Movement becomes accustomed to the Party accepting union demands automatically. Probably few rank and file members would really expect Labour to give in to every union demand when in power, but they are constantly encouraged through Party propaganda to expect more of the Party than it can ever reasonably give when it is in office. The shrewd ideas that union leaders have developed of the difficulties which may arise under a Labour government, in the course of long discussions with Party leaders over economic policy, have not even begun to percolate down to the ordinary member.

Throughout the years the unions have constantly been able to show their independence by negotiating freely with governments of every shade. The Party has not had the same opportunities. It has had only a few years in which to show what is to be reasonably expected of the Party in power. The popular conception of its duties to the unions still rests essentially on fifty years of opposition. This is a dangerous anachronism.

The tone of much union discussion seems to suggest that the unions are asking an unwisely high price for their support of the Party. In fact it seems clear that from time to time Labour governments will be faced with union demands which they will not or should not accept. The idea that Labour may sometimes say 'No' is not heretical; it should be thoroughly normal if infrequent. In fact the alliance with Labour is probably still worth while even if the Party says 'No' relatively often. But emotionally and intellectually the alliance seems ill-prepared to meet such a test. It clings to an outmoded notion of what one partner can do for the other. This may not be a recipe for disaster, but it seems bound to increase the strain on the partnership when Labour is in office.

Yet the collapse of Labour's partnership with the unions has been prophesied as often as the demise of English cricket. There have been the early discontents because political action did not win the millennium overnight, the general strike, the 1931 disaster, the breakdown of wage restraint and the Bevanite quarrel. Yet even sixty years of premature obituaries is no guarantee that the prophets of doom will always be wrong; simple survival is among the alliance's most remarkable achievements. Clearly, however, the ties of doctrine and sentiment, of inertia and self-interest, which keep the Movement together are powerful.

Confirmation of the strength of these ties may be found in the post-war years. From the opening of the campaign for wage restraint under the Labour Government to the end of the Bevanite struggle a rupture never looked probable. Even had the Party adopted a programme of widespread nationalization, rejected German rearmament, and elected Mr Bevan first Treasurer and then Leader of the Parliamentary Labour Party, though the right-wing union leaders might have thundered, tightened their purse strings, and dropped dark hints about secession—not one union would have left the Party. Occasional musings about the benefits of independence after the fashion of the American unions, or the formation of a separate trade union party never seriously emerged from the smoking-room. Arthur Deakin put such talk in perspective: 'I want to say with very great emphasis that I am certain that there is no trade union affiliated to the Party which would for one moment consider any disaffiliation or divorcement from this Party'.[1]

Not one of the irreconcilable right-wing leaders could have felt really confident of carrying disaffiliation through his union even in 1954–1955. Their rank and file would not have followed them. Even to make the attempt would have plunged their organizations into bitterness and division for relatively little gain. The experience of these years suggests that the alliance still has vitality, and that it is unlikely to founder on purely political issues. Its collapse could only come from a conflict so bitter that active members and their leaders were left furious and completely disillusioned. Few issues can generate sufficient feeling to make them cast aside the arguments and beliefs of a lifetime. For years union leaders have been expressing themselves in such terms as these:

'The relationship of the unions with the Labour Party is not just something that happens for the moment because it is politically advantageous to the unions for the time being. . . . The two movements are of the same material, and the history of one is the story of the other. The fundamental principles of trade unionists over a hundred years ago were the natural origin of the Labour Party itself, and side by side, in good fortune and misfortune, the two organizations have been intertwined and inseparable. The faith of the one is the faith of the other.'[2]

[1] *Report*, 1953, p. 194.
[2] Mr W. B. Beard, *Report*, 1956, p. 116.

To turn and break with the Party would involve the personal humiliation of admitting their Conservative critics to be right— a partial rejection of their own past. Such a crisis could only be provoked on an 'industrial' issue, under a Labour Government (no rational Labour leadership would risk such a rupture while the Party was in Opposition). Few industrial questions are large enough to endanger the survival of the Movement: wages policy, perhaps a strike in an essential service or (remembering 1931) social service benefits.

There is small wonder that some of the most anxious meetings between the unions and the Party have turned on means of avoiding such a head-on clash over wages. As usual there was ground for pessimism. Frank Cousins' views on wages policy seemed a far cry from Arthur Deakin's: 'We have said that we do not accept and would not accept a policy of wage restraint'.[1] It was evident that hopes that the unions might be persuaded to withhold wage demands in return for pledges to pursue certain policies were vain. Yet the deterioration was possibly more apparent than real. A Labour Government will have to create conditions in which there is either little pressure for wage increases or they can safely be financed from expansion —unless it is content to let inflation swell. The arbiters of whether the Party had paid a sufficiently high price for their support would, of course, be the unions. Yet they would doubt-less show as much loyal moderation in framing their demands and pursuing them as was possible. While differences between a Labour government and the unions over wages could easily lead to bitter ill-feeling, many would expect Labour to concede too much rather than too little in such a situation.

Caught in a major crisis, with no room for manoeuvre, a Labour Government might be forced to refuse the unions' demands completely. The 1931 crisis is a warning. Labour has never fully realized how fortunate for its unity was MacDonald's departure, which turned aside the inevitable storm over the cabinet's handling of the economic crisis. Can one seriously conceive of the alliance breaking without a major crisis within the Labour Party? If the unions went part of the political move-ment would certainly follow; the Labour vote would be just as

[1] *Report*, 1958, p. 165.

surely split. The ending of the alliance would shatter the Labour Party as an effective political force.

While such a headlong collision is possible, the gravest danger is probably not explosion but decomposition. This is the process we have been witnessing since the war. It is clear that the unions have been less willing to make sacrifices for political action, whether we look at their attitude to the political levy, to organizing the widest possible discussion of policy, or to letting officials go into Parliament.

For all the multitude of affirmations of loyalty to the Party, the repeated unwillingness to pay the full price for political action implies that the game is not worth the candle. Although left-wingers often attack the trade union leadership for 'dragging their feet', it is abundantly clear that the pressure for parsimony comes primarily from shop stewards, branch officials and conference delegates—even if many leaders have not done all they could to overcome their apathy. Left-wing unions are no more ready to make sacrifices for the Party than any others. In all but a handful of unions the belief that the unions should have their politics on the cheap has become an ingrained tradition.

Perhaps this reluctance to make genuine sacrifices has been only a passing phase. Throughout the Party's history the unions have tended to swing between emphasizing political and industrial action. In the years immediately after the Second World War the industrial side seemed relatively more important. The unions found that they were stronger than ever before, while supporting the Labour Government brought home to many militant trade unionists for the first time the lesson that political ties could be embarrassing. Then came the rule of Sir Walter Monckton at the Ministry of Labour, coinciding with the Bevanite battle. On the one side the unions were courted, on the other they were embroiled in an interminable quarrel which brought them a torrent of abuse. As full employment continued, and the unions discovered that Conservative rule had not put the clock back to the thirties, the militancy of leaders and members alike was dulled. Labour could apparently do little for the unions while in opposition, and they were coaxing more from the Conservatives than they had ever hoped. What point was there in making sacrifices to maintain their political efforts?

But the unions' confidence in their industrial strength was undermined as relations with the Conservatives deteriorated during the 1955 Parliament. The era of easily-won wage increases came to a close, while a series of Pyrrhic strike victories, culminating in the London bus strike of 1958, cast doubt on the unions' ability to 'go it alone'. Slowly the re-appraisal of the value of political action began. Obviously the attitude of governments had had a greater influence on the unions' success or failure than the movement had been in the habit of thinking for some years. The trend of union thought was evident in an extreme but symptomatic reflection by a member of the AEU:

'The moral (of the London bus strike) is that it is upon the government as such that the unions must exert pressure if they are to protect the living standards of their members. Industrial action may be needed from time to time, but political action is at least as important and is much cheaper. Poor Mr Gaitskell may be calculating how many more marginal seats might have been won for Labour if the £1,500,000 spent by the TGWU on strike pay during the bus strike had instead been contributed to Labour Party funds'.[1]

The unprecedentedly generous contributions most unions made to the Party's 1959 election fund were the most striking expression of a general shift in attitudes. Yet in other ways their efforts were still modest in relation to their capabilities— on such questions as Parliamentary candidates there were few signs of a thaw. This was a danger signal. For Labour was in opposition, supporting the unions zealously, and their anger was concentrated on the Conservatives. This could well be the high water mark of the unions' affections. With Labour in office again, and the inevitable compromises and half-measures that would bring them, their ardour might soon be dampened.

For the long term trend is for the unions' part in the life of the Labour Party to slacken. While the movement has felt the need for a Labour Government its conception of the role of such a government has become increasingly diffuse. At one time the

---

[1] *AEU Journal*, August 1958.

unions looked to Labour not only to produce a generally favourable economic climate but to accord them full recognition,
nationalization, and the welfare state. Of Labour's new policies
only the pensions proposals touch on ground which is central to
the unions' own aims. Municipalized housing and the comprehensive school mean relatively little to trade unionists *as trade
unionists*. Mr Cousins put the unions' hopes in these terms:

'Our TUC colleagues are well-satisfied that the Labour Movement intends to create the background in which we can cooperate with them in increasing productivity in order that the
standard of living of the people that we represent, both Labour
and Trade Union, goes forward. . . .'[1]

This deceptively mild demand expresses one of the unions'
traditional expectations. In the past it has been surrounded by a
catalogue of major reforms with which the Party could also hope
to satisfy the unions. Now, as the unions come to think of a
Labour government almost wholly in this role of a benevolent
creator of a framework within which they can successfully
pursue their activities, this expectation is an onerous and
never-ending burden. When Labour fails this exacting standard
the unions will become irritable and frustrated; when it succeeds
its efforts may well pass unnoticed. It is doubtful whether the
unions appreciate the advantages of having a government which
is basically sympathetic until they have to cope with a hostile
one.

In this situation lies the alliance's gravest danger. The unions'
hopes from Labour are less and less directly and immediately
related to their industrial needs. Today their support is based
much more on general political grounds. Are such considerations sufficiently powerful to enable trade union leaders to 'sell'
political action to their members? Is there any hope in them that
trade unionists can be persuaded to make sacrifices in such a
cause? Unless Labour can find ways of persuading the unions to
give a positive answer to these questions there seems little hope
that the unions can be persuaded to pull their weight within the
Movement. A decline in the unions' participation does not spell

[1] *Report*, 1958, p. 166.

the ending of the Labour alliance. Indeed, it is hard to see how, under the Party's present Constitution, the decline in the unions' political interest would ever induce them to sacrifice their prerogatives. And so Labour might be left with the worst of both worlds. On one hand social change could make the Party's association with the unions a wasting electoral asset, and even an embarrassment. On the other hand, the unions' continued withdrawal from participation would leave the Movement like an ageing elm. Though outwardly it might be sound its heart would be dead.

# INDEX